THE VISUAL LABORATORY OF ROBERT LEPAGE

THE VISUAL LABORATORY
OF ROBERT LEPAGE

LUDOVIC FOUQUET

TRANSLATED BY RHONDA MULLINS

TALONBOOKS

Talonbooks
278 East First Avenue, Vancouver, British Columbia, Canada v5T 1A6
www.talonbooks.com

First printing: 2014
Typeset in Arno Pro
Printed and bound in Canada on 100% post-consumer recycled paper

Interior and cover design by Typesmith
Images used in the interior and on the cover are copyright the photographer
or creator credited. Further credits appear on page 393.

Talonbooks gratefully acknowledges the financial support of the Canada
Council for the Arts, the Government of Canada through the Canada Book
Fund, and the Province of British Columbia through the British Columbia Arts
Council and the Book Publishing Tax Credit.

This work was originally published in French as *Robert Lepage, l'horizon en
images* by L'instant même in Quebec City, Quebec, in 2005.

Ludovic Fouquet extends special thanks to the team at Ex Machina, who have
opened their doors so often since 1996: Robert Lepage, of course, but also
Lynda Beaulieu, Louise Roussel, and the whole team.

In quotations, ellipses are set within square brackets ("[...]") to show gaps in
the text quoted. In the notes, "– Ed." marks those added to update the English
edition.

LIBRARY AND ARCHIVES CANADA CATALOGUING IN PUBLICATION

Fouquet, Ludovic, 1973–
[Robert Lepage, l'horizon en images. English]
The visual laboratory of Robert Lepage / Ludovic Fouquet ;
translated by Rhonda Mullins.

Translation of: Robert Lepage, l'horizon en images.
Includes bibliographical references and index. Issued in print and electronic
formats.

ISBN 978-0-88922-774-3 (pbk.).—ISBN 978-0-88922-775-0 (epub)

1. Lepage, Robert, 1957– —Criticism and interpretation. 2. Theater—
Production and direction—Québec (Province). 3. Theaters—Québec
(Province)— Stage-setting and scenery. 4. Performing arts—Production and
direction—Québec (Province). I. Mullins, Rhonda, 1966–, translator II. Title.

PN2308.L46F6813 2013   792.02'32092   C2013-907200-4
                                                C2013-907201-2

*To Jacquie Bablet, who inspired my visual
laboratory with her infectious curiosity*

*To Michel Bonsaint for his steadfast friendship
and for a nighttime tour of Quebec City
on the trail of films by Robert Lepage*

*To my little sister, Marie, for all the
images we didn't have time to share*

We find beauty not in the thing itself but in the pattern of shadows, the light, and the darkness that one thing against another creates.

JUN'ICHIRŌ TANIZAKI
In Praise of Shadows

Almost too near at hand one vast bare page quivering in scorched earth light holds out until once more with one another we close.

ANDRÉ DU BOUCHET
Where Heat Looms
translated by David Mus

CONTENTS

INTRODUCTION

In a bedroom, glimpsed through an opening in the
stage set, a man sits on the bed, in conversation on the
telephone; then the stage opening moves sideways to
reveal another part of the bedroom while the actor's
conversation continues in voice-over.

A front-load washing machine transforms into a
goldfish bowl when a video image of a swimming
fish is projected onto the windowed door, and then
later opens like the portal of a space capsule that the
actor climbs through.

A TV screen spins around, blinding the audience;
when it turns back toward the actor, he has become
an old woman, asleep in a wheelchair.

A mirror inclines and the actor takes flight, pirouettes,
and disappears.

These visually exciting images from Robert Lepage's solo show
The Far Side of the Moon (2000) have elicited "fascination and
wonder"[1] from audience and critics alike. Theatre reviews expound
the pleasures of the show, referring to "inspired scenography, a
brilliant performance, and a wealth of ideas beautifully rendered
in an elliptical text full of metaphor."[2] As director, actor, designer,
and dramatist, Lepage has been called a magician of images, with
one critic pointing out that Lepage's stage design "continues to
demonstrate [...] magical versatility throughout the performance."[3]

 Theatre is a celebration for Robert Lepage, and his main
instrument in that celebration is the stage. After *Vinci* (1986), most

Lepagean projects have been built around a specific idea of the stage, fostering a wide range of distinctive effects, from the stage box, to the puppet theatre, to the screen. The stage is the source of a developing theatrical language, a visual, sound-based, musical, and only incidentally text-based language.

This is why Robert Lepage's dramatic universe must be approached from the point of view that stage design is a visual laboratory and the theatrical image is its apparatus. Further, we can better understand the source of Lepagean theatrical images by questioning their relationship to technology. Many influences – photography, virtual reality and virtual environments, film, video, and soundscapes – shape their creation, and while Lepage's stage design draws on traditional theatre, his practice in image-based theatre, which he quickly made his own after starting out in 1979, is now iconic.

The evolution in Quebec theatre that occurred at the end of the 1970s showed uncommon connections between a society and its theatre. From those early years, Quebec theatre has been strongly marked with collective works (fuelled by improvisation), a demystification of the text, and a broad notion of the creator. Since the late 1970s, these approaches have been used and accentuated in experimental theatre performances – collective creations that explore other forms of language. A very open relationship with the text developed at the same time, and multidisciplinary theatre that encouraged creative encounters resulted in continued collective exchanges. Lepage entered Quebec theatre during this time of major upheaval, experiencing, drawing from, and supporting its evolution.[4] In many ways he positioned himself as the heir to three aspects of and phases in Quebec theatre – which can be traced back to 1825 when Montreal's Théâtre Royal opened its doors – using first, the spectacular; second, the collective; and third, the experimental in a practice that rethinks ideas while drawing inspiration from them. These historical models would serve as the basis for Lepage's spectacle, and it is within this memory of collective experience that Lepage established his own collective practice; his explorations are the direct descendants of experimental theatre practices in Quebec. But his field of inquiry is also broadened by a wide range of references and experiences, multiplying and disrupting influences and heritage, as echoes that recur in Lepagean stage design.

MACHINA

The reference to the Latin word "*machina*" is explicit in Lepagean theatre practice, including in the name of the multidisciplinary company he founded in 1994. Lepage chose "Ex Machina" as its name, deliberately avoiding the word "theatre." It was not an innocent decision; Lepage justified it by saying that theatre is "no longer our exclusive concern."[5] A further argument: "the name Ex Machina evokes machinery. But for me, machinery is not only the harness that makes poet Jean Cocteau fly in *Needles and Opium* (1991), it's also inside the actor, in his ability to speak the text, to engage with the play; there are mechanisms in that, too."[6] The name retains some reference to theatre: "we removed the '*Deus*' from the expression, which originally heralded an unforeseen outcome, although I think we've preserved a mythical dimension and a sense of spiritual quest. The outcome and the narrative mechanism are still unforeseen, mysterious, and it's now up to us to uncover them."[7]

The word "*machina*" in Lepage's work effectively suggests an etymological mix of trick and invention,[8] with an emphasis on the device and on the mechanics of acting – things concrete and material – from which he extends the relationship with the object: Lepage starts from the concrete and uses his sensitivity and curiosity to develop the work. The name "Ex Machina" does not so much evoke the *deus ex machina* denouement – and therefore the presence of machines or machinery in their contemporary form, technology – as much as it evokes the experimental, creative impulse prompted by contact with the machine.

Dropping the *deus* from the phrase *Deus ex machina* means doing away with illusion and the stage's wings, as well as with the gods. The machine is present onstage alongside its product: machine and its effects (projection, sound, movement). The question is no longer "How does it work?" because how it works is in plain view; rather it is about observing the evocative and poetic power of the machine. The magic remains, but its role changes.

The repeating echoes that characterize Lepagean stage set and image are also at work throughout this practice: a characteristic creation process, the widespread intersection (weaving and cross-breeding) of different forms of media, and the look of the whole fed by both formal and technological models. Technology feeds the entire practice. It provides vision and lets itself be seen, and most importantly it offers something to think about in a masterful practice that questions the image, while revealing the tools used in the questioning. It is a visual laboratory in which we see both the images and ourselves as audience looking at the image as it echoes to the point that we are drawn into the image's centre. It is taking the visual laboratory as a backdrop or using the image as an apparatus so that in viewing Lepagean theatre of images, we essentially go into a box and discover the infinite.

PART ONE

Puppet Theatre and Quarry:
Two Models in the Visual Laboratory

Lepage's first efforts in directing at the beginning of the 1980s distinguished themselves for their scenic design and the connection they forged between audience and stage. Quebec audiences and critics were unanimous: they talked about the power of the gaze (or the power of perspective, in a sense), the influence of film, and a new use of the imagination. In a few years, an entire universe would emerge. Only three years would pass from the first directing project in 1979 to the one that marked the end of an apprenticeship, *En attendant* (1982), in which Lepage created theatre out of nothing except a suitcase and a sheet. From these first shows sprouted a special relationship with the object and set design independent of the stage, which became entrenched as Lepage's practice evolved: a puppet theatre using Chinese boxes, a sort of frame within the frame of the stage that creates a *mise en abyme* or Droste effect. The stage design is based on these two strong instincts – which are more the result of the artist-in-training's intuition and experimentation, as well as a few decisive encounters – than of an obvious aesthetic. Later on, because often it is only in hindsight that things are named, Lepage would create his own mythology of the theatre, a way of justifying the other scenographic tension: the quarry wall as a set for shadows but also as a space that can serve as a screen.

The object, the quarry, and the puppet theatre were the first landmarks of this creative world. They marked out the

architecture of the stage and stage elements and paved the way
for the approaches that would follow: technological environments
as part of the storyline for the creative shows; as well as acting
and the creative process. This would all be contained within a
territory delimited by these instinctual landmarks. Each creation
would explore a new parcel of land, trying to see these landmarks
from different angles. What saves Lepage from repetition and
being derivative of other works is the fact that these instincts are
also a way of asking questions and that the territory he marks out
undergoes astonishing transformations.[1] Lepage juggles with the
territorial markers he has set out on a hunch, without being afraid
to move them and even pile them on top of each other. It's a game
of construction that is much less innocent than it seems.

THEATRE OF THE OBJECT

In 1978 Robert Lepage (a few months before his twenty-first
birthday) and Richard Fréchette graduated from Quebec's theatre
conservatory, the Conservatoire d'art dramatique de Québec,[2]
and completed an internship with Alain Knapp at the Institut de
la personnalité créatrice in Paris. In 1979 they founded Théâtre
Hummm...[3] with the only means at their disposal being their will
and the incredible energy resulting from the internship in Paris.

 The three years Lepage spent at the Conservatoire gave him
a chance to try out different practices and repertoires, and to explore
his abilities as an actor. The reserve, modesty, and "non-acting"
often used to describe his performance style were already apparent.
At the Conservatoire at the time, they were experimenting with
"observation days" that ended in short improvised plays. Teacher
Marc Doré also introduced students to a poetic approach that
allowed Lepage to discover "the poetry of the body, the poetry of
space, of objects, of words."[4] The impetus given to the invention
of new narrative forms would find an extension in Knapp's approach,
requiring the actor-creator to combine improvisation, observation,
and the exploration of inner resources.[5]

 Drawing on this education, Lepage and Fréchette staged
L'attaque quotidienne (1979) in café-theatres, colleges, and arts
centres around Quebec City. The show was improvised based on

stories published in the tabloids that were popular in Quebec at the time. From these café-theatre productions, they went on to stage *Saturday Night Taxi* (1980), a series of comic situations set in a taxi: a woman about to give birth while her husband remains oblivious to what's happening, a retired couple bickering, and so on.

Like the next generation of the collective creations that had swept through Quebec in the previous decade, these first two shows stood out for their rejection of repertory texts, indeed of written text altogether. The approach used was a practical one: a sort of comedy of manners born of observation, the shows were founded mainly on resourcefulness and produced on very small stages on a shoestring budget.

Improvisation was an important part of this practice. While writing and acting in his own shows, Lepage joined the Ligue nationale d'improvisation, the LNI, or the national improvisation league, whose popularity helped introduce him to the general public as an actor. In 1984 he received the O'Keefe trophy, given to the player awarded the most stars, and the Pierre Curzi trophy for rookie of the year.[6] Improvisation would contribute to the conception of Lepagean objects, but in fact two collaborations with Quebec companies would be the real turning point.

The first seems natural, from the vantage point of hindsight on thirty-five years of creative work, but it was also one of those requisite moments of chance, when an unlikely encounter marks a creator's trajectory. For Lepage, these moments were as plentiful as his journeys. Between 1980 and 1985, he mounted four shows for the Marionnettes du grand théâtre de Québec. The experience was important for him in that it helped him to develop his own theatrical language through a process of discovery; it left an indelible mark on his idea of scenic design and acting. His work with marionettes would be echoed in his practice, and, as for many directors, it would be an opportunity for enriching encounters. Like Artaud and his interest in Balinese theatre, and Craig and Yeats with their interest in different forms of non-European puppet theatre, Lepage developed a deep interest in Indonesian *wayang kulit* and Japanese *bunraku*, two traditional forms of puppet theatre that would appear on his stage in varying degrees of orthodoxy. Before objects began to appear in his work, puppets provided Lepage with his first introduction to the inanimate.

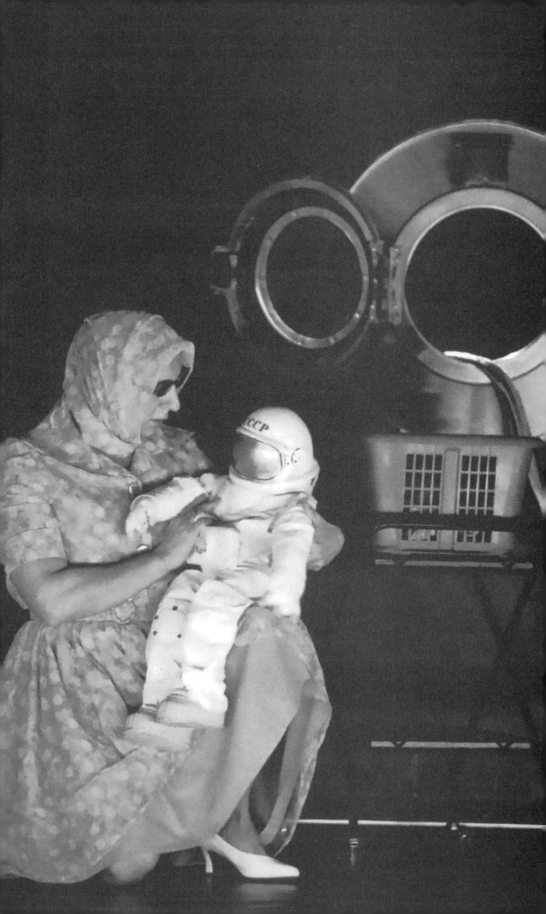

Oomeraghi ooh! (1980) was Lepage's first experience with rod puppets, likewise for the company that hired him to direct. The rods extend out of the puppets' heads and are manipulated similar to *bunraku* puppets. The actor-puppeteers work out in the open, often talking to themselves, like children playing. Lepage saw individuals bringing objects to life, exploring possibilities, and attributing feelings to the puppets. He experimented with the poetic possibilities of puppeteering and tried it himself, in addition to directing *À vol d'oiseau* (1983).

This experience was more than just a step in his education as a director. Lepage would use puppets in four productions: *Coriolanus* (1992, one of three plays in the Shakespeare Cycle), *The Seven Streams of the River Ota* (1994), *The Far Side of the Moon* (2000), and *La Casa Azul* (formerly titled *Apasionada* [*Que viva Frida*], 2001), often with the team from the Grand Théâtre de Québec, now called Théâtre de Sable. He also used puppets for the witch scene in *Elsinore* (1995) and in *The Andersen Project* (2005); the main character, a Quebec librettist, thinks he might stage the Hans Christian Andersen folk story that he is adapting for the Opéra de Paris using puppets.' Throughout these works, Lepage uses a whole range of puppets: string puppets, hand puppets, *bunraku* puppets – a multitude of figures that coexist onstage with the actors. Working with puppets left its mark: Lepage developed a clear rapport with objects, even in the plays where the puppeteer is seemingly not present, as in *The Geometry of Miracles* (1998).

At the same time, Lepage was collaborating with a newly formed company in Quebec City, Théâtre Repère, whose founder, Jacques Lessard, was one of his professors at the Conservatoire. Lepage took part in a first school show and then, in 1982, in a last-ditch effort because the theatre's financial situation had become precarious, Lepage created *En attendant* using only a sheet and a suitcase. The sheet, painted with a motif in the spirit of Japanese *sumi-e* (ink painting),[8] served as a backdrop. The three actors, Fréchette, Lessard, and Lepage, played people waiting in a train station, three characters with nothing in common.[9] In this show, Lepage created theatre out of nothing: just the actor, two objects, and a few costumes. Financial constraints were basically sublimated and transformed into aesthetic intention. Lepage's education was complete; he was confidently exploring a

The puppet object: the astronaut mother and child in *The Far Side of the Moon.*

PHOTO

Sophie Grenier

theatre of the actor manipulating meaningful objects. *En attendant* demonstrated a precocious maturity, a synthesis of the teaching going on around the actor-creator and his early experiments with puppets as objects.

Working with Théâtre Repère and participating in the collective creation of what came to be called the Repère cycle made Lepage more formally aware of an approach that begins with a concrete concept and combines the use of instinct with a process that involves specific stages. The result provides almost objective management of a sensitive piece of information. Lepage would retain from this collaboration the idea of the work in progress and the resource object, but would abandon the fixed structure that characterized the Repère cycle, while keeping their spirit, as *The Geometry of Miracles* would later show.

In Lepagean theatre, poetic impact is inversely proportional to the importance of the set and props. It resides mainly in the ability for evocation that the actor-creator develops with each object. A world emerges from next to nothing: the measuring tape in

Vinci brings about all sorts of "artistic creations that [go] beyond the rigid rules of the measuring tape,"[10] from the Great Wall of China to the trombone, by way of the Pyramids, photographic film, the car, and Michael Jackson's moonwalk. The world is created right in front of the audience's eyes, virtually out of nothing. Lepagean theatre is essentially a genesis; it is fundamentally in the present.

As in the biblical Genesis,[11] many of Lepage's shows open on an empty stage, where only the earth is defined, set in opposition to a sky represented by a floating screen. For example, the stage is empty at the opening of *Elsinore* except for a screen of floating clouds, as was the stage for *The Geometry of Miracles* when it was staged at the World Stage Festival in Toronto in April 1998: nothing but an expanse of sand, topped by an inclined screen the same size. The earth and the sky, as raw material, share the darkness. And then there is light and the universe on the first day of Creation comes into view.

Once the light reveals the stage, the audience is faced with a new, blank universe, a starting space in which the elements will be separated and transformed gradually to create the earth, the show's universe, and the show in its entirety. In many respects, the same principle is at work with the set for *The Far Side of the Moon*, a solo show about two brothers, their dead mother, and a Russian cosmonaut: a rotating partition screen (when the show deals with the cosmos) and a rectangular surface marking out the ground (when the show deals with the story at home on Earth). The universe for the initial versions of *The Dragons' Trilogy* (1985) and *The Geometry of Miracles* was reduced to essential elements: the earth (sand), fire (in the form of smoke in *The Dragons' Trilogy* and flames suddenly shooting up from the sand in *The Geometry of Miracles*), and water (in the form of artificial rain in *The Geometry of Miracles*). Shows like *The Dragons' Trilogy*, *Needles and Opium*, *Elsinore*, *The Geometry of Miracles*, and *The Far Side of the Moon* start with relatively open spaces, which are then populated with objects.

A theatre of the object revitalizes that object, postponing its inevitable banality by reinjecting or injecting it with poetry. Lepage's object is first and foremost the etymological *objectum:* "the thing put before," as an obstacle (in case of defence or attack). It is the "object encountered." The actor comes to terms with it, which is the first step in the Repère cycle. The object cannot

The Dragons' Trilogy opens with a stage set empty as the universe on the first day of Creation: light and darkness, air and sand.

PHOTO
———
Claudel Huot

be circumvented or ignored, mainly because it is often brought
onstage by the actors themselves. At its essence, the object is
singular: the actor encounters, isolates, and designates "an" object.
The stage plays the same role; it is a space for showcasing and
illuminating the object for the person, actor, or audience who
encounters it. The stage is the showcase, literally the surface for
presenting the object.[12] The stage is a site for genesis and an offering. *Objicio*; that is, to present, to expose to, but also to offer. It
is a strange gift this "obstacle is put before," an exhibition related
to the offering.

      Lepage's object is small enough to be manipulated and
moved. It is a close encounter between matter and flesh. The
object is approached, observed, and manipulated. The German
term *Gegenstand* ("object") suggests this physical contact even
more effectively: literally, what stands against (*stegen* = stands,
gegen = against).

      This meaning can be found in the evolution of the puppets
Lepage uses onstage, but it applies to any object as the object moves
closer to its manipulator. In *Coriolanus* (1992), it was string puppets,
held at a distance by people who cannot fully be seen. Then in *The
Seven Streams of the River Ota*, the court of the Chinese emperor
is manipulated using a simplified version of *bunraku*, but with
real contact. And it is not an innocent choice that in *The Far Side
of the Moon* Lepage, dressed as an old woman, cradles the little
cosmonaut puppet and then makes it walk like a child, holding
its hands to help it lift one foot after the other. The mother rocks
both the child and the child's toy, which will be discovered later
in the adult Philippe's closet. As the performance progresses, the
puppet loses more and more of its attributes and becomes more
like an object. At the same time, objects become actual characters;
for instance, the ironing board is "dressed" in a shirt.

      One of the objects that turns up most regularly in
Lepagean theatre is the suitcase (*En attendant*, *The Dragons' Trilogy*,
Tectonic Plates [1989], *The Seven Streams of the River Ota*, and
The Geometry of Miracles) or its equivalents: the backpack and
the duffle bag (*Circulations* [1984], *1984* [2005], *Vinci*, *The Seven
Streams of the River Ota*, and other shows). Often the object is even
smaller, for instance, shoes, a glass ball (*The Dragons' Trilogy*),
a flask, a small basket with a lighter and cigarettes, or a doll

The empty stage set in
The Dragons' Trilogy is
quickly populated with
metaphorical objects.
The barber's chair
represents the business
used as stakes in a
poker game; the shoe
boxes around it are
laid out to represent
St. Joseph Street.

PHOTO
_____
Ludovic Fouquet

(*The Seven Streams of the River Ota*). The object is by definition
more held in the hand than manipulated. This tactile quality is
essential as it is the source of emotion; in contact with human
flesh, the object cries out to be touched.

For Lepage, this relationship with the object is repeatedly illustrated through the figure of the blind man. Three shows
have blind characters: the Florentine guide in *Vinci*; Hanako, the
hibakusha, a Hiroshima survivor in *The Seven Streams of the River
Ota*; and Olgivanna Lloyd Wright in *The Geometry of Miracles*.
The Florentine guide develops a special physical relationship
with the object using his body as a resource when he leads a tour
of the cathedral in Florence. His body becomes the object: in turn
a nave, transept, heart, and choir, like the two women who touch
different resource objects. Unlike the guide, neither woman was
blind from birth, which is why their touching becomes almost
visceral. Touching the thing evokes its shape and the memory
of seeing it. The blind fetishize the object that exists only in its
uniqueness, through sensory contact. Because of their disability,

their senses are highly developed. Hence, Hanako smells the flowers long before Pierre offers them, long before she touches them. When she encounters the object or obstacle, she develops a relationship that privileges the impression of it over the idea of it. This is central to the way the Repère system works, and, more broadly, it is the guiding principle of Lepage's artistic approach. The object is both what it is and what it evokes for the individual, with theatricality residing in the difference and in the possibility offered by two ways of seeing. The object viewed is simultaneously perceived as something else, transformed by the act of seeing and thought. Through the actor's cerebral activity, the object even becomes a screen for thoughts, a tangible resource that moves the imagination.

In three shows, *Circulations*, *À propos de la demoiselle qui pleurait* (1985), and *The Dragons' Trilogy*, the object was very much the starting point. Objects were selected before any thought was given to theme, based on a vague sense of their poetic potential. The resource, whether visual, tactile, sound-based, or olfactory, initiates the exploration. Lepage's object is ordinary, banal, quite often a crude piece of reality, that has dropped onto the stage as if in error, a puzzle that the show slowly pieces together.[13] *Circulations* was built around two objects: a cassette tape and a road map. The cassette tape contains the English language lessons played by Louise, a young Quebecer travelling the east coast of the United States. Her trip is tracked on the road map, which offers a panoramic view of the country. Using the cassette tape gave the actors the idea of the train and the trip ("When does the train to New York leave?" the cassette recording asks), along with a motivation for leaving; in this case, a disturbing rape. From absurd juxtapositions of series of "words with similar sounds,"[14] they "had the impression that the words hid a girl's rape at the hands of her father."[15] The rape or the memory of it makes Louise want to embark on a trip to "take stock." Travel and the rape feed into talk about circulation: the circulation of blood mingles with the road network. And so the receptacle objects invite justification and rich exploration.

In *The Dragons' Trilogy*, the resource object gets even bigger: "The point of departure is the parking lot [covering the old Chinatown in Quebec City]. [The team had gathered] to make it talk, to explore its surface and depth."[16] A resource object is clearly defined: the old Chinatown; its residents and its relationship to Quebec City of the 1950s, but the creators base their exploration on a personal resource object: a glass ball that will link the characters together and cut across the plot. Such a receptacle object is a substitute, an avatar of the performed text. Its use grows out of a spare and well-conceived idea of the stage. Objects are both scarce and omnipresent. This feature distinguished Lepage's first productions from those of his contemporaries. Shows like *Circulations* and *Vinci* were surprising for the physical simplicity of their stages, a presentation space in which just a few objects create an entire world.

A solo show in fourteen scenes, *Vinci* retraces the coming-of-age travels of Philippe, a Quebec photographer, who, after the suicide of his filmmaker friend, starts to question his life and his practice. He interrupts his psychoanalysis to take a trip to Europe, where he meets a series of colourful personalities: an Italian guide, a British guide, the *Mona Lisa* in person philosophizing about the virtues of Burger King, and, finally, Leonardo da Vinci, whom he meets in the public baths of Florence. After this education, Philippe returns to Quebec: "I came to Vinci, and I saw, but I have yet to conquer," he says with a Caesar-like verve, strapped into one of the many flying machines da Vinci dreamed up.

The stage set is minimal: a low wall of glass blocks along which an electric toy train runs, a screen for projecting the shadow figures of the cities Philippe travels through, a psychoanalyst's couch, a seat on a plane bound for Europe, a few books, a tent, a camera, and a white cane for the blind. As in all of Lepagean theatre, there is "maximum use of minimal props."[17] The stage holds a few props (the tent, the chair) that contain within them an environment. They are emblematic objects with evocative elements of reality ripped from their context yet signifying it entirely. The *Mona Lisa*, sipping her Coca-Cola, is an amusing expression of the potential of this sort of empty space: "What I appreciate most of all is that there is no furniture, so anything can happen."

In fact, Lepage plays a great deal with empty space. In it, the prop becomes more meaningful and even takes on a multiplicity of meanings. Lepagean theatre is built on objects that in turn are based on an ongoing use of metaphor. The object is the box that the actor as Pandora opens, releasing a volley of mental or physical images, using the immediate presence of the object and a multitude of associations, the connections it suggests as it is progressively decoded. It becomes a sort of guide for the actor's inspiration.

The Dragons' Trilogy is the show that delves deepest into the symbolism of the elements, multiplying the number of referents and with them the semantic scope of each object. Characters and objects are caught in a web of tightly woven connections that intersect and superimpose metaphors. For instance, chairs acquire a metonymic function. They form the kitchen scenery and then evoke a train trip, with their imitation leather backs reminiscent of the tall benches of old train cars. Chairs often play this role in Lepage's shows; chairs create automobile interiors in The Geometry of Miracles and airplane cabins in The Far Side of the Moon and Zulu Time: A Cabaret for Airports (1998). The chair has metaphorical and initiatory functions, on which it superimposes its practical function.

In the same show, shoes – or their surrogates, boxes – keep popping up in conversations and games and as stage elements. The pregnant Jeanne, who as a child played with shoeboxes, is given little white booties. Later, on a train, Françoise tells the English-man Crawford that a good pair of shoes will see a person through any hardship (Françoise is in effect the character who is present throughout the trilogies). They have to be carefully chosen, like a good bed "because when we're not in one, we're in the other."[18]

Shoes take on a talisman-like power. In the second scene, Jeanne is tending a shoe store where she sells the Englishman's products. Later on, the two young women take off their shoes, one to put on ice skates to go meet her fiancé, and the other to dance with the young Bédard symbolically re-encountered. The shoes are thus the source of one of the play's most moving scenes, the skater's waltz. How better to express the regret of a love affair that was not meant to be than with a few steps of the waltz, its embrace, and the everyday act of placing shoes in pairs! Later, when Françoise meets Bédard again, after she has married Lee, he is taking care of his shoe store in Toronto. In hesitantly placing shoes in different places on the sandy surface (a woman's shoe near a man's shoe), they evoke their relationship, the love story that never was, the moments they never shared. Bédard runs toward the young woman and hugs her with all his might. Jeanne's cries are at once cries of suffering, of relief, of feeling overwhelmed, and of the end of a long wait.

The intensity of her cries suggests her fight against an illegitimate love that is stronger than she is. Then Bédard leaves; later Jeanne has contractions and gives birth lying on the table, attended by Lee, her husband, who is not the child's father. But by placing a bootie between each pair of shoes the lovers set out in the sand, Lee shows that he will accept the baby as his daughter. She emerges from beneath the parting table – extensions are slid into it – and puts on the last pair of shoes, while the remaining pairs evoke the march they will watch as it passes. Soldiers pillage the little families of shoes, scatter them, and slash them with sharpened skate blades, suggesting war. Then, quite significantly, Jeanne removes her shoes before committing suicide. Just before she hangs herself, she takes off her shoes, relieving herself of the objects that accompanied and guided her in life. She gets up on the table, rope in hand, and looks up, breathing heavily. Blackout.

Not just shoes, but every object comes alive with the character who comes into contact with it. The death of a character who has developed a particular relationship with the object therefore results in its disappearance. After Jeanne commits suicide and offers her shoes as a legacy, all shoes and shoeboxes disappear from *The Dragons' Trilogy*. For Lepage, the object doesn't exist independently; it exists only in relationship, subordinated to a consciousness that encounters it.

This subordination doesn't mean that the object can't exist as a relic. It may remain onstage, embodying the memory of someone who has died, but, unlike the shoes, it is present only as a memory: the audience doesn't see the individual in question develop the primary relationship with the object. This is particularly clear in *The Seven Streams of the River Ota*, where many objects – photos, a baseball glove, a camera, and a kimono – outlive their users, creating a memory for generations to come. These objects are filled with a story that the survivor will tell the audience. As synecdoches, they personify the deceased. For example, for Jeffrey Yamashita, or Jeffrey 2, the glove symbolizes his father, G.I. Luke O'Connor, and the games he was never able to play with him.

"Okay, let's change." At the opening of *The Dragons' Trilogy*, two little girls in short dresses and white sockettes bustle about setting out white shoeboxes in two parallel lines. These smooth, identical rectangular shapes on the sand floor suggest a city in miniature. The two little girls who open *The Dragons' Trilogy* use the boxes to construct a familiar reality: St. Joseph Street in Quebec City. Each box represents a store: "Lépine the undertaker," "Morin the barber," and so on. The audience is quick to understand the game and integrate the convention, based on mimicry: imitation not so much in the shape of the box to suggest a store, but in using the box unit as a standard dwelling unit and "rearranging" it to reflect the actual layout of the street. There is confusion or synecdoche between the store and its owner. "That's Talbot's," Jeanne exclaims looking at the largest box, "because it's the biggest." The ideal container, the shoebox, is opened for each new scene and closed when we move onto the next store: "Okay, let's change."

> JEANNE: Okay. And then, a man arrives who makes shoes and he wants them to sell them.
>
> […]
>
> FRANÇOISE: And he comes from England, okay?
>
> […]
>
> FRANÇOISE: And so then, he goes to Paquet's, and then Paquet sends him to Georgette's, but then, fat Georgette Matte, she hates English people, so she plays a trick on him, and she sends him to Pettigrew's …
>
> JEANNE: And he doesn't know that Pettigrew's burned down …
>
> FRANÇOISE: So he ends up in front of a crater at Pettigrew's, and then, he goes to the house next door, and then …
>
> […]
>
> FRANÇOISE AND JEANNE: He ends up at the Chinese laundry![19]

As soon as the little girls mention the English character, he appears in the flesh walking along the street outlined by the boxes. Two universes intermingle: the children's game and this sales representative's meandering, and both lead to the Chinese man's establishment, at the mention of whom the girls run off, while the Englishman has a first conversation with him. This game of childish imitation, combining the use of found objects as props for play and repeating things that they've heard, is not just an amusing interlude. It marks out the performance space and summons the characters; these are introductory scenes during which one by one the figurines are taken out of their boxes.

In *Vinci*, Lepage uses a very free visual approach with shapes. Philippe's photography books, which are stacked, aligned, and standing upright, become a mimetic reference to Vinci's village, as he perceives it in the hills. This game of architectural mimicry was already apparent and even more pronounced in *Tectonic Plates*, with the towers of books, at once stools and skyscrapers, recreating New York's famous skyline, as a couple looks for a public bench on which to sit. The playfulness comes in mainly through the difference in scale between the performer and the object used. The ability to group and combine objects provides Lepage with a range of opportunities for mimicry, exploiting the wide range of meaning latent in his objects. On the empty stage in *Circulations*, two fly cases (shipping containers for light and audiovisual equipment), are used to create everything: beds, changing rooms, train cars, and restaurant tables.

Lepage's theatrical practice uses the objects that surround him, and starting with its shape, the object evolves notionally through delightful musings that consider the visual, symbolic, and sound-based aspects of the object, as is the case with the enchantingly simple train of postcards in *Circulations*. The physical nature of the postcards is explored: "We would rub them together near a microphone, and the electronic keyboard would use the sound to create the clack-clack of the train."[20] Postcards suggest both the sound of a train and, by analogy, the missives Louise writes throughout her journey. But the mimicry becomes visual when the six cards are lined up to form the cars of the train on which Louise travels. And yet an analogy between postcard and train is a bit of a reach. But the little train doesn't stop there. The audience has just barely grasped that this is a train when the cards are turned over to show photographs of scenery as seen from the train. Scenery starts to roll by; then the cards are joined "and take flight: gulls, the sea, and Provincetown suddenly appear."[21] This approach using the object is at once formal and semantic, a visual reading at the crossroads of the immediately palpable and pure thought, is inspired by the general shape of the object. This is how, during the architect Frank Lloyd Wright's meal at the Taliesin Fellowship, Wright's school of architecture, the wine glasses and plates are grouped to form a model of the Johnson Wax Building.

This symbolic, playful mimicry can also be based on a grouping of elements used separately. The object creates meaning through its synchronic relationship with other objects. This is what occurs in *The Dragons' Trilogy* scene with the typewriter that Françoise uses while listening to her typing lesson on tape. The machine is broken down into different metaphorical levels, the analogy transforming the window blind in the cabin into the typewriter's roller (physical mimicry). There is also sound mimicry (bicycle bells and a camera shutter release) and more conceptual mimicry (ideological conflict for the separation of the keyboard for the two hands). These unusual illustrations weave several threads of the story together that simultaneously unfold during the typing lesson.

Lepage's images abound in resource objects as vessels that render their content through the actor-manipulator. The image is created through manipulation, but also through the combination of objects. This manipulation is very similar to the manipulation of puppets and even goes further, because quite often the object is manipulated as an object, with no anthropomorphism. Lepage's object is the offspring of both the puppet's strings and the imagination. But what about the set?

A PUPPET-THEATRE SET

Alongside this "objectification," which suggests puppets but no true effigies – they will appear starting with *Vinci* – Lepage's world is based on an architectonic view of the stage. The puppetized object creates a puppet-like space, by making references to the puppet theatre through a geometric structure that isolates and frames the action and the characters. The first productions didn't feature this signature set or put the set in a box. The significant change of direction occurred in 1986 with *Vinci*, after a transitional phase that began in 1980 with the first forays into the world of puppets. It seems paradoxical that Lepage discovered the puppet theatre just when the puppets of the Grand Théâtre de Québec stepped away from it.

Gradually, from performance to performance, a new acting space was defined, moving closer to that of the live actor, but at the same time reintroducing fragments of or references to the old puppet theatre. Then, in 1985, *Histoires sorties du tiroir* plunged into fantasy world of the cock-and-bull story.[22] Here the action takes place in and around a tubular metal structure that evokes in turn a windmill, a house, and a glacier without any real outside intervention. All the necessary elements are contained in the structure and are in plain view from the beginning of the performance: horizontal ladders serve as floors or bunk beds, the windmill's wheel is set at the top, and so on. The hollowed-out structure that results is a puppet theatre and set piece at one and the same time.[23] The puppet theatre no longer hides the puppeteer and puppeteering tools; it offers its structure up to view, to the imagination, and to symbolism.

There is a kinship between the puppet-theatre productions and those with live actors that Lepage created during this period. The most obvious influence, and one with the greatest potential for exploration, is found in *The Dragons' Trilogy*. Produced in the same year as *Histoires sorties du tiroir*, this marathon six-hour show is for the most part based on a central structure, a wooden kiosk, very much like a puppet theatre, and Lepage delves fully into its rich semantic possibilities. Most often the structure coexists with other spaces onstage – a large sand surface. Unlike puppet theatres as traditionally used, the action doesn't take place exclusively inside the box's frame, but is connected with an entire outside environment. Lepage integrates and combines what he learned with the puppets at the Grand Théâtre de Québec with a formal reference to a Québécois reality: the stage, with this central puppet theatre, is a replica of many Quebec parking lots, stretches of dirt or concrete surrounding a parking attendant's booth of varying size. The wooden structure of the show is rectangular with a glass half-wall. All that's needed for a puppet theatre is to replace the glass with a curtain or to mount a blind above the glass to unroll as the curtain falls. And this structure has a novel addition: the puppet theatre has openings on three of its sides, like three windows.

The action begins inside the parking attendant's booth. Smoke fills and streams out of it, while a projector set on top lights the glass wall. A parking-lot attendant enters the booth and – adapting the possibilities of the central puppet theatre for the actor – becomes a puppet moving in slow motion, bathed in intense red light, while reverberating music. The other characters appear, approach the booth, and look at "the guardian of eternity," noses pressed up against the windows, like an audience of children gathered around the puppet theatre. Later on, two little girls bring clothes to the Chinese laundry, and the parking attendant's booth / puppet theatre becomes the laundry. The little girls walk around the parking booth, knock on the door, and call out as if calling out to a puppet. Jeanne's "Mr. Chinese Man" is reminiscent of children stamping with impatience and calling out "Punch" in traditional *Punch and Judy* puppet shows. Then, at one point in the third act, the action changes to a scene in the Vancouver airport terminal, where a young Japanese girl, Yukali, runs the news and souvenir stand. Again, it is a kiosk. She emerges from the newsstand through a raised window in the wooden door, just as, in Lepage's later production *La Casa Azul*, Frida Kahlo will emerge from the inclined roof of her canopy bed. The two characters are only visible from the waist up, expressing themselves with arm gestures, like a glove puppet with just the bust emerging from the puppet theatre. The comparison is all the more clear when Yukali addresses the audience as if they are a customer, in this case, a French pilot who keeps bothering her:

> YUKALI: What do you want? [...] This is the third
> time you've come here this week ... [...] This is
> my space, it's a small space, but it's mine, and I can't
> breathe when you're here. You take up all my air."[24]

"It's a small space, but it's mine" could reference the puppet theatre as defined by a talking puppet.

The wooden parking booth has all the features of a puppet theatre, with the added benefit of integrated wings and lighting. What's unique about this puppet theatre, like the tubular structure from *Histoires sorties du tiroir*, is its diversity of meanings. Normally the puppet-theatre structure is neutral; it is the compartment that delimits the performance space, mimicking the Harlequin's cloak in Italian *commedia dell'arte*. And yet, for this show with its minimal equipment changes (opening and closing the door, raising and lowering the blind), the puppet theatre incarnates different places through mimicry. As with puppet shows at the Grand Théâtre de Québec, every surface, every possible space in this box and the opening of its door is used, providing very deft switches between interiors and exteriors, up and down. So when Crawford enters the Chinese laundry, Wong comes out of the hut to make room for him, and the scene resumes as if the inside of the shack were now the street outside, with the stage representing the inside of the shop. Later on, the puppet theatre becomes a stairwell: Crawford and Wong, both in the hut, pretend to go downstairs, turning around and lowering themselves bit by bit, a classic technique used with puppets. The characters re-emerge onto the stage the opposite way, which has turned into the basement of the laundry.

The puppet-theatre box is a regular feature on Lepage's stage, sometimes even referencing itself. There is the puppet theatre in the form of a phone booth in *The Seven Streams of the River Ota*. There are red English-style phone boxes in Lepage's design for the *Secret World Live* tour (1993–94), the first Peter Gabriel concert that Lepage staged, and there are phone booths in his adaptation of Gay's *The Beggar's Opera*, titled *The Busker's Opera* (2004). The booth is a modular set that evolves from a small narrow booth into death row, depending on how the sides of the box are unfolded, or rather, how the sides of two phone booths united into a single form are unfolded. In *The Andersen Project* (2005), the same shape is found in the form of the sex shop / phone booth that in one scene becomes a sort of calèche that Andersen travels in. Like a puppet, he is visible from the waist up.

It was while working with puppets at the Grand Théâtre de Québec that Lepage appropriated the structural and scenographic possibilities of the puppet theatre. An evolution is evident beginning in 1986, when we see the puppet-theatre box expand to take over the whole stage. The stage becomes a large box, with each performance exploring its own theatrical possibilities.

The production *Vinci* was created in 1986. It came on the heels of Lepage's solo show *Comment regarder le point de fuite* (1985), the first part of a multidisciplinary show, *Point de fuite* by Théâtre Repère. Lepage, who interrupted his work with the puppets of the Grand Théâtre de Québec, moved away from having the puppet theatre visible onstage. But this didn't mean that he dispensed with every reference to the puppet theatre: the same year, he directed *Comment devenir parfait en trois jours* (1986), an adaptation of Stephen Mane's *Be a Perfect Person in Just Three Days*. Once Lepage stopped directing puppets, his stages gradually became great puppet theatres.

Projections began to appear in *Vinci*, as did the beginnings of a physical delimitation of the stage. Even more symbolically, a low wall of glass blocks circumscribes the background, emphasizing the demarcation created by the backdrop screen onstage. A thread would run through all of Lepage's solo shows: moving walls, forming the sides of a hypothetical box. This was the case in *Needles and Opium*, *Elsinore*, and *The Far Side of the Moon*.

The thread is clear in the solo shows, which increasingly make plain a puppet-theatre box around a solitary puppet actor.

From the opening scenes of *Needles and Opium*, the audience faces a screen that takes up the entire width of the performance space. Like the central puppet-theatre set in *Comment devenir parfait en trois jours*, the screen is a boundary between two spaces. It is also a turning point, because its rotations reveal new places. Most often it represents the walls of the character's location, specifically a room at Hôtel La Louisiane, during a visit to Paris. The screen represents one side of this room that is as cramped as a box, which Lepage sets in opposition to an expansive exterior (city noises, the panting of a couple making love, the character's dreams). Physically there is only one wall – in addition to a checkerboard floor that is hard to ignore – and yet the idea of the theatrical box is clear, as is the idea of confinement, demonstrated by the actor regularly breaking out of the box. Directing himself, Lepage performs in a small set, in a box he can walk on, hide behind, and appear in the centre of, in short, a small theatre, the size of the actor, a reassuring box, a puppet theatre.

With *Elsinore*, the stage box is even more clear. It appears larger: four panels mark the four sides of a form that is the performance space. The far panel, which was made of light fabric in *Needles and Opium*, can still rotate, but in *Elsinore* it is more mobile and heavier. The far panel is a large, 600 kilogram plane surface supported at each of its four corners by industrial wires wound up and down by a set of motors. This is the iconic Monolith, which can revolve in any direction and will be in turn vertical, horizontal, and inclined. The side walls move only laterally, framing the Monolith with a large screen wall that cuts off the stage as would a curtain at the beginning of a performance. This screen or wall becomes a rampart of the Elsinore castle, when the credits are projected onto the backdrop of the wall of the medieval Danish fortress. In *Elsinore*, however, Lepage seems to have wanted to exhaust all possibilities of the three walls, one of which can incline to horizontal position. Thus the central wall becomes the ceiling of Ophelia's bedroom, the upper deck of a ship, an inclined floor with a turntable attached during the face-to-face encounter between Hamlet and his uncle, or a wall with the throne of the king or the queen, who are treated as playing-card characters.

From parking attendant's booth to phone booth, the upright rectangular box appears often. *The Busker's Opera.*

PHOTO

Ludovic Fouquet

   Elsinore is above all a technological show. In the version
staged in Créteil in August 1996, Lepage is hemmed in by the panels
moving around him, as well as by the conditions of the manipulation, which are invisible to the audience. In the London version
in January 1997, he gave the impression of performing in a space
that is the same size as him – the mark of his solo shows. The set
changes had become fluid.[25] Many of the play's spaces were enclosed
spaces. The mobile walls, reflecting the internal dramatic tension,
had taken on a special power and meaning: characters are endlessly
spied upon in this play, and the walls close in on the protagonists
to the point of shrouding them. The box that is formed frames the
protagonists more and more tightly, becoming the character's tomb
or coffin, a box at any rate.

   Even though the box has evolved to the point of having
its walls removed, it doesn't abandon its puppet-theatre origins.
But rather than having an actor suspended from wire, an amusing
reference to the puppet as the basis for unusual images, the walls
now seem to be floating. The Monolith is suspended, as was Lepage

in *Needles and Opium*, and is therefore capable of the same rotations. The only difference is that when it is suspended it becomes a new performance area, a small stage for the actor. It's a stage in miniature and a reference: Lepage as Hamlet climbs onto the stage and manipulates puppet objects.

The puppet theatre, expanded to fill the entire set, is also found in the collective productions. The set of *Alanienouidet* by Marianne Ackerman (co-written with Lepage in 1992) is an actual rectangular box, set on an angle, with windows and doors, and with the actors standing on its "lid." There are two acting spaces inside and on top of the box, reminiscent of Aboriginal dwellings and those of the first settlers, depending on the level. In order to be seen, the actors who perform inside the box are positioned in front of the openings – as in a puppet theatre. *Alanienouidet*, like Shakespeare's *Coriolanus*, builds on initial ideas for the sets for *Vinci* and *Needles and Opium* and foreshadows the ideas for *Elsinore* with the panel that opens like the opening of a puppet theatre. But in this case, the box structure doesn't change. The central panel is no longer a reversible part of a theatrical box with its insides on display. In *Alanienouidet*, an actual brick wall 2.5 metres high, like the wall in *Le polygraphe* (1987; in English, *Polygraph* [1987]),[26] occupies the entire width of the stage, and the panel suggests the walls of the dwelling, the corridors of the metro, the Berlin Wall, and, more broadly, the frontier between reality and fiction. In contrast, the set of *Coriolanus* is the facade of a theatrical box with both puppet theatre and movie-screen influences. The entire play unfolds behind the rectangular opening, like a puppet show. The opening is waist-high to the actors, and it can be altered through the use of trestle tables that become stages or performance spaces.

For Lepage, the ideal model for a stage is the geometric shape he encountered when working with puppets. It is his main starting point, and this shape allows his imagination to run free as he considers how to make the action visible and how to highlight the protagonists within this structure. The geometric puppet-theatre shape is Lepage's first solution. But he progresses from using it as a direct reference to a broader exploration of changes to the puppet theatre, applied to live actors. The puppet theatre grows, its performance space becomes more varied, and its structure opens up and becomes mobile. At times all that remains is the core, as in

The brick wall in *Polygraph* occupies the entire width of the stage, suggesting the frontier between fiction and reality.

PHOTO

Emmanuel Valette

The Geometry of Miracles, with a large sandbox similar to the set in *Alanienouidet* and *Polygraph*. The box is the stage: there is nothing else. We have moved from the puppet-theatre set on the stage, to the puppet-theatre stage.

An ideal figure emerges from all these attempts to define a theatrical space: the square box. Lepage prefers the square (part of *Vinci, Needles and Opium, A Dream Play* [1994], *1984*) to the upright rectangle (the parking attendant's booth / puppet theatre in *The Dragons' Trilogy, Comment devenir parfait en trois jours, The Busker's Opera*) or its horizontal cousin (*Alanienouidet, Coriolanus, The Seven Streams of the River Ota, The Geometry of Miracles*). The square, and later, the cube, is the ultimate, irreducible shape. It is the tangible trace of combining the properties of the puppet with a humanization of the puppet theatre. This shape is often found when researching Lepage's sketchbooks – a perspectivist vision of a cube that he evokes as his ideal scenic design – but quite often the cube is tweaked by the "will of cinema" that lengthens it into a rectangle to produce a rectangular frame. In either case, the cube is truly "an object for serving up images."[27] With the cube, anything is possible; it represents nothing and everything. The cube is a shape that is easy to recognize and an "eminent tool of representability."[28]

The wall of a symbolic stage box, the screen the actor floats in front of in *Needles and Opium*, like the Monolith in *Elsinore*, is square. The original box, with its walls intact, is square, which the metallic structures suggest. It is therefore not surprising that the modular stage Lepage uses at La Caserne, the production centre established in his hometown of Quebec City, is itself within a cube 18 metres square. The creation space is a large black box, a cubic space that can be completely transformed. In his earlier stagings and with this black box, the square box is a perfect and autonomous shape, even more so than the rectangle.

The cube also has human dimensions, a bit like Tony Smith's sculpture *Die* (1958), a six-foot black steel cube (the height of an average man). The dimensions of the human body are suggested through proportions of what could be a man's body, or his coffin. In Lepage's stage designs, the man is the measure of the set or vice versa. Setting a cube onstage is evidence of a human presence and intervention. As a set designer, Lepage sees the stage as an architect

would, organizing human modules: "The square and the cube represent [...] the world, architecture. If you find cubes and rectangular
boxes in my sets, it has a lot to do with my desire to structure space,
to make architecture out of it."[29] While Lepage's universe fits inside
a cube, the human body is at the centre of this universe, so it seems
appropriate to have Leonardo da Vinci's famous *Vitruvian Man* appear
projected onto the Monolith in *Elsinore*. In this illustration from an
unpublished treatise on anatomy da Vinci depicts man in a square,
in turn within a circle, showing the rotation of arms and legs. The
same image, this time rendered by Oskar Schlemmer, can be found
on the back wall of La Caserne in Quebec City: etched on black stone,
vanishing lines suggest the drawing of man in the universe.[30] But in
this case, man is no longer alone at the centre. The lines designate the
heart of this universe: the stage, man's medium. The cube becomes a
sort of sacred receptacle of a dual mystery: stage and man.

Lepage speaks of architecture when mentioning these
stage designs, clearly an intentional move. His quest is part of an
aesthetic heritage that, since the end of the nineteenth century, has
made the stage an architected space, a functional space, coherent,
and fitting with a vision of a world that can be shaped. The notion
of architecture is common among creators today such as Lepage
and Robert Wilson, but it builds on the thinking of Craig and
Svoboda. At a time when no one yet talked about the structure
of the action – as would be done with Meyerhold and Piscator –
Craig conceived the stage as a distinctively built working drawing.
Since Craig, architected spaces have been popular, supported by
lighting but particularly playing with a kinetic space, to which
theatre designers assign different names: "kinetic" for Craig, who
sees this as a fifth essential stage in the history of stage design,[31] and
for Svoboda, "psycho-plastic," meaning elastic in scope and alterable
in quality.[32] All scenographers are tormented by this question of the
stage image, its depth, and its constitution. They probe it to better
explore it, but without questioning the anchoring point of these
experiments: they remain anchored on a proscenium-based scenic
design, on a box of illusions. And it would be perfectly natural to
see hints of the silhouette of the actor in effigy emerge in these
theatrical spaces. This is definitely what underlies Craig's visions;
the screens he dreams of as well as the stage design for the Moscow
Art Theatre production of *Hamlet* in 1911–12 are echoed in Lepage's

practice, specifically his staging for *Elsinore,* and Yannis Kokkos's scenic design for Vitez's production of *Hamlet.*[33]

　　　The description of the screens – partitions covered in canvas or in solid wood, capable of producing "a thousand sets in one" through their movement and changes in lighting – could apply to the stage design for *Elsinore.* For Vitez, as for Lepage, mobile panels are constantly moved about to redefine the space. They too are white, but they don't have the magical mobility claimed by Craig. He wants the audience to remain in ignorant awe of how this celebration is accomplished, an approach that is diametrically opposed to that of Lepage. In *Elsinore,* he leaves the mechanism that lifts the Monolith in plain view – even exploiting an aesthetic of connector technology when the Monolith is turned around – along with the metal beams that form the outline of a puppet theatre around the stage. In *The Seven Streams of the River Ota,* we see ricepaper doors called *shoji* screens and other set pieces glide along rails, pushed by technicians or actors in plain view. In *The Geometry of Miracles,* technicians pull on cords that slide the set elements into

sight and that move the large screen in the distance. The machinery is even more clearly on display once the sand is removed from the pit and the action takes place on bare wood: the revolving stages and ropes are in full view. With Lepage's work, the elements of stage design have a greater range of movement, whereas they move in only two directions with Craig's work. But they have the same minimalism, with the projection of images playing the role of lighting on the white panels. Architected in this way, the stage forms both the box for the object and a puppet theatre as well as a symbolic shape that contains the actor. While it is architected, it is no less modular and sometimes mobile.

THE BOX:
THE SEVEN STREAMS OF THE RIVER OTA

In January 1994, upon his return from a visit to Hiroshima, Lepage began work on *The Seven Streams of the River Ota*. Along with *Elsinore,* this production would feature the most closed, most inventive, most transparent, and at the same time the most evolving stage box. The set is a magnificent compromise between the imperviousness of the ideal box and the stage's needs for transparency. The show is also important for the mastery and fluidity of set changes that use and easily get around the closed box. *The Seven Streams of the River Ota* is an unusually long marathon show: seven hours with intermissions. The published script[34] involves seventy-six scenes; in other words, seventy-six theatrical units, with their sets, their lighting, and their characters. However, many scenes unfold in the same place, exploiting the initial set to the fullest.

A sloped tile roof, seven sliding *shoji* screens, and a wooden porch create a traditional Japanese house for the set in *The Seven Streams of the River Ota*.

PHOTO

Emmanuel Valette

Before the performance begins, the set is visible, waiting. The exterior walls of a Japanese house stand out against a dark backdrop. A variety of traditional elements are recognizable: a sloped tile roof, wooden door frames, and seven sliding *shoji* screens. A wooden porch and a garden of raked stones that are of identical size and separated by two steps extend the facade of the house. With this stage set, Lepage and set designer Carl Fillion return to the idea of the box, but on a larger scale than with the initial puppet theatres. This box offers new possibilities for entrances and exits and for action in front of the set. Unlike *The Dragons' Trilogy*, where action revolved around a small puppet theatre, in *The Seven Streams* we are plunged into a box the same size as the set. Everything is seen nearly head-on, because the elements have little depth – less than 2 metres for the garden of raked stones and the wooden porch – and the performance space is very close to the audience, at the edge of the stage or right near the first rows.

The set is soberly realistic: the empty wooden space divided by sliding ricepaper doors situates the action in the Orient, but at no specific time. The Japanese structures, secular and commonly used, are timeless and archetypal. The only temporal reference is a harsh one: seven neon lights under the porch cast a cold, white halo that contrasts with the soft colours of the set. The first scene foreshadows how tradition and technology will cohabit in this show: seven *shoji* screens, seven neon lights, two diametrically opposed relationships with light. One is almost ethereal, tranquil, and soft – and weather dependent – and the other is immutable and electric in its stark coldness.[35]

Proscenium, screens, opening *shoji* screens: these are all elements that run through the stage design for this show in a broad exploration of the initial set. Lepage uses the rectangular opening of the puppet theatre as a starting point and, around this opening, throughout the show he builds a form that is the extension of the puppet theatre. Leaving certain partitions invisible, he manipulates a rectangular box and manages to display it from every angle without a revolving stage. This principle was used beginning with the show's genesis: the entire creation team called each scene of this marathon show a "box." Each version of the production would see new boxes added: three at the Edinburgh International Festival and other 1994 performances, and then five in Vienna and other 1995 performances, and finally seven in Quebec City and other 1996 performances. From a dramaturgical point of view, the story itself is also a sort of game of forms; from version to version the scenes are thought of as interchangeable elements and sometimes as nesting boxes. Thus the box takes on a variety of semantic forms: it designates the part, the place, and the prop that occupies the place in this show.

The *shoji* screen is the baseline measurement for all the elements of the set: screens, panels, and so on, in the same way that architects use a single element or component in different ways in

In *The Seven Streams of the River Ota*, the *shoji* screen is the baseline measurement for all elements of the set.

SKETCH
Carl Fillion

The facade, floor, and ceiling make up three walls of a rectangular box, with the audience viewing the action through the open shoji screens. *The Seven Streams of the River Ota*.

SKETCH
Ludovic Fouquet

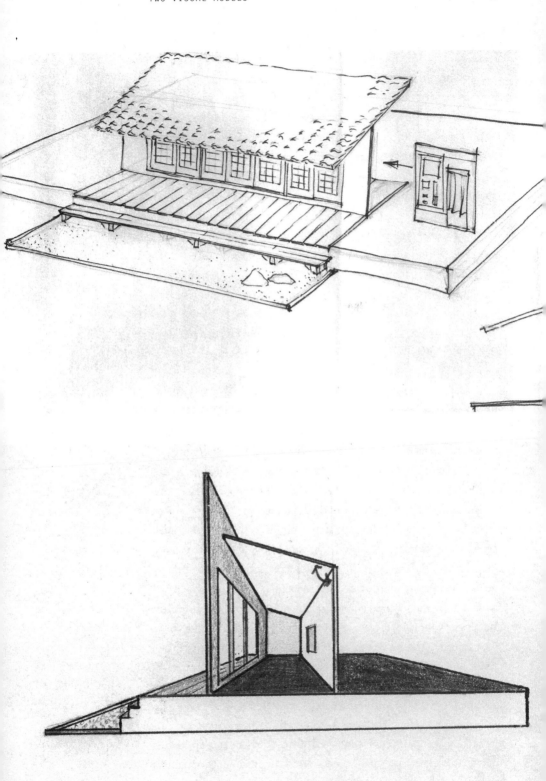

their practice. The Japanese unit of measure is the *tatami* mat, the size of which is based on the height of the average man – another example of the human body-as-yardstick Lepage uses to build his sets. The rooms of the Japanese house normally are separated by partitions, but here, by convention, they are not given form. The opening in the *shoji* screens corresponds to an equivalent room: the living room or the bedrooms of the tiny Japanese house. The opening reveals a space at the same time as it delimits it, which is the attribute of the frame (theatre, photography, painting, and cinema). The *shoji* screens slide in and out to reveal an apartment, a recording studio, a restaurant. In the third part, "A Wedding," the walls become increasingly concrete: in the initial versions tulle, Plexiglas, or a two-way mirror close out the performance space behind the wooden frame, but remain transparent.

The first scene of the third part unfolds in the red-light district of Amsterdam. The wooden frame walls of the tiny house become the front of any house lining the streets of the district with their one-room sex shops. The Japanese tile roof is raised. Now only the facade is visible, which, because of its great sobriety, lends itself well to the changes of scene and shifts in time and place, while providing a sort of permanent reminder of the oriental theme.

To suggest the red-light district, four women prostitutes rip the screens from the wooden frames, which now suggest sex-shop display windows. The prostitutes dance within the wooden frames, and their white lingerie stands out lit by black light against the black background. Slowly, panels filled with books slide onstage to close the box: the panels act as both set and curtain, hiding the display windows of the sex shops and closing the box behind the wooden frame. Likewise, the porch becomes an interior space; for example, a bedroom, a space delimited by the same *shoji* screens. The *tatami* mats are no longer behind the wooden frame, but in front of it, for the audience to see. The facade acts as a spatial reference point and as a partition to delimit the area and the form of the box being used.

When the prostitutes exit in scene 5, the backs of the display windows are lit, revealing a wall covered with soundproofing material. The performance space behind the frame has become a recording studio, with a sound booth bordered by a long glass wall, a symbol, like the earlier display windows. Two spatiotemporal frames are juxtaposed, but more importantly the two spaces play with different ideas, one with the idea of enclosure – with the closed space of the soundproofed recording studio – and the other with the idea of fluidity and passage – with one character passing by on the porch without stopping, like a memory. And then the studio partition rises and reveals another box with more physical partitions. This performance space is gradually built in the third part, with partitions added to the box in each scene forming a "mezzanine box."

After the recording is finished, the studio's partition rises and reveals a new partition, that of an apartment in Amsterdam. The partition of the previous box tilts to 135 degrees and becomes the top of the mezzanine box. The panel of the studio's soundproofing reveals its reverse side: wooden boards that suggest the sloped ceiling of a closet under the stairs. The scenery panels are stacked, waiting to be unveiled, and the scenery change is as fluid as the sliding of the *shoji* screens. The Amsterdam apartment is marked out on four sides: the floor, the back wall, the ceiling, and the wall on the audience side, a large wooden frame hollowed out to match the dimensions of five of the *shoji* screens. The last two screens, stage left, remain closed and represent a part of the facade, with an opening for a door. The box is almost perfect, and it creates an impression of intimacy: an apartment in Amsterdam where Jeffrey O'Connor, G.I. Luke's son (Jeffrey 1)[36] will live out the days leading up to his death from AIDS, surrounded by his loved ones. It is difficult to see this virtually perfect wooden box as anything other than a coffin, into which one may ultimately, serenely lie down.

In contrast to this ultimate confinement, Lepage attempts to add depth to the forms as if stretching each to its limits. The set ends up overflowing, with people leaving the box and the frame, and therefore the limits of the mezzanine box. In the fourth part, the scene takes on a dreamlike quality when Jana Čapek, the Czech Jew who has survived a Nazi concentration camp, reveals a wall of mirrors as she slides back the *shoji* screens lining her room (the porch). As she kneels before the wall, the mirrors show the audience what is behind; a change in lighting reveals Jana as a little girl lying in the same position. The two-way mirrors, like the *shoji* screens, are both impervious and transparent, in addition to having the power of reflection. Jana watches her memories pass by in the mirror, as pale and ephemeral characters. This is more than a mere penetration behind the mirror; it is an immersion inside the mirror because the new characters also find themselves in front of a reflecting surface. Two lines of mirrors face each other and frame the mezzanine box. At first this space is relatively shallow: a narrow corridor the panicked characters run down, a women's dormitory, and a design studio. When the adult Jana moves the *shoji* screens, the mirrored space gains depth. She looks across a mirror at the child Jana, who opens the mirror panels and discovers Sarah Weber, an opera singer held at the Terezin concentration camp, getting ready before a large mirror. Three rows of mirrors are visible, reflecting to infinity when the doors are slightly angled.

The box in *The Seven Streams of the River Ota* therefore develops along a perpendicular axis to the house facade. It expands and grows deeper on the mezzanine side of the box. But a reverse movement is also possible, and the box can open on the audience side, on the porch and the garden of raked stones. Thus, in the second part, "Two Jeffreys," the cross-section of apartments on one floor in a New York apartment building appears behind the wooden facade. Where there was an empty room, broken up by a few *shoji* screens, three boxes are lined up, each corresponding to a room and a reference to the principle of the fourth wall.

The shared central bathroom is the common room in the apartment building and the heart of all scenes in this part. People run into each other in the bathroom while performing their ablutions, when someone visits the apartment, to take drugs, and to spy on the neighbours. People meet there to make music, to talk and dance during a party, and to develop pictures. It is an autonomous box, tacked on to the opening of the facade, around which the other spaces are organized. The two other rooms – the hallway and the bedroom facing the bathroom – are formed by the bathroom's three walls. Despite the narrow space, many characters circulate within it. In contrast, the porch seems a vast expanse with only a scenic model or a solitary character on it.

Two spatial and temporal spheres are juxtaposed: within the house facade, the action takes place in the United States in 1965; on the porch, it is 1945 through 1946 in Japan. In a dreamlike scene, Jeffrey 2 leaves the New York apartment and in a dream meets his father for the first time on the porch. Later on, he sits there with his mother's body in remembrance. Once the American setting has been established, the scenes can alternate between New York and Japan. The wooden facade is the common element of the two juxtaposed spheres; it is the point of juncture, the hinge, and sometimes even the curtain. The juxtaposed spheres create sets with distinct energies: an axis parallel to the facade for New York, and a perpendicular axis that seems to emerge from the frame and continue on the porch, outside of the box, like a second temporal sphere superimposing on the first, for Japan. The first axis explores the stage design possibilities inside the box; the second emerges from the box and juxtaposes a new fuzzier and more blurred spatial and temporal frame.

When G.I. Luke O'Connor arrives in front of the Japanese house, he is a metaphor for the audience's experience of trying to find out what's going on inside. The entire first part is based on waiting for the *shoji* screen to open. There is a metonymical shift at work between the box and Nozomi, the Japanese woman who lives there. The *shoji* screens are barely open, but Luke will end up drawing them back to reveal the secret of this dwelling and take photos of it. Penetrating within this house takes on a carnal connotation, underlined by the kissing scene in the shadows. From a symbolic point of view, this penetration unites death with fertility. This woman is connected with death: a survivor of a nuclear holocaust, she shuts herself in with her mother-in-law, living in worship of the dead. This *hibakusha*, whose flesh is scarred and who has been rejected because of her exposure to radiation, will become a mother after the G.I. enters the house. Life and death and life in the midst of death are tensions and themes that date back to cave paintings.

Then the prop boxes grow to contain the actors. The first to grow is the magician's box, deceptive in its small appearance. The young Jana Čapek becomes an assistant to a French magician, Maurice Zimmermann. The first performance takes place in the concentration camp before an audience of prisoners sitting on two levels of barrack bunk beds, facing Maurice and the audience.[37] The magic trick involves putting the young Jana in a cardboard box decorated with paintings of stars and the moon, set on a wooden cube, and making her disappear and then reappear. While the magician is saying the magic words, she slips through an opening in the side of the cardboard box opposite the audience and therefore visible to them; young Jana then hides in the wooden cube, and finally repeats her movements all in reverse. Throughout, the audience for *The Seven Streams of the River Ota* is in on the magic trick. In a concentration camp, magic, spectacle, and joy reside in a box. And symbolically, freedom also resides in Maurice's magic box, because it serves as Jana's hiding place during the last shipment of prisoners to the final solution. The box acquires oxymoronic values.

In the final part, "Thunder," the box takes on different forms, starting with the Japanese house, the largest box in the show, to the smallest, a *kabuki* makeup kit Hanako shares with Pierre. She opens it and shows him the gestures for applying and removing the makeup, adding colour and, with the same circular motion, erasing it. Once open, the kit unleashes colours and characters. The kit is a symbolic puppet theatre and opening it starts the kimono dance: the protagonists emerge from behind the *tokonoma* (display alcove) and inhabit the kimono, for the time of a dance movement. The actors are not physically inside this box; they are there in spirit, immaterial beings that a gesture or thunder, like a flash, will materialize.

As architecture on display, the stage of Lepagean theatre is constantly being redefined and is purposely kinetic, although often, instead of the whole thing moving, one element slides or another suddenly breaks away from the rest of the set, like a satellite going into orbit. The set is never entirely realistic or fully built. On the contrary, it leaves a great deal to imagination. Lepage plays with the idea of a form signifying a place. The viewer can already detect the reverie, the leeway, the possibilities for exploration this offers. This is not exactly one of Lepage's hallmarks, but he does give it a great deal of rein in his practice. He plays with the stage set, just as he plays with anything that enters into his thinking about the show. And the solutions for showing the interior of the house or for moving from one room to another are far more exciting. This becomes even more obvious in his stage experimentations with the cube.

THE CUBE

Lepage's 1994 stage design for Strindberg's *Ett Drömspel* (*A Dream Play*) at the Kungliga Dramatiska Teatern in Stockholm is a watershed moment, being the first incarnation of the idea of the cube.

As in *Alanienouidet*, the cube, like the puppet theatre, is already onstage before the performance rather than being displaced or progressively assembled to create the stage box. *A Dream Play* is the story of the descent of the daughter of the god Indra into the mortal world, where she meets many characters, including those symbolically representing theology, philosophy, medicine, and law. "So I represent the world with a cube: the sites Strindberg uses are human places like the theatre or the home."[38] The cube is unadorned, with openings for a door and window, and with a few props to designate different places. A simple geometric shape, designed with folded paper, is the foundation for the stage design, and that foundational shape is cubic. Assembled only on three sides, the cube is closed off only symbolically. It floats in the air as if it were a complete cube that a demiurge (Plato's creator of the universe) would hold in his hand.

Lepage's stage design for *A Dream Play* started from the observation that the idea of the Trinity, and therefore a triangular structure, runs through many religions. If the square represents civilization or the result of human activity, then: "The meeting of the square and the triangle creates a church, a meeting ground for the earthly and the heavenly, a contact between humans and God."[39] The free-floating cube has a counterweight so it can tip and turn on its own axis. The cube tips over and the lawyer's house is inclined 45 degrees, making objects and characters slide about.[40] The cube is pushed and pulled in every direction, like objects being studied from every angle. In a minimalist but obvious way, the cube in *A Dream Play* becomes "a place to blur the vision, because of the impermanence [to be taken literally, because the cube never stops turning, which disrupts both understanding and visibility] of the things seen."[41] Beyond the essentially mimetic representation of the cave, the cube's rotations are the equivalent in duration and to the eye of a curtain dropping. For Lepage, the action is no longer set at the turn of the century, but crosses the entire twentieth century. In practically every scene, the cube rotates and we change eras.[42]

The scenic design for *A Dream Play* is thus evidence of a major evolution in form. In it Lepage is the closest he has ever come to articulating his first instinct that the set is a box, even before seeing it as a puppet theatre or a theatre in miniature. The formal approach is almost abstract, virtually stripped of realistic details. There are a few props, but the overall impression is of an empty, almost cold, cube that even the colour of the brick wall cannot warm up, and that will become meaningful with each rotation. *A Dream Play* revisits the simplicity of the parking attendant's booth in *The Dragons' Trilogy*, but expands the puppet theatre to the entire acting space. Like the earlier boxes, this one is not very big, and it grows even smaller when five characters play a scene together in it. The closed stage box is not yet a reality in *A Dream Play*, but the progress is clear and sets the stage for *1984*.

At Lepage's request, the opera *1984* features a truncated cube that can be manipulated inside a large circular rotating set. The form starts out circular and then opens to reveal different structures for performance, buildings or cubic interiors, and circular towers. It's a pure play of shapes, a play of geometric forms that rotate on their own axis, fit together, embed in each other, and conceal each other. Each panel, like Craig's movable screens, reveals another space or changes it. Lepage's design has settled into a pattern: while the set is inspired by the box, it is made up of a group of geometric elements – sometimes three-dimensional, but more likely two-dimensional – that will be assembled in different ways throughout the performance. Like the object, the set element is modular, polysemic, polymorphic, the overall shape changing through sequential combinations of elements.

THE ACTOR AS PUPPET?

"The actor no longer exists; instead it is the image." "The screen has consumed the actor." Or "Technology is sucking the lifeblood out of ..." While such statements about the role of technology onstage are commonplace, today they are undoubtedly less frequently heard about the relationship between the set and the actor. But with the set relying on an entire underlayer of technology, as is the case with Lepagean theatre, a debate about dehumanization has quickly re-emerged. Because technology and the actor coexisted with the projected image, actors were said to disappear in front of the image; they would be nothing more than a silhouette or a shadow. These remarks are an updated version of the discourse about the actor as effigy that took shape at the end of the nineteenth century and at the beginning of the twentieth century. However, at the time, this dehumanization was understood and asserted as a form of progress in the dramatic arts. The efforts of Jarry, Maeterlinck, and Craig were intended to create the character in effigy in place of the actor, who was seen as an obstruction between the author and the audience: too mortal, too fickle, and too present. With Lepage, the use of technology hasn't grown out of an anti-actor stance. He doesn't deliberately substitute the puppet for the actor. But there are similarities, including frequent use of shadow play and a pliable vision of the actor, who is often seen in silhouette. These similarities are reinforced by direct use of the puppet and by a whole host of puppeteer influences, both in the design of the set – influenced by the puppet theatre – and in the actor as puppet, or more often as silhouette.

There are similarities therefore, or rather relays, but with marked differences. In particular, unlike Craig, Jarry, or one of the Futurists, Lepage has not written a manifesto and doesn't claim a visionary approach; but then he doesn't belong to the same era. However, there are many similarities between the approach of the avant-garde and its aesthetic of opposition, and Lepage's approach after leaving the Conservatoire; in his own way, he was setting out to kill his forefathers. Supporters of the effigy reject the overly imperfect actor. Lepage rejects repertory texts. There is also a major distinction in that Lepage has been able to realize his utopia or get very close to it, while the models of the avant-garde – Craig, of course, and then Artaud, but also Jarry and Maeterlinck before them – developed a model of dramatic art and placed the text at its service, without creating satisfying theatre.

Puppets appear on Lepage's stage alongside actors, a coexistence that tends to give rise to metaphor, the puppets' presence influencing the reading of the stage, and therefore, of the live actor. In *Coriolanus*, actors and puppets share the puppet-theatre set. Sitting on a table that serves as a floor, women weaving a tapestry are seen through a gauze-covered rectangular opening, an allusion to a theatre curtain and a TV or movie screen. In fact, the entire show uses dual readings. A servant arrives holding a string puppet, but we see only his legs and feet walking on the table that serves as a floor because the size of the opening is intended for the puppet and not the actor.

The humans in this show are too big to be fully visible. After this scene, the stage goes black, the gauze opens, and the puppet show begins: the battle in Act One is waged by string puppets. Alongside the silhouettes and the puppets in performance are the bodies of the puppeteers, represented by barely perceptible glints off leather boots and the lamé of an evening gown, very large and juxtaposed against the little army. The dress and the boots become armour, and the legs become spears: all are dynamic lines full of meaning. In this play about persuasion, manipulation, and promises, actors in plain view manipulate the puppet characters. The actors' and puppets' roles are interchangeable. An actor, playing the character Marcius, of whom we see only his legs, takes a puppet in his arms and lifts it out of the frame while talking to it. When the actor Marcius kneels down, the puppet is replaced by an actor, who kneels facing it. Playing with the frames makes it possible to explore the powers of incarnation and interpretation of the two media: puppet and actor. This is the sense in which the puppet theatre as object is used onstage to create metaphor. The puppets end up giving up their place to the actor, who uses the same spaces and props.

Similarly, *The Seven Streams of the River Ota* recounts a Chinese legend about the invention of gunpowder using *bunraku*-inspired puppets. Onstage, a small wooden and gauze structure forms the canopy bed of the emperor and his courtesan. The diplomat couple, Walter and Patricia, climb on the bed and the scene turns to the domestic dispute, carrying on an argument from the legend. Walter then goes to the red-light district in a sedan chair. He is carried by the same puppeteers dressed in black, but more specifically by their puppets, representing the emperor's slaves manipulated by the men in black. The image of the legend re-emerges, as a puppet ambassador standing in for the emperor, driven by his chauffeur. This action, which is comic because the actors move about in the midst of set elements that are too small for them, provides irony and sets the stage for the puppetization of the actor. Patricia, who wants to get past the quarrel by assuming the lotus position on the bed, is lifted up by the barely visible hands of the puppeteers. She levitates. Surprised, she cries out and disappears behind the curtains of this minuscule theatre.

In *A Dream Play*, the actors are turned upside down, lifted up, and forced to stoop by the cubic set. They must adapt to its rotations. The characters are toys of the gods, the cube being a metaphor for their higher powers and their whims. The cube's rotation is often what provides the meaning for a certain posture or space onstage by perfectly rendering the strange metamorphosis of the space anticipated by Strindberg. A man enters through one of the openings; his chest is bare and he wears a loincloth. The actor does a headstand, and in this action places his head toward the floor as the set begins to turn. It quickly becomes apparent that this is Christ on the Cross, who with the revolution of the cube winds up upright at the top of the set. The other actors perform in front of him as if he were a statue, albeit a very large statue that is very close to them, hemming them into the corners.

The same effect is created with the moving stages in *Jean-Sans-Nom* (1999), based on the adventure novel by Jules Verne, *Famille Sans-Nom* (*Family without a Name*), that follows a young patriot fighting to liberate Lower Canada from Britain during the rebellion of 1837 and 1838. The moving stages in *Jean-Sans Nom* move the actor within the proscenium arch – symbolizing the frame of a vertical painting, as in a museum – behind the scrim on which 3-D images are projected. The actor is manipulated by the set, which lifts him up so that he appears to be at the right height for the image projected onto a catwalk, in the hand of a character, or in front of a fireplace. Beyond the technical need for placement in a 3-D set, having a set manipulate the actor means that the actor doesn't move, but *is* moved as if by a puppeteer. This manipulation is a serious constraint in that the actor can no longer change positions at will on his small platform, because he could disrupt the overall image by being misaligned with it. This precise and constraining placement of actors harkens back to Craig's desire to plot out their movements onstage, but with Lepage the actor is subject to a stage image and its technical requirements, as required in image-based theatre.

This is not just a matter of placement or movement, but of the power of incarnation that the set gives the actor. The set manipulates him and even defines him: it fills him with movement and identity, as would a puppeteer. The movable panels in *Elsinore*, particularly the Monolith, manipulate the actor in this way, who, since *Needles and Opium* seems to have faded to make way for the effigy or the puppet capable of all sorts of gymnastics, and who can

adopt any personality, don any costume, and speak in any voice. The Monolith raises the actor seated in a chair, and the projection completes the identity: the king – played by Lepage – is a play on the idea of the portrait gallery, sitting on his throne while images of playing-card backgrounds are projected, with Lepage inserted as the figure for the king, the queen, and, for Hamlet, the joker! The solo actor is staged as subject and as object. He is the object that is manipulated, and sometimes the manipulator. Passing his head and arms through a spandex surface stretched on the Monolith, he becomes Ophelia in a white lace dress, but the only thing he has done to bring about this change is to be in the right place at the right time because the Monolith drops to horizontal around him. When the Monolith rises again, still horizontal, it suggests Ophelia's tomb, first by conjuring the deck of the ship Hamlet stands on; then the white fabric detaches from the Monolith; Lepage rolls himself up in it while the Monolith rises around him like the water that drowns Ophelia. He lies down in the opening that becomes his tomb. When the Monolith rises again, all that is left onstage is a body wrapped in a shroud.

Like the string puppet used only in *Coriolanus*, the actor often finds himself suspended, in fact increasingly so, given the many acrobatic scenes in *The Geometry of Miracles*, *Zulu Time*, and *The Damnation of Faust* (1999), as well as the stage designs for *La Celestina* in Barcelona (2004), *Kà* (2004) and *Totem* (2010) in Las Vegas for Cirque du Soleil, and *The Andersen Project*.[43] This approach fits with the mobility of the set, manipulated in every direction and explored from every angle, but it also fits with Lepage's thinking on feelings of ecstasy, flying, and the screen. Inside the puppet theatre, the actor lifts off and is suspended. He is weightless and capable of light, sweeping gestures similar to those of puppets. Because the puppet theatre is a small theatre that contains its own grid and rigging systems, it isn't surprising to see mechanical effects, and because everything is an object, everything can be manipulated.

Needles and Opium, a show that opens on an acupuncture session followed by opium and heroin trips, is very hypnotic. This power is in the projected images, but even more in the visual thought in action and the tremendous dexterity of the actor. He incarnates vignettes in turn as a barker, a flying character, a

The shadow object in *Needles and Opium*, created using an overhead projector as an image machine.

PHOTO

Ex Machina archives

The puppet actor, suspended in *Needles and Opium*.

PHOTO

Claudel Huot

swimming character, an actor with four arms – parodying Halsman's
famous photo of Cocteau – therefore transformed into a puppet.
At one point, an actual living puppet is suspended in front of the
projected facade of a building. Lepage must have trained physically
to be able to maintain his balance while performing the series of
pirouettes required. In the falling scene, the actor jumps into the
void and then, after a pirouette, manages to rise again, and we see
the facade go by in the opposite direction! From the fall to the
ascent, the set and the actor share the task of making the action
intelligible. There is a division or sharing of tasks that is a way of
creating a sort of hall of mirrors of the theatrical image and the
action onstage. Lepage uses this approach again for *The Damnation
of Faust*, a splitting in two of the physical and the vocal in the scene
of the race within a race. Faust and Mephisto stand on the edge of
the stage structure, each on a different level, when four suspended
stuntmen mount a horse and one of them pirouettes before falling
into the abyss. Apart from the fact that this is a powerful image,
this borrowing from puppetry demonstrates a familiarity with the
lyric actor and the difficulty of singing in uncomfortable physical
positions. It also offers the actor new movements and a new range.

    Contrary to this range and command of movement, the pup-
pet-like suspension of the actor suggests incredible pain or a dream
of freedom and mobility rather than a hallucination or a fall. *La Casa
Azul* tells the life story of Frida Kahlo, her painting, her illness, her
accident, her many operations, and her tumultuous relationship with
Diego Rivera. Confined much of her life to plaster corsets, she painted
self-portraits while looking in a mirror hung under the canopy of her
canopy bed. To recreate this setting, the designers imagined a vast
scaffolding structure that would serve as a bed but also as a puppet
theatre. In Kahlo's notebooks, on which the text by Sophie Faucher
is based, this immobility turns into an obsession with movement and
flight – synonyms of political activism – which Lepage rendered for
the most important scene of the show. "What do I need feet for when
I've got wings to fly with?" says Kahlo, grumbling about the surgeons
and referring to her body as a trampled garden.[44] Her easel, which
doubles as an X-ray machine, when inclined becomes an operating
table. A hook descends with a sort of large drill to screw metal rods
into Kahlo's back. The easel is straightened, Kahlo is suspended
like a doll, and the blindfolded surgeon Diego Rivera prepares to

hit her, as did the couple with the pinata during the party at the beginning of the play. Rivera first hits into the void and then hits Kahlo, who screams. In the next scene, Rivera gives her two little string puppets, echoing an earlier scene where Rivera plays with a ventriloquist's monkey, manipulating it like a hand puppet in front of the dumbfounded civil servant who has to register their remarriage contract in the United States.

The Lepagean actor, to use Bouchor's idea about the "Petit-Théâtre des Marionnettes," doesn't grab all the attention to the detriment of the character he is playing; instead, the actor gives the character an even broader scope because it is not an exclusive relationship. Lepage's productions feature many characters played by a limited number of actors using hairpieces, costumes, and accents so effectively that the actor is unrecognizable beneath the character. This non-exclusivity between actors and their roles may be the clearest mark of puppets on Lepage's work. The actor connects with the effigy for the flow and flexibility of identity and, therefore, status.

While playwright Sophie Faucher played the main character, Kahlo, in *La Casa Azul*, Lise Roy played all secondary roles, making fast, impressive metamorphoses: the nurse, Kahlo's sister, a civil servant, and others. She also played Death, *La Pelona*, "the bald whore," to use Kahlo's expression, and it is significant that she shaved her head for the role. Her face is blank like Lepage's,[45] ready to adopt any identity, either female or male. When she enters the stage as Trotsky, she is absolutely unrecognizable; as far as the audience is concerned, she is just another actor.

Having actors play a number of characters is a useful approach in dramaturgy that uses doubles, which Shakespeare did extensively, and it also suits financial requirements. However, for Lepage, the use of doubles becomes a valid foundation for all productions. The actor is at the service of a story, prepared to do anything and play any part. In *The Geometry of Miracles*, which chronicles the life of architect Frank Lloyd Wright, a whole troupe of secretaries dressed in identical Charleston dresses and little hats flit around the industrialist Johnson and his secretary, Marge. This swishing crew then transforms and is replaced by a studious group of Frank Lloyd Wright apprentices, and then by Gurdjieff's absurdly disciplined cult followers. For the actors involved, it would take until the final run-throughs and then only with mad dashes against the clock to get the costume changes down. Often multicasting makes it possible to connect the double through family ties; for example, in *The Seven Streams of the River Ota*, Rebecca Blankenship plays Sarah Weber and also her daughter Ada, who, forty years later, is also an opera singer.

Actors playing multiple roles do not have inalienable rights to their roles, however. Roles disappear or are traded between actors, who are unusually at the service of the story. These changes are often a source of stress for the actors, who, a few hours before the premiere, can see their role eliminated or altered, often dramatically.[46] Lepage, like a puppeteer over his figures, tries new combinations in a shared manipulation, which means that the designer needs to be present as the play evolves. It's no surprise that the actors for *The Geometry of Miracles* took it hard when Lepage was absent during performances. They found themselves without the puppeteer who could approve new changes inside the box.[47] A character's identity and existence are never set in stone: depending on the version of *The Seven Streams of the River Ota*, Hanako Nishikawa and Jeffrey Yamashita are husband and wife, mother and son, and then sister and brother, requiring at every change a complete redefinition of the character. Likewise, Pierre Lamontagne, the central figure in *The Dragons' Trilogy*, is a student of calligraphy and then of *butoh* dance; similarly, he is gay and then straight. So there is no guarantee of continuity for the character, particularly in the sagas.[48] Plays like *The Seven Streams of the River Ota* and *The Geometry of Miracles* underwent massive changes during their run, which meant that the audience, depending on where the show was in its tour, didn't see the same show or the same characters. Roles were also exchanged within each performance, either to suggest the passage of time, as in *The Seven Streams of the River Ota*, or to transcribe a larger metaphor, as with the role of the lover in *La Casa Azul*.

In passing on a character, the actors are actually passing on its effigy. Kahlo is dumbfounded when she sees her sister enter the stage while she is kissing Rivera. Then Rivera places the two sisters face to face, hands clasped, and undoes the back of one's dress to put it on the other, without them releasing their hands. Slipping the lover's dress from Kahlo to the sister is a puppet gesture, passing on the effigy onstage itself instead of in the wings or above the puppet-theatre opening. Giving actors no exclusivity over their roles is no doubt central to what Craig advocated with the *Übermarionette* ("Superpuppet"), as Bablet sees it.[49] This is not a matter of simply replacing the actor, but of "proposing the marionette as a model, so that the actor can acquire some of its qualities and free himself of the constraints."[50]

However, the marionette as model is not fully asserted. Based on his training, Lepage proposed such an environment and range of statuses to the actor. The model is not so much a model, a gesture, and a form of presence, as much as a freedom of incarnation; not a mechanics of acting, but rather a new way of thinking about the cast, inspired and sometimes constrained through the experience of the effigy.

All of this is concentrated in *The Geometry of Miracles*, which could be seen as one big and varied expression of the notion of the effigy – effigy in the treatment of characters, who are first and foremost dancing figurines and malleable figures, particularly when Gurdjieff's disciples dance. There are non-realist ideas of movement and purity of gestural intensity that could suggest the dream puppet of the avant-garde. This impression is created through biomechanics and Gurdjieff's sacred dances. The actors are primarily silhouettes, tensed bodies using severe restrained gestures that suggest both the cosmos and the architecture of Wright, whose sketches are projected behind the bodies in motion, making them part of their geometric figures. Gurdjieff gets annoyed at the disciples' imitation, calling them puppets. Olgivanna, teaching Gurdjieff's dances, turns in the middle of the apprentices, standing on a revolving stage with a cup of tea in her hand. Everyone marks time and makes mechanical gestures. More defined characters stand out among these silhouettes, incarnated by actors who also have other characters to play. And these characters are above all symbols, effigies, but also automata, mannequins. The lexical field of the actor's work centres on the notion of the puppet, more visual than aesthetic and more practical than dramaturgical. The Lepagean actor is a silhouette (that is, all silhouettes), and his solo show *The Andersen Project* is proof of Lepage's capacity for metamorphosis as an actor. He in turn plays a Quebec author, the programming director at the Paris Opera, an American neighbour, and Hans Christian Andersen,

but also one of his female love interests, a young Moroccan janitor,
and others. Throughout the show, the transition between roles is
done in plain view, when changing props. Multifaceted, the actor
is what he makes of the object, making himself an object; in other
words, absolute polysemy, with receptiveness and sometimes with
a few props that facilitate the shape-shifting. This hallmark has
been apparent since *Vinci*, the stage for which was set through
Lepage's improvisation work at the Ligue nationale d'improvisation.
One example from *Vinci* is the transformation of Mona Lisa at a
Burger King sipping her soft drink, with her jeans, stiletto heels,
and long hair, and that enigmatic smile. Like a number of plays
since *Saturday Night Taxi*, *Vinci* draws from stand-up comedy,
with a series of caustic portraits: the taxi driver, the *Mona Lisa*,
libidinous Leonardo, and others.

    All these figures have often led critics to comment on this
being a theatre of snapshots with weak storylines, but the whole
point of this theatrical form is to play with silhouettes as one would
play with received ideas, or as one would stage the very power of the

theatre, the mystery of incarnation, convention, and imagination. Although Lepage is also an incredible mimic, as he often proves in his solo shows, it's the image more than discourse that is duplicated. This choice doesn't mean the actors don't have to contribute; on the contrary, they have to be totally "inside" while being jostled about or an element of the whole, an element of a score that can only be understood in its entirety. They have to accept the uncertainty of their status as character and the motion and danger of the set that manipulates them. Some claim that all this is also incredibly stimulating and a great exercise in acting. However, if the effigy is the reflection of the Lepagean actor, it is above all a space for experimentation that is so vast it can be dizzying. The puppet theatre allows the actor to experiment by becoming effigy, very much akin to puppet utopias. This creation of an effigy exploits actors onstage, but also draws out their shadows, creating one more link between the avant-garde dream and the theatrical mythology that Lepage invents.

The mannequin in the form of a dressmaker's dummy suddenly comes to life in an unusually sensual scene in The Andersen Project.

PHOTO

Érick Labbé

THE SHADOW AND THE QUARRY

Light is essential to many image-based theatre directors: Langhoff started out as a lighting technician; Wilson designed many light installations; Lepage devised the lighting plans for his early productions, including *The Dragons' Trilogy* and *Circulations*. Designing the lighting allows them to give their worlds a visual identity (space, colour, material) and lays the groundwork for other technological interventions. Lepage even won the 1989–90 Dora Mavor Moore Award for best lighting design for *Echo*, his theatre adaptation of Ann Diamond's *A Nun's Diary*.

Lepage's relationship with light is based primarily on an original stage, a foundational element that strengthens his first broad strokes (the object, the box, and the effigy or puppet) and renews them at the same time. Fuelled by heritage and myth, Lepage has created his own origins, in a cosmogony of the theatre that is like the legendary birth of the act of painting evoked by Pliny in *Natural History*.[51] "Theatre begins in a quarry, and we light a fire. A storyteller gets up and begins the dance; he tells a story."[52] The quarry is the ground zero of theatre and the contained space that serves as the stage; a man gets up in front of an audience.

Fire is always what brings people together. In the great black of the night, we gather around a fire to tell each other stories. Fire is used to inaugurate important events: the Olympic Games are opened with the lighting of a torch, which, however, does not illuminate the whole stadium. Fire is the symbol for gathering.[53]

This fantasized origin of the theatre underlies all of Lepage's creations; he goes on to say that the standing storyteller is understudied by his shadow, which is projected onto the wall behind him. This shadow has a certain degree of autonomy, in that it can convey something other than the story being told; it is pure effigy and, as such, has its own discourse. In the quarry there is therefore the story and the shadow, the storyteller and the understudy, a shadow seeking autonomy. The crucible of the quarry also explains the presence onstage of light, not only to light the stage, but also to create shadows and produce dark silhouettes. It shows off the nighttime dimension of his theatre, a festival of light, but also solitude, demons, reverie, moonlight, and firelight. Lighting technology is just a modern substitute for primitive fire. It's not surprising that when Lepage read multidisciplinary artist Laurie Anderson's *Stories from the Nerve Bible*, he picked up on the idea of technology as a gathering place for modern societies in the place of the bonfire.[54] It's no great leap from there to seeing theatre as an incarnation of the cave. Lepage happily makes that leap in describing the use of shadow, closely related to Plato's *Allegory of the Cave*. The quarry in this case is explicitly a cave: the same mineral presence, the same space made of rock with blank walls that can be used as screens. The first screen was thus the wall of the cave.

There are nonetheless major differences between Plato's cave and the quarry. With his "myth of the quarry," Lepage describes action and a set that are close up, with a light source that is visible and the elements projected drawn from within the group. With Plato, the outline of the shadow doesn't belong to a member of the group: a man gets up to leave the cave and discovers that the forms he thought represented reality are just shadows. In the quarry, on the contrary, there is no trickery or projection of elements from the outside; everything happens inside the circle. The seated audience can see the fire, the subject, and the shadow all at once; the theatricality operates in plain view. Lepage does everything he

In a modern representation of the quarry, the shadow of a Zulu warrior is created with a spotlight instead of fire. *Zulu Time.*

PHOTO

Ludovic Fouquet

can to avoid alienation: members of the audience can turn their
heads and see the light source. His "myth of the quarry" is first and
foremost a desire to reveal the illusion.

But what is common to these two tales is the presence of
the shadow as a cut-out of the light and testimony to a presence.
Grotowski's theatre laboratory is similar to the "myth of the quarry."
In his idea of "poor theatre," he positions the actor-audience pair as
the heart of theatre. However, Lepage introduces a third element:
actors move in front of the audience, leaving their shadows visible.
For Grotowski, the fundamental relationship of the actor to the
audience is a vital experience. It allows for disclosure and conse-
cration, not of the content of the exchange but of the exchange
itself, when the image becomes the medium of the ceremony and
the scene of the quarry, which makes the image possible. A trilogy
is thus created: light plus subject plus screen surface, which are
primary and, as is said of prime numbers, irreducible elements.
The sets and the use of technology allow subject and the source
of light to be close together, a sign of a presence.

For a shadow to leave its mark, there has to be a wall. Each part of the trilogy of light, subject, and screen surface goes through many variations, which sometimes seem to be the rationale behind particular shows. A desire to work with 3-D images was behind the making of *Jean-Sans-Nom* and its environment that featured new screens with intangible projections. The wall that is the descendant of the quarry is simply one of the walls of the box onstage, one of the sides of the puppet theatre built to whatever degree on the stage with all of its sides used, with openings and the screens that hide them, as with the parking attendant's booth in *The Dragons' Trilogy* and the exterior walls of the Japanese house in *The Seven Streams of the River Ota*. The puppet theatre and the quarry come together in the design of a form for the stage, a highly mobile form and the result of endless combinations, in a geometric alignment. It is basically a celebration of theatre, a *mise en abyme* or Droste effect, marvelling at its ability to make an image at the same time as it stimulates an inspired gaze. A stony backdrop is added to the box of the puppet theatre and it becomes a quarry. From one to the other, the actor becomes a malleable silhouette and the walls display shadows. It's even the quarry wall that lays the groundwork for the puppet theatre, and it's in the meeting of theories of shadows, as in the theory of the puppet, that the particularity of the actor and his space onstage is situated, a space that pursues the shadow and presents it to us in effigy.

Where there are fire, actor, and screen, Lepage offers other combinations, particularly once he starts working with translucent screens. To become the quarry, the puppet theatre had to expand. When it takes on human proportions in *The Dragons' Trilogy*, a human-sized puppet theatre, it expands to contain both the actor and his projected shadow, with a gap required between the two to be able to distinguish them. The theory of the quarry requires that Lepage stop seeing the set as a presentation space for the object and the puppet theatre, but as a space, even a three-dimensional form, that combines the puppet theatre and the quarry. The Japanese house in *The Seven Streams of the River Ota*, in essence a light box flanked by translucent panels, effectively synthesizes puppet theatre and quarry. Lepage keeps moving between these two initial forms, enlarging the puppet theatre but bringing the light sources closer, as in *Jean-Sans-Nom*, finding a balance in sets in which the stage is

Translucent panels turn the Japanese house into a light box in *The Seven Streams of the River Ota*.

PHOTO
Emmanuel Valette

the same size as the box, without being too big – about 14 metres long and 3 or 3.5 metres high in *Elsinore, The Seven Streams of the River Ota*, and *The Far Side of the Moon*. The quarry space is most clearly defined in *The Geometry of Miracles*. There the sand, the large screen, and the actors are gathered around a fire that rises up from the desert. Lepage doesn't stray far from the box, and the set suggests a three-dimensional shape with only the base visible. A wall from the Lascaux caves is right at home here, projected onto the large screen bordering the upstage end of the set. The screen becomes the wall behind the primitive storyteller. While the blank walls of the café-theatre and the theatre were used in Lepage's earliest shows, the space would later always be minimally marked out, drawing the box as a reference point or border, tracing a surface on the ground as one would draw a magical shape. What is marked out is the space for the ritual and for theatre itself.

The actor who performs in the quarry set exists as a storyteller and a shadow, which is sometimes the only one of the two visible. Silhouettes appear throughout *Vinci* with the silhouettes of people and monuments that Philippe encounters in London. Silhouettes are part of the beginning of *The Seven Streams of the River Ota*: only the shadow is visible on the *shoji* screen, while the *hibakusha* Nozomi remains invisible. In this sense Lepage's actors are silhouettes and, since *The Dragons' Trilogy*, they have had to deal with this larger and more dramatic double, both a reflection and a shadow that the actors themselves contemplate at times; this relationship with the double pops up again in a detour to the use of live video.

"The shadow" are other words for "the effigy," and it's not surprising that they have been evoked by the avant-garde in their thinking on the puppet. Maeterlinck wondered whether human beings will one day be "replaced by a shadow, a projection of symbolic forms, or a being that has the aura of life, without being alive itself."[55] What image-based theatre offers instead is a cohabitation of the shadow and the actor, the projection and the person, with a gap that allows for an exploration in manipulation, which is where the puppet portion resides. The quarry makes this shadowy place a space that refers back equally to the origins of the image and of theatre, by way of musings about puppet, which are only a more extreme way of seeing the actor as an image. The stage is set for new images to be created within this box, playing with and scoffing at its walls, adapting to it, and circumventing it.

Inside the box, the images echo, like technological musings. The stage box becomes a receptacle, a frame, a sacred outline for a ritualistic performance, more ritual than it appears at first, in Claudel's meaning of the stage potentially containing an entire world.[56] Puppet theatre, quarry, and altar, the form holds the mystery of this celebration. Opening the box means releasing all the imaginary images that turn this box into a vast world.

The box and the quarry are two models that populate Lepage's visual laboratory, and two models that form a single result and connect in a single set that generates images. Or we should say, they are two models that coexist on the same set, or even that are its sources of power, tension, and resistance. The whole point of the presence of Lepage's actors or objects on the stage, or inside the stage box, is in making that presence an image, under the aegis of the quarry. Actors find their space, or perhaps become an image, in this tension between the box and the quarry and in the tension between a form and a surface or, more accurately, a space bordered by screen surfaces.

The simplicity of the stage in the form of a box showcases its dialectic, like the simplicity that painter Barnett Newman found in the mud walls of the native *tumuli* in Ohio, another confrontation with an architected whole. "This experience of 'simplicity' requires – or better reveals – the productive ambiguity of a twofold rhythm, a *dialectic*. The experience of a *here ... and beyond* and the experience of a *visible ... and beyond*."[57] The *here,* in Lepage's framework, is the box; the *visible* is the quarry. And the *beyond* is the tension between the two. The beyond is a place for producing images.[58] The Lepagean image – because his theatre clearly is about images – is above all "the experience of a place," even the experience of a dual, ambiguous place. This fact underlines the extent to which any image, and the theatrical image in particular, is an exercise in space. Whether in front of mud walls or in front of Lepage's images, the place *is* the experience, the moment, the instant of the meeting, and therefore of time. Newman talks about a "physical sensation of time"[59] in referring to these ancient spaces. Something takes shape a bit like Benjamin's aura, a phantasmagoria of space and time.[60] The Lepagean image can no doubt explore itself using the idea of Benjamin's aura, as long as "the unique phenomenon of a distance, however close it may be" finds echoes in it. Apparition, mingling of a near and a far-off mystery, even ceremony, space, and time: an aesthetics that calls into question our reception of the image, its materiality, and its proximity. This is a standpoint that we could adopt, at least for a moment, as we stand before the Lepagean image. We would see that there too the shift is possible and that, standing *before* the image, we can quickly be *inside it,* thanks to an opening that could no doubt be the very fold of this original dialectic between the box and the quarry. This fold is not only a transition but a break, a break like a dialectic space, like the only possibility of expression of this dialectic, like an ambiguous space that is at once volume, surface, depth, and threshold. In the visual laboratory of Robert Lepage, puppets, the box, and the quarry are clearly not a single apparatus among many but rather an assemblage of the whole.

PART TWO

The Visual Laboratory of the Imagination: Technological Echoes

Lepagean theatre, whether the repertory texts or the collective scores, is a theatre of the present, based on an idea of "a universal culture in Panavision"[1] and on a localized code of reference. Technology, whether or not it is present onstage, provides an ongoing reference to and an echo of our world. An implicit language underlies all of Lepage's projects, based on a global audiovisual culture and on the "perceptual habits created by the technological environment we live in."[2] The audience is assumed to be primarily television viewers, movie buffs, Internet users – essentially people who understand technology and the video era, which, since television, has seen an unprecedented evolution in information-transmission networks – a form of knowledge transmission that is now screen based but soon will be interactive rather than oral or exclusively print or book based. At the same time, Lepagean theatre is fuelled by its relationships to film and photography.

Through technology, Lepage looks at the evolution of the history of the image and its many incarnations. This is the first way in which he uses technology: as a history of image techniques that include drawing, painting, photography, cinema, video, and digital images, rooted in the audiovisual.[3]

Lepage puts theatre through a hall of mirrors in the stage box, making each technology he adopts resonate. The box becomes an echo chamber – like the recording studio with its acoustic panels in *The Seven Streams of the River Ota*. Or the box becomes a visual laboratory of images that borrows both from older techniques and newer technologies that revive these older traditions. A characteristic perception equipped with technology-induced ways of seeing and thinking about the image is at work in this resonance chamber that is the stage box.

Lepage embraces the vast field of the image, from the gesture that sketches to the number that draws, an abstract language that creates a virtual universe. In a broad reflection on the process of creating images, he moves from the most concrete gesture to the most abstract. Calligraphy is often used in his shows – the first stroke illustrated by the art of *sumi-e* (Japanese ink painting) in *En attendant* and *The Seven Streams of the River Ota*, and on the cave walls of Lascaux in *The Geometry of Miracles* – while the computer-generated and 3-D images in *Elsinore, The Tempest* (1992, one of three plays in the Shakespeare Cycle), *Jean-Sans-Nom*, and *The Andersen Project* form an abstract language. Before creating technological images and offering a history of the technique of the image and its perception, Lepage infuses the image with different origins; for example, a word's etymological roots.

Since Plato, the image has been "the result of an imitation:"[4] *imago* means "portrait, image, imitation," the root of which is found in the verb *imitare*, "to imitate." The imitation can be concrete when it uses a physical medium as its foundation, or abstract when the medium is our mental universe or our brain. Lepage uses ambivalence and a contra(di)ction that draws the object and thought, matter and codex closer together, a contradictory shortcut that contains the essence of Lepage's theatricality, between matter and thought.

The place left to the imagination in processing the object is found in the conception of the image. This process begins with the materiality of the object on display: a page of calligraphy, the simulated development of a photograph onstage, a handwriting lesson on a glass plate, and so on. Lepage moves on to the widespread use of projection – the projection being at once material and immaterial – and later moves toward virtual reality (*Elsinore, Zulu Time*). The screen becomes the physical medium for the imagination transmitted by technology. Lepage's evolution forms a practice based on the creation of images that increasingly requires the intervention of machines. Rather than slapping on representations and freeze-framing an imaginary world, machines enable a computer-assisted imagination. For Lepage, the technology of the image is the materialization of a dream and a starting point for poetry and a visual language.

THE IMAGO

The etymology of the word "image" is multifaceted and primarily designates anything but an aesthetic reality: a reality of the world of beliefs, imaginary devices to which we attribute agency. A technical term, the *imago* is the face of an absence or the materialization of a disappearance and is used in ancient Roman funeral rites: a wax cast of the face of the dead, a funeral mask, therefore an image by impression.[5] *Eidolon*, another etymological source, this time from ancient Greece, first means: "phantom of the dead, spectre and then image, portrait."[6] Achilles, when he wants to seize the image of Patroclus, seizes nothing: smoke disappears underground, with a small cry, like a bat.[7] The *eidolon* evokes absence, as well as the notion of "a deception or a snare":[8] Patroclus is present while being irreparably absent. For the ancient Greeks the image is in the order of apparition and not of resemblance. Inspiration, ghost, the flight of a bird, or haze, the *eidolon* suggests a sudden, ephemeral vision or sound. A vision or fleeting moment, the *eidolon* is nonetheless an apparition, an irruption into the visible, and raises the question of the sudden appearance of the invisible into the visible, so more broadly the visual.

The coincidence between this definition of *eidolon* and Lepage's definition of the confrontation between the actor and technology is compelling: "It's good to have a character acting in real time, but we need to feel the trail of his shadow behind him, the ghost, the action in slow motion, or a complete halt, even though the character keeps moving."[9] The Lepagean image is like the ghost of the dead, the spectre, a physical representation that relates to presence and memory. The image makes a memory. It does so by having technology take over the representation. The image is an attempt or a technique to fill an absence or to make the absent present, which goes back to the very definition of the "re-presentation," presenting again. "To present" is to place before, *objicere*, the Latin verb constructed from the same root as the word "object": the object and the image therefore have a single deictic root.

Absence, apparition, imitation, representation. The image is used to fill an absence and to create a presence. This is how Pliny describes the origin of the art of painting, in Book 35 of *Natural History*.[10] A shadow may be at the origins of painting; it was apparently born of the sadness of Kora, the young daughter of the ancient Greek potter Butades of Sicyon, over her beloved's departure. As they were saying their goodbyes, she noticed the shadow of his face on a wall, projected by the diffuse light of a candle, and she traced its contour.[11] The image is the fixed shadow. A silhouette created by light is the source of photography, another way of making images materialize, with all the ontological ambiguity of this fixed shadow. Any image, in theory, but also generally in practice, is "tormented by the question of the index, that is, by the question of the presence and proximity of the referent"[12] or, at least, by the issue of the imprint – for those who reject the idea of index when it comes to photography. Pliny's reference to the contour of the shadow also creates an opening in the form of the abandonment of the subject to its contour, a distance, and a divestiture. Contact or loss, imprint and distance, the image begins an examination of the relationship.

For Lepage, the image is a celebration of the shadow encountered or found. Images are explored in this relationship with the shadow, an idea that makes them traces of shadows or attempts to capture a shadow, particularly in the later virtual environments.

Lepage is brilliant in how he uses the fact that images endure only in our memories and are distorted by them. He draws from the substrata of images accumulated over centuries, borrowed from painting, sculpture, photography, and cinema, and rooted in our myths, fears, and realities, which involves a journey to the very roots of our imagination. Lepagean theatre of images touches us deeply because his source is an ancient well into which so many musings about the representation of the shadow have been thrown. Lepage summons all these substrata on a foundation of origin within the unconscious. His stage images begin as purely visual and then are anchored in dialogue; for example, in *Needles and Opium*. This isn't meant to suggest that grounding the images

in words is secondary; for Lepage, images and words are essential
to a theatre of images, as important as sound, the materiality of
things, and the trace of their shadow.

The image lays "bare the composition of the space," as
has been said about Wilson's universe.[13] This statement applies to
the many creators of image-based theatre (Dumb Type, Matthias
Langhoff, Peter Sellars, The Wooster Group, François Tanguy,
Dominique Pitoiset, among others) and particularly to Lepage.
In Lepage's work, the stage and the technologies used expose the
process of theatre as a whole, including the creation of images.
The image is constructed through unveiling or upon this unveiling
itself: it's in revealing its structure that it is constituted, by unveiling
how it works and, at the same time, how it acts and is displayed.
Every technology used onstage becomes an opportunity for a practical, active reflection on the image that it helps create. Beyond the
image, it encourages a discourse about theatre and, more broadly, a
meta-reflexive discourse: "making the image" and "making theatre"
are experienced simultaneously.

Image-based theatre is primarily a theatre of perception: a
history of the image is contained in this practice, as is the history of
all senses of prehension and comprehension, grasping and decoding
a visual, sound-based, or other form of message. Merleau-Ponty's
essay "Eye and Mind"[14] raises sense, presence, visibility, and imagination in talking about the reception of the image, and is relevant to
the Lepagean image. The most solicited sense is sight, which comes
as no surprise since we are talking about theatre, therefore a world
perceived from "a place for viewing" (*theatron*). "As an indirect
result and by very reason of the organization of image-based theatre,
the audience's eye is put to the test."[15] This theatre offers new ways
of building icons. The intrusion of technology onstage can produce
new organizational systems unrelated to perspectivism, particularly
in the juxtaposition of images, superimposed projections, the
reference to virtual environments, and so forth, but perspectivism
can use technology as a frame. Image-based theatre stages the
seeing. It's also a chance to explore the very act of thinking as well
as imagining: beyond the seeing, it's the analysis, the extrapolation,
the connection, the dreamlike drifting, basically, the power of
reflection and imagination that are at play. The blind Florentine
guide from *Vinci* is in this sense the symbol of Lepagean theatre:

> If any of you, like me, can't see the stained glass, the
> domes, the masterpieces, but if you can see them in
> your mind's eye when someone merely suggests them
> to you, then you are as great as Leonardo da Vinci,
> because imagination gives you wings.[16]

Lepage's technology intervenes in real time, "a language with a diversity of meanings, the syntax of which is created before the audience's eyes."[17] From Aristotle to Artaud and Valéry, the purpose of the image in theatre has been said to be to make people think, to encounter a "place of imaginative logic."[18] This is the territory that Lepage explores in using technology, a place to rest and then analyze the audience's gaze, for resurgence and connection, knowledge and novelty. This exploration involves reflecting on how the image is constituted and how it is perceived by the audience, while showcasing an imaginative logic that functions using stimuli and technology, influenced by memory. The memory of a presence, the memory of an absence, the memory of a confrontation, and above all memory created from shared images, like so many memories and so many echoes. And the echo reminds us of the extent to which the practice of the image primarily uses a spatial language. Now it's time to delve into these memories by moving closer to the images and diving into the ways in which they echo throughout Lepage's body of work. The repeating echoes that characterize Lepagean stage set and image can be organized into six categories of technology: light, photography, cinema or film, video, virtual environments, and sound.

FIRST ECHO

LIGHT TECHNOLOGY

If, as according to Bablet, the first revolution in stage design was essentially pictorial, making scenery a painting and ballet an animated painting,[19] then clearly innovations in lighting are what enabled this evolution. These innovations lifted the image off the painted canvas to occupy space, which is similar to the practice being analyzed here. First there was an exploration of and a search for lighting. Light as a presence onstage moves toward the object, and then toward the technological, following the example of stage lighting that becomes increasingly complex and heavy.

Light is the first technology to appear onstage, displaying its source as a scenic object. After Lepage's first café-theatre productions, light becomes the most important element onstage, around which everything is organized. Naturally archaic, light is primitive and non-technological. It recreates the fire of the quarry, a primitive, ancient presence.

 "THEATRE BEGINS IN A QUARRY AND WE LIGHT A FIRE"

From *The Dragons' Trilogy*, which marks the end of the apprenticeship years, to *The Geometry of Miracles*, to the firestorms of *The Ring*, fire is used consistently. With it Lepage introduces a real element, a foreign one, that he connects back to our origins: the panorama of a cave against a backdrop of night is what develops. It's no coincidence that *The Dragons' Trilogy* is about origins and delves as far away as distant China. The hangar where the play was created in Quebec City in 1987 becomes the modern equivalent of the cave when the curtain rises on seven flaming barrels. Burning on an expanse of sand, they add to the ritual aspect of the theatre. Lepage exploited fire a great deal during this era, and it persists in various forms. *The Dragons' Trilogy* is the show that most uses real flames. The fire that burns in the American desert in *The Geometry of Miracles* can be said to have the same origins as the projected wall from the Lascaux site at another point in the show. The fires are in fact the fires of the quarry, and the image of apprentices gathered around the flame is a direct reference to this.

Fire appears in the form of torches, candles, and paper in flames in *The Dragons' Trilogy*, but also in *Macbeth* (1992, one of three plays in the Shakespeare Cycle) and *Tectonic Plates*: candles placed on suspended chairs create a dreamy Père Lachaise Cemetery. Fire becomes portable and private: it moves with the person carrying it, an evolution of the quarry set, where, logically, only the actor moves amidst the fire and the fixed walls. In these plays, the storyteller carries the flame as a source of light with him. The actor is lighting himself, which gives his shadow new mobility. He is a new Prometheus, bringing fire to the people, other actors, and the audience.

Along with fire, the scenic design requires many other sources of light, mainly electric, all variants of the original fire. In the first productions in particular (*Circulations*, *Vinci*), but also up to the techno-cabaret *Zulu Time*, which developed under the working title *Cabaret Technologique*[20] and features, among other light effects, divers with headlamps, for which Lepage uses battery-powered light sources. These headlamps are the ultimate manoeuvrable object, ontologically deictic light sources. They outline and isolate an object, a space to be seen, and are a modern version of the candle or torch. Flashlights and torches are used in *Le bord extrême* (1986), the only shafts of light amid the theatre's seats that served as the performance space.

Some luminous objects are electrical, making them as manoeuvrable and durable as fire. Modern, portable fires appear up until *The Geometry of Miracles*: the parking-lot attendant in *The Dragons' Trilogy* wanders around in the dark not with a simple flashlight, but with a portable light, its cord snaking around him. The same waves are created by the portable light's winding cord as

in the lines traced with a rake in the sand of the Zen garden in *The Seven Streams of the River Ota*. The electrical cord finds a meaningful variation in the telephone cord in Room 9 of the Hôtel La Louisiane in *Needles and Opium*, the only connection with the outside world. Scene changes are introduced by manually turning on and off a light bulb that hangs over the stage.[21] The constantly moving electrical cord can be seen as the rope Robert clings to, perhaps tempted, in his desperation, to hang himself with it. Connector technology is an important part of the aesthetic in many of the technology shows.

Equally discreet are the lighting and the scenery. The white rectangle that floats for a few instants in the dark during *The Seven Streams of the River Ota* is the light table Sophie Maltais uses to view Hanako's slides. In the darkness of the scene change, the rectangular halo, immediately recognizable as an echo of the bomb dropped on Hiroshima that blinded Hanako, is one of the most terrible images of the disaster. Her blinding is rendered by a white light directed at the audience, a curtain of light that masks what's behind it. Overwhelmed by the light, the audience doesn't realize that this technological fire throws no shadows and meets no obstacle other than their eyes. The audience becomes the actor caught in a halo of light and then realize that their shadow must be visible behind them on the theatre walls or on the other rows of seats.

Similarly, as the parking-lot attendant makes his rounds in *The Dragons' Trilogy*, the halo of his lamp illuminates the acting space, creating shadows and revealing the central parking booth. The booth takes the place of the original fire: both are made of wood. So it's no surprise to see smoke rising from it and a red light appear, the smoke of an original fire now in electrical form. The protagonists press up against the windows, like a circle of people drawn close around a fire. Later on, a power failure at the laundry justifies the use of traditional light. Each person takes a candle in hand and sets it on a barrel, creating the impression of small hearths filling the space.

The even more traditional and ephemeral candles that surround Lee and Jeanne are like memories of Stella: a paper junk and house that they burn to mourn her. When the flames go out, black forms freed from matter, memories that a breath can scatter, Stella is dead. Jeanne and Lee blow out their candles, darkness falls over their accepted grief, and when Stella reaches heaven in a final blaze of light, the torches become the stars:

The red sail of a junk captures beautiful shadows from an ancient fire. *The Dragons' Trilogy*.

PHOTO

Claudel Huot

LEE: And now, she will go like a flying star.

JEANNE: Et maintenant, elle s'envolera comme une
étoile filante.[22]

Likewise, the paper airplane that pilot Philippe Gambier sets ablaze
in front of an indifferent Yukali's news kiosk foreshadows the disappearance of his plane at sea in the first of the trilogies. The streak
of flames that crashes into the sand is also the image of Halley's
Comet, which features in Philippe's final message to his passengers.

It's amazing to think that at the same moment that
the sun sets in Vancouver, it rises in Hong Kong. […]
In a few hours another miracle of nature will occur:
Halley's Comet will pass, streaking through the sky
and trailing a long gash of light behind it.[23]

Sun or comet, fire is a pervasive simile, a protective figure that dominates *The Dragons' Trilogy* and helps create many dramatic objects.

CREATOR OF SHADOWS

The major strength of this use of light is the graphic images it creates: Lepage draws with light. The pervasive light on the quarry wall serves a steady gaze, using areas of shadow with light breaking through, like the outpouring of light from the parking attendant's booth in *The Dragons' Trilogy*, with a simple projector piercing the dark and providing a hint of the luminous intensity of the rising sun:

> Lighting is part of the emotion of a scene. [...] in the scene in the kitchen where a pregnant Jeanne gets up and sees the sun rise, Marie [Michaud] creates a great deal of the emotion, but the sun does just as much, if not more. [...] I'm fascinated by light, and I work with shadows a lot: lighting is part of the writing.[24]

Fire is used mainly to throw the night into relief and to play with shadows. There are plenty of references to cinematic lighting, but these light objects are more often reminiscent of chiaroscuro painting and art.

The candles and flashlights are used facing the audience, creating an enormous shadow for the actor. When he turns around, he appears as a shadow neatly silhouetted in front of a fire now invisible to the audience. The quarry fire is often small so that it can more easily be obscured behind the actor it lights. The portable light in *The Dragons' Trilogy*, equipped with a movable shutter, creates chiaroscuro without the need for a light source behind the actor. The shutter allows the parking-lot attendant to be visible and lit, behind a layer of shadow, with the small movable plate facing the audience to mask the light.

The most beautiful chiaroscuro effect occurs during Stella's death scene in the first of the trilogies. Holding her ball of light close to her one last time, she is forced to lie down on an iron bed by a male nurse who intimidates her with his flashlight and strikes her with a blow of light as if delivered by a billy club. She approaches the bed, dying, wrapped in a coffee-stained sheet, and the portable light turns on under the bed; the portable light's shutter is placed on the audience side so as not to blind them. Whether Stella is

Chiaroscuro in *The Dragons' Trilogy* expresses the balance between life and death. As Stella dies, her silhouette is projected on the wall behind.

PHOTO

Claudel Huot

standing or lying on the metal structure, she is partly lit from below and is visible as a shadow, still alive and yet already dead. She curls up, creating an enormous shadow figure on the wall behind her, a motif overlaid by the motif of the bed's metal slats which become lines of shadow converging toward Stella. Her death occurs at the centre of very dramatic graphics: patterns of shadows that for one last time suggest a star-shaped figure.

From the chiaroscuro to playing with Chinese shadows is just one step, and Lepage takes it in his early productions. Light is used to create shadows; its use in chiaroscuro is one way to do this, but sometimes it's used in conjunction with the projection of this chiaroscuro on a translucent surface. This is the principle behind the scenic design for *The Seven Streams of the River Ota*, with the house as a luminous box. The silhouette of the shadow is visible only through a cloth screen that makes it more spectre-like.

Nozomi, the *hibakusha*, is visible only from behind when the panels of her house slide open, or she appears in shadow behind the panels. For having seen the source of the light too closely, she is condemned to being nothing more than a shadow in a light-based recording device, reminiscent of Hiroshima's nuclear flash. The G.I. photographer, pointing a projector at her face, inflicts a new form of light torture upon her. The candle that goes out during her wake is laden with meaning: it sends her back to the world of shadows, releasing her from the light. The G.I. talks to her shadow through the *shoji* screen, and only after several meetings is he able to penetrate to the very heart of her suffering, cross through the shadow to discover the obliterated face. Here the light takes on a painful power for creating shadows, but also for recording the shadow on the flesh of the body it meets. From chiaroscuro, Lepage moves completely to the shadow, without any other nuance than the opaqueness of the dark.

The dance of the kimono in *The Seven Streams of the River Ota* demonstrates the staging of a light object (the photoflood).

PHOTO

Emmanuel Valette

BETWEEN SHADOW AND LIGHT: THE MIRROR

In *Needles and Opium*, the light from an overhead projector is used to create shadows. It outlines objects – cups, a trumpet – placed on the glass plate of the machine with their contours reflected by a mirror. A shadow is inscribed on the receiving surface: with the overhead projector, the image in the mirror is not visible directly; it requires a medium, some sort of screen. The mirror therefore reveals and carries things; it is a medium, a surface that reflects all that form or light offer. The fire of the quarry produces shadows; the mirror does as well, sometimes in the most primitive form: the simple reflection in the water, a surface that reflects back the shapes cut out of the clouds by a beam scan (*Elsinore*) or that draws perfect reflections in *Bluebeard's Castle* (1992). In the latter case, the audience can even dive into or emerge from the mirror, because the mirror of water is an actual pool from which the hapless spouses emerge and return to, torn from their shadowy sanctuaries for a few moments. They end up bringing with them the last spouse, recently dead, who has become a shadow.

Mirrors are part of Lepage's world and appear in every form. The silver or aluminum tint of the mirror is a substitute for the mineral colours of stone. The fantastical set of the quarry evolves: its walls become polished surfaces, in a modern, industrial version of its original walls.[25] As a new reference wall, the mirror takes on all of its meaning in the light that outlines the forms to be reflected, potential shadows.

The mirror is related to light, shadow, and sight, all themes that help define each of the Japanese protagonists in *The Seven Streams of the River Ota*. The Hiroshima bomb blew up mirrors, pulverizing shadows in a mere second and transforming walls into permanent mirrors of a shadow that has disappeared. It ravaged Nozomi's face, from whom all mirrors have been removed from view; it extinguished Hanako's eyes, who now puts on her makeup using a mirror and hides her eyes behind mirrored glasses. Hanako and Nozomi are inverted reflections, connected in opposite ways to sight and to the mirror and to an overabundance of light.

In Latin, *miro* is primarily a reaction of wonder, related through a second meaning to sight. "To see with wonder," suggests admiration in Latin. In Lepage's work, the apparition in the mirror often generates surprise, even wonder, through changes in lighting. Fascination with the mirror is nothing new, nor is surprise at the reflected image. This idea was used in theatre in the nineteenth century with Pepper's ghost effect (1862),[26] which was merely an update of the work of Hero of Alexandria (first century CE)[27] and many imitators: the reflection of an image using tilted mirrors to create the illusion of an image floating without a screen. In a pit in front of the stage, an actor moves lit by candles with reflectors, while his image is reflected on a glass plate inclined 45 degrees out of the sight of the audience, although on the edge of the stage. The figure thus appears vertical. This trick was reproduced almost exactly in the *Secret World Live* tour, when Peter Gabriel, supposedly in his room under the stage, becomes visible via the reflection of a long, inclined mirror. Lepage had already demonstrated his mastery of this trick in *Polygraph*, *Coriolanus*, and *The Far Side of the Moon*, each of which make spectacular use of inclined mirrors.

In Lepage's work, this dramatic response of surprise at the mirror is expressed through the use of two-way mirrors, the most perfect illustration of which is in *The Seven Streams of the River Ota*. A change in lighting delivers the magic and the poetic force of the suddenly transparent mirror. Jana Čapek, sitting in front of the mirrored wall, cuts two locks of shiny red hair. When she lies back on the floor, the light changes or, more precisely, the back of the mirror is lit by white sources revealing the mirror space, the Terezin concentration camp, while the intensity of the light drops onstage. Jana's hair as a child has the same fiery hue. The two Janas

When the mirror turns in *The Far Side of the Moon*, it takes with it not only reflected light but also the audience's gaze.

PHOTO

Ludovic Fouquet

face each other. The source of light, the fire, located behind the mirror, makes the reflection or the shadow disappear from the wall. As long as the fire burns, the mirror can't be seen, even though it is there, which is what creates the discord. The flame behind the mirror makes it possible to travel through space and time: Jana sees herself as a young girl. A particular spatiotemporal frame is created around each flame. The mirror transports this frame and, in the case of the two-way mirror, twists it, batters it, inverts it, shattering the frame of reference without breaking the glass.

If the image lays bare the composition of space, light lays bare the composition of the theatrical image. Light allows for a reflection on space, playing with the idea of the surface, adding depth to the stage image and compressing it. Light is what creates this dramatic change. "Without light, there is no space," Wilson says.[28] In Lepage's work, examples of beams of light are legion, from the flashlights in *Circulations* that outline the contours of a skyscraper or the prison bars, to the divers using their headlamps to search for the black box from a plane that crashed into the ocean in *Zulu Time*,

not to mention the headlamps and flashlights in *The Dragons' Trilogy* and the relentless neon lights in *The Seven Streams of the River Ota*.[29]

The stage becomes a flat, vertical surface on which dynamic lines are drawn. Exposing the theatre process is connected with exposing the image and the set, helped along by lighting. The box and the quarry are reunited in a two-dimensional composition on a surface of shadow. The shadow soothes the tension created by the dialectic of the box and the quarry. Lepage throws shapes made of fire, signs of pure light on to the surrounding darkness, in ephemeral, violent bursts. In *The Seven Streams of the River Ota*, this is what the unyielding prison bars or the light table do, suddenly breaking the recreation of the Japanese home. These signs are discourse and blazing comments on the action itself, as if Lepage, using superimposition, tacked an inscription in fire onto his initial image as a subtitle. Light takes on a new expressiveness.[30]

The actor / light bearer outlines the performance area using rudimentary tools, like Yukali, in the first of the trilogies, surrounded by three candles when she paints her dragons. The first productions rarely use lighting effects offstage, instead using them in plain view onstage. This became apparent in the first café-theatre productions, and continued in *Circulations* and *The Dragons' Trilogy*. After that, the use of onstage light sources drops off. The lighting effects become mere references to what was at one time a poetic and aesthetic trademark. Candles are still lit in *The Seven Streams of the River Ota*, fire emerges in *The Geometry of Miracles* and is used in various forms including a simple flame from a lighter, torches blaze in *Jean-Sans-Nom*, and the minuscule lanterns held by walk-ons shine in *The Damnation of Faust*. But after *The Seven Streams of the River Ota*, the use of light onstage dwindles and becomes increasingly technological.

It is significant that in *Jean-Sans-Nom* – a show that explores projected 3-D images with live actors – fire, as a light source that pierces the darkness of the night, is technology based, in the form of a projected video image. A theme that runs throughout the show, fire, which destroys the traitor's house, is reminiscent of the colour of the heroine Clary's hair and is found in every indoor set. Fire consumes the heroes' sinking boat, suggested by the image of a flame rather than by a real flame. "He is the red-haired torch no wind may blow out,"[31] with the flamboyant

colour red used since *The Dragons' Trilogy*, like Stella's and Jana
Čapek's hair, the ultimate souvenir of fire.

Twice, however, an actual torch is superimposed over the
image of fire; a flaming torch is placed behind the scrim screen,
in a gripping shortcut from the ancestral source to the spectral
double. For the glimmer of an instant, tradition and modernity
are superimposed. Lepage returns to the original fire of the quarry
in this show, but expresses it technologically. Theatre and video
come together in a single celebration of light. The light source has
often been technological for Lepage, but had never before been
filmed in its primitive form. An image, a reference to fire, that lights
the stage, the technological artifact takes on the properties of the
object represented.

As a further example of the use of light, the represented
objects the houses in *Needles and Opium* and *The Seven Streams of
the River Ota* are like light boxes, lit from the top or from upstage,
making their two-way mirrored walls transparent. The light reveals
the dynamic structure of the stage, which is shown in its entirety or
broken down into sections, because the shadowy areas are where
scene changes are prepared. This division is done without walls, and
it's as if the spike-tape stage markings have volume. Lighting carves
the empty insides of a dwelling into rooms. The Japanese house in
The Seven Streams of the River Ota and Philippe's apartment in *The
Far Side of the Moon* materialize when needed and as characters
move through them.

Like shadow effects, this carving with light is often made
possible by the proximity of projectors fixed on the set and not
necessarily on the grid. The stage set as a puppet-theatre box brings
the actor closer to the light sources. The parking attendant's booth,
the houses, the multifunctional shelving unit, and the rectangular
opening in a wall: all have different light sources that suddenly move
closer to the actor. This is theatre on a human scale, containing the
humans while lighting them, and scrutinizing them from every
angle and in every position. While the lighting onstage remains
hidden, often in the wings, the actor finds some of the proximity
with it that he had with the luminous objects. There is now real
closeness in addition to contact.

In this respect, *Jean-Sans-Nom* is the ultimate outcome of
having lighting close by around a small stage. No matter where the

actor is, he is lit by a projector less than 2 metres away, because the stage is 4 metres wide and is flanked by a column of six projectors along the entire 6-metre height of its opening. The actor is hemmed in by the light of the Super Scan Zoom projectors, a technological light based on an ancient technique: the reflective power of light on a mirror, offering a strange analogy between Lepage's set designs and the mirror at the heart of a projector. Lighting has always been based on the use of reflectors. A back mirror captures the light flow, which can then be directed by another mirror located at the front of the projector or the lenses, almost in contact with the light source. The mirror has a special place in this quest for shadow situated between a source and a projection surface. The wall serves as a mirror, capturing reflections like so many shadows, in the same way that the Super Scan mirror captures them, but at the same time is totally mobile. Unlike other projectors that have a limited range of movement on moving heads, the Super Scan has a remarkable range of movement because a moving mirror directs the light beam. The mirror can pan 150 degrees and tilt 110 degrees. The seemingly independent section at the end of the projector that contains the mirror can turn up to 360 degrees. The wall is therefore reflective *and* mobile. Instead of the lighting simply framing the action taking place in a stage box, it watches and tracks it.[32] It makes sense that this type of projector would first appear in *Elsinore*, a play about being under surveillance. Lepage, alone onstage, is stalked by lenses and projectors, like undercover spies trying to reveal Hamlet's secret thoughts. The way the projector operates takes on a whole new semantic value; it becomes a roving eye that scrutinizes. The source moves closer to what it is watching, which fits well with the study of the relationships between the set and the actor.

Lighting makes increasingly precise outlines of the actor's silhouette caught in its beam; the light frames him tightly. The light from the Super Scan Zoom is exceptionally intense. In *Elsinore*, Lepage appears in these clear outlines, the intensity of which is reinforced because the light is reflected on his white shirt. In *Jean-Sans-Nom*, the shape of the Super Scan suggests a missile, even a missile launcher.[33] The actor becomes the target of waiting projector warheads, targeted by the projector's little mirrors with relentless precision. Upward movements are adjusted as minutely as the lateral movements of the actors. With a battery of projectors set in six rows, the Super Scan Zooms are no longer limited in height. The proximity is as real as the fluidity, because a single projector is capable of a range of effects in a given performance: different sizes of beam, colour, position, shape of the gobo (go-between or go-before-optics) screen, movement of the shape, and so on. The ubiquitous fire takes on many forms.

 ## TECHNOLOGICAL EXPERIMENTS

The Super Scan Zooms in *Elsinore* and *Jean-Sans-Nom* and the Mac 500s and 600s in *Zulu Time* offer more flexibility and precision than traditional lighting. They are used mainly in experimental "technological shows," which demand a high level of technical skill.

Elsinore, Lepage's first true technological show, after *Vinci* – which relied more on ingenuity than technology – uses five Super Scans in a simple projection scheme around a single actor. Lepage also uses an infrared camera, so that the surveillance of Hamlet can continue in the dark. The character is surrounded by experimental lighting, and the audience sees him through the filter of technology.[34] With *Jean-Sans-Nom,* the lighting is simplified; Super Scan Zooms are used along with a bit of front lighting on the opening of a small stage and a few droplights on the narrator and his musical instruments. But things get more complicated when it comes to configuration. Each of the Super Scans requires setting eight parameters per effect, and there are a total of fifty effects in this show: so six thousand parameters have to be adjusted for light alone during set-up. This show pushes the logic of the puppet theatre to its end point; the technological stage acts on behalf of the actor.

In 1993–94 Lepage stage designed Peter Gabriel's *Secret World Live* tour, which involved 140 dates in 26 countries. Turning rock concerts on their head and using lighting as the main effect on a stage populated only by instruments and musicians, Lepage creates a stage design that is visible and mobile, light and ephemeral. The stage has different spaces, and the approach to it, with a kinetic screen and musicians, is eminently Lepage. The central set is a circular stage, featuring in turn a tree and then a boulder, covered with a half sphere, while behind it, there is a second raised stage with a large screen over it. Lepage experiments mainly with powerful lighting: stripes of light, droplights, patterns of light on the ground, extensive use of gobos, and a battalion of projectors far larger even than what he uses for theatre. It wasn't so much that he familiarized himself with the metal structures the projectors are affixed to, the baffles, and rebroadcast screens, now commonly used in theatre, but more that he grew accustomed to using them in plain view. This exhibition of steel structures adds a rock-poetic to the purely practical aspect of attaching things. This type of set would find its way into the elaborate scaffold structure in *Zulu Time*, as well as into *The Damnation of Faust* and the *Growing Up* tour, another Peter Gabriel concert that Lepage designed the set for: a mobile batten lowers fabric that holds the performers, turning elements upside down, and so on. After this incidental experience, in which Lepage was in charge of stage design only, lighting becomes more powerful, even intense. *Elsinore* and *Zulu Time* followed in the footsteps of the *Secret World Live* tour in terms of lighting (very white Super Scan Zooms, blue front lights and profiles); their precision (droplights creating very dramatic lighting effects on the walls, which double as screens); and their general aesthetic.

In 1999 the *Printemps du Québec* was celebrated in different regions of France.[35] This mega event showcased the cultural and artistic output of Quebec through a variety of events in theatre, dance, music, cinema, and exhibitions, with Lepage acting as commissioner-general. In addition, he was commissioned to produce an original creation. This was an opportunity for him to experiment with complex technologies on a large scale. The first thing Lepage did was to come up with an idea for a 3-D production, before deciding specifically what the creation would be; in the end it was a musical drama, *Jean-Sans-Nom*. The technology came first, continuing on from efforts made in 1998 (while producing Shakespeare's *The Tempest*), in which Lepage tried to make actors part of a 3-D environment.

From the point of view of lighting, which took a back seat to the 3-D technology, Lepage would have the means to use twelve Super Scan Zoom projectors. His technicians experimented with lighting ideas. Starting from the premise that the 3-D glasses used for *The Tempest* didn't let through enough light and left the actor in the shadows – prompting members of the audience to remove their glasses from time to time to watch the action – the lighting was rethought, moved closer, and intensified. From one project to the next there was clear progress in terms of visual comfort. However, some of the lighting was still too raw and too white on the actors performing within a projected image. The light was not always properly balanced between the greenish hues of the xenon lamps and the bluish hues of the HMI spotlights. But a great deal of progress was made due to the fact that the production was so heavily subsidized. The concerts and official commissions both involved performances, technological experiments, and musical and virtual environments, for which every instance of lighting, image, sound, and acting were rethought, regenerated, and revitalized. These experiments fuelled and consolidated Lepage's universe, serving as an experimental breeding ground on which other productions could grow.

Light is the essential condition of Lepagean theatre, along with its corollary, the dark of night. If the theatre is a place for viewing – *theatron*, designating the semicircle surrounding the stage – then it is a place for viewing light. Initially drawn in by the fire that creates fleeting shadows, the actor moves from being a storyteller in the light to a carrier of light. A carrier of fire, he becomes "one who interprets" through light, according to Greek etymology, the actor who plays with fire and who exists through the fire he carries close to him. Lighting is used alongside darkness because of the need to create shadows for the projection. Actors and projections are made to coexist, in the case of videos or slides, on a dark background or in a dark space. Lighting therefore has an essential role of outlining, as projections grow in number and become more refined. Luminous objects, flames, and electrical objects were used to pierce the darkness; now they are used to find shadows.

In contrast, the creation of a 3-D universe brings light closer to the actor to the point of erasing his shadow, contradicting the artificial depth into which he is inserted. In *The Seven Streams of the River Ota*, annihilation through light is suggested by bringing the mini dichroic halogen bulbs that are installed in the Japanese house and lateral batteries of Super Scan Zoom projectors as close as possible to the actor, erasing his shadow and thus his existence. These little bombs recreate the blinding moment of the impact.[36]

There are many light-based weapons in the history of twentieth-century conflicts; for example, the U.S. Air Force's magnesium
flashes and electronic flashes were used for light but also to blind
enemy troops. In an offensive of stun grenades, light becomes a
killer, in a sense, just like it was in Hiroshima. "But few have pointed
out that the bombs dropped on Hiroshima and Nagasaki were *light
weapons* that prefigured the enhanced-radiation neutron bomb,
the directed-beam laser weapons, and the charged-particle guns
currently under development. Moreover, a number of Hiroshima
survivors have reported that, shortly after it was detonated, they
thought it was a *magnesium bomb* of unimagined power."[37]

Does the actor still exist amid these technological experiments and sets that act on his behalf, scrutinizing him and freezing
him in a shadow or an image? The primitive fire that creates the
actor's shadow is intended to burn him, as with Stella's symbolic
combustion in *The Dragons' Trilogy*. The chiaroscuro, variations of
which were seen with Chinese shadows, is nothing more than a
symbolic combustion that suggests the ashes of the dead. Lepage's
light, whether a luminous object or actual lighting, compromises
the actor's usual visibility, outlining him and turning him into
something else. From *Zulu Time* to *The Damnation of Faust*, the
actor performs on a total set that includes projections, sounds,
manipulations of space, and variations in light and shadow as
sources of images. He is just one part of the score, a physical form
revealed by the light, a sound form, moving and changing. In his
quest for shadows, Lepage has burned the actor in the fire of the
quarry. Frédéric dancing in a white shirt in front of a white screen
in *The Andersen Project* seems to burn in a blinding, stroboscopic
fire, foreshadowing the immolation of another character a few
scenes later. And the mirrors in *Elegant Universe*[38] recreate this
bedazzlement faced with the wall, the incandescence of the light,
purposely sending us back to Hiroshima, and also to an entire universe of the image: the confrontation with the image, the reflection
that blinds, and the image that stuns.[39] Lepage's image emerges in
a flash, and strikes in a dazzling light. And the trace it leaves is our
understanding of the work.

SECOND ECHO

PHOTOGRAPHY

Photography is the primary and most common of image technologies used by Lepage. Photographs are used as a reference art, as indicative works related to memory, but above all as metaphors for the psychic apparatus – where Lepage's mark is most obvious.

PHOTOGRAPHY AS A REFERENCE

Photography is used *physically* onstage in the solo shows, beginning with *Vinci*. Explicit references to the world of photography appear earlier, in the form of objects, such as postcards in *Circulations*, and shadow play, such as Chinese shadows and the use of the overhead projector that brings the luminous image into play. After *Vinci*, photography is used more often, both in terms of the number of photos projected and in references to the process of imprinting with light.

Lepage first underlines the reference to photography through the many passing justifications for the medium. For example, his work features a number of photographer protagonists. In *Vinci*, Philippe leaves for Europe with his camera. He looks at things around him through his lens, and he develops a body of conceptual photographic work. He tries to express the soulless world he is living in through empty bathrooms and porcelain sinks. G.I. Luke O'Connor is charged with creating the photographic record of postwar Japan in *The Seven Streams of the River Ota*; in this case, photography from the point of view of photojournalism. The protagonists take many photos and private snapshots in these plays. Camera flashes go off during the party in New York and in the Dutch apartment in *The Seven Streams of the River Ota*. Robert takes a picture of himself in the solitude of his hotel room (*Needles and Opium*), just like the protagonists in *The Seven Streams of the River Ota* have photos taken in photo booths. The third Yukali in *The Dragons' Trilogy* is a young model seen several times in a photo shoot, for which the stage becomes a set.

Photos are taken and developed in plain view. Philippe in *Vinci* and Jeffrey O'Connor, the son of the G.I., develop photos

onstage in similar scenes. Philippe works alone in the darkroom above his tray of developer, while Jeffrey teaches the second Jeffrey to develop prints in the inactinic light[40] of the shared bathroom. After Jeffrey O'Connor sells Jeffrey 2 his father's camera, they develop the father's films. This is how the half-brothers get to know each other.

Photography onstage is a way to get acquainted; it brings the protagonists' worlds together. In *The Seven Streams of the River Ota*, fifteen of the fifty-five scenes include references to photography. Generally this involves one protagonist showing another snapshots: Luke showing them to Nozomi, Jeffrey 1 showing them to Jeffrey 2, and so on. They carry these pictures with them, like a portable world, a quotidian universe that follows them everywhere, or they send themselves photos to circumvent distance and postpone forgetting (*The Dragons' Trilogy*). Using real photos onstage provides an efficient introduction; it creates a self-contained discourse with raw data, like a presentation on an index card lending depth to the character: how many brothers and sisters they have, where they live, and so on. It creates an offstage existence that goes beyond the timeline of the story presented.

Photography is a common, underlying thread that touches each of the protagonists. The snapshot Luke takes of Nozomi underpins the whole story. A photo session opens the play, is the purpose of the first box, and a reason for Luke and Nozomi to get closer. A photograph from this photo session recurs through scenes in the rest of the play over several decades. Luke offers one of the photos to Nozomi, who sees in it her ravaged face. Ada Weber searches for a historical work on the war in Japan in an Amsterdam library and then steals it. Tucked into its pages, she finds a reproduction of a photo of Nozomi's face and offers it to Jeffrey 1 at their reunion. Because Jeffrey 1 is dying, he passes the photo on to his half-brother. The photo circulates among the story's protagonists and unites them.

It is no coincidence that photography, a substitute for presence and a derivative reproduction of familiar forms, appears most in the solo shows and is the only activity happening around an actor in an empty space. These solo shows are productions that use references: the reference to an artist and his career in *Vinci*; *Needles and Opium*'s combined reference to jazz musician Miles

Printing photographs in *Vinci*.

PHOTO
———
Claudel Huot

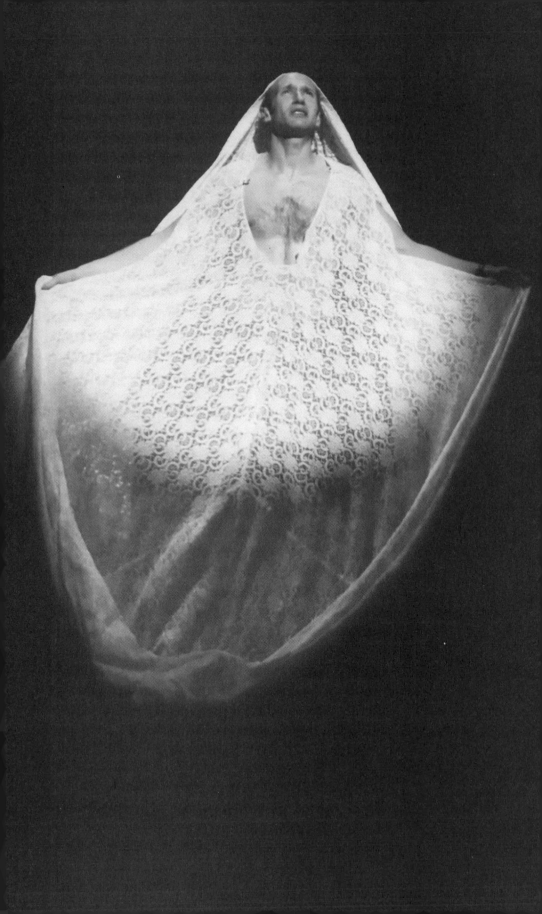

Davis and Cocteau, and again in *The Andersen Project*; a reference to a dramatic work, *Hamlet*, in *Elsinore*; and a reference to an epic event, the conquest of the moon, in *The Far Side of the Moon*. Lepage chooses a few scenes from the artists' lives and a few important events from the conquest of space, in the same way that he boils down the intrigue in *Hamlet*, while emphasizing specific aspects of the story. No matter what the format, Lepage rarely tries to make us forget that photography is representation. It's basically the reference to the forms that pass before the lens, a reference to a piece of reality. It's a reference that announces itself as such and is frank about its declarative role. It doesn't try to create an illusion. When there is an illusion, it is conscious. Lepage chooses to project drawings, paintings, and famous photos and to work the image less imitatively, playing with synecdoche and the enlargement of detail like he does with the lace pattern on Ophelia's dress in *Elsinore*.

In *Vinci*, Philippe discovers Leonardo da Vinci's *The Virgin and Child with Saint Anne*, which is the source of inspiration for the show. We see him onstage taking a picture of the projected image.[41] Likewise, *Needles and Opium* features the famous photo of Cocteau that appeared in *Life* magazine, showing him with three sets of arms, holding scissors, a cigarette, a pencil, and a little red book.[42] The photo illustrates how Cocteau dabbled in just about everything.

Drawing on his practice at Théâtre Repère and his relationship with the object as a source of inspiration, Lepage's shows offer a journal of their own creation, particularly the solo shows. Photography reveals the creative and cognitive processes at work and the important stages of connections, memories, and links made in developing a show. These connections are visual. They are memories of fixed or animated images, much more than memories of texts or events.

Photography is easily used to refer to other things because it isn't cumbersome. From the first shows, photography offers an economical and aesthetic solution: all that is required is a projector, a canvas screen or a wall, and a stock of images to project. Using photography provides a sort of magic lantern, or an inexhaustible supply of apparitions. Like a hawker commenting on his illustrated scenes, Lepage uses luminous apparitions as source figures, as anchors in space and time, and to suggest the setting for the story. The reference to the hawker finds an effective illustration

Passing his head and arms through a spandex surface, the actor becomes Ophelia in a white lace dress. *Elsinore*.

PHOTO

Claudel Huot

in the choice of projection equipment used. The projectors –
most commonly Kodak Pro slide projectors – are intended for
conferences rather than the stage and are merely used with greater
distance between the projector and the projection surface.

With time, the sources of projection multiply and cover
the entire stage. Nine slide projectors are used for *Elsinore*, seven
of them set up in the house facing the stage, with two on the
sides, handling cross projections from the wings. The set is
designed as a neutral, undefined space that the projection of
photos will provide with an identity. It is significant that the
panels in *Elsinore* are white, at one and the same time a screen
and an empty, undefined surface, a large blank page like Craig's
screens. Lepage doesn't just move these panels to create different
spaces within or around the medieval Danish fortress, he adds
projection. He uses photography as one of the ambiguous means
of exploring the drama: the use of projection is underscored each
time something is projected, to break the illusion and make the
audience aware of their perception of space.

When Lepage uses projection, he always underlines the
artifice by a reference, whether in the form of allegories or the projection of synecdoche, an element detached from everything it refers to.
The photo is sometimes used as a stage direction specifying location
or providing insight into a character's personality. The projection
of the king, queen, and joker playing cards is a way of presenting
Claudius, Gertrude, and Hamlet, while the actor who plays these
three characters sits at the centre of the projected cards, his chair
attached to the screen panel. The protagonists of the drama, the
holders of power, are shown like playing cards.[43]

Often photography occupies only part of the set, a
synecdochic projection that transforms the entire space. The
projection of a heavy wooden door transforms the Monolith and
the neighbouring panels into a wall. The same applies with the
projection of stained glass and tapestry. These stage-direction
vignettes projected onto a neutral set give it an identity, like
a painted canvas. But close-ups and serialization give this set a
decidedly modern character, bringing it closer to Brecht's panels
than painted canvases. The shelves of a bookcase or the lace on
Ophelia's dress are examples of the "loop effect" that photography
can create. These elements aren't scaled to the characters, but are

instead enlarged references, making the photographed object a
symbol and a structural rhythm, used particularly in *The Damnation of Faust*. In *The Geometry of Miracles*, photography is used in
the form of structural rhythms made up of architects' drawings,
models, and photos, which appear disproportionate on the screen.
A stage direction vignette can also indicate time: time passes as
we watch the evolution of a building from sketch to completion.

The main purpose of the projected image is to cover the
set or a specific surface in a veil of light. The image as light uses
relief, hollows, and projections of the screen set, and it recomposes the sides of the stage box. In *Elsinore*, the projections change
space. Using computer processing, the designer can modify an
image's scale, erase elements, or reproduce a detail indefinitely.
"For *Elsinore*, it was essential for the transformation: we had to
make it as if the projection [of the heavy wooden door] was on an
angle."[44] Computer processing the image according to the chosen
angle of view makes the desired distortion possible. Projected
onto the central panel of the Monolith, the reworked wooden-door image suggests a central perspective for the audience.
Without recomposition, the door image would not have appeared
so perfectly, given the slant of the panel. Images projected at an
angle from the wings receive the same computer processing, a
treatment that played with the initial angle of projection, creating
an ambiguous image.

A paradox thus exists: the photographic image is always a
reference or meta-enunciation. At the same time, the reconstitution
of the image's spatial information allows it to blend in with the set
and to appear realistic. Representation and illusion: this is also
the direction the placement of the projectors takes. They encircle the
stage in *Elsinore*, and the beam of the projectors reaches every part of
the space; then they become central to the set in *The Seven Streams
of the River Ota*. Six projectors are used: three surrounding the stage
and three others camouflaged on the mezzanine side of the box. The
projection of photos becomes more predominant: projections in any
direction become possible, changing the appearance and therefore
the role of the screen set in a variety of ways.

Illusion is used to disrupt perception and play with
theatrical conventions. In two cases, photography more openly
vies with the scenery as an illusionist *toile peinte* (or painted

backdrop). One scene in *The Geometry of Miracles* uses panoramic photography, serving as scenery for the action that unfolds in front of it. We see an actual photo of the cave in Lascaux, at the same time as we see a photo of cave paintings, a midway solution that still relies on the ontological ambiguity of the projected image, simultaneously illusion (the photo) and representation (the painting). Even more illusion is involved in the effect in *The Seven Streams of the River Ota* with the projection of the Bay of Miyajima and its *torii* arch. The mezzanine box becomes a porch overlooking the bay. The characters look at this landscape in the twilight and the contours fade upstage. This panorama appears again after an initial video version is projected onto the *shoji* screens at the beginning of the performance. In this instance, the projection appears on the cyclorama at the back of the stage, creating the impression of opening the stage up to the world. Photography becomes more than just a backdrop; it creates depth and a landscape from which the boatman and his watercraft emerge in front of a waiting Pierre. A small 3-D image of the Torii of Miyajima is placed in front of the landscape: it intensifies the impression of realism, while creating a contrast with the photo. The backdrop of the scenery from which the *torii* has been removed and a magnificent reflection of the landscape are seen in the rainwater on the porch, the reflection making the ghostlike image of the *torii* seem real. Pierre, seen from behind, joins the boatman: the two stand out, clear shadows against a darkening greyish yellow gash of sky, and everything vanishes in the darkness. With the shadow, the stage becomes uniform and disquieting. The luminous veil becomes a landscape.

A panoramic photo of the cave paintings at Lascaux appears as a projection in *The Geometry of Miracles*.

PHOTO
Emmanuel Valette

PHOTOGRAPHY AS AN INDEX

The Bay of Miyajima with its *torii* arch. The stage box opens onto a landscape. *The Seven Streams of the River Ota*.

PHOTO
Jacques Collin

Lepage's use of photos seems to come from a fascination with how they are produced: a luminous imprint created by contact. The focus is on physical connection, which dominates his thinking about scenic design. More than a mirror, the photo acts as a trace of the real. Since Benjamin and Peirce, photography has been seen as an index, a trace, a mark, or a deposit, like an engraving; from the printing of money to the creation of death masks, imprints are made through direct contact.

We are familiar with the idea of the index through the photogram, the essence of photography for László Moholy-Nagy: a negative imprint of objects in contact with a sensitized surface, created without any equipment, using simply the action of light. The objects placed on the glass plate of the overhead projector in *Needles and Opium* are an obvious reference to such photograms. This minimalist definition of photography, a straight line from the origins of painting and drawing through a projected and fixed object, makes contact between light and a subject and the dazzling speed of this contact the heart of the process. "Representation has to be accomplished in a single stroke, the image of the shadow captured in a single instant,"[45] the shadow struck by lightning.

Lepage's scenic design fits in perfectly with this movement toward the index, cultivating metonymy. The traces of shadow, as physical contact and questioning of the presence, are central to this practice. The idea of the quarry, the reference to cinema in large part, and the photographic design of the productions all flow from this. Each show is built on the traces, most often visual, of objects and events the director attempts contact with. This explains the set designed basically as a sensitized space, like photographic paper: a place for fixing prints made from light. Shadow, video, and the photo make the stage a place for examining traces of shadows. It's how those traces are managed that makes Lepage's productions, particularly his solo shows, memories of his own life combined with other collections of potentially more noteworthy traces. "My interest in certain episodes of the conquest of space forced me in spite of myself to revisit my childhood and a large part of my adolescence," he writes in the program for *The Far Side of the Moon*, which has a feeling of "déjà read" in reference to the theatre programs for solo shows, which have always associated the broader artistic sphere with the private sphere. This same association appears in the introduction to *The Andersen Project*, with Lepage even saying that what inspired its creation was discovering a hidden face of Andersen that resonated with him. As with photography, not surprisingly, Lepage returns to the sign as an approach to production. In *The Far Side of the Moon*, he doesn't look at the conquest of space beyond his experienced perception of it. He commemorates the historical event and how it was recorded, based on his memory. Getting in touch with this memory is often like psychoanalysis – an index of memory and its effect on our lives.

The reference to Hiroshima, a source for *The Seven Streams of the River Ota,* is also a reference to photography as an index. Hiroshima is often represented as the ultimate photogram: an imprint of the outline of a reality that has disappeared created through contact with light. The photo by Eiichi Matsumoto, published in the Japanese national newspaper *Asahi Shimbun,* shows shadows of a man and a ladder projected onto the wall of a wooden house by the energy of the atomic bomb at Nagasaki; their shadows were frozen in time. What should have been ephemeral becomes enduring, while the referent disappears. Similarly, at the Hiroshima museum, a stone step still has the shadow of the man who was sitting on it at the time of the explosion. The disparity is terrifying. In a terrible way, Hiroshima is the realization of the myth of Orpheus that symbolically defines photography:[46] Eurydice literally dies for having been seen.[47] References to Hiroshima and photography appeared in Lepage's work as early as *The Dragons' Trilogy.* The young Yukali explains that her mother's body vanished, making it difficult to grieve. And she has never seen her father, the American soldier who spent time with her geisha mother. On August 6, 1955, the tenth anniversary of the bomb, she takes part in the ceremonies and follows the advice of burying a substitute object, in her case the dress the officer gave her mother. This same effort to symbolize compels her to photograph her absent father as he leaves or returns to the sentry box, in a dream scene. Despite the symbolic presence, she is still photographing an empty space instead of her father. She then buries this *imago* by burying the film in the sand so that she can forget him. The sentry box's blind goes up and the father has disappeared. Once again, a flash makes a body disappear, or, in this case, a memory or fantasy.

The photograph is primarily a chemical impression with origins in shadow games, although it's different from shadow games in that it's a fixed image. Photography emanates from and is an index to its referent. It testifies to a presence, and this is essential for Lepage's notion of photography. It is a tool of memory, evoking a time gone by.[48] It requires the interval between the moment the photograph is taken or fixed, and "the present moment of the gaze upon the photograph."[49] This gap is a chasm that the fastest Polaroid cannot fill: the photographic instant is ontologically in the past.

The photo booth in *The Seven Streams of the River Ota* is a particularly apt reference to this dual aspect of time gone by and the proof of a presence. The booth is part of the stage set showing a train station concourse in the four scenes of Part Five, entitled "Words" and set in Osaka. Passing by the photo booth, Walter Lapointe suddenly remembers that he needs ID photos for his pass to the World's Fair. The audience enters the privacy of the booth with him, through a camera that replaces the camera in the photo booth. At the moment the flash goes off, the projected image is fixed to imitate the photographic rendering. While Walter's image is fixed, we see him moving in the booth preparing for another shot. Patricia, his wife, picks up the photos and gets annoyed at how mediocre they are. Neither Hanako nor François-Xavier, who also use the photo booth, picks up their snapshots: Hanako, because the train is about to leave; and François-Xavier, because he doesn't want to have a run-in with Patricia, who just missed her train. The images of these subjects disappear by the time the photos are developed, despite how quickly this is done. The hybrid photo booth illustrates the photographic interval, taking literally an affirmation of proximity, of identity one could say, all the more obvious because these snapshots, just like any photogram, cannot be reproduced.[50] The role of the device itself suggests the index: one expects representations of oneself and, in the case of the photo booth, what's expected is imitation, which is why Patricia gets upset when she sees the "bad pictures" of Walter. If the photo testifies to "what was," then the photo booth illustrates the temptation to control it. Because it actually involves a photo in the mirror: the lens is behind a pane of glass that protects the camera and reflects the subject. The reflection is what makes it possible to control the pose before it is set by the flash.

Before taking the train for Hiroshima, Sophie also goes into the photo booth. We have just seen her crying. She is unhappy with her performance in Osaka, she knows that she's pregnant and that her boyfriend doesn't want children, she is irritated by François-Xavier's insistent pursuit, and she ended the night with Walter! In the phone booth, Sophie reveals her distress and her hurt self; in the photo booth, she reconstructs her social self, showing

The photo booth at the train station in Osaka is a metaphorical starting gate and a place for introspection. *The Seven Streams of the River Ota.*

PHOTO
———————
Emmanuel Valette

how she lies to herself. The two booths act as a sort of confessional, but with different results. Sophie's face appears sad in the first shot, still streaked with tears. Then from shot to shot, she musters a smile and ends up radiant. The photograph is *not* an index of Sophie's true feelings; the audience isn't fooled and laughs at the difference between the photo and their understanding of the character's state of mind. Sophie reconstitutes her social image by checking herself in the mirror and, more importantly, by authentication through a supposedly objective process: smiling for the camera means receiving the seal of authenticity. This is why she doesn't need to wait for the photos: stamped with the seal of light, captured in full light, she is able to put together an illusory face that will hold until her next bout of sadness.

The role of the photographic image as index makes a particular use of memory, around relics. Photography is the ultimate *imago*, "a physical trace of unique people who were there and who have a particular relationship with those looking at the photos."[51] What people seek from a photograph is testimony of the proximity

that was: think of the pride people take in pictures of themselves
with their favourite celebrity. Pictures of someone at a distance
from his or her hero, separated by a crowd or by security, are even
more revealing. The snapshots show the distance, but the person
sees the trace of contact and remembers it fondly. This explains
the common, emotionally charged practice of the family album,
a collection of images, "a catalogue of our most shared snapshots
that sum us up."[52] The photo, while emphasizing irretrievable loss,
is the last connection with the object photographed, an object
as if embalmed, taken out of time, but subjected to the aging of
the medium of photography. It fuels and revives memories, even
substituting for them at times.

In a scene from the first part of *The Seven Streams of the
River Ota*, Nozomi's mother-in-law is looking at the damaged
photos of her loved ones that she has removed from an old file
folder. This scene then begins to use referencing as the snapshots
she looks at are projected onto the *shoji* screen panels. The projection begins at the height of the file folder and then moves, in
time with the movement of her arms, miming the action of taking
out the photos. She looks at wedding photos – an occasion for
families to gather – no doubt at Nozomi's wedding. And she can
see how many have died. The projected image turns into a film,
as if the old woman were reliving a series of memories. But the
image shrinks in front of her as she screams, hands outstretched.
This poignant impotence evokes both the irreparable nature of
human loss and the loss of memories. Regularly looking at photos
postpones this loss somewhat, a pathetic period of grace before
forgetting. The scene underlines the ambiguity of photographic
memory, "a physical film of consciousness, [...] developed in
the place of a durable trace of our memories."[53] An ambiguous
memory, therefore, "or if you prefer a memory prosthetic,
signifying a failure to record traces, and which shows both the
holes in the psyche and the impossibility of their repair."[54] Jean
Guerreschi's analysis goes to the very heart of Lepage's approach
to screen surfaces and relationship with the image: "The *homo
photographiens* creates a sort of 'surface' history and a history of
surfaces, realizing the dream of a memory on the same level as the
operations of the consciousness."[55] The use of images has often
been seen as a way of addressing the imagination directly and

making reference to an associative syntax connected to dreams and the unconscious. The impossibility of mending is clearly demonstrated in this vanishing, in this shrinking of the image. Photography is like an artificial memory or index to the scene. It showcases traces of memory and even competes with memory, making it in a sense a protagonist.

In *The Geometry of Miracles*, photography tells the story of a number of buildings being built. This epic in images runs through the creation of a building from sketches to completion. In counterpoint to the action, in a suggested "offstage," the photographic narration is like a messenger speaking. Photography operates like a character's intervention in the story because it is profoundly deictic. As Barthes suggests, it is a succession of "see," "and see."[56] More effective than a traditional story or dialogue because of its concision, clarity of intention, and speed of conveying the message, photography is used for short informative sequences. But it finds its true dramaturgical place in *The Seven Streams of the River Ota*. The show grew out of the need to commemorate the fiftieth anniversary of Hiroshima, an event symbolically connected to the camera's use of light. Lepage talks about a "photon-graphic"[57] disaster, reviving the widespread idea of a light-related catastrophe, a sort of giant photolysis.[58]

Photography takes on the discourse of memory. In the last part of the show, Pierre and his mother, the European protagonists, visit the Peace Museum accompanied by Hanako. It's one of the rare moments when the bombing is referred to directly through the simple and terrible recognition of well-known images: the mushroom cloud, the Atomic Bomb Dome, and others. Earlier we followed Hanako into the photo booth, first alone and then accompanied by her husband. In the most recent version (performed in Quebec City and elsewhere in 1996), she remains single and the little girl who plays her as a child joins her. She is blind and doesn't see her reflection in the photo-booth mirror, but she jumps when the flash goes off, a reminder of the explosion underlined by the mushroom cloud projected onto the central panel. This is how we understand that Hanako did in fact lose her sight in the bombing. The most recent version is explicit on this point from the beginning, with a nurse taking care of a little girl with bandaged eyes.

Photography evokes the bomb in the characters' stead. Rather than talking about her memories of that day, Hanako describes the garden of her childhood or brings her visitors to the museum. In the same way, the images Nozomi's mother-in-law looks at act for her. The protagonists assign photography, with its disturbing resemblance to the murderous device, the mission of memory, allowing them to forget. The event is omnipresent, its consequences are palpable and affect all the protagonists, but it's only partially addressed by the text and by the descendants of the protagonists who witnessed the catastrophe. The survivors try to obliterate that moment, and when they return to the past, mainly through photographs, they turn their minds to those who died and to what came long before the bomb. Technology provides the account of the greatest disaster of the last century, a meta-reflexive narrator that draws a line between the photo's and the mind's capacity for memory and revelation.

PHOTOGRAPHY AS A METAPHOR FOR THE PSYCHIC APPARATUS

Along with the notions of presence, interval, and the disclosure and management of information, photography, in how it works and its pragmatics, introduces symbols similar to Hiroshima and, more broadly, to the process of human thought in the relationship of the subject to the world. Photography evokes the idea of assimilation. In this sense, "the darkroom is the technological prosthesis that man has most effectively adapted to his psychological need to assimilate the world."[59] A need for photography thus emerges from the heart of Lepage's productions, even more evident because it grows out of an understanding or profound intuition about the psychic apparatus.

Traces of the *camera obscura* can be found in the box in Lepage's scenic designs. Every projection space is inspired by the *camera obscura*,[60] a use of lenses that predates photography and that made it possible to control the sharpness of images. In the eighteenth century, this device for capturing images provided a sketch or a picture and "was also used to project painted or drawn images on a screen."[61] A dark chamber recreates the mechanism of the *camera obscura*, but on a much smaller scale, as man no longer has to enter it.

Lepage's sets are inspired by the camera's dark chamber, with the human dimensions of a *camera obscura*: an empty box that receives the image on a screen, like on the paper *shoji* screens in the first set, a box pierced with an opening like the rooms in the New York apartment, the Monolith, the set in *Coriolanus*, and so on. There is always an entrance, a place for capturing images, and a surface on which they are shown. The rotation of the screen wall in *Needles and Opium* is similar to the shutter of a reflex camera. In both instances, the mirror moves. The structure of the camera provided Freud with a key concept for understanding the psyche, "an apparatus to which we ascribe the characteristics of being extended in space and of being made up of several portions – which we imagine, that is, as resembling a telescope or microscope or something of the kind."[62] The set in *The Seven Streams of the River Ota* bears the mark of these theories.

The camera's viewfinder finds a psychological equivalent as a system of perception/consciousness, through which all information passes, while on the other hand the recording surface is like a system that traces memory and the unconscious, where everything rests: in the black box, as in the psychic apparatus, impressions are recorded and stored. In this sense, Yukali opening the camera and inserting the film underlines the analogy between the darkroom and the psychic apparatus. This device is found in the set of the New York apartment in *The Seven Streams of the River Ota*, a scene in which photography is central. The doors to the small rooms are like viewfinders that frame a subject; there is one actor per door. This viewfinder delivers information about the eye of the conscience. Facing these doors, on the audience side, there is a symbolic recording surface in the unconscious. At her wake, Nozomi emerges from this symbolic space that will later be analyzed as film, while Jeffrey 2 is looking in the viewfinder of Luke's camera that he recently bought. Nozomi lies down on the porch, in front of Jeffrey's room. This action is thus the metaphor for developing the image and the daily work of the psychic apparatus, a phase of reconstructing an image that is detaching from the inscription surface. The porch is a site of memory, as is the idea of adding depth to the box, which is like a zoom image in a telescopic darkroom.

The problem of resurging traces of memory is at work here, and it's interesting to look at the recording surface, the screen, whether symbolic or real, and, more broadly, at Lepage's sets, as a psychological place that stages unconscious processes; for example, in *Needles and Opium*. "Freud's use of the model of the photographic apparatus is intended to show that all psychic phenomena necessarily pass first through an unconscious phase, through darkness and the negative, before acceding to consciousness, before developing within the clarity of the positive."[63] To clarify, say the preconscious corresponds to the negative – an inversion, as with the *camera obscura*, and not a very recognizable image – and the conscious corresponds to the positive – "the final, luminous image."[64] What is happening in the psychic apparatus is similar to the path of the image in photography. The snapshot doesn't have to be developed and can remain the ultimate latent image, just as the psychological process can remain unconscious. If developing reveals what was on the film, then with the psychic apparatus this visibility is less linear and less necessary or dialectical. It is not a matter of finding a buried meaning, "always already there,"[65] but of constructing a meaning that never existed; this is the goal of psychoanalysis, but also a recurring part of the dramaturgical vocabulary of the shows. It is also the path that the protagonists' stories follow.

In *Vinci*, Philippe is seeing a psychiatrist when he decides to take a trip to Europe. We sense his preoccupation with psychoanalysis in the photos he takes there: understanding the world, himself, his place in the world, and his identity. The moment the picture is taken is experienced as a questioning of the world, but also a way of verifying that one is part of the world. For Philippe, photography, through the act of taking pictures, is intrinsic proof of his presence in the world. This is also what Robert tries to achieve alone in his hotel room in *Needles and Opium*, even more clearly because he is taking self-portraits with his Polaroid. In both cases, taking pictures is a form of resistance to the self-isolation of the psyche. The black box of the camera and the psychic apparatus contain a piece of information: an image of the world or a representation, an affect, a state of the body "related to a situation that cannot be assimilated,"[66] a psychological movement of incorporation, wanting these elements to come back to the surface to be internalized. The box retains, and the screen – photo paper, the stage screen, or the actor who mimics its imprint on a surface – reveals its contents. Thus Nozomi passes before her son's

lens, while the son is reminded of her death when his father's death
is announced. In both the psychic apparatus and the photographic
apparatus, the tension between box and screen is essential.

These photography metaphors are an extension of the
archaeology metaphors from *Civilization and Its Discontents*, which
Freud uses to illustrate how traces of memory are managed. Freud
points to Rome as an "immense archaeological palimpsest,"[67] a
site of accumulation, fragmentary stratification, and endurance,
where something new is superimposed over traces of the thing
that preceded it. For Freud, if Rome were a psychic entity "in
which nothing that has once come into existence will have passed
away and all the earlier phases of development continue to exist
alongside the latest one,"[68] a visitor could see buildings from every
era superimposed all at the same time. In his analysis of Jensen's
novel *Gradiva*, Freud presents, through Pompeii, the possibility
of a complete and unchanging representation of the past.[69] He
compares instant capture to the durability of Rome: whereas
Pompeii presents only fragments, Freud sees the totality. Like
Hiroshima, the Pompeii disaster suspended a city in an eternal
instant, a disaster that also occurred under particular light conditions. "Pompeii gives us only an image, but virtually intact."[70]
Rome is the antithesis of Pompeii, multiplicity set against the
whole, the duration as opposed to the instant. And yet, Freud sees
them reconciled in any psychic apparatus in which the traces of
memory are both "always all there and always whole."[71]

These ideas find unsettling echoes in the treatment of
photography in *The Seven Streams of the River Ota*. Applying Freud's
thinking, the photographic positive is like Rome, an exposed ruin,
subject to the unrelenting erosion of time, while the negative is like
Pompeii, a "buried ruin, therefore relatively intact."[72] In this show,
the positives and images revealed are vestiges that a protagonist
exhumes while thinking. It isn't an innocent design decision that the
family photos that Nozomi's mother-in-law contemplates are damaged, partially destroyed, perhaps by the catastrophe itself. What she
mimes taking out of her file folder are residues of representations,
ruins exposed to the storm that would shake Hiroshima. The same
applies to any photograph that, while removing the subject from
time, is nonetheless, through its materiality, subject to unavoidable
erosion due to the fragility of the medium of photography.

Conversely, keeping the snapshot in negative form is effectively illustrated in the film that Jeffrey 2 leaves Jeffrey 1 when he returns to Japan. The final scene in this box shows Jeffrey 1 developing the film in the bathroom, now transformed into a darkroom. When he takes the image out of its developing bath, he drops the snapshot, having just recognized his father in it. Jeffrey 2 had told him that the film was left in Japan by his own American father! The film is twenty years old and reveals its contents once it is exposed to the light and the image has stabilized. This scene perfectly illustrates the idea of the negative as a buried ruin. In fact, it is only a ruin once it is developed and exposed to the light. Freud effectively sums up this fact: "the destruction of Pompeii is beginning only now that it has been dug up."[73] This again points to the creative and destructive aspect of light, seen in Hiroshima and in Lepage's light technology. More than a simple buried ruin, the negative is a latent image, trapped in the interval between the time the image was captured, which is no longer, and the appearance of an image, which is not yet.

In "A Note Upon the 'Mystic Writing Pad',"[74] Freud attempts to reconcile Rome and Pompeii. With his mystic writing pad, the *Wunderblock*, he has them coexisting in layers. Freud describes the *Wunderblock* as a child's toy consisting of a wax tablet covered by a sheet of cellophane "as a protective layer to avoid ripping the thin wax paper that is under it."[75] A stylus is used to etch an image into the receptive wax surface. When the cellophane sheet is pulled away, the image on the tablet disappears and it returns to its original blank state. Freud points out, though, that the wax tablet retains a trace of the image after it has been erased. In fact, the wax surface retains both the message and the layers of all messages, the accumulation and the whole. Traces of writing, memories of a message may be understood more clearly than the latent image ("because there is something to see")[76] – although it is less obvious than a positive image where the message is clearer – this inscription is instead like a negative, using a "trough between the order of the eye and of memory. A memory of the eye and an eye of the memory."[77] The *Wunderblock,* the perfect point of articulation between the Roman and Pompeiian visions, is the definition of a palimpsest, a reusable surface and durable traces of the elements that appear on it; in other words, where memories of new experiences are superimposed over memories of the experiences that have gone before.

This surface is found in the dwellings created for several Lepagean stage sets, but more importantly the surface is one of the sources of image processing in Lepage's work. In Pierre Lamontagne's house (*Le confessionnal*, 1995), the camera, like the Freudian visitor to Rome, superimposes different realities, bringing together different spaces and times. In the same shot, we can see the Lamontagne couple in the bath, in 1952, and the son working around the house more than thirty years later. The outlines of the photo frames that Pierre can't manage to cover up, despite many coats of paint, are a perfect illustration of the *Wunderblock*: the message of the frames persists despite being covered by the new coat of paint, a symbol of a new layer of time. The same goes for the kimono scene in *The Seven Streams of the River Ota*, in which all the protagonists parade by in the costume that Nozomi wore during the photo session. The same scene also includes the flashes that are at the origin of the story, both Luke's and the bomb's. These flashes come from the walls, more precisely from the *tokonoma*, the decorative recess of shadow where the kimono is on display.

The reference to photography is a profound and prolific justification of the stage box. It is a dark chamber that releases exposed images, photographic memories that emerge in disarray, delivering the representation again or after a time lag. It also helps to understand the analogy with the psychic apparatus. Using this analogy, we can say that photography is the box, which indirectly legitimizes the narrative's intersections and meanderings that seem to be the result of a mind plagued by slowdowns, selection, and resistance in the process of resurgence. Lepage's narrative and space are conditioned by a central mental activity, a protective agency organizing all sets, hence the themes of quest and investigation. This particular memory more broadly influences the relationship to the projection and the shadow. The image is never considered in isolation, but, as a palimpsest, in relation to the other images or elements over which it superimposes the new.

Something is at work between the eye and memory in this desire to fix a shadow while underlining the duration of the gesture. Similarly, something is at work between the eye and memory in this reference to the inevitable time lag between the photo and the disappeared reality it captures, in all of these photographic conceptions of space and the apparition, and in the different temporalities that accumulate on a single surface or in a single space. It is the same between the screen and the box, which foreshadows the extent to which the Lepagean screen operates between visibility, latency, and memory. Everything occurs as if Lepage, projecting on screens (*Elsinore, The Seven Streams of the River Ota*) or using walls as real or psychological screens (*Polygraph, Le confessionnal, The Seven Streams of the River Ota, The Far Side of the Moon* …), is pushing us to consider them as mystic writing pads; in other words, to see the instantaneity of representation of the icon all the while remembering what was already imprinted on it. The image, which is latent, often represents a fantasy, a still poorly defined construction occupying a protagonist's psyche. Spandex – one of the materials commonly used for Lepage's screens – becomes wax, etching what the photos, videos, and shadows offer as if they were inscriptions made by the stylus.

The idea of the palimpsest, of new experiences superimposing themselves over traces of experiences that have gone before, is central to the iconic organization of the stage and narrative design and makes this reference to photography an essential detour, a trace of light opening up a psychoanalytic backdrop, an alteration of the box into screen layers. Photography is an appeal to memory, an open door on memory, an index-based questioning that fuels and makes possible the ontological quest. All of Lepage's protagonists are on this quest. The image, the screen, and, more broadly, the stage design, become the site of a Roman archaeological dig, making the many and often fragmentary Pompeiian vestiges of our image-based society emerge entirely through photography.

THIRD ECHO

CINEMA

While photography is the image technology most often used, cinema is the one most referred to in Lepagean aesthetics. Lepage sees cinema as "an account of what happened to the light in a particular place at the time of filming," while "the actor, in film, is only a luminous impression."[78] For Lepage, references to cinema enrich the theatrical narrative and provide new possibilities in scenic design. References to cinema contribute to the trajectory of the gaze, and start a cross-dialogue that becomes all the richer when Lepage begins directing films in 1994. Three of his six films are adaptations of plays or excerpts initially created for the stage. While ontologically the stage presence and image owe a lot to photography, their pragmatics are first and foremost cinematographic.

 ## A FILM NARRATIVE

Whether through allusions to film trades, particularly post-production, beginning in *Needles and Opium*, and shooting a film in *Polygraph*, or through allusions to composers of film scores such as Miles Davis in the development of sagas such as *The Dragons' Trilogy*, *The Seven Streams of the River Ota*, and *The Geometry of Miracles*, cinema appears repeatedly in Lepage's narratives. It is primarily "an art involving both the combination and arrangement of elements,"[79] and this well could be Lepage's definition of theatre, about which the notion of editing is frequently raised.

Editing can be defined as being "that which assures the connection of the elements of an action according to a principle that is, quite globally, a relationship of causality and/or diegetic temporality."[80] In his narratives, Lepage uses many threads to weave together two or more themes in patchwork narratives whose fragmentation has drawn from the narrative techniques of screenwriting. Cinema embraces the instant rather than duration, and this turns up in Lepagean theatre, where the scenes are designed as small independent and movable units. In shows such as *The Seven Streams of the River Ota*, *The Geometry of Miracles*, and *Zulu Time*, scenes are short and come in rapid succession, punctuated by blackouts. Lepage works with the story like a director in the editing room: he moves shots and rebuilds sequences in different orders. He has total control over the final order, or the final cut. Well before 1994, his narratives were like film scripts, and their final meaning is created more through editing than through the scenes in and of themselves. Editing isn't concerned with chronological sequencing; his approach is the antithesis of it.

For Lepage, public rehearsals are the equivalent of the rough cut before the work leading to the final cut. The rough cut is "an end-to-end placement, using directions in the script, of shots with the clapperboard removed from the beginning and the 'cut' from the end, which can be shown to certain collaborators – producers, musicians [and, for Lepage, the audience] – to give them a sense of the film"[81] and get their reaction. Lepage always reserves the right during a show's run to rework the story or the order of the scenes. The first version corresponds to a rough cut. He begins a show's run with a rough cut and edits while on tour. This ability to move entire scenes without necessarily changing them, with a particular skill for connection, is definitely a cinematic approach.

Thus, beginning in 1996, once the seven boxes of *The Seven Streams of the River Ota* were created, changes in sequence would occur; for example, Lepage reordered the scenes of an intrigue, which itself remained static. It is significant that the boxes that were moved weren't changed internally in any way, while the boxes that weren't moved underwent profound changes. Boxes three, four, and five moved to fourth, fifth, and third place, as if this were filmed material or Lepage was reusing the rushes left on the floor during the first edit.[82]

The fragmented structure of *Polygraph* is borrowed from the detective film. It puts the audience in the role of the investigator who traces the facts back to reveal the murderer. The title itself points to the lie detector that suspects can be subjected to. Etymologically, the word "polygraph" suggests multiple scripts, like the many paths belonging to each of the protagonists: the screenplay was written by Lepage and Marie Brassard.[83] Beginning with the first version of the show, four threads intersect. The first involves the police investigation of the rape and murder of a young Quebec woman. The second develops the end of the thesis that François Tremblay has to defend, a thesis about the symbolism and reality of the Berlin Wall. François, a friend of the victim, is the primary suspect in the police investigation. A third thread follows the progress of a project to make a film inspired by the crime. The fourth thread places, "in counterpoint to the action, a pathologist [who] comments on the anatomical charts illustrating the bloodstream and physiology of the heart, which evokes the autopsy done on the victim and explains the violence she suffered."[84] The two symbolic ventricles of a city divided between east and west correspond with the ventricles of the heart. The words of the student defending his thesis and of the pathologist teaching a course connect perfectly into a single text about the reality of the wall, the functioning of the organism, and indirectly, the young dead girl, without us knowing which is the metaphor for which:

> PROFESSOR: [...] at the hand, at the wrists, with a blow to the rib cage; and we can assume that the fatal blow was here.
>
> FRANÇOIS: ... in the heart of the city ...
>
> PROFESSOR: ... between the fifth and the sixth rib. The septum is this little wall located beside the heart that prevents the passage ...
>
> FRANÇOIS: ... from East to West.
>
> PROFESSOR: ... from the left ventricle to the right ventricle [in the film version, we see the professor crossing over to the West, producing his passport to the customs officer].
>
> FRANÇOIS: The crossing can only happen in one direction.
>
> PROFESSOR: In fact, a sophisticated system of doors that open and close, makes it possible to filter ...
>
> FRANÇOIS: ... the visitors from the West.[85]

The theatrical narrative is also film-like in the importance it assigns to narrative instances, in an effort at symmetry that boils down to playing with conventions while drawing attention to them. Like a story within a story, Lepage tells tales in loops, around the voice of a witness narrator who opens the space of the story (*The Seven Streams of the River Ota, The Dragons' Trilogy, The Far Side of the Moon*) or around a recurrent image (*The Seven Streams of the River Ota*). This is a common technique in detective movies. This manner of ending a narrative on a repeated speech immediately underlines the narrative instance, while pointing to its cyclical nature. *The Dragons' Trilogy* opens with the image of a parking-lot attendant who finds a ball of light, an image we would expect to see at the end of the performance. The circular effect is reinforced by the text: at the opening, three voices recite in three different languages "I have never been to China," and they tell the story of the plot of land that has become a parking lot. At the end of the performance, Pierre announces to his mother, Françoise, that he is no longer going to England, but to China; Françoise then continues the opening passage, in a trembling voice: "I have never been to China. But when I was little, there were houses here. This was Chinatown. Now it's a parking lot. Maybe someday it will become a park, a bus station, or a cemetery."[86]

The story within a story is a narrative technique of the novel that, when used in cinema, is rendered most often as an ongoing voice-over against the backdrop of a long panoramic shot. Lepage adopted this technique for the opening of his films *Le confessionnal, Polygraph,* and *Nô* (1997). But the technique is also found in some of his plays, with a narrator or voice-over in a space treated like a panoramic shot; that is, during the storyteller's prologue in *The Seven Streams of the River Ota*, the *shoji* screens part to reveal a screen and the panoramic view of a bay, a landscape that appears again at the end of the performance. The same thing crops up in the solo shows, particularly in *The Far Side of the Moon* (a travelling shot created using set panels that replace the frame). *The Andersen Project* updates this opening with the announcement before an image of the Paris Opera (Palais Garnier) that a modern tale will be told. Frédéric Lapointe appears onstage to explain that the evening's performance has been cancelled and that instead he will tell a story, which turns out to be the story of his trip to Europe and his research on Andersen.

There is a part of Lepage's work where the narrative influence of film is more direct and its techniques bring something to the world of theatre: the film transition that provides "the articulations of the story"[87] for syntax. Lepage inserts them in his narrative, most often without using projection, as if he were editing it, because all of these technical transitions appear concrete only at the editing stage, when the material is organized. The first type of technical transition changes scenes through a cut. It is the "most basic transition, the most common and the most essential as well," in that it is symbolic of the foundation of cinema itself, which is not a simple recording of reality on sensitized film, but the organization and connection of different *pieces of recordings* "separated at the moment of the shot."[88] Between these different sequences, there is a separation that signifies only a change in point of view. Lepage often talks in cinematic terms when building a story, which he imagines in an interrupted continuity: "We have to do jump cuts. We make a film," he explained, during the second phase of rehearsals of *The Geometry of Miracles*.[89] Many cuts can be detected in his plays, called "cut noir" instead of "blackouts" when Lepage chooses to underline his intervention. In *Coriolanus*, all the scenes are separated by very short blackouts, signifying changes of scene again used in film aesthetics. The same goes for *The Seven Streams of the River Ota*, in which, within each box, scenes are separated with blackouts. Turning out the lights becomes part of the action. In the New York apartment, we move from one room to another as a camera operator would change shots, and as soon as lights are turned out in one room, they go on in the next room and the action starts.

Another gentler way of suggesting the passage of time is the dissolve.[90] This transition is used a great deal in *The Geometry of Miracles*, because of the frequent use of a revolving circular platform on the stage, a metaphor in action. The movement and rotation of a wooden drafting table signals the scene change. We see Frank Lloyd Wright working at the drafting table in the middle of the desert, when Beelzebub appears. They start to discuss the Faustian contract.[91] During the discussion, the actors begin to exit the stage, and the industrialist Johnson jumps on the turntable and tap dances. His secretary, Marge, arrives with a chair and sits down at the table, pretending to type as the entrepreneur dictates. The movement of the table becomes a synonym for the dissolve. It keeps one shot visible in front of another while the second is being set up.

The wipe is a less common narrative transition in cinema today. With a wipe, "an image is replaced with another that sort of slides in front of it (either laterally or like a fan)."[92] The new image sliding in from the side, while artificial, plays similarly to the curtain, while the fan displays the new image with an additional level of artifice. The stage design in *The Seven Streams of the River Ota* is based entirely on the idea of the wipe, with

panels sliding along rails to move the action underway to another
action underway; in other words, a superimposition of images.
At the beginning of the third part, "A Wedding," sliding bookcase
panels obstruct the prostitutes' windows. Once the panels are in
place, Ada removes a book from the shelf: the curtain has depth.
The panels act as a wipe, a "curtain" whose surface includes the
directions about a new space onstage. Lepage is acting like a film
director in designing the transitions between scenes as movements
from one shot to another. These transitions crop up again in
his films, with a real fluency, as if their use onstage had been an
apprenticeship for possible editing techniques.

Credits are clearly borrowed from the visual narrative of
film and television, and they were rarely used in theatre until recent
years. Today it is increasingly common to see theatre reproduce the
canons of film and television. The credits are a metatext that show
the title of the film and the people who take part, to whatever extent,
in making it. The list scrolls by on a neutral background or a still shot
from the film and a soundtrack. Credits can also be integrated into
ongoing action. Traditionally, the credits appear at the beginning
of the film; sometimes only the title and names of the main actors
and director appear at the beginning, with the names of the other
contributors left until the end. On occasion, the story begins before
the credits are presented. In either case, the metatext is displayed.
Thus in the film *Polygraph*, the title of the film and the names of the
actors and the director appear several minutes into the action, after
the first scene with the lie detector test. This effect is very common
today in film and in the 1960s was widely used in television to grab
the viewer's immediate attention. Credits have been a Lepagean
signature since *Elsinore* and now appear in all productions; as with
cinema, they appear at different points in the story. In *Needles and
Opium, The Seven Streams of the River Ota, The Far Side of the Moon,*
and *The Andersen Project* they appear after an introductory scene, a
sort of prologue recited on the side of the proscenium or in front of
the curtain (however symbolic). In *Elsinore* the solo actor has already
started the play, incarnating the king, the queen, and then Hamlet,
corresponding to the second scene of the first act in the original text,
before the credits appear. The credits make a spectacular appearance
when the three panels come together to form a large screen wall
in the foreground, hiding the stage. In the case of *The Geometry of*

Miracles, the title only appears on the background screen after the first scene with Frank Lloyd Wright and the complete credits appear at the end. While transporting the ashes of the architect and his wife, two of Wright's former apprentices stop for a drink in what they think is a café but what is in fact a nightclub. As in film, the credits are superimposed over the action. The story isn't over, but already a text appears signifying the end. The text appears behind the actors, but it is projected from the house and consequently is superimposed on the actors. The audience's perception of the show is therefore disrupted, and they are surprised to find themselves momentarily in front of a movie screen.

 ## A MOVIE SET

Lepage's definition of cinema as "an account of what happened to the light in a particular place at the time of filming" while "the actor, in film, is only a luminous impression"[93] is reminiscent of the quarry and gathering around a light source that creates an image on the wall. The quarry is as much the storyteller's theatre as is the movie theatre. Words are important, but what brings people together is the light, the "public lighting" to which Virilio refers.[94] In Lepage's universe of the imagination, the stage is a space from which light springs to create images, even a box (a hodgepodge reference to the camera obscura and the 35 mm projector) that releases a thin ray of light cutting through darkness to an awaiting screen. The theatre mimics cinema, an empty frame within which everything happens; for example, there is an ongoing allusion to the movie theatre in *Coriolanus*. The screen is suggested at the beginning by a sheer curtain: transparency that passes for projection. Lepage shrinks the proscenium opening in this show. It literally contains the action and recreates a different performance space. The movie set doesn't change: it is the unadorned frame for the whole performance like a traditional screening room. The same constancy appears in *National, capitale nationale* (1993), a show that criticizes the failings of Ottawa bureaucrats, but with a changing set. A large frame on a black wall is a reference to the movie screen, although its borders move to recreate zoom effects, still in rectangular shapes. The framing of the actors is close, with the heads of those who are standing cut off, and even framing at ground level to show a woman on a leash. Movie-theatre allusions are found in at least three of Lepage's other shows (*Coriolanus*, *The Seven Streams of the River Ota*, *Elsinore*), although with more fluidity and diversity of meaning. He moves from ongoing reference to rapid allusion, from a reminder of the conditions of viewing to the actual use of images.

In *Coriolanus*, as in *Elsinore*, the set can take the audience by surprise, by momentarily creating a film structure. The stage changes at the end of the credits, but it introduces, quite effectively and dramatically, something that is more cinema-like through the suggestion of large screens that plunge the audience into an enveloping image, like those found in cinema multiplexes. The size of the screen, be it real or symbolic, tends to grow from performance to performance. From the modestly sized opening screen in *Coriolanus*, we move to the screen facade in *The Seven Streams of the River Ota*, and then to the wall in *Elsinore*, to end at the 17 metre-long screen in *The Geometry of Miracles* and the wall screens in *The Damnation of Faust*.[95] These screens offer enormous, unified images that occupy the entire proscenium opening of the Paris Opera (Palais Garnier). In *The Geometry of Miracles*, as with the credits in *Elsinore*, Lepage competes with cinema through large-format projections: the image of the inside gallery of the cave at Lascaux is a rendering of materials and colours reminiscent of high-definition film. In the opening of *The Damnation of Faust*, when a giant book fills the large mosaic screen made up of eight Plexiglas screens or when twelve screens arranged in three rows of four show images of stained glass, the audience has the feeling of seeing a projection on a giant screen.

However, once cinema begins feeding the narrative and visual substratum, the presence of the means of dissemination as a reference is no longer necessary. The production uses another space related to the world of film: the movie set. The films *Polygraph* and *Le confessionnal* are constructed around a film being made, a film within a film. In the theatrical version of *Polygraph*, the film shoot remains essentially offstage. Only a silent scene in which we can see Lucie (played by Marie Brassard), stripped to the waist, facing a crane, displays a moment of it. The camera is replaced by a projector.

At the time *Polygraph* was staged in 1987, Lepage had already acted for movies and television, but he had not yet directed

The screen in *Coriolanus*, a rectangular opening that is a symbolic reference to cinema.

PHOTO

Emmanuel Valette

a film. As this world became more familiar to him, he became more
inclined to refer to cinema in his work. By the time *The Geometry
of Miracles* was in production, Lepage was urging the actors to see
the show as if it were a movie, he himself having directed three
films by this point in his career. In fact, the set of *The Geometry of
Miracles* is designed as a large movie set. The artifices are clearly
visible around the performance space: the shell of the stage, the
flies,[96] the technicians pulling the ropes attached to the wooden
table, the gas ducts, the turntables, the different set-ups on the
floor, the audio speakers, all things that disappear in the image
because of the camera's accurate framing. This becomes even
more evident in the versions produced after first performances
at Austria's Salzburg Festival (October 1998), at which point the
sand that filled the bottom of the wooden pit disappears, revealing
the machinery that was buried in it. During the meal at Frank
Lloyd Wright's school of architecture, the Taliesin Fellowship, the
industrialist, Johnson, and other guests gather around the table.
A light box decorated with geometric shapes in tinted glass, very

dear to Wright, is suspended over the table. The steel chain and hook that hold it are from a movie set. With its position above the guests, the light box is a reminder of the light boxes used in detective films, a rectangle of light the exact size of the table cutting through the surrounding darkness. In general, this box is located slightly above the table, and the cigarette smoke – as demanded by the genre – masks the area of light that illuminates only what is below it. Everyone is seated at the table underneath the light, some with their backs to the audience. Lepage shows us the entire set, as if we were on a film shoot. The back screen remains neutral or can be a medium for later superimpositions. The rest of the wooden pit is left undifferentiated out of theatrical convention, and the few realistic elements (cutlery, chairs) are chosen with care and placed very close to the table and the light box. The audience facing the stage is in the position of the camera that selects a very well-defined frame. On-camera, without more props, this scene could be very realistic. Similarly, in rehearsals and the initial performances, the architect's burial provides the opportunity for an emphatic nod to cinema. His loved ones are huddled around the coffin, dressed in long raincoats and black hats. It's raining, of course. And the rain is supplied by showers or, more precisely, by a long hose pierced in five places over the stage. The water doesn't rain down on the entire set, but only in the places needed to create the illusion of rain "onscreen." As on a movie set, the machinery is clearly visible.

The imitation on Lepage's sets, playing with the site of viewing and the site of recording, combines these initial associations with something more symbolic: film, the cellulose strip, the symbol and medium of the movies. The film strip is a series of small rectangular frames (boxes) separated by thin vertical lines: photograms. Each box corresponds to an image. The film-strip projector scrolls the boxes at such speed that the bar separating them is eliminated and continuity is achieved. The white panels of the Japanese facade in *The Seven Streams of the River Ota,* separated at three points by vertical wooden strips, imitate the film strip, or more precisely, a length of film with three frames (as used in silent films). The seven white neon lights under the porch could symbolize the perforations in the cellulose. The audience watches a giant film strip with images, or rushes, just like the first editors of silent films.[97] Plus in this show, as in *Coriolanus,* the cuts to black between scenes are like jerky images, simulating the jumpy uncoiling of silent films and the first talkies. On this set that simulates a screen, rapid changes alternate acted scenes and cuts to black, and sometimes acted scenes and filmed scenes (*The Seven Streams of the River Ota*).

This reference to the actual uncoiling of film is particularly noticeable in *The Geometry of Miracles*. In one sequence, the drafting table, which Svetlana Wright uses as a piano, makes a dozen rotations between the two ends of the stage. While Svetlana continues her movements and the piano moves farther away, the drawing table reveals its contents: two naked apprentices, each lying horizontally as if on bunks. The table turns and provides only a peek at the action taking place within it on each revolution: an apprentice looks in the direction of the other, lying above him, extends his hand, and then grabs the other's hand and joins him on the upper bunk. This rotation fragmenting the action between two blanks – when the table turns – is an allusion to the irregular frames of silent movies and movies at the beginning of the twentieth century (sixteen images per second in 1895 with the first Lumière brothers films). The rotation of the drafting table is a metaphor in action of the actual unwinding of the film that, at each splice,[98] projects a blackout, creating breaks in the action that are perceptible within the continuity. This continuity is constructed with fragments, like film.

Film has no depth; it is a thin cellulose skin less than 2 millimetres thick. But like any representation, it can suggest or represent depth and volume, like the screen. What all of these references to film do is to confuse the small recording medium, film, with the disseminating medium, the screen, the size of which can change. In fact, in the examples provided, the film strip takes on the same dimensions as the actual or simulated projections, occupying the place of the screen. What is shown on this symbolic piece of celluloid is shown on the scale of projected film and, more precisely, on a human scale, with the actors creating depth. Thus Nozomi emerges from the 50 centimetre-deep scenery facade, sliding sideways, from stage right, as the screens did before her along the same rails. She is the projected image, the shutter, and the film. The action is in fact contained within the depth of the seven rails, incredibly narrow from the point of view of the entire set. Nozomi moves by on this film and then detaches herself from it, to lie down at the front of the stage. Like all of Lepage's effects, this idea of the film is ephemeral, but it is also connected with a common fantasy: having filmed characters detach themselves from the cellulose, or more broadly, from the screen.[99]

From the first instances of pictorial representations, the autonomy of the work to rival life has haunted designers. Film gives rise to this temptation of stripping the photographic image from the collodion film on which it is bound. Lepage gives the representation life and releases it from its medium: Nozomi, freed from this symbolic film, performs a perfect film stripping (the technical process for removing the image is called "stripping film"), with an ease that leaves the technical difficulties of its photographic equivalent far behind. Photographic stripping is a delicate operation, done in very specific conditions of heat baths. Lepage's stripping gives flesh to the immaterial and releases the figure from its background by offering it autonomy and a new range of movement.

 ## A CINEMATIC GAZE

Lepage uses the world of cinema to organize his sets, reassured by the shared references of a universal medium, references that are easily recognized by the audience. Starting from the very shape of the screen, he explores endless variations in the frame. Cinema leaves its strongest mark in the work of the gaze within this frame.

Film editing has been described as the essential and founding act of cinema: framing must also be considered as fundamental; it is the director's raw material. The frame is delimited by a natural boundary, that of the little box and that of the lens, but within this frame, the distribution of elements; in other words, the composition is essential to the notion of framing. The film image is a surface to be organized.

This organization of the image is the basis of the scenography in image-based theatre and, for Lepage, this organization is based on film and not just on pictorial representation. In the cinematic world, one refers to composition rather than framing. There is a strong analogy between the definition of framing and the idea of the stage as a space to be architected, through three-dimensional elements that are like frames. These frames contain many references to the puppet theatre, the stage box, the proscenium, and the screen.

The deictic action of the frame dovetails with that of the box. Three frames side by side, three film frames, and three boxes in the cross-section of the New York apartment building are depicted at one and the same time. Framing is the art of organization within a space during a shoot, and within a surface, the surface of the image. Lepage functions within the box as he would within a frame, using the constraints he has created for himself: to contain, frame, and compose within the square (the ideal shape in Lepage's spaces), which passes for a simple frame. Lepage's frame is always being pulled toward the screen.

In *Coriolanus*, the rectangular opening (the screen) is a little more than 1 metre from the ground. A table is used as a parapet walk or a platform, revealing the legs of Coriolanus, whom a man kneeling on the ground and visible from the shoulders up has come to beseech. The framings are original, one could say daring, even for cinema, and inspire other variations in framing in *National, capitale nationale* one year later, offering a chance to modify the opening and vary the takes. Framing is also a matter of cutting, indeed sectioning bodies, to reproduce close-ups or close-medium shots, roughly from knees to head. These productions extend the organizational possibilities within the frame,[100] delimiting a portion of the visible stage and leaving the rest in darkness.

Characters regularly step outside this box frame. In *Coriolanus*, a banished character goes through the rectangular opening to "come out of the screen," in the same way that Jeffrey 2 leaves his frame in the bedroom of the New York apartment to go off into his memories and attend his mother's wake. What makes it possible for characters to leave their frames is that the frame acts as a threshold, a point of passage, or a transition point between two worlds. The most common frame is the door, which, in one instance, aided by a change in lighting, becomes a delimitation isolating and visually highlighting the character.[101]

The use of the door is an old theatre tradition: a place for characters to enter and exit, it's a separation and an airlock to the outside. For Lepage, it's a stopping point for the character, an in-between space that can be very thin, like film. The door's dramaturgical importance is revealed within the thickness of the barrier it symbolizes. It collects roles and functions through metonymic shifts.

The door of the Monolith in *Elsinore* is an allusion to both a screen and the door of the medieval Danish fortress, and then becomes the hatchway of a ship, the proscenium of a small theatre, and Ophelia's freshly dug tomb. Under surveillance, the site of passage and the site of observation in this show combine: Hamlet speaks standing in the rectangular opening that frames him perfectly. Later on, the door isolates what is to be filmed and projected onto the Monolith. The frame becomes the camera lens. This connection becomes clear when Lepage is sitting in the doorway, as if on a windowsill, and is filmed from the house. The image is framed by the door frame. The image of Hamlet seated is projected enlarged and inversed, creating the impression that the actor is sitting in the lap of the filmed figure, who adopts the same posture. With this materialized frame, the actor is the simulacrum, and the image is the real thing on which a vignette or an image is superimposed. The actor framed by this door tends to merge with the projected image. When Hamlet evokes man, he is framed by an image from the study of human movement by nineteenth-century photographer Eadweard Muybridge, a frieze of three men taken in time-lapse photography at three stages of movement. The actor, framed in profile by the door, creates one of the four stages in this series of movements. The overall image is unified, and the openness of the set and the image is counteracted by the open door in the middle of the Monolith. The frame becomes an image and a surface. The emptiness becomes a manifestation and material for a screen.

Lepage sits with his screen double in *Elsinore*.

PHOTO

Richard-Max Tremblay

In "Words," Part Five of *The Seven Streams of the River Ota*, we witness the end of the performance of Feydeau's play *The Girl from Maxim's*. Lepage offers a literal interpretation of the commonly held notion that this theatre is a "theatre of slamming doors." The intrigue is marked by the untimely bursting in and sublime entrances and exits of "amazement and legitimate indignation."[102] The set for this hall of mirrors is a succession of three doors, separated by panels of the same size. The action is supposed to be seen from the wings, behind the scenery: either we see the actors waiting behind the scenery or we follow their performance through the door frames. By convention, gestures and movements remain within the dimensions of the doors. In the New York apartment, a world appears and exists only through the door of the bathroom. We see the hallway, the door of the

bedroom across the way, and tenants in their doorways through this frame. Scenes acted simultaneously in the hallway and in the boxes are very realistic because of these openings. This impact is reinforced because of the frame's ability to condense space, to create perspectives and depth through a small opening.

Lepage develops a stage language that is very much inspired by framing in film through playing with depth of field, points of view, and the movement of the frame itself. Most commonly, he underlines the physical presence of his frame, even if it means having it descend from the flies for specific purposes, like during the rehearsals for *The Geometry of Miracles*. Once the frame is defined onstage, everything within it is likely to be changed as in an image. Without using projection, Lepage literally changes the depth of field, using the broad palette of shots available to the lens.

In *The Seven Streams of the River Ota*, Nozomi's shadow appears hazy and then is clearly outlined within the door frame of the *shoji* screen. It goes from hazy to clear and then returns to hazy. The technique of shadows has always used the potential of different depths of field, including them in the dramaturgy itself. In Indonesian *wayang kulit* (a puppet show with painted and worked leather puppets that Lepage knows well), the leaf of the tree or the tree itself, symbol of the creation of the world, emerges from nothingness (in darkness) as an imprecise, blurred shape, and then is clearly outlined (in the light), before it disappears. The manipulator, the *dalang*, forms an ellipse with his wrist that brushes the screen, and then steps back from it. Lepage knows how to create stage images using different depths of field, visible on a single screen surface: during the G.I.'s dream, his profile in shadow, in a close-medium shot, takes up the entire length of the screen while, facing him, is the little doll that was a gift from Nozomi. The doll comes to life and moves toward the G.I.'s face to caress it, and then it disappears in the soldier's shadow, as if penetrating his head. The two actors are not the same distance from the light source that creates their shadows on the screen: the G.I. is very close to the back wall of the stage (the wall that supports the projector) while the actress playing the doll is virtually plastered against the facade of the house, therefore the screen panel. The two actors perform as if they are face to face. When the doll caresses Luke's face, the actress simulates the gesture in empty space, and when it "penetrates" his head, she merely passes in front of her partner in profile and exits.

In these stage images that do not involve projection, rather than playing with clearness and blurriness through changes in depth of field, Lepage changes camera angles, as in the image for the credits in *The Seven Streams of the River Ota*, a large projection of the Bay of Miyajima. When he does use depth of field, it is to project an image in *sfumato* (a soft-focus Renaissance painting technique), as seen from a light atmospheric perspective, dissociating the shots. The image grows deeper; it creates a very deep background, while the foreground doesn't change. And for good reason: the actors seen in silhouette can't change size! Because what is happening is in fact changes in size and scale, which the filmed image allows. When Lepage doesn't use projection to change the size of the shot, he uses toys or puppets that create a change of scale. The small-scale model (car, plane, or boat) creates a Lilliputian version of the world. A toy appears and suddenly the reality of the stage changes, the set becomes a visual laboratory for the audience who, by convention, agrees to consider a certain portion of the scenery as a wide shot.

Shadows and depth of field: the G.I.'s dream in *The Seven Streams of the River Ota*.

PHOTO

Claudel Huot

At the end of *Zulu Time*, one of the suspension bridges in the elaborate scaffold structure is raised as a model airplane attached to the bridge takes off. While the plane slides along its rail and the bridge gains height, the plane lifts off the runway. We see the classic final shot of a movie with the plane taking off, a wide shot becoming increasingly blurry until the plane finally disappears. What's happening is a radical change of scale. The space above the stage becomes the sky, when it previously represented the confined cabin of the plane: interior shot, exterior shot. The Dinky Toy rolling along the edge of the set in *The Geometry of Miracles* performs a similar function. Behind this miniature car, the audience no longer sees sand in a wooden pit but a panoramic view of the desert. Like the puppet, the toy allows for these changes in scale. In fact, where the toy implies a reduction of the world, the puppet represents a reduction of the individual.

This is particularly evident in *Coriolanus*. We move from medium-long shots framing the head and shoulders of real actors to full shots, even wide shots of the puppets, which appear in

their entirety. During the battle scene, we see an exterior scene, a traditional wide shot as used for the Battle of Agincourt in Kenneth Branagh's *Henry V*. The playful dimensions of the toy or the puppet recreate film effects without using projection.

With the frame Lepage creates, he tries to vary the position of the camera that in his theatre is merged with the gaze of the audience. With or without the use of projection, the audience's gaze no longer depends on its location in relation to the stage, and this is one of the most obvious differences between theatre and cinema. Lepage, like most directors using moving images, blurs the two worlds from performance to performance. When Lepage uses projection, the effect is obvious because he borrows the angles of view from cinema that he creates using the camera, a vertical overhead shot, for example. The camera is omnipresent in Lepage's film work, located above "the box" (the house, the sauna, the bathtub, the car, and so on). This angle of view is new to the theatre which, at best, can only reflect the action and not enlarge it. In the elaborate scaffold stage set for *Zulu Time*, aluminum bar tables are placed while the screen is unrolled. Cameras hidden in the flies secretly film the gestures of a man and a woman, each seated at a table. Hands, cups, ashtray, and sugar bowl are visible in geometric compositions that are reminiscent of the ballet of shadows from *Needles and Opium*. This scene provides a reversal of perspective, accompanied by a simultaneous vision: the audience has both a horizontal perspective, from their seats, and a vertical perspective, from the camera. Because the screen is above the tables, the audience sees two angles of the same reality at once. They forget about their obverse view and move above the stage. With the close-up, the audience can even indiscreetly read the newspaper the woman is leafing through[103] or follow the line of the drawing the man is making in the sugar sprinkled on the table. Following the curious camera, the audience leaves their central perspective and flies around the stage.[104] This movement is obvious in Lepage's films, in which he stalks his characters around a set.

However, most of the allusions to camera angles are in scenes that don't involve projection. This is when they are at their most spectacular, corroborating the idea that Lepage bases his work on a common audiovisual culture. In the early days of cinema, the audience, unable to understand that a given close-up followed from a given long shot, or that one shot was the reverse

Video cameras camouflaged in the flies provide an overhead view of the stage. *Zulu Time.*

PHOTO

Emmanuel Valette

angle of another, were helpless faced with editing cues to the action onscreen. Visual codes and syntax had not yet been shared and absorbed. The mental translation done with film is immediate today, but it sometimes requires a few seconds when an equivalent effect is produced in the theatre.

The ability to create new angles of view also occurs in theatre through the use of mirrored panels, which often go further than simple surfaces that reflect the actor. The mirror puts the gaze and the set onstage, in reverse. One of the most brilliant examples of this is Svoboda's stage design for *Hamlet* in 1965.[105] A mirrored panel, inclined 45 degrees, is set at the top of the geometric set, extending the set in new perspectives: what is inclined, that is, the staircase, the catwalk, and so on, appears vertical, and we don't immediately realize that it is an aerial view. The mirror provides a new perspective on the set, creating a hybrid space, half real, half spectral. It prepares a shift in the gaze, a new and still partial ubiquity of the audience's gaze. It foreshadows the projection, reflects what the director and then the audience will see behind the camera. A mobile surface, it rediscovers anamorphosis through camera angles.

The actor changes roles with each rotation of the table, a plane surface supported at each of its four corners by industrial wires that are wound up or down by a set of motors. *Elsinore.*

PHOTO
———————
Claudel Huot

The first clear use of film angle is in *Circulations* in the form of a reversal of perspective. It's also the first sequence in which the idea of film editing is so evident; this practice began with *Saturday Night Taxi*, but only from a narrative point of view. In *Circulations*, young people are smoking locally grown pot, it's nighttime, and they are lit from the side as if bathed in moonlight. Everything goes dark and suddenly the scene tilts: we see the same sequence but from the ceiling or the moon. This passage requires a blackout and a physical reversal of the actors. The chairs are on the ground, and the actors are still sitting in them; they are actually supported on their sides, as if lying down. It's a simple trick, but it works. It merely requires seeing the audience's gaze as a camera lens and, rather than raising the stage, inclining the actor.

In *Elsinore*, Lepage makes the set incline as well as the actor. Only a part of the set moves: the Monolith. Symbolically, it's the screen that is moving around the action, the movement illustrating the mobility of the camera and its lens. First the Monolith inclines 45 degrees, lifting its contents: a rectangular table with Lepage sitting at the end of it. In the audience's eyes,

The plane tips to frame a high-angle shot as used for film. *Elsinore.*

SKETCH
———————
Ludovic Fouquet

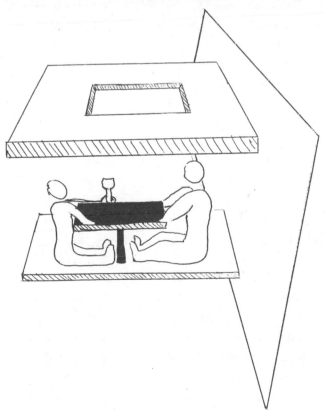

the action is seen from a slightly low angle. The table turns and, with each rotation, Lepage changes roles: he is Claudius holding the wine goblet, and then Hamlet. At one point the magnetized wine goblet is at the end of the table, opposite him. The low-angle shot is combined with reverse-angle treatment, created through the rotation of the table at the end of which the camera would be found during a shoot, but here, it's where the audience is. Lepage takes on the two roles with an ease and rapidity that changes a play meant for several actors into a solo performance. Of course the audience reacts enthusiastically.

This scene lays the groundwork for the later 90-degree tilt, a brilliant reproduction of a vertical shot. The Monolith turns back into a frame that moves in the place of the camera and a screen on which a map is projected. In *Circulations*, Lepage only tilted chairs; here he raises the entire stage behind a black frame that cuts off the wings and the machinery to create the appearance of a film image. Broken up by a door, the panel of the Monolith is vertical, as is a small stage in the back, which rises along with the actors who are on it. The audience therefore sees Hamlet talking to his stepfather at the same table, but they see them as if they were at the same height. Lepage and his double are both harnessed to the small raised stage to keep them in position, half lying or half upside down depending on their position at the table. The image is entirely cinematic, without the use of projection.

What's special about the cinematic gaze, compared with the photographic gaze, is its mobility, which also includes mobility within the sequence shot. The director's eye, through the eye of the camera, not only composes before the shot, but also intervenes during the shot. The camera's lens roams by travelling or rotating on an axis (a panoramic shot) and sometimes both. The camera's mobility is nicely rendered in the sequence in *The Geometry of Miracles* in which the drafting table is meant to represent the apprentices' bunk beds. The bed/table isn't supposed to move; logically it's the camera that turns around it. But onstage, it's the table that turns and moves. Like a rotating shot, which dramatizes a moment between lovers, the final image is rotating. Olgivanna Lloyd Wright is a witness to this scene. She follows it, staying right behind the moving table, like the audience, but also like a camera or a camera operator behind the camera. The camera operator moves during the shot and turns around the subject, circling it to better capture it.

Beginning in *Needles and Opium*, the vertical travelling shot appears, by scrolling the overhead projected image. This movement is a nod to the cinematographic processes of illusion, creating the sensation that it is the actor who is moving and not the background of the image. In front of the image of the building façade scrolling from bottom to top (an image simply drawn on acetate and rolled on a tube so that it scrolls uniformly), the actor seems to rise up into the air. Then he changes direction, and the movement is reversed, creating the effect of free fall. In *The Andersen Project*, pieces of scenery are pulled onto the stage using ropes from the wings (the solo actor sometimes enters or exits this way as well). One sequence opens on Frédéric moving sideways, seated on a stool, sliding behind the proscenium which at that point acts like a table. As he moves, he sets up empty glasses in front of him, and then when he stops, he only has one left in his hand. He drinks and starts talking, leading us to understand that we are in Stockholm, at the meeting where he is presenting the broad strokes of his book about Andersen. We also realize that his movement not only provided him an entrance, but also introduced the travelling shot presenting us to the people attending the meeting (each symbolized by an empty glass). In his use of projection onstage, Lepage sometimes chooses to indicate the actual movement of the camera to evoke movement and carry the story along.

The sequence in the Guggenheim Museum in *The Geometry of Miracles* starts with the image of the building in close-up, projected onto a sheet of paper set on the raised panel of the drafting table. And then, as with a dolly-out shot, the image expands, the visual laboratory inspires the imagination, and we see Central Park surrounding the museum. To accomplish this, the background screen of the mobile stage is inserted between the source of the projection and the drafting table. We move to a view of the entire park and the city. On the panoramic screen, we have a view in 16:9 aspect ratio.[106] The move from one screen to the other, from a sheet of paper to a large 17 metre screen, shows the evolution of an idea toward its realization, from the sketch to the finished building, at the same time as it creates a visual enlargement in plain view, breaking down the steps.

Lepage's stage vocabulary is nourished by very different worlds, but one of its main sources is cinema. It stimulates the story, enriches the syntax, and influences the set, with movie-like framing, which works as much through the gaze as through a discourse on perception. Lepage seduces the audience by drawing perception into a hall of mirrors – and the gaze opening on both an empty and a full door, as with the Muybridge time-lapse photography sequence in *Elsinore*. The audience's moments of recognition enrich his vision as he experiments with different elements, inputs from film onstage, elements from theatre in his films. Because each of his productions is inspired by, refers to, and integrates another universe, different to varying degrees from our own, this provokes images and creates a new discourse. The work is built on this essential clash or overlap. It was perfectly natural that Lepage should move on to directing films by developing a similar theme and the same aesthetic through a cinema of non-transparency. For Lepage, cinema is more than an inspiration, more than a breeding ground; it is a foundation or a spectre that understudies any space. Behind the mirror of the stage, a movie set sleeps, lies, and watches. The influences intersect; the echoes melt into one another and multiply. The echo of film is a way to vary the stage design and narrative solutions. The screen of the quarry acquires a new mobility while remaining in the frame or the shape of the box. The dialectic remains valid, but it is constantly transformed and revolving.

FOURTH ECHO

VIDEO

For Lepage, video is a paradox in that it is a medium frequently used onstage without clearly being recognized as video. When it is used it falls within the scope of cinema or photography, like a more practical expression of other media of representation, the symbolic effect of which interests Lepage more. Video first appeared only in *Needles and Opium*, in the form of recaptures of 16mm film, and in *The Seven Streams of the River Ota*, with the combined use of projected images and recorded images. In 1993–94 during Peter Gabriel's *Secret World Live* tour, both projected and recorded images appeared on the screen. Previously Lepage had used moving images in peripheral undertakings (except for *Needles and Opium* where video sketched out a few passages). Peter Gabriel's concert was the beginning of a movement that would grow, to the point that today one cannot imagine Lepage's work without the moving image, as confirmed by projection designer Jacques Collin, who until recently created most of the images: "In his vision of things, we can no longer do without video, a common and accessible technology. There's no longer any reason not to use it."[107]

Video began to appear on Lepage's stage only when he was no longer satisfied with photo projection or shadow games on the overhead projector; in other words, only after working with shadows and initial projections of coloured shadows and slides. Video makes the occasional, but increasingly regular, appearance: it is featured in the four productions created in 1999 and 2000: *Jean-Sans-Nom, Zulu Time, The Damnation of Faust,* and *The Far Side of the Moon.* It is the only image technology used in *The Busker's Opera,* alongside music and an adjustable box. And it becomes the necessary complement in solo shows, as in *Vinci.*

One can gauge the evolution of image technology in comparing *Vinci* with the other solo shows. The ingenuity in *Vinci* is not in the animated images, but rather in language and photography. The other productions are built on an image-based narrative, make the gaze and surveillance central to the drama, or use fluid evocations; hence the almost natural presence of video. *The Far Side of the Moon,* one of Lepage's finest solo shows, returns to a narrative theatrical performance and a predilection for wordplay that comes straight from *Vinci,* while video stands in for the character, using the reverse side of the set. *The Far Side of the Moon* brings together *Vinci* and *Elsinore.*

 FROM THE MONITOR TO THE MOVIE SCREEN

Even though Lepage uses projected moving images with video, his basic universe doesn't adopt all of video's characteristics. He essentially projects live or archived images, often shot in cinema format,[108] onto all sorts of surfaces. Instead, the monitor, which the so-called technology productions and video installations familiarized us with, appears only in two productions: *The Seven Streams of the River Ota* and *Zulu Time,* and it is used also in the

form of a flat screen in *The Busker's Opera*. However, Lepage
emphatically uses a monitor in all his films, in the form of a
computer monitor (*Polygraph*) and a surveillance screen (*Nô*),
but above all in the form of a television screen.

A television screen used as a monitor introduces the
action. It revives the function of the messenger in tragedy, with
stark juxtapositions against a background of surprises, connections that multiply coincidences. The common analysis of the
"image-window of the cinema" as an invitation "to leave the
room, to forget about it by plunging into its opening" contrasts
with that of the television monitor, "an electronic screen [that]
functions not as a window, that is not part of a wall, does not bring
the inner gaze outward; on the contrary, it brings the outside
inside, in an intense centripetal movement, to where the viewer
is found. It operates by *superimposition*."[109] In filming a television,
Lepage tries to blur its properties. Television forces the world
inside, and at the same time it attracts us, grabs us, and engulfs
us. This is the price for us to emerge in a new space and time. In
the film version of *The Far Side of the Moon*, Lepage tries to film
the television from behind in a scanning motion: the TV set acts
as a mask revealing the characters seated before it, in the 1960s or
today. Lepage's television is like a guide, a decorative backdrop.
It uses its resemblance with the film image, while emphasizing
its attributes: colours, edges, and TV shows.

Instead, onstage, Lepage is wary of the monitor. He uses
other situation-based artifices: narrator actor, voice-over, and
projected images. He doesn't exploit the video aesthetic of the
onstage monitor. When the monitor appears, it's simply part of
the set. He seems to have spurned it in part because of its rigidity,
but mainly because of its resemblance to the television set. For
Lepage and his team, the monitor can only express a television,
a strangely reactionary idea that doesn't take into account the
productions of The Wooster Group and Peter Sellars, to name
only North Americans. "When you introduce a cathode-ray screen
onstage," projection designer Jacques Collin explains, "aside
from using it as a TV, there's not much else you can do. You can't
intervene: its dimensions are set."[110] What he is hinting at is the
need to disrupt. With the quarry, the body must be able to intersect with the echo of technology; in other words, the creator of

shadows. The light from a monitor can't really be disrupted except by standing in front of it. Video or film projection is based on the sudden appearance of light on a surface, creating an opening that is central to Lepage's productions.

Aside from being a reflection on the spectacular or spectral presence, video is above all a light event. Nonetheless, in a number of productions, Lepage uses video monitoring and the presence of video equipment, particularly in the first version of the interview in *The Seven Streams of the River Ota*. But the final image never appears on a monitor;[111] it simulates a monitor. Thus, at the opening of Part Two, the Japanese house appears as an immense monitor during the famous Abbott and Costello sketch "Who's on First?" projected onto screen panels or during the editing of an interview with Patricia Hébert. A light table symbolizes a monitor, while a vignette projected onto the canvas surface, placed on the rails of the facade, is the size of a monitor image. The three levels of stacked boxes that fill the height of the proscenium opening in *The Damnation of Faust* also suggest a wall of screens. Each box is rectangular, with proportions similar to a monitor. At times the audience has the impression of looking at twelve monitors, like a wall of TV screens (monitors) in an electronics store window.

This aesthetic of a wall of screens is used with the plasma screen in *The Busker's Opera*, a hanging, movable screen, particularly when it is at the forestage. But more importantly it is a flat screen, a metaphor of the permanent tension between box and screen because the screen is, by definition, a monitor box, that, when shrunk, becomes increasingly flat, in any case as flat as a screen. Through its shape, this screen is more of a reference to cinema than to television, but in intermediary form. The heads it presents are enlarged and shown in close-up: "affection images," according to Gilles Deleuze: "in a face that fills the entire screen, that invests it completely to the point of transforming it into a face."[112] The flat monitor carries on the idea of silhouette, and it's not surprising that what it shows are portraits, and that these portraits are mobile, surface images. This is definitely an avenue that Lepage will take again, starting to manipulate this surface monitor like a screen. The video monitor is a window that acts as a magnifying glass and its border, at the proscenium opening, inspired by the mirror.

A monitor is used as a television set in two productions. In the New York apartment in *The Seven Streams of the River Ota*, it shows baseball games and a propaganda film about a nuclear attack. The monitor is even the object of a dispute, when Jeffrey 1 believes that the other Jeffrey is spying on him from the bathroom window, when in fact the other Jeffrey is trying to watch the baseball playoffs. Exasperated, Jeffrey 1 places the television in front of the window, which hides the rest of the apartment in the opening. The monitor acts as a curtain and forms the side of a box both for the monitor and for the scenery box it appears in, drawn toward being a surface. The monitor, real or symbolic, as in the Abbott scene, is part of a reconstitution. It provides an anchor in time, both through its appearance (an old TV set with rounded corners like those of the 1960s) and what it is broadcasting. Here, video, through archive images, is used as a stage direction and intermediary.

When the image is projected, it is reworked. The gap between the source of the image and its projection surface offers an opportunity for all sorts of interventions. When the image appears on the monitor, it's left raw. It mimics television in how it is presented and because of the fact that it isn't changed. Images could be manipulated in video on a monitor just as they are with projected video. Technically, nothing prevents this from happening. The decision not to make changes demonstrates a desire to emphasize the television aesthetic by respecting the image on the monitor, which can only be manipulated by being turned off or changing channels. We do not interfere with the luminous plate.

The second time a monitor appears is in *Zulu Time*, as a permanent fixture on the elaborate scaffold stage set. Monitors are fixed to the metal structure, on either side of the audience. Lepage is using an aesthetic of monitors on display, combined with technological clutter: cables, control devices, the control room, and instruments, all visible in the lighting towers that frame the stage. But the presence is justified dramaturgically, whether by a video screen giving safety instructions in an airplane cabin or showing televised documentaries and news, or by an information screen in an airport. In either case, the monitor isn't integrated into the recording device, but is used instead as a televisual reference to the broadcast of recorded images. On flights, everything is recorded, even televised news. In *The Far Side of the Moon*, a monitor delivers

The hanging, movable screen in *The Busker's Opera*.

PHOTO
Ludovic Fouquet

the news about an international contest to pick personal videos to be sent into space. Philippe is ironing his clothes while he watches the television facing him, so his back is to the audience. At first he listens distractedly and then he notices the news about the international contest. But the monitor has no electronic instrumentation; it's just a sound and light window[113] without the variations that a moving image would offer. A stimulus for the drama, the monitor is treated as light technology before it is treated as an image,[114] characteristic of image technologies in Lepage's work and in particular characteristic of the use of video: "There is a tremendous desire to integrate this luminous object to the life of the show."[115]

Beyond the monitors that are part of a televisual logic and pragmatic, a television semantic, even a syntax, is also at work, with the interview scenes that parody journalistic jargon in *The Seven Streams of the River Ota*. Video, television's heir, has a small frame. For Lepage, video also lies in the historical wake of the puppet theatre and its ability to reveal a world through a 1 metre opening. Lepage, combining his knowledge of puppets with this abiding feature of video (the size of the monitor), uses small vignettes onstage. He used postcards to create a landscape and the train in *Circulations*, and the entire audience could follow this minuscule image. And he used the same approach with television in *The Seven Streams of the River Ota* and *Zulu Time*. But the effect is more impressive, because a show like *The Seven Streams of the River Ota* played to houses of almost eight hundred seats: the Maison des arts de Créteil, the BAM Majestic Theater in Brooklyn, and Salle Denise-Pelletier in Montreal. And yet, images of the little turtle narrator or American children training in safety drills, from the scene involving the propaganda film *Duck and Cover*, are easily understood by the entire audience, even those seated in the back.

Video for Lepage, therefore, revives film's method of presentation: the projection of light, a scrolling strip, a similar screen, and a necessary separation between the two. This feature made it possible to detect an architectural thread in the sets: movie theatres or movies on an airplane. The structure of *Zulu Time* offers a spectacular reproduction of how filmed images are viewed in an aircraft cabin.

There is a lightness in the way Lepage sets up and presents video and how it evolves: the screens and the projectors are mobile and take up as little space as possible onstage. Projected video makes it possible to render many images virtually freed from physical media. Next to the weight of monitors, the scrim and spandex screen appear ethereal, particularly because they make transparency possible, as Lepage said in interview with Rémy Charest:

> Expressing something using relatively light means may be what distinguishes us from video specialists: they see everything through this frame. We integrate it into a larger stage frame. They will try to achieve greater flexibility in their images, for example, with three-lens projectors, but this requires too many adjustments. We use LCD projectors: they don't provide better quality, but they do offer more flexibility.[116]

This statement points to how video must melt into a whole, the larger set, and how it must remain flexible, a flexibility that Lepage's team doesn't seem to find in the monitor. Video is seen as something to be used from time to time on a set, part of which will serve as a screen, or to be used with one or more monitors. Video is just a means, whereas cinema and photography are used for deeper reasons.

For projected images, Lepage often uses amateur or basic conferencing equipment, such as slide projectors. Lepage's image designers achieve astonishing results with relatively little investment using widely available equipment, exploiting its limitations or using it in ways other than originally intended. For *Elsinore* and *The Seven Streams of the River Ota*, three VHS projectors are placed in front of the stage, one per panel. *The Seven Streams of the River Ota* uses an inexpensive video camera for the photo-booth scene and the interview scene. This standard equipment offers the advantage of being fairly light-sensitive. *Elsinore* uses four VHS cameras – two placed on either side of the Monolith, one behind the Monolith, and one dedicated to an image of an oscilloscope – and a Panasonic mini-camera attached to the end of a sword during a duel. *The Far Side of the Moon* uses the same VHS projectors (Sony LC300s). These three devices not meant for the stage, which is not always lit well enough for projections on a black background, as is the case in this show. Image quality is not a concern in this use of video.

Four cameras frame or occupy the stage: Philippe uses a simple Sony Hi8 video camera. Three surveillance cameras that measure 3 centimetres square are hidden on the set. This equipment was developed for the FBI and CIA but is now marketed to the general public for surveillance and was sourced through the Internet. The surveillance cameras are even smaller than the Panasonic mini-camera used in *Elsinore*. Like the camera installed behind the ironing board, these cameras need only a tenth of a lux to record images in black and white.

Projectors generally cover the entire set or a large part of it, with a back panel generally delimiting the performance area as in *Needles and Opium, Elsinore, The Seven Streams of the River Ota, Zulu Time, The Far Side of the Moon,* and *The Damnation of Faust*. Video becomes part of the scenery. In *The Far Side of the Moon*, it is integrated into the round washing machine and dryer door, a little porthole that becomes a moon or an aquarium, but it is also projected at a large scale onto the grey partition. In *The Seven Streams of the River Ota*, video appears in its actual size, the occasional substitute for the painted canvas that enables light scene changes and low-cost illusion, like in *The Damnation of Faust*, where more images are used, generally in the dimensions of a box and therefore on human scale.

Period images in large-format video may be used as an interlude. For example, in *The Far Side of the Moon*, rare archival images of the Russian space program are shown during scene changes and share intermissions with the puppets, which perform a similar function, this time for the American program, a reversal that is full of meaning. Similarly, film excerpts, including from *Ascenseur pour l'échafaud*, and a song by Juliette Gréco, both old recordings shot in 16 mm and transferred to video, occupy the large screen in *Needles and Opium*. At times they evoke a movie screening in Saint-Germain-des-Prés, a Paris neighbourhood filled with movie theatres.

Video could logically be part of this body of work by operating in plain view. We have already looked at how Lepage's theatricality uses shared knowledge of an object or a part of the scenery, and movements in plain view. With video, Lepage exploits a similar opportunity of the "immediate confrontation between the production of the image and the image itself live."[117] This is often how video is integrated into conceptual works, in which "the device [video] is both the concept of the work and an instrument of its foundation."[118]

In fact, Lepage doesn't really exploit the possibilities of monitoring and disseminating with video in a hall of mirrors approach. He uses live monitoring with simultaneous projection, but never along with projection on a monitor, except for in *The Busker's Opera*. There he uses a stage design involving video, which dramatizes the device, by introducing a "theatre of seeing/perceiving," which already crops up in his relationship with the object and, more broadly, with theatricality. This is the approach used in the photo-booth scene, the interview scene, albeit less so, and in *The Far Side of the Moon*. With this dissociation of vision and perception, the elements of the representation are separated, and then juxtaposed. The image is no longer presented with normal perceptual settings, Anne-Marie Duguet says on the subject of video installations.[119] This is also true of video devices and, more broadly, of perception in Lepagean theatre.

VIDEO AND THE MIRROR

The photo booth in *The Seven Streams of the River Ota* uses video as an ontological mirror. The characters in *Elsinore* are under observation, like the protagonists in Lepage's films. In the medieval Danish fortress, they are spied upon by cameras and by the screen panels that keep being repositioned as if to better trap and obscure the protagonists. In addition to playing with doubles, video makes the disappeared reappear, creates ghosts with archive images like so many testimonials (*Needles and Opium*, *The Seven Streams of the River Ota*, *The Far Side of the Moon*). In short, the camera "changes the screen into a mirror and a crypt [...] into a reflecting surface and a place of return."[120] Video is thus a meeting with the shadow, but a figurative, lifelike, animated, and colourful shadow.

The actor faces the projection surface, which is similar to the reflecting surface of the mirror. With the monitor, scale is often respected; with projection, the representation is generally enlarged: the video mirror offers a disproportionate reflection, huge and spectacular, intended for the gaze of an entire audience rather than simply of the person reflected in it. So when Lepage as Hamlet is standing in the opening of the Monolith, the two video images that frame him and that he talks to are simply reflections, as if two large mirrors were reflecting the profiles of the person they frame. Lepage plays with this misalignment in the line of sight in the mirror, like a three-panel mirror that reflects both his face and his profiles. What actually surrounds him are cameras and not reflecting surfaces rendered autonomous through a video connection. Rosencrantz and Guildenstern, school friends of Hamlet, appear as his potential reflections, as suggested by the queen when she presents them as shadows of her son:

> Good gentlemen, he hath much talk'd of you;
> And I am sure two men there are not living
> To whom he more adheres.[121]

Exploiting their past connection, Hamlet questions his school friends, scrutinizes them as if he were looking at himself in a mirror to detect something: "Nay, then, I have an eye of you. If you love me, hold not off." The reflections are silent, and don't reveal their secret. Hamlet does it for them – and with good reason – speaking as he would in the place of the reflection in a mirror. Hamlet wants to hold up a mirror to his close friends so that they can see the extent of their darkness. He wants, through theatre, to trap the king's conscience, which the reference to the mirror, through video, expresses perfectly.

The relationship with the mirror video continues and is refined with the mini-camera during the sword duel. This is in fact a trick with mirrors: Hamlet fights with his double, each one successively donning the different identities of the protagonists. Both are dressed in the same white outfit and hidden behind a fencing mask, obscuring their identity. For this scene, Lepage's understudy was chosen specifically for the similarity of his silhouette.[122] The filmed image is projected onto one of the back panels. The person holding the camera/sword holds up both a mirror and a weapon to the other, like a bizarre camera operator filming his reflection. The reflection created by this camera is poisoned, and it is perhaps the reflection that kills as much as the poison on one of the two tips. Death is signified by a video still of the face of the dying man. It is a metaphorical duel, a video duel. This perfect use of video and the screen underlines

Video images appear to be two large mirrors reflecting Hamlet in profile. *Elsinore.*

PHOTO
Jacques Collin

In a video duel, in which the sword and the camera are a single deadly object, the image freezes on one character's death grin while the actor gets up and plays another character in the carnage that closes *Elsinore.*

PHOTO
Emmanuel Valette

the extent to which the filmed face, at this point the image is all face, is essentially independent, emancipated from the actor. This is what the faces on the screen say, frozen in a final grimace, while the actor has gotten up to play other characters.

The notion of the mirror keeps popping up in Lepage's efforts to recreate reality, whether through photography, cinema, or video. These media have a direct relationship with reality and have as a medium a strip or sensitive surface exposed to light, which is similar to the definition of the mirror. Nothing changes with the appearance of digital and computer-generated images. Photography, cinema, video, and mirror are media that mimic. Lepage uses these qualities. He combines them with the use of the mirror, blurring the differences and underlining the similarities.

Video offers new possibilities: it is a mirror whose reflection can be manipulated. The reflected image can be slowed, accelerated, reduced, frozen, turned upside down, and so forth, moving beyond the simple magnifying glass effect. The reflection gains new autonomy; it frees itself from its subject and operates according to other rules. The control booth modifies the images, or video reflections, in real time. The technical director becomes a demiurge (Plato's creator of the universe), controlling the reproduction of the mirror. An additional interval is created between the subject looking at his reflection and the surface that shows the reflection, and this is when the technical director intervenes. So the reflection of the duel is slowed; the reflection on the glass plate of the photo booth is frozen, prefiguring the photo. This is also how Lepage as Hamlet can play with juxtaposed, inverted, and enlarged reflections, appearing to be seated in the lap of one reflection.

These effects have long been available in film, but film rarely employs them except alongside other frames of reference that use different compositions and approaches such as screens within a screen or the hall of mirrors video effect used in Jean-Luc Godard's *Numéro deux* (1975). There a monitor or two are visible in the frame. For Lepage, the mirror's frame contains another time and other laws, dividing up space and time onstage, whether through two-way mirrors or symbolic mirrors, such as the use of video.

In addition to reflecting a protagonist's image in the mirror, video turns the set upside down; it circumvents it by offering new reflections. It acts as an informer, because it is highly mobile: "the ubiquity of the gaze," as we said. Video often crops up as the result of a play of many symbolic mirrors surrounding the set, and their reflections within reflections allow a further reflection to reach the audience's eyes. Giving the audience super-vision, because they see what they shouldn't, video renders visible what until then had been invisible. It "distends the visible through the power of the invisible,"[123] but it is an invisibility that has visibility latent within it, what Jean-Luc Marion calls the *invu* (the "unseen").[124] Thus sudden emergence, revelation, unveiling, and the expansion of the visual field.

Like cinema with all its cranes and television with the Louma crane, the inquisitive camera that roams the set, video is imbued with the fantasy of Icarus: "See the world from *somewhere else* (specifically from above) and decipher it as uncharted space. Carry the audience toward new and exciting perspectives."[125] The fantasy of Icarus is very much at work in Lepage's universe: the suspended actor, high-angle views, the object on the set that lends the stage a new scale, and so forth. The use of video is direct testimony to this. In video, we find the same aerial movement of devices, and particularly the same effects of floating spaces. Whether in the film version of *Vinci*, in *Zulu Time*, or in *The Far Side of the Moon*, shooting the actors from above is like putting a mirror above the stage to create a high-angle image.

In *Elsinore*, these properties of video also appear throughout the show: the audience can simultaneously see the scenery, its opening, and its reverse side. The door on the surface of the Monolith opens, a panel serving as a screen for the image shot from behind. Hamlet, with his back to the audience, opens the door, while at the same time the audience sees him from the front on the threshold of this door/screen. By splitting the person in two, video offers another angle. This is a common feature in video installations: the viewer who sees himself from behind, as Bruce Nauman did in his 1967 to 1971 video installations *Performance Corridor*. Video tries, through its very apparatus, to shift, delay, reverse, refuse, and deny the reflection. It is used as a visual prosthesis of individuals who can normally not see their back. It endlessly reveals their "unseen."

This is how the camera in *The Busker's Opera* playfully films the back of the flat screen. The screen hides the upper body of the protagonist, but because the camera is located on the reverse side, it films from behind, showing what the screen hides. Visible

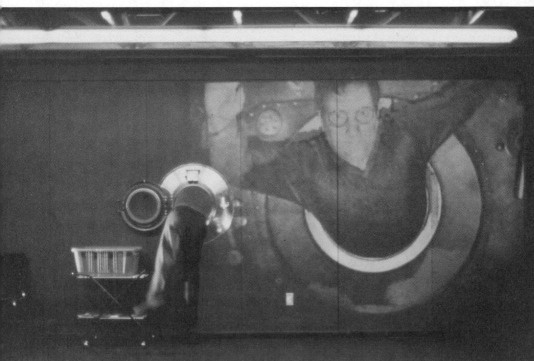

and invisible are confounded, inversed in a playful representation within a representation that creates the impression that the screen is a magnifying glass: the image of what is hidden, the face, appears enlarged on the screen.

In *The Far Side of the Moon*, the cameras, placed behind the grey partition at the back of the stage, film the individual once he puts his head through the opening. When Philippe throws his laundry into the washing machine, the audience sees only the open window of the drum, whereas a camera lets them see the inside. This image is visible on the partition beside the opening of the machine. The audience can see the hidden reality, Marion's *invu* (the "unseen") of an action that they saw only from the front, here the back. Later, Philippe climbs into the drum that has turned into the capsule of a spacecraft, or he looks through the porthole again during the countdown to liftoff. The camera, now live, shows us what is going on behind the grey wall, and the framed image creates the impression of a capsule of a rocket. Later still, because the porthole has become the opening of a computed tomography (CT) scanner, we see Philippe's face as he lies down for an exam on the ironing board. His head goes through the opening and is rendered visible by the camera. The partition marks a rupture, a frontier, and video repudiates it.

Video reveals the front and back of the same reality. Within and sometimes above the set, a screen panel extends space as would a mirror. This is not a simple division of the space into parts, using simultaneous action, but rather a division of space into simultaneous images, either multiplied or slightly staggered. The part when Philippe, with the noise of the engines and the countdown, becomes an astronaut in a space capsule makes magnificent use of these time lags, of the halting image, as if the images were really coming to us from very far away via satellite. Suddenly, this action, perceptible onstage through the little opening of the porthole, no longer belongs to this sphere of space and time, but is a long way off.

The audience no longer has to move, the space no longer has to change: everything is visible in a single instant, like a juxtaposition on the screen of a shot and its reverse shot. Video, like a space of "multiple mirrors," divides up space to present simultaneously different facets of the same reality. It therefore reveals the set like "visual architecture of the story."[126] This effect

Video from front and back in *The Far Side of the Moon*. At the laundry, Philippe observes the cosmos from the window of the washing machine – or a spaceship.

PHOTO

Emmanuel Valette

In *The Far Side of the Moon* Philippe climbs into the washer/dryer and it becomes a space capsule.

PHOTO

Emmanuel Valette

is more common in cinema, and it was used with magnificent results in Richard Fleischer's *The Boston Strangler* (1968), where alternating kaleidoscopic images or split-screen technique and montage images share the frame of a single shot.

The ability of video to turn things around has an effect on how scenes are treated, in particular in certain reversals of viewing angles in *Elsinore*. The dialogue between the queen and Hamlet is seen from the point of view of Polonius, hidden behind the tapestry, on the audience side. In a scene in *The Far Side of the Moon*, the person being addressed is symbolized by the ironing board set upright, a standing panel "dressed" like a mannequin in a cap and a shirt. At the exact location of what would be Philippe's left eye as a child, the back of this table has a miniature camera that is about the same size as the diseased eye examined by Lepage as the doctor. What the camera films, subjective video, is projected in the porthole, the eye of the protagonist. Lepage also plays with the camera, bringing it closer, moving it away, masking it with his hand, and so on. The audience therefore sees what the child sees through one eye. This ironing board is also a smaller image of the large partition that has a camera set on top of it. So every panel shows us its reverse side.

This simultaneous exposition even works in the absence of light and, in this, video differs from the mirror. The tiny cameras in *The Far Side of the Moon* require very little light, barely a tenth of a lux. Like super-vision, the infrared camera pierces the darkness that reigns in the medieval Danish fortress in *Elsinore*. This monitoring or instance of creating images, therefore shadows, doesn't use the main element of Lepage's mythology: fire. With infrared film, a light source is no longer needed. Generally speaking, video replaces the light source with a recording source. In this instance, the shape is recorded without light; in other words, without anyone knowing, despite the ever-present surveillance. Infrared takes on even more importance once we know that for Lepage it is connected with war machines:

> So with the infrared system, the stage manager is in
> control. He can look through the lens and make sure
> the actor did leave before cueing the lights again. So
> this infrared system is much appreciated in theater

circles. It's used just about everywhere for just about anything. But the U.S. Army invented it to shoot at illegal immigrants who were trying to cross the Mexican / U.S. border in the dead of night [...] And as artists we should rehabilitate these things and turn them to good use [...] Technology is often a product of the swamp.[127]

With the infrared camera, the enemy is captured first by being seen. Video puts the entire stage under surveillance, even splintering it by sending different images to another space, even another time. Video generally shares many characteristics with the mirror when the image is shot live with a camera, whether or not it is visible onstage. But there are exceptions, in particular in faux live passages, as with the washing machine in *The Far Side of the Moon*. Recorded video plays on memory, as an archive image, or on dreams. This is the only case in which the technical director intervenes and manipulates the recorded image live. The recorded image increases the live layering and manipulation, moving from mirror to palimpsest.

VIDEO PALIMPSEST

The layering of the image is like a palimpsest, in which memories of newer experiences superimpose themselves over memories of experiences that have gone before. The layering of image, which makes what is projected more complex, could have a dreamlike conception of the image behind it, a sort of mental flow or visual maelstrom. In *Needles and Opium* video is projected in large format on the background panel, offering a narrative in images without words: the portraits of Robert are superimposed over those of Cocteau and Davis; a line drawing in Cocteau's style is erased as the pencil passes, as if the pencil were absorbing it; a man in a black balaclava dives; a Capitol record turns, and so on. These images are combined with acted sequences. Sometimes they are even used side by side with them, extending the actor's body, and the actor's body extending the image: the image of a trumpet sliding through the water is followed by an image of a man swimming. When the man surfaces, it is Lepage's head that emerges from the screen, perfectly aligned with the filmed body.

Here video is used as a sort of dream, or a dive into consciousness, even the unconscious. It is integrated into the set as a visual layer, but never the only one; it generally interacts with other layers. The final theatrical image is layered. Sometimes the set is a box of images, justifying their superimposition in advance. The set of *The Seven Stream of the River Ota* could be seen as the black box of a camera, a movie screen, or an archive box, in turn or all at once.

Lepage exploits all of video's technical possibilities. He even pushes its limits, through his collaborators' experimentation. This device for projecting renderings is used on occasions other than those originally planned, in the Shakespeare Cycle, for example. Many effects create interventions in the form of new layers on the image. Lepage is perfectly comfortable adding a video image to an initial film, leaving the latter visible, as was done with early negatives. This was the case in the scene from *Elsinore* that combines video and slide projection, doubles of Hamlet, through Étienne-Jules Marey's time-lapse photography. Spectral bodies superimpose, with intervals of darkness. Running bodies appear on Lepage's front or back, slightly paler. The image is effectively layered. It even incorporates the live actor into it. This effect is even more common in Lepage's films, where he uses the dissolve in passages that leave two images on the screen.

During the hospital CT scan scene in *The Far Side of the Moon*, the video images provide a psychoanalytic reading of the palimpsest. We see Philippe's face filmed in close-up, as if he were stunned. There is a moving fragility about him, like that of an old woman, his mother perhaps, whose death he just learned the circumstances of. And then another sequence is superimposed: childhood memories, with the family gathered around the Christmas tree and gifts to open. The Super 8 image is an old one, and the colours run and fade. Philippe is reliving a memory.

Video's flexibility lies mainly in the possibility for manipulation and online editing. The 8 mm video image is frozen in the photo booth as in *Elsinore*, and the image is slowed. Discs burned with the sixty-three image sequences in *The Far Side of the Moon* make it possible to pause the image for as long as needed without it jumping and with no loss, which eliminates any separation between video and slides. In *La Casa Azul*, two projectors are no longer needed for a single surface, depending on whether a photo or a moving sequence is being projected. The projector, in this case a Sanyo Pro Xtra X, specifically a multimedia projector, is used indiscriminately, even for projections of light that create simple coloured backgrounds on the canvas on Kahlo's easel when she talks about colour.

In the photo booth in *The Seven Streams of the River Ota*, a processor is used to make black and white possible with a colour camera. This same device, a Panasonic Audiovisual Digital mixer shrinks the image for the photo album scene. This effect, created directly by the console, is called "picture in picture." As with the previous effect, the live intervention of a technical director is required. He or she selects the image with a joystick, reduces it to the desired size, and then moves it to the projection surface in the same way that the technical director in *The Far Side of the Moon* creates a jerky and fragmented effect for the image by pressing the strobe button, while filming Lepage in the drum of the capsule / washing machine. The image can be reworked while it is visible, without interruption, which digital video cameras can do today. This is how the filmed view of the bay with the Japanese *torii* is animated, through simple manual quasi-graphical retouching of the initial image: a wave effect is created by moving the cursor, as if the camera were on a rocking boat. The audience has the impression of being on a boat that is nearing the shore.

The video is mainly constructed in successive layers laid over the earlier visual layers. Basically, the medium is one of superimposition and of coats of colour applied by a mixer, as in the sequences of the boat, train, and repainted planes, actual archive footage shot by G.I.s. The image of the plane on which one of them, the flesh-and-blood actor in front of the image, paints a cheesecake image of a pin-up, is bathed in colour just as he pretends to throw his can of paint on the projected cabin. The impression is then created that the image reappears as the G.I.'s paintbrush passes over it. And yet, the brush merely follows the apparition of the image under the layer of colour, creating the impression that the actor is in control because of the speed of its reaction. His movements are precise as he paints the image of a young woman on the cabin, because he knows the approximate proportions of the drawing. The image doesn't reappear randomly; it is controlled by the mixer, through an effect that reacts to the image's light waves. The lighter parts of the image are revealed first, followed by the darker parts. Seeing the image re-emerge from under this uniform layer of green creates a strange impression for the audience.

The G.I.'s gestures with his paintbrush on the image that he has just covered in paint are like the gestures of a scribe scratching the surface of papyrus to try to bring out an earlier layer or a buried representation. The etymon of "palimpsest," from the Greek *psan* (scratch) and *palin* (new), is similar to the activity of these characters on a layered image. The characteristic feature of the use of video is to leave the scribe visible in front of or behind this crowded and then cleared surface. Every time projected video appears, actors are added, like elements of the set are added for the final image of the bay. When an actor is visible behind the projection surface, he is perceived both as a projected shadow and through the screen. These two pieces of information are added to the projected video, which may use the same range of colours or similar patterns.

The Seven Streams of the River Ota takes the idea of video as palimpsest the furthest, using it in every projection. Even when photos are used, there are always actors in front of them, in shadow. "We wanted to manipulate video images to make them dramatic and to adapt video to theatre rather than adapting theatre to video."[128] The video image can be modified; it can be layered because it is modified. This is similar to the idea of video projection as a source of light, with several coats of colour, that connects with the idea of painting based on the transparency of superimposed colours. Video becomes light and colour. It undergoes the treatment of a colourist, before any semantic, historical, or other connection. This treatment is the ultimate throwback to the treatment of shadows and their transparency with the puppets, layers of elements, whether figures or pieces of scenery. Lepage's video images are reminiscent of this accumulation. They turn the technical director into the puppet master, superimposing visual elements for a single projection.

Lepage also draws on early colourization techniques for film. Where designers used to paint each photogram with a brush or a stencil, today video mixers make automatic colour washes possible. However, Lepage never uses such recorded video effects. The technical director intervenes manually by painting using the cursor. The video manager revives the film colourist's work. But this work isn't done before the performance or in the moments before the projection. The intervention of colour and palimpsest is part of the very pragmatic of the image. With video, coating and layering occur in real time, distinguishing it from cinema where everything is done before the projection. Video in Lepage's universe remains live and manual.

More colours independent of the medium are laid on top of these layered video images in *The Seven Streams of the River Ota* with red, green, and blue lights. But the best example is in the scene in *The Far Side of the Moon* in which Philippe is snowmobiling on the Plains of Abraham in Quebec City. After having attached his camera (which he carries with him everywhere to produce a film to send into space) to the back of the chair that stands in for a vehicle, Philippe heads off. A wooded landscape appears on the grey wall: the bumpy image that he is supposedly filming. It is projected in double on the screen, with a slight lag in time between the two images. Two projectors project the same image with the

Video effectively recreates the Plains of Abraham. *The Far Side of the Moon.*

PHOTO

Jacques Collin

lag synchronized by Dataton WATCHOUT, a digital, multiscreen
display technology. The image is in negative, making trees appear
white on a black background, as if covered with snow. Philippe
talks about the evening of December 11, 1972, the lunar landing
and first moonwalk of the seventeenth Apollo mission. While he
is talking about the stars and about becoming aware of his place
in the universe, which happened that evening in the park, the
image is enriched with layers as translucent as fog, one created by
a large-format slide projector like a PANI-type projector and the
other by a mirror: an image of light and a reflection. Clouds pass
by over the image of the Plains. What we think is a video image
of clouds is in fact a black-and-white image drawn on a glass slide
and tinted blue with a gelatine slide, projected by a Strand Lighting
projector. This is true light projection, and an additional visual
layer that is independent of video. The projector is set just behind
the proscenium opening, stage right, and the image is particularly
visible on the left side of the grey partition, covering a portion of
the video image. But because these are clouds, the delimitation of
the two images is not very clear. A second even more diaphanous
veil appears: the mirror panel is hoisted horizontally above the
stage; the light from the Strand projector is therefore reflected in
it slightly and is diverted onto the grey partition. This movement
creates subtle rays of light that suggest a roadside in the cloudy sky.
In the end the grey partition displays an image with three layers
of light from different origins. During this scene, the audience is
drawn into the fog of the Plains of Abraham, fog that seems to be
the shortest route to the clouds and the moon.[129]

Lepage continues the layering offered by the technical
possibilities of video equipment by adding another visual layer.
This is sometimes a coloured background behind the image: the
screen is lit from behind; it becomes translucent and reveals a space
at the back of the stage, at the same time as it displays the image
projected onto its surface. The screens are made of a material that
allows for projection and transparency. Since the painted sheet in
En attendant and the first screen in *Vinci*, the screen surface uses
backlit effects, varying degrees of transparency, but that one can
see through every time. In *Vinci*, Lepage even uses an "immaterial"
screen, accomplished through the persistence of vision created by
the blind person's white cane turning very quickly. Slides of works of

art are projected and can be deciphered. When the screen is opaque, it either has a door (*Elsinore*) or a porthole that in turn becomes a surface for projection or a screen (*The Far Side of the Moon*), or it can be raised completely to reveal a space (*The Geometry of Miracles, The Far Side of the Moon*). To create a simple sheet or the rear or front projection screen, as in Chinese shadow play, Lepage uses spandex, tulle, rice paper, laminated tulle (*Jean-Sans-Nom, The Damnation of Faust, La Casa Azul*), all materials that, with the right lighting, can be opaque or transparent.[130] In *Jean-Sans-Nom*, as in *La Casa Azul*, the show in its entirety is seen through a surface of laminated tulle, a reference to painting in the first case, and to painting and cinema in the second. The screen thus coincides with the proscenium opening, but in *Jean-Sans-Nom* the tulle rises at the end of the show to allow the actors to take a bow, the final curtain.

Instead, in *The Far Side of the Moon*, the screen partition is opaque. The grey wall has openings, but transparency is never used to reveal what's behind it. But throughout the show, Lepage draws symbols on it in chalk, which remain visible for several scenes. They remain visible through the video images projected over them and become the framework for later images, a framework on a partition that had no pattern on it at the beginning of the show.

The screen acts as a curtain, but a particular sort of curtain that doesn't need to move to perform its theatrical duty and that becomes a medium for projection, an impetuous intervention that can't wait for the curtain to open. The light on the canvas surface, whether or not its origins are video, replaces the technician who opens the curtain. The screen, because of its potential transparency and the manual and live processing of the video image, compresses different sorts of visual layers, united in the small space of a single frame. But sometimes this frame is itself integrated into a set that in general is based on the idea of the palimpsest. Because screens in Lepage's work always have a certain rigidity, unlike the curtain in a theatre; they are never left floating, fluid, or slack, but are stretched on a flat, or "framed."

The set for *The Seven Streams of the River Ota* is built entirely around the movement, superimposition, interchangeability, and transparency of panels set on three rails. The very idea of rails placed side by side shows a desire for a layered vision. Like productions that use proscenium-style machinery, the set uses a perspectivist system broken down into different ground plans, in one very close setting, to use the traditional terms: wings made up of a flat, a set piece or a backdrop. In *The Seven Streams of the River Ota*, the interiors built behind the wooden facade all function on flat systems, forming angles and delimiting a space, while limiting visual access. In proscenium theatres, this type of setting suits an illusionist conception of the scenery, panels and scenic elements superimposing over one another for the audience, who reconstitutes a space with depth. This perspectivist space, organized along a central vanishing point, corresponds to the monarch's location, the famous "œil du prince," the great organizer and central axis. While Lepage no longer performs on stages with rues and trapillons, once again for this show he finds a way of breaking down elements and plans. He creates an illusionist set, one that also creates a virtually perfect illusion for the audience in the centre of the house. However, being seated slightly to one of the sides is better for seeing the video projections displayed on the central panels. In fact, the "œil du prince" suffers from seeing the trace of the light source in the form of a white halo that breaks through the image at the same time as the video image itself.

Inset:

Sketches for fire for the video scenes in *Jean-Sans-Nom.*

SKETCH
_____
Carl Fillion

    The layered perspectivist design receives special treatment in *Jean-Sans-Nom*, a show made possible through layering in which video plays a significant role. Video acts as an additional layer for a three-dimensional system of projection of ancient engravings. The filmed image occupies the exact spot as the engraved and therefore fixed drawing, introducing, aside from an impression of realism, a strong effect of vitality. A number of times an image of flames is overlaid on the same engraved pattern, giving it movement and colour: torches, blazes, hearths, and chimney flues. The engraving is brought to life. The video projection is laid on top of the projection of the photo. Here again, the video is a palimpsest, leaving visible the different patterns that previously and simultaneously occupied the tulle screen.

    During the fire onboard *La Caroline*, the ship in distress carries the heroes away. The image is composed of filmed flames, the illustrations of two actors, and the actors themselves. Jean is both an illustration, because his legs are projected, and a real actor with the rest of his body. The flames don't cover the entire illustration, but through an impressive game of hide-and-seek, whether with video

Testing the computer-generated fire effect in *Jean-Sans-Nom.*

SKETCH
_____
Carl Fillion

or the illustrations, they emerge in the middle distance and the background. A unified image is created by merging entirely different elements: two-dimensional and three-dimensional, black and white and colour, printed, filmed, or incarnate. With the addition of relief, whether real or fictitious, the visual layer acquires new depth, and video, which has no relief, gains volume and life, through movement and colour, as do the actors. It may gain even more than the actors, because they are treated in colours that suggest black and white, like figures emerging from the illustrations.

Video takes on a new role in this show. It is no longer merely a counterpoint, a blow-up of a recorded reality or outside reality intruding; it becomes a malleable pictorial element. And it is used precisely for this malleability, for its rapport with the apparition and the projection of light, and by virtue of its potential colours and its changeability: enlarging, shrinking, the projected vignette moving. Video is a decorative element just like the painted canvas, scrim, and light. Lepage paints with video; he cuts it up as he would a canvas or a decorative panel and integrates it into other elements.

Much was learned from the production *La Casa Azul,* which was performed only three times, confirming the extent to which each show is part of a constantly evolving and changing practice. *La Casa Azul,* a theatrical extension of *Jean-Sans-Nom* and *The Tempest,* uses video in the same traditional perspectivist space; in fact, when no one is performing onstage, one has the impression of being in an old-style set-up, with a system of pulleys and legs (tall, narrow stage drapes that mask the wings on either side of the stage). However, the show once again uses tulle and the possibilities of digital technology for creating images. *La Casa Azul* is an effective illustration of the work of the palimpsest as Lepage intends it, that is, the legacy of a *commedia dell'arte* theatrical tradition and successive, ephemeral superimpositions, layers of light, photo and video, of which the actors become a part. The set is inspired by the most *commedia dell'arte* of construction plans: curtains, legs organized in perspective, that is, five on each side of the stage, between which are inserted mobile panels along an elliptical track. These panels are mounted on runners, a modern version of the trapillons and costières of the proscenium stage, but here they are controlled from above. The first ellipse is visible at the back of the stage, in the form of a small curtain that hides the cyclorama and the scene that can be played between this curtain panel and the cyclorama. Two other ellipses are also visible, between the second and third legs. These panels advance onstage and make it possible to shrink the break in perspective and, at the same time, hide what is being prepared behind them. The panels surround the visible portion of the stage like a diaphragm.

Layering is an organizing principle to this layout, whether as the point of departure or as the show develops. In total approximately ten veils are added between the background of the set and the audience's eye. Quite often the audience can't count the layers. The theatrical palimpsest, in particular Lepage's, is deceiving.

The stage only stages its very materiality, a monochromatic black space that when seen through the scrim appears dark blue. In reality, only the floor and the back screen are blue. Decorative figures aren't placed in the foreground, middle ground, or background, but instead silhouettes are cut out in one colour, that is, in a single symbolic surface, from the layers that will be at once accesses, wings, reserves, and curtains. The perspective of the space is used to camouflage how small the stage is,[131] and the space is punctuated with exits, another sort of black hole that absorbs actors, props, and images. This is the function of the legs taken to extremes.

Video is used as an intermediary to allow for scenery and costume changes, as in *The Far Side of the Moon*. During Rivera's speech in the United States, extolling the virtues of Mexico and prompting the Americans to proclaim "the aesthetic independence of the United States," two vertical panels frame the artist. Archive images of Ford enterprises are projected onto these panels: assembly-line work, details of manufactured parts, and so on. These screens are the most vertical and narrowest of all of Lepage's screens, sort of animated columns. The vision of Rivera, behind a microphone on a stand, talking to the audience and surrounded by screens on a black background, is reminiscent of the set for Svoboda's *Laterna Magika* (1958). Set on an angle, the screens create the same effect of depth, which is accentuated by an effective reminder in the form of a tulle surface on which the translation of Rivera's speech is projected, in the foreground. The impression of shallowness coexists with the opposite impression of depth. And then the surface becomes blurred, while being accentuated, with the appearance of Mae West on the scrim. These slightly bluish images show the actress in different outfits before a large curtain, of which we previously only saw a detail of the reflections, a lightly glittering screen background, used during the translation of the speech. This is a pure screen sequence: there are no actors left onstage, just a ballet of images. A veil of light, the image onstage is made up of layers of images, the first of which is completely porous and transforms the appearance of the following ones. Mae West, a symbol of success, but also a symbol of the American people, who see themselves in her stardom (she is dressed as the Statue of Liberty), allows the exact opposite of success to filter through: assembly-line work, intensive production in repetitive movements that brings to mind alienation and mass production more than the American dream. From this ephemeral palimpsest, only the image of Mae West remains, applauded by invisible spectators, because the scrim becomes more like a movie screen and then everything disappears.

Video and palimpsest raise the question of space of the image. Lepage takes a new step in *The Tempest* with another medium: 3-D Betacam. Lepage's desire to work with 3-D projected images is what was behind this show. What results are the beginnings of work with computer-generated images and video, all in 3-D, hence a particular rapport with the layers that make up the theatrical image. The idea used for the set is detachment from a surface: the stage is defined by a checkerboard tilted toward the house, the corner of which extends beyond the proscenium. Stretching the original checkerboard could free figures from their base, like pieces flying off an upended checkerboard.

The Tempest creates a dramaturgy of the invisible and the fantastic, through Prospero's magical powers. The use of 3-D video offers an obvious solution for scenic design: it expresses the actions of an invisible Ariel and scenes of magic, like at the masque or banquet, along with the scenes that don't strictly take place on the island, such as the opening scene in which the ship sinks.[132] Prospero summons a whole host of spirits to foment his vengeance. He says several times that "These our actors, As I foretold you, were all spirits," and "insubstantial pageant,"[133] and he explains at the end of the play that they "are melted into air, into thin air": "Ariel vanishes." He remains invisible, except to Prospero, to whom he reports on the progress of events.

The use of 3-D projections, which in many respects is part of an aesthetic of the hologram, makes it possible to show the spirits on the island vanishing, as opposed to the physical presence of Ariel onstage when he is alone with Prospero. For these moments of apparition, the presence is video, but in the form of a hybrid image: projected onto a screen wall and detaching from it. The filming is done by two 3-D Betacams calibrated the same way on a tripod, each sending images to a Sony projector, equipped with a polarizing filter. Each of the projectors present what one of the two eyes is supposed to perceive. The dissociation is accomplished naturally through glasses handed out to the audience. These images are projected onto a large, slightly concave wooden screen 14 metres long.[134] Lepage had planned to have the spirits perform, particularly during the banquet, in a space offstage that would serve as a film set. During rehearsals at La Caserne in Quebec City, union issues made managing a dual set complicated.[135] The video images were therefore pre-recorded, but controlled in real time, creating the effect of an ethereal apparition disappearing as if by magic, an effective rendering of Shakespeare's stage directions: "claps his wings upon the table; and, with a quaint device, the banquet vanishes."[136] Filmed objects actually seem to be moving in the foreground during the magic scenes. The shipwreck offers a convincing relief with waves and drowning victims surfacing one last time before going down, and the image truly appears to be jumping off the screen. This scene is projected onto the left half of the wooden screen, while a background of old-fashioned cards on slides is projected onto the entire screen.

In order to increase the 3-D effect, the perception of distance is magnified. So while fruit or a scythe turn in space, a starry background creates an immediate sense of distance between the background and the object. Here 3-D video is translucent, a blurred image, a veiled effect that has particular depth and realism. Video tries at the same time to reconcile the set and the actor, the theatrical background and the human figure. It also tries to jump off its surface, which has an impact as part of a practice that keeps adjusting the possibilities of a surface for shadows and projected images.

The actors sometimes cast parasitic shadows on the projections they appear in front of and that are supposed to move in front of or around them. Although they create the impression of being released from their surface, the 3-D video images sometimes remain at the back of the stage, which makes it difficult to establish an effective rapport between the performance and the projection. Besides, to better see the actors, the audience tends to take off their glasses, which make things look darker. The magic of the 3-D video image is thus lost.

In *The Tempest*, Lepage was testing a piece of equipment and a theatrical impulse – to play with 3-D images, which fit perfectly with the idea of a layered stage. He experimented with each layer to explore new variations. He tried video in relief, bringing together the moving image, relief, and the testimony of a presence that video provides. It became clear that he preferred projection to the monitor. Aside from its resemblance to film, it was the very notion of the opening or breach that made projected video an obvious choice for Lepage's theatricality, in this malleable conception of the palimpsest. For Lepage, video is also an incredible mirror, splitting the actor in two, becoming part of a dramaturgy of the presence of the other and oneself. It opens up the visual architecture of the story and the set to close examination and is an active part in a dynamic understanding of the environment. Every time Lepage uses video, he wants a certain degree of transparency, so once again we see a preference for projection and screens that can become translucent. Video is not an object of investigation or a dynamic component of an introspective dramaturgy; it becomes material, a malleable element that forms the stage, drawing from older set techniques. It achieves a sort of dream world via the spectacular.

FIFTH ECHO

A VIRTUAL ENVIRONMENT: THE ULTIMATE PALIMPSEST?

From *Elsinore* to *Jean-Sans-Nom*, processing the projected image requires virtual reality software, and not just conventional graphics editing or live manipulations in the case of video. This virtual environment takes the form either of modelling through the creation of an image, a contour, and so on, out of nothing, or of digitization, through the capture and modification of a pre-existing image, resulting, through the transformation of the object, in a new creation. Between these two productions, a need arose that went beyond technological evolution: the virtual environment marks a new chapter in Lepage's thinking on the stage palimpsest.

 ## THE MODELLING ROUTE

Lepage's first incursion into the virtual world was by way of an awards ceremony. The organizers of the inaugural *Soirée des Masques*[137] gala (1994) invited him to put together a short number, working with Softimage, the 3-D computer-graphics application. He chose to wear a suit equipped with motion sensors ("DataSuit"),[138] which animated a computer-generated character in real time and generated preprogrammed sequences based on behavioural algorithms. At the end of his performance, Lepage removed part of the suit, causing the character to break down. It was intended to be a live performance, but the gala director ended up opting for a recorded sequence.

When creating *Elsinore* one year later, Lepage thought he could use Softimage's technology to become both actor and manipulator, echoing Hamlet's role. The virtual has something in common with puppetry, particularly with the motion capture software intended to be used in this show. Lepage kept the idea of manipulation, but through more traditional means: the equipment necessary for this sort of animation was still much too expensive in 1995 and would have put a serious strain on the show's budget. Over time, with the drop in price of this technology virtual environments eventually became possible for Ex Machina designers. They began to work on Macintosh computers using Maya 3-D animation software to create virtual environments using Silicon Graphics Inc. (SGI) 3-D visualization processing software.

Modelling is used in the genesis of *Elsinore*, a show that sees *Hamlet* through the filter of technology. The creative team got the chance to try out all sorts of technologies and equipment during a residency at the Musée d'art contemporain de Montréal. One of the museum's technicians, who had access to modelling equipment, suggested creating a sequence that would serve as an intermission. It was a passage merely evoked by Shakespeare: Hamlet's interception and substitution of the letter from the king, entrusted to Rosencrantz and Guildenstern. In the result, it is significant that a computer-generated image introduces the scene of Hamlet's journey: the image is in fact a pure mathematical language. Unlike video and photography, modelling, when not the result of digitization, is completely detached from the world; it is nothing more than an optical trace. Computer generation connects with the world of ideas and doesn't confront reality or what is – in this case, the words of Shakespeare – but expresses the virtuality of it. After reworking and cutting, this sequence was no longer projected onto a smokescreen, but on the curtain: a slightly bluish translucent ship emerges on the curtain of the theatre and moves from stage right to stage left. A map of the coast of Europe is then superimposed, with the ship's advance shown in dotted lines. When the curtain opens, we are on the bridge of the ship, in the middle of the night.

The modelled image also uses its role and virtual appearance to stage a part of the story in which Hamlet finds himself outside of Elsinore. The only other scene that takes place outside the castle is the meeting with the gravedigger, during Ophelia's burial. But the cemetery could very well be located within the walls of the castle, or just around it, in its shadow. This is what Lepage is suggesting when he stages this scene at the centre of the inclined Monolith, surrounded by screen walls. The only "true exteriors," to borrow a term from film, are those of Ophelia's drowning, performed in front of the curtain, and the voyage on the ship that was to carry Hamlet to his death. Exteriors (here, offstage) signify death.

Modelling is part of Lepage's effort to update Shakespeare's text. Every staging is in some way an update or an opportunity for directors to mark their own path through the landscape of *Hamlet*. Two years later, in *The Tempest*, modelling was used with three-dimensional work. This involved an immersion in a landscape and free movement.[139]

We are no longer confronted with a fixed representation, but with a completely polymorphic universe. Modelling doesn't always involve 3-D processing of images, but their perception is helped along considerably by the roving gaze that acquires a new ubiquity. In Lepage's work with virtual environments, he follows a similar path to that of Mark Reaney, head of the Virtual Reality Theatre Lab at the University of Kansas and the creator of many virtual stage designs that use 3-D. As in the case of Lepage and *Hamlet*, a virtual environment is the tool that allows for the reading of Elmer Rice's 1923 expressionist play *The Adding Machine* (1995). Virtual reality is used to create backgrounds, and then to integrate elements in relief: desk, chairs, and so on. Their texture and their definition are still fairly basic, because Reaney wants to use virtual reality generated in real time, unlike Lepage, who had tried real time with his 3-D video project.

In *The Tempest*, the 3-D images are created using video and then using computer-generated images on slides. For the slides, the texture work was done using Adobe Photoshop, but the basis of these images is virtual, using the SGI environment. These are occasional objects: scythes floating in space, fruit, and so on, or landscape elements such as boulders. Modelling provides a great deal of flexibility in the creation of these "slide loops": the choice of shapes, textures, and such, and a new rendering of detail.[140] The boulders appear in relief against a background of waves and sky. Modelling is used more as a simulation of an environment, an object more than a representation – the term "representation" being overly associated with an analogical relationship to the real. The modelling of these scenery elements truly allows for a "virtual simulation."[141]

Simulation was effective and therefore was integrated into other virtual elements, as well as to a traditional image background or real stage space. With his images, Lepage exploits a new medium to "plunge us into a fictional illusion of the real."[142] This is a double illusion: the one that the magician Prospero uses and the one that is specific to the theatre and its elements of scenic design, the former again being a metaphor for the latter. Lepage uses virtual simulation to speak to us of illusion. This virtual simulation doesn't try to be hyperrealistic, instead using a great deal of illusion, which the use of 3-D reinforces.

Lepage doesn't use modelling as an opportunity to dive into imaginary abysses, throwing open the doors of non-real figures and spaces, which computer-generated imagery from laboratories and graphic design firms has accustomed us to. Whether *Elsinore*'s ship or a few slides, modelling simulates reality; it doesn't invent another one. Lepage's virtual images are created in close relation to the real. In 2005 with *The Andersen Project*, the grand staircase of the Paris Opera (Palais Garnier) was used as a model for the modelled environment that surrounded Lepage. Real locations were the starting point, and were then simplified through modelling.

THE DIGITIZATION ROUTE

The production of *The Tempest* wasn't satisfactory, despite its odd success. It offered limited visual comfort, and stray outlines and shadows disrupted the reading. And yet, the effect Lepage was after in combining 3-D imagery with a virtual environment was immersion. He had to find new stage and projection solutions to immerse the projected elements in the scenery image and, hopefully, immerse the audience in the show.

Lepage and Reaney follow the same evolution in this area: the second phase in their virtual approach is all about immersing the audience, in *Jean-Sans-Nom* as in *Wings* (1996). For *Wings*, Reaney used head-mounted displays and Virtus WalkThrough Pro[143] software to make it possible to walk around in the environment. Lepage, for whom shadow is an archetype, realized that he had to go against his usual approach to theatre and, more specifically, against his approach to the set; in other words, he had to get rid of the shadow, something that has long fascinated him, in particular with the productions of Sankai Juku and Dumb Type.[144] "Getting rid of shadows" meant getting rid of the projection surface that until then received not only images but also, unintentionally, the projected shadow of things that came between it and the light source. Rather than having the actor perform in front of a screen that displays images of things that are supposed to surround him, in *Jean-Sans-Nom* the actor was placed behind the screen, at the heart of the echo chamber, behind the image but in the image. This approach is not a new one for Lepage (*Coriolanus*, *The Seven Streams of the River Ota*). What is new is the purpose: a race against the shadow as parasite.

In *Jean-Sans-Nom*, Lepage tries to make the screen invisible, to recreate the conditions of visibility of a virtual environment, in which we normally see the visual result without seeing the screen. In *Wings*, there is only one screen onstage, but the audience, seeing the stage through a vision helmet, sees the actress as being surrounded by multiple screens, persistent memories of the "Polyekran."[145] The scrim, used for the screen in *Jean-Sans-Nom*, has the same properties of opacity and transparency as the small translucent screens of the head-mounted displays.

Translucent screens have been part of the theatrical tradition since the mid-nineteenth century, with false reflection behind them to create the appearance of reflecting surfaces, or mirrors. This stage solution got rid of the parasite shadows from the performance area, because it doesn't necessarily correspond to the angle of light suggested by the 3-D projected image. Shadows would reveal the fakery, making different light arrangements clash, as if in a universe with many heavenly bodies or one in which light is randomly organized, which is common in virtual environments. I have mentioned how for this show Lepage brought light sources closer to the more constrained acting space. The actors took a little heat, but it was all for the good cause of making their shadows disappear.[146] Shadows are neutralized onstage by flooding the area with light. The quarry is thus completely reversed: where there used to be the light source, a subject, and a wall displaying the shadow or the image, there are now a source, a wall, and a subject. The wall, unlike the subject, is transparent and porous, and the subject appears to no longer receive the shadow, letting the screen receive a shadow that it no longer helps create. The black-and-white image doesn't show on the actors' grey costumes; the use of masks also prevents superimpositions. The shadow (the image) is totally freed from the subject that it no longer intersects with: it is no longer the image of the subject, or the image is no longer the shadow of the subject. The disruption of the archetype, necessary for effective 3-D projection, could explain, beyond obvious economic and material reasons, Lepage's loss of interest in this sort of environment in later productions. His last two solo shows bring back the shadow and a stage design that celebrates and explores it (*The Far Side of the Moon, The Andersen Project*).

With *Jean-Sans-Nom*, Lepage wanted to place the actor in a 3-D environment. Lepage used the same technical team as for *The Tempest* to find stage solutions for aspects of *The Tempest* that were disappointing: "*The Tempest* showed that the relationship of the actor to projected environments could be effective, but there were problems with integration."[147] It was no longer a question of creating virtual environments through modelling, therefore out of nothing, but of processing existing images in a virtual environment to give them an effective 3-D appearance. In this case modelling was followed by traditional digitization: capture and processing, scanning, and recreation. Ninety per cent of the images projected onto the laminated, semi-transparent scrim are drawn from George Tiret-Bognet's illustrations for Verne's adventure novel *Famille-Sans-Nom* (1889). With Tiret-Bognet's illustrations as the backdrop for the stage on which the actors perform, we simultaneously find ourselves within the world of *Jean-Sans-Nom* and within the book – the author/narrator is onstage pretending to turn the pages of a giant projected book. To create this effect, the initial illustration was scanned and sectioned into planes using Photoshop. By cutting the illustration into layers, depth is destroyed through fragmentation, and each plane is dissociated. Jacques Collin explains that this is really a matter of laying flat pieces side by side in space, without curving these fragments, to harken back to the book-based origin of the illustrations, while referring to the proscenium theatrical tradition, with legs, set pieces, and other flats. These fragments, layers of a dissected space, are then remounted into an image in the SGI environment. The use of the virtual environment is essential in that it makes it possible to work with the original image, with flexibility, speed of execution, and the technical possibilities of gradients, shadows, and textures that digital editing software cannot rival. Plane by plane, each fragment is projected in a 3-D environment on a virtual screen.

Stage set and George Tiret-Bobnet illustration to be projected in *Jean-Sans-Nom*.

SKETCH

Carl Fillion

The result is close to the original illustration, but a space has been created for the actor to interact with the image. The depth is more pronounced, and the baselines appear closer together. In this way, to heighten the impression of the immensity of the night sky that a troupe of horsemen jumps off, the entire section of the sky is inclined, creating a false perspective. This reconstitution, a true virtual model of the traditional set, requires the designers to recreate the textures of certain elements that were not visible on the illustration. This is a logical extension of the work of "texturing," which, while not actually part of the virtual environment, is more easily realized because it offers greater sharpness than the 3-D rendering. This hybrid process results in greater visual comfort for the audience: the actor is visible in the projected image and the impression of relief is convincing. The actors perform in an unsettling space. This space is within the realm of 3-D simulation, with a strong impression of form, but it also is within the realm

Storyboard showing the modular platforms and landings that move the actor around the 3-D image in *Jean-Sans-Nom*.

SKETCH

Carl Fillion

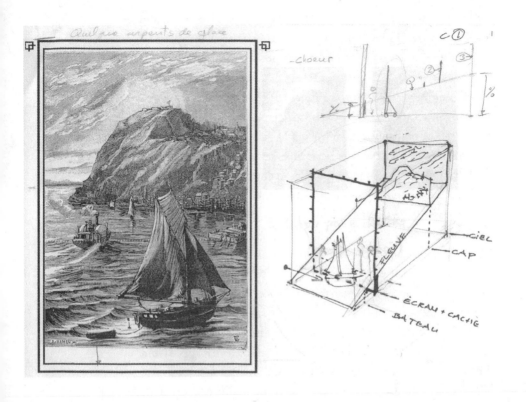

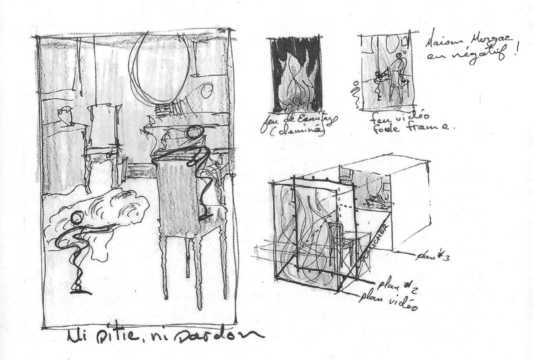

of books, with a flat treatment of motifs, the choice of black and white, and the desire to keep the texture of the illustration. If modelling simulates the real, then Lepage's digitization simulates theatre. Lepage doesn't try to create non-Euclidean spaces through modelling; in digitization, the model of the theatre is used as a starting point for reconstructing images.

The only purpose for using 3-D slide loops in *The Tempest* was to create a frame for the performance, within a set-up drawn both from the proscenium arch and leg technologies. This approach is used more often in *Jean-Sans-Nom*, which is an illustration of the propensity for virtual environments to become part of a perspectivist tradition.

The actor, at the centre of a reconstituted proscenium theatre, purposely too small relative to the projections, is immersed in an image, which is itself space. The third dimension makes penetrating the image possible, which Lepage emphasizes by holding back on the 3-D projection and then progressively introducing depth. *Jean-Sans-Nom* begins at the forestage, in front of a large vertically oriented painting with no discernible motif, and then a three-dimensional map of Canada, an illustration of the leaders of the rebellion at Fort Chambly, Quebec (1837–1838), and a newspaper headline appear. Then only the shape appears in the projected image, during the passing of ships on the background of a bay. The sails appear to be filled with wind, and the projected ship passes behind the actors, who are supposed to be on a barge.

When the overhead shot into the image occurs, the actor, surrounded by elements that could mask him, is performing in a three-dimensional space. During the suicide of Simon Morgaz, Jean-Sans-Nom's father, the impression is created of a window opened onto a landscape. The actor performs within an environment and not just in front of or behind an image. The audience forgets the projected reality that they perceived until that point. The projected engraving is of a forest landscape under snow. There is a road, different perspectives between trees in the foreground and background, and the knotty trunk of a large tree in the background. Simon Morgaz walks through the projected snow and his feet disappear, thanks to a system of masks on the floor. The tree in the background, behind which Simon shoots himself, has a visible density, created using a mask of the exact dimensions of the tree.

The projection is so effective that it creates the illusion that the character really stands beside the imagined chair. *Jean-Sans-Nom*.

PHOTO

Jacques Collin

In this stage design, the projected element has both volume and density. But the approach doesn't allow actors to move about freely, as is often the case with virtual environments, in a 360-degree view. Using several angles or points of view repeats one of the features of Lepage's practice developed primarily with video. By plunging into these images, we observe an actor immersed in a space that keeps changing. In a number of scenes the frame expands or perspective is reversed. During his escape, we see Jean running in profile toward stage left. There is a short blackout onstage and Jean runs in the other direction. Again a blackout, and we see him running upward, as if we were above him. Throwing the gaze into disequilibrium, which occurs frequently in Lepage's stage universe, is now a characteristic of virtual environments rather than indicative of the influence of film. Beyond being immersed in the image, the audience observes actors performing in virtual universes. However, 3-D makes the separation between the stage and the house less obvious and makes the stage spill over into the house, which allows the audience to penetrate the space.

Lepage thus dramatizes the immersion of the user of a virtual environment. This is obvious in *The Andersen Project* when Frédéric, the Quebec author, walks around in the entrance of the Opera, watching for a presence, reluctant to climb the stairs. The virtual scenery, projected onto the screen facing the actor (but a specific sort of screen with rounded edges on which the actor can walk), changes in time with Lepage's movements. The immersion works; it is quite astonishing to watch Lepage pretend to go up the stairs or turn and see the image of the stairs moving with him. Like video games with levels to be accomplished, at the end of the sequence we return to the starting point, a crossroads that opens onto possible directions for walking about in a virtual world. This virtual movement, like that on computers, uses only a two-dimensional image, although a moving and changing one, to create the impression of immersion, while in *Jean-Sans-Nom*, 3-D glasses were required.

The glasses give the audience the feeling of having a privileged view. They allow them to see images not visible to the naked eye and offer the sensation of super-vision and a new perspective on the image. In fact, the person defined as the user, that is, the actor, doesn't even see the space he is performing in!

Immersion in a virtual environment is demonstrated as Lepage arrives at the entrance to the Paris Opera (Palais Garnier) in *The Andersen Project*.

PHOTO

Érick Labbé

He doesn't see the images projected onto the scrim, or else, with traditional projection, he sees a vague halo of light. If the actor experiences vertigo, then it isn't a vertigo created by the infinite, modular spaces of virtual immersions, but a vertigo that comes from performing in front of a blue screen, unable to see the space he is supposed to be in or the person or creature he is supposed to be talking to. He is playing a sort of blind man's bluff, without the audience knowing it. Except for very rare moments of stiffness, the actors in *Jean-Sans-Nom* know how to perform the illusion they see. Modular platforms and landings move the actor around in the image, up and down the screen. The movement of the user of the virtual environment is less free here: he who in a head-mounted display can move his eyes and neck and have the impression of moving is instead moved within the image – manipulated and moved around by the set. Lepage's immersion, while it assumes a super-vision by the audience/voyeur wearing a prosthetic device, doesn't abandon convention completely. In that it remains theatrical.

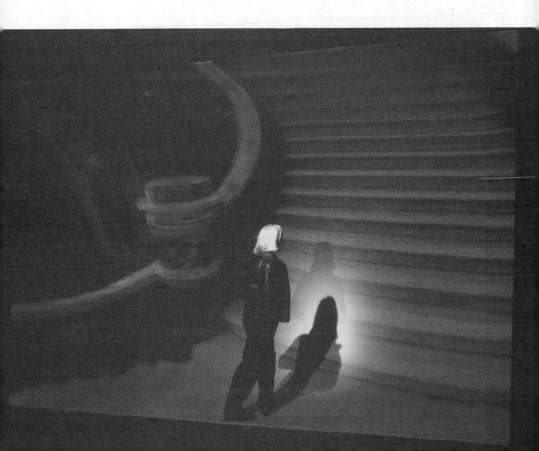

THE PALIMPSEST SPACE

We have pointed out the vividness of immersion and integration into Lepagean theatre. These are part of a broader reflection on the relationship of the actor to the screen or the actor onstage to the nearby image. The image is no longer facing the actor, in front of or behind him, even if, in reality, the actor is standing in front of the screen for *The Tempest* and behind it for *Jean-Sans-Nom*. The actor is so immersed in the image that he becomes its prisoner. The set for *Jean-Sans-Nom* has been studied as a box with one translucent side that displays the image that appears to be contained in the box. The actors pointed out the difficulty of acting in this context. Because the screen literally closes off the stage box, they felt as though their acting was not reaching the audience. They were aware of being part of an overall image, and they were conscious of acting with the impalpable. But not only did they not control anything, they also recognized the extent to which this high-angle perspective went against traditional communication and the communicative trajectory of the theatre. But they weren't taking into account what 3-D brings to the equation: allowing the audience to penetrate the image. With their glasses, the audience breaks through the surface of the screen and is receptive only to the relief of the image, a relief that neutralizes the boundary. Even before relief appears in *Jean-Sans-Nom*, this palpability of the surface is already apparent: depth and superimposition exist before 3-D imagery appears. In fact, the opening of this show is a ballet of images in the form of a palimpsest.[148] When a price is put on Jean-Sans-Nom's head, the portrait is enlarged, image by image, on the page of the newspaper projected. And then Jean's silhouette is obscured, and in this hollowing-out Simon Morgaz appears talking to another man, through the transparency of the screen. The two actors play on the platform raised midway up behind the screen. Even before the scene fades, an illustration in relief passes by the silhouette, suddenly acquiring depth, visible in the opening cut-out against the dark background of the screen. Then an illustration, a video image, and actors are all visible at the same time. Like intangible strips, these images reveal unexpected layers and sudden openings. Projected layers aren't always superimposed. Sometimes, as in this silhouette effect, an opening is created in the first image, as if the film has been removed from the image, as if the projected image has suddenly acquired a depth that allows the image to be peeled off it, reminiscent both of photographic stripping and the etymology of the term "palimpsest."

A palimpsest is also achieved through the intervention of actors, another form of layer in addition to the projected layers and the layers of scenery. The layer of actors uses confusion with the projections and scenery, by creating the impression of transparency in part of the projected image: the actors are black-and-white figures, and their faces are white.[149] The costumes are in shades of grey, with a single stain of colour, Clary's red hair, while her dress in the ball scene is the exact tone of the paper of the illustration. When Jean and Joann find themselves in their children's room, in her black cassock Joann blends in with the shadows of the illustration. The effect is ghostly, the strange impression of a hybrid figure that is neither completely present nor completely absent. And the end of the scene, when the two actors are erased, leaving nothing more than the empty illustration, creates this ghostly impression. The form is the same colour as the background, diluting and partially blurring it: it is incomplete visibility or partial invisibility. In either case, the silhouette becomes almost transparent, and this is where the palimpsest effect comes in and where the virtual environment re-emerges symbolically. This notion of hybrid presence is in fact a central idea to virtual environments; it also echoes the very origins of the image and representation. What the audience experiences is the duality of the palpable and the intelligible, the simultaneous and continuous flip-flop between what they see and what they know, between what they can observe and what they can deduce.

Through this treatment of the projected image, through these hybrid appearances of the actor, through this layered conception of space echoing perspectivist traditions, but with volume and relief that "keeps its promises,"[150] what is created is the space of the palimpsest. Previously, perspective merely provided two dimensions for viewing. In the case of the virtual environment, volume is penetrable. The palimpsest space combines all sorts of layers, which tend to camouflage themselves in what they cover and leave partially visible what they hide. This is the perfect coincidence between instincts for stage design and the possibilities of new technology that gives them expression.

Virtual treatment is an opportunity to experiment with 3-D, which Lepage uses exclusively in these environments. *The Tempest* and *Jean-Sans-Nom* are the final execution of the idea of the palimpsest, in that they propose solutions for scenic design and uses of technology that aren't used in later productions. *Jean-Sans-Nom* offers answers to the questions raised in *The Tempest*. And the goal is achieved: the actor is convincingly integrated into the image. In virtual universes, integration even becomes immersion. The image appears to have freed itself from its surface, because the surface is now practically invisible when something is projected onto it, and the depth of the elements projected is relatively convincing. However, the problem of balancing lighting and awkward shadows remains. When the image of a ship passes behind the actors, the sail seems full, but at the same time the ship's shadow shows on the background of the bay, which becomes a simple panorama in the pictorial and two-dimensional sense of the term, disrupting the illusion of depth in the landscape.

The projection of images created in a virtual environment is a satisfying response to this quest: a light screen, as suggested by the apparent void of the scrim screen at the beginning of *Jean-Sans-Nom*. However, Lepage adds form, masks, and physical components that counter this desire to derealize the set. The "dream of the diskette" – Lepage's recurring fantasy of working with a virtual set stored entirely on a floppy disk – is a technological dream and expresses Lepage's ongoing drive to reconcile creating sets that have the lightness and mobility necessary for international tours. Lepage continues to pursue this ideal but in another form: he's no longer seeking derealization, but rather a certain sobriety, a spareness in sets that use very little or nothing at all beyond the structure. There are very few props in *The Far Side of the Moon, The Damnation of Faust,* and *La Casa Azul.* All of the projected images in *The Far Side of the Moon* are stored on disk, sixty-three images or films, the order of which can be changed almost instantaneously using the same projectors. The grey wall and the mirror are, on the other hand, very real.

Lepage's ideal of derealization relates to that of immersion and the palimpsest, ideals that are not always equivalent. What he is after with the palimpsest is not simple immersion, but rather simultaneous and translucent resurgences, making earlier images visible. Why would Lepage pursue this ideal in ways other than the apparently satisfying virtual environments and 3-D? There are the financial considerations. Virtual reality and 3-D technology had previously been very expensive. Technological experimentation was only made possible by *Jean-Sans-Nom* being included in the well-funded *Printemps du Québec en France* festival. Of course high-budget experiments are not possible for every production. For *The Tempest*, the designers had a hard time managing all the static scenery images, and then adding video images. Preparing the virtual universe required weeks of image processing.

Further, working in 3-D increases the amount of equipment required. Everything has to be doubled: the number of images, the time for their creation, the number of projectors, and the amount of connection equipment. In every performance there is the danger of a time lag in settings which, even if slight, would ruin or disrupt the effect. This is what happened in the second performance of *Jean-Sans Nom*, on June 4, 1999. A vertical alignment error was identified before the performance, but the team preferred to keep the error rather than trying a risky adjustment that could have seen the show cancelled outright. During the first evening, the visual comfort was real, whereas it was relative during the second performance. That said, the effect of relief was still perceptible, with the different layers working perfectly.

This story raises a concern long held about any technology applied to shows. A breakdown can paralyze the entire production and render the spectacular impossible. Clearly a fully virtual set on diskette – today it would be a CD or a high-speed connection – requires a technical reliability that is never 100 per cent guaranteed. Lepage's designers and technical managers, aware of this uncertainty and risk, create opportunities to intervene, troubleshoot, or replace things in real time; if there is a problem with projection, a virtual set is hard to replace. Such technical vulnerability would hardly work for a show on tour and is better reserved for the lab or an experimental one-off performance, such as *Jean-Sans-Nom*.

Besides, getting rid of shadows, which emerged as a necessity at one point in Lepage's quest, is contrary to how he normally works. Lepage has always used objects as dramaturgical drivers.

While experimental, these shows connect with a recurrent idea, which seems to have developed in the memory of theatre images. Once more, the "dream of the diskette" – "arriving at the theatre and only having to read the diskette," explains Lepage – is similar to the practice of hanging paintings on flats,[151] and is a throwback to the first sets that used the lightness and the possibilities of a hung painting (*En attendant, Vinci*). The technological whole, the virtual whole, connects with the crafted whole and the illusionist whole. The virtual image connects the painted image, the impalpable, and the lightness of a painted representation to a density that is quite different from its actual weight. The virtual object and the image projected onto the screen share this with the painting, which can create the illusion of materiality and permanent scenery.[152]

In experimenting with these environments, Lepage continues his thinking on the relationship of the actor with the screen and the notion of immersion. The idea of the palimpsest comes up quickly, which contains and reveals realities or representations in fragments: scraps of memory perhaps? While the set suggests a puppet theatre, it can also be seen as a metaphor for the cranium, for the brain revealing its psychological activity, which the use of photography confirmed anecdotally, but also symbolically. The palimpsest video seeks the same thing, like cinema with its ongoing coincidences and resurgences. The virtual environment is another way of becoming part of this echo chamber, in the camera obscura that the different technologies of the image propose, using ongoing metaphors for the psychic apparatus. The virtual environment even offers the resurgences new flexibility and points of view.

The image technologies mentioned earlier correspond to memory, which was meaningful within the framework of "magnetic technologies." Tapes can deteriorate, be modified, or erased. Optical traces and memory traces worked hand in hand. With digital and virtual technologies, the relationship to memory may change, because there are no more tapes, only logical-mathematical sequences that are not easily altered. We don't yet have the hindsight to understand how long these media will last.[153] What is certain is that these technological media, "which were supposed to retain our memory of history have instead accelerated the process of amnesia."[154] This would justify the palimpsest of environments in *The Tempest* and *Jean-Sans-Nom*: it reinjects memory into a virtual or purely mathematical universe, unaffected by time and unaltered, like video did on a set conscious of its own alteration. While virtual-reality environments offer new possibilities for creating images and diving into the performance, as a technological tool, they merely return, with virtually unlimited power, to the examination of the memory and recollection, of which the palimpsest – a montage using successive, translucent strips that can be erased but that are always present – is a lasting metaphor. But paradoxically, the palimpsest created by virtual environments offers no room for memory or distortion. And yet, this is actually what Lepage is after with the layered, fragmentary, and resurgent images. Mark Reaney's virtual-reality environments have been described as unchanging, programs that can be downloaded. Their media can be damaged, but they can be infinitely reproduced. The echo in this virtual chamber is merely an unaltered reprise, even otherness. Given the loss of oral memory in our societies, Lepage has remarked on the use of "written or visual documents […] to store the things we remember […] as a result, our memory doesn't function anymore because it no longer has to make the effort to store things. So, memory no longer distorts facts by filtering them, which makes it all the harder for history to be transformed into mythology."[155] For Lepage, poetry and the strength of the artistic creation depend on "our ability to recount events through the imperfections of our memories."[156] This is a long way from the truth of archives. On the contrary: Lepage counts on the "distorting lens of memory."

The Lepagean palimpsest could also be called an echo chamber, which we observe from every angle and through every resonance. While photography reveals its technical principles, video puts the palimpsest into practice, while virtual environments communicate Lepage's attempts to dive into the interior of the palimpsest and its space. Photography is essentially an object of resurgence and erasure. Lepage agrees with this characterization, letting all the different phases of an event emerge on the real or symbolic surface. Freud's *Wunderblock* is the model for many boxes, Lepagean dwellings, black boxes that make photos re-emerge randomly, reminiscent of a photographic chamber and a psychic entity. The spatial metaphors initiated by photography are taken further by video, increasing the number of resurgences and layers on a light-sensitive screen. A source of light and representation, video adds successive, ephemeral coats, with other visual layers over them. The echo becomes coloured light. Video tries to cover the image with a coat of colour or with another sequence, and at the same time it tries to pierce the image, by outlining and erasing. While the screen moves effectively between visibility, latency, and memory, latency can be understood as a gaping maw, an opening or breach in the tightly woven image.[157] Like memory, the echo rises to the surface. But it isn't only space or a breach that Lepage wants to introduce in his onscreen images, hence his logical move into 3-D virtual environments. These projected images activate the audience's memory, because they are seen at different angles. They are repeated, echoed, and distorted, prompting the memory to work through the similarities and differences. So in the last box, the image of a couple intertwined in shadow on the *shoji* screens refers back to the shadows formed by the G.I. and Nozomi that we see in Hiroshima. The audience remembers the first image, compares it to the current one, no longer really knowing whether it is the same couple, or Pierre and Nozomi, or Pierre and David, depending on the scene in the show. Everything transpires in the same house, but fifty years apart. The echo, like a tool for the memory, has time to sketch a few memories before fading away. "People complain about the unreliability of memory, but we should rejoice in it, use it as a creative tool."[158] The palimpsest, when it appears in the form of photo or video, is based on this idea and this intervention by the audience. Lepage reinjects memory into 3-D environments through other sources of images, but these intervene in an immersion that is anything but vague and imprecise. The audience sees a layered weaving, but without any gaps. Everything is too controlled and verified for openings other than those allowed. The audience is no longer free to play its own memory. The echo can no longer resonate. This would also explain why Lepage abandoned these environments: he simplified the technical to put memory and convention back to work instead. Because, since his first use of photography, which shadows laid the groundwork for, Lepage has been developing a work of memory, a memory of the gaze through a memory of the image, in multiple plays of resonances. The palimpsest, the fourth porous wall of Lepage's stage, closes off the box. And it's through these openings that we can plunge into the echo.

SIXTH ECHO

SOUND TECHNOLOGY

Lepage's stages are above all visual surfaces for all sorts of inscriptions. As in most image-based theatre, sound is also important, because it allows for full participation in the show. It is a more or less conscious legacy of the total work of art. The total work of art advocated a new complementarity of sound and visual effects, with poetic intentions that provided them a new visibility and vividness.[159] While Lepage stages image-based stories, he also stages sound, and not just in operatic productions. His shows demonstrate a technological reflection about the function of sound, another way of thinking about the dimension of the stage image and its impact and an obvious way of making the echo resonate. The sound echo is of course a creator of images.

THE ISSUES OF AMPLIFICATION

Sound technology in Lepage's world primarily involves microphones surrounding the stage or attached to actors' costumes to amplify their voice. Basic equipment in most theatrical stage sets, microphones, like projectors, seemingly serve no dramaturgical purpose and are considered only for their practical aspect of revealing or diffusing sound. For Lepage, microphones are laden with potential for metaphor.

The stage starts to be miked beginning with *Vinci*. The later solo shows (*Needles and Opium, Elsinore,* and *The Far Side of the Moon*) use stage or HF (high frequency) microphones. Likewise, these solo productions are "technological shows." Alone onstage, Lepage feels the need to bridge the distance and create a feeling of intimacy with the audience through this prosthetic device. The audience hears the actor without the actor having to raise his voice. The autobiographical aspect of solo shows – suggested by a character who is both Lepage's double and the access "door" to the audience – no doubt explains this need for proximity: "All one-man shows, no matter what your theme or subject is, are about solitude … How can you tell people increasingly personal things and let them peer into your soul, when theatres have become so huge? And that's the reason why … I use technology onstage."[160]

Beyond the notion of intimacy and confession, there is the theatrical reality of the room where the show is staged. *The Dragons' Trilogy* marked Lepage's first national tour (1985) and international tour (1986 to 1991), while *Vinci*, a solo performance, received kudos and awards around the same time, in different countries.[161] The tour brought with it a batch of new venues, the capacity of which required the microphone to maintain intimacy. They were a long way from Quebec City's café-theatres, the venues for Lepage's first productions.

The impressive array of microphones in *Elsinore* – an HF mini-microphone on the ear, a miniature microphone attached to the sword, shotgun microphones placed at the forestage by sound engineer Claude Cyr – make Hamlet's true monologues perceptible, in opposition to the feigned or indirect monologues in which Hamlet, in talking to someone, is in fact talking to himself. In Peter Gabriel's *Secret World Live* tour, every performer, singer, guitarist, or bassist has an HF, which lets them move between the two stages and the footbridge that connects them. This mobility, although commonplace today, at the time turned the HF microphone into the audience's ear, glued to the performer and never leaving its prey.

In *The Seven Streams of the River Ota*, like the lighting, the sound equipment frames the set and penetrates the stage box. Sound technology surrounds the actor it observes and amplifies. Three shotgun microphones are placed in front of the gravel parterre, and four microphones are hung behind the facade of the Japanese house. The sound technician doesn't use them all the time, only to harmonize the voices of the protagonists at the forestage and upstage. Thanks to hidden microphones, we can hear what is said behind the mirrors and the *shoji* screens, as well as the singers behind the scrim screen in *Jean-Sans-Nom*. The microphone surmounts the barriers; it reconstructs a perspective without spatial limits for the audience. In the last version of *The Seven Streams of the River Ota*, the interview between Patricia and her ex-husband is inadvertently prolonged by the HF microphone that Walter still has on him, while Patricia waits in the yard until her assistant has retrieved it. Not realizing he is being overheard, Walter paints a caustic portrait of Patricia, which she hears through her headphones.

Shotgun microphones are used most commonly. But sometimes the protagonists act with HF microphones, like the narrator in *Zulu Time* at the top of her scaffolding tower, Olgivanna Lloyd Wright describing an inner vision in *The Geometry of Miracles*, and the entire cast in *The Busker's Opera*. It's the classic concert situation, with the character musicians singing over live music. The HF microphones for the *Secret World Live* tour are connected, through a mixing table and powerful amplifiers, to a multichannel diffusion array. The central circular stage with an audience seated in a U-shape provides widespread visibility, and this stage is surrounded by speakers arranged in clusters, which deliver universally good sound. Just as Lepage offers the audience's gaze ubiquity, he offers the ability to hear from any angle or position.

Sound amplification is also a chance to use technology that works with an actor's voice as raw material. It makes it possible to affect the colour, range, and general aspect of the sound message.[162] Plus in solo shows, sound amplification increases the effect of characters. Amplification underlines the slightest sound modulation by the actor, which we see in both *Vinci* and *The Far Side of the Moon*, productions in which Lepage adopts different accents and vocal ranges. He plays an English taxi driver, Leonardo da Vinci, a young Quebecer, an Italian guide, and a Parisian Mona Lisa.[163] The amplification isn't responsible for the metamorphosis alone; the actor's voice and the props are needed: a cane, glasses, wig, cap, and so on.

Through abrupt changes in volume, sound amplification also allows for scene changes. In *The Far Side of the Moon*, we see André present a weather report on TV. He speaks into a high-frequency microphone that slightly amplifies his voice, using television-style processing. In the middle of a sentence, while he is talking about having to travel far to see the sun, André's voice suddenly stops being amplified. The microphone being switched off and a change in lighting signal a change of location: we go from the television set to Philippe's apartment, where Philippe is having a discussion with André. Amplification transforms the space by processing the ambient sound of the stage. The voice treatment is like the slides projected onto screens in *Elsinore*, providing a new identity for each acting space.

The transformation of sound as stage direction is generally sufficient information, but it can also be used as a complement to and an illustration of a spatialization whose identity is derived from projections or scenery elements (footlights facing the audience, amplification and projected image to suggest that Frédéric, the Quebec author of *The Andersen Project*, is braving the Paris Opera the night of a strike). The clearest example of this is found in the Florentine guide scene in *Vinci*. All of Lepage's words are amplified and mixed to suggest the voice of someone talking in a church with an echo, creating the impression of high archways, and so forth. This effect is created live by the sound technician working with a mixer. At the same time, lighting creates the effect of light coming in through window panes. Sound is particularly important insofar as it affects a blind character. The effectiveness onstage is the result of a dramaturgical reflection on the effect, with sound creating the space.

A good example of changes in volume is in the use of the telephone,[164] a favourite tool of the solo actor, and a contemporary

and dramaturgical embodiment of the megaphone. The telephone breaks up solitude through an oral connection between two protagonists. For the solo productions, it is an obvious way to bring another person to life or create another place offstage. It's no surprise that the telephone appears in *Needles and Opium*, in the solitude of the hotel room, and even less so in *The Far Side of the Moon* and *The Andersen Project*, where it is omnipresent. The first phone conversation in *The Far Side of the Moon* is expository. We discover that Philippe has a brother and that their mother has just died. Lepage plays both Philippe and André, one phoning the other, whose replies we can infer from what the actor onstage says. Lepage has mastered the trick of phone communication.[165] Later on, André also uses the phone when he is stuck in an elevator, in this case a cellphone. As soon as he is confronted with an unforeseen problem, André calls his friend Karl, and this happens several times: when an elevator breaks down; when he discovers his mother's goldfish, Beethoven, dead, that Philippe had left in his care during a trip to Russia; and so forth. Finally, the phone is an instrument for reconciling the brothers and the link between Quebec and Russia. This connection is emphasized even more in the film version that frames the two brothers in the same image, one in Quebec, the other in Moscow. The wall of a phone booth hears the conversations and confessions of the characters in *The Andersen Project*, nine cells in which the protagonists share their solitude.

In *The Seven Streams of the River Ota*, the telephone forges a connection between Japan and Quebec, and between Osaka and Hiroshima. In this show, the words of the person on the other end of the line are recorded – Marc, Sophie's friend, is heard as a voice offstage – or are performed onstage, for instance when Hanako, in her interpreter's booth, answers Sophie in the phone booth. Sound amplification increases the number of characters by borrowing the situation of the phone conversation from reality, a substitute for dialogue, played by only one of the two protagonists involved in the exchange. Whether by telephone or by microphone, for example, during the lecture to the empty room in Moscow, sound amplification increases intimacy.[166] The protagonist drops the mask, whereas the words spoken without amplification are more public and social, more of a rant. By creating distance, we touch the

The way cellphones are used in *The Blue Dragon* is typical of the links Lepage builds between characters.

PHOTO
Ludovic Fouquet

heart of the message and the individual; by moving away, we move closer, which explains how Lepage manages to keep the humanity in his technologically based shows.

Sound is also an opportunity for opening up new avenues through voice processing. The sound message is not simply retransmitted; it is transformed to take on another identity, for example, an artificial, synthetic, quasi-robotic timbre in *Elsinore*. As in *Vinci*, Lepage was confronted with many characters, except that he didn't have the same latitude because it is a repertory play, the only instance of this in his solo shows. In the opening scenes, after the credits, the king and the queen speak, each in their own voice. Hamlet and Ophelia have their own voices as well. The actor's voice is transformed through the filter of technology to sound like there is interference. A gap is therefore created between what the actor says and the voice that we hear, which is not exactly his because it has been through the mixer.[167] This practice partly explains certain criticisms about the distance of the acting as well as its limited use in Lepage's work. However, he doesn't fall into the trap of a strict alternation of voices, a Ping-Pong game of sound that is supposed to render the otherness and energy of normal exchanges of lines. As happens in some solo stagings of repertory plays, the sound score is the score of a consciousness plagued by questions. Every protagonist incarnates, or, rather, gives voice to, one of the facets of this consciousness. Sound amplification captures the voice and transforms it before letting the audience hears it. The actor's voice is modified, held back for a moment during which it is doctored. Communication is thus adversely affected. This time lag allows for theatricality, while underlining the artificiality, the ambiguity, the very limits.[168] Sound amplification makes the scenic design palimpsest possible, because while vision cuts through the layered surfaces, hearing has more difficulty working its way along a straight path. In this sense, the microphone is the tool necessary when screens are used, mainly when the performance area is behind it.

SOUND TECHNOLOGY, OR THE
ART OF ACCOMPANIMENT

Sound technology in Lepage's world creates an environment, whether a tape or live music played onstage, often on its periphery. Amplification borrows from cinema: "Film-editing has taught me that what really shapes film is sound."[169] Whether in film or theatre, Lepage designs his soundscape the same way. Sound is used as stage direction, delivering an immediate, ephemeral, and very supple colour.

> The same connection to sound exists in my stage work, too. The skaters' waltz scene in *The Dragons' Trilogy*, in which soldiers on skates act out the destruction of the war by scattering groups of shoes representing families, would not have the power it has without Robert Caux's music. The same thing applies to many of the scenes in *Needles and Opium*.[170]

Just as photography draws from universal heritage, the sound in these productions uses sound memory, whether of music or noise. This memory is constructed within the sphere of influence of film editing, but also in the sphere of influence of stage direction, provided by projected sequence titles and pure stage direction: the title "Enter Hamlet" could be read on the Monolith in the English version of *Elsinore*. Thus the voice-over plays the role of narration. Several voice-over narrations run through *Vinci*, delivering information about Leonardo da Vinci as would a tour guide, in oral or written form, or specifying the frame of the action through clearly identifiable messages. When Philippe is leaving for Europe, he is seated on the couch at his psychoanalyst's office. The soundtrack creates the new setting of the airplane, and the message intervenes as stage direction and a transition: we hear "Please buckle your seatbelts." In *Zulu Time*, the audience hears boarding announcements and safety instructions in different languages, reproducing the sound environment of an airport or aircraft cabin. Ada Weber opens a scene in *The Seven Streams of the River Ota* by reading a letter, after Jeffrey 1's death. The narrator's avatar, the voice-over, introduces the new space and time.

The soundtrack plays on the audience recognizing a component of sound and on the world that this sequence conveys – an era, a geographical area, and so on – which effectively performs the function of stage direction. Koto music opens *The Seven Streams of the River Ota*, foreshadowing the anchor location for the show, even before the light hits the set. The same approach is used during the party in New York, and with the Led Zeppelin hit in *The Far Side of the Moon*. Excerpts of recordings of speeches or shows can also be used. There are a number of archived sounds from the Russian and American space programs in *The Far Side of the Moon*: television and radio shows, countdowns, astronauts singing "I Will Go to the Moon One Day," and so on. The soundtrack is like an information banner. Historical accuracy is not the main concern in the choice of pieces, but it shows a desire to add local colour. These archives are often used partly because of the requirements of solo shows but also because of the film approach to stage production and the use of sound references that in turn intersect with multiple references. Offenbach's music was chosen for *The Seven Streams of the River Ota* for its reference to light comedies, to "door slamming" theatre.[171] In the middle of the Terezin concentration camp, the singer Sarah Weber recalls her performance of *Madame Butterfly*: like the heroine, she kills herself. The memory of the opera underlines the coincidences between the different realms of *The Seven Streams of the River Ota*. Music reinforces the emotional impact of the scene.

Traditionally, the soundtrack allows for changes of space. Throughout *Vinci*, we hear traffic noises for the London bus sequence, water noises and conversation for the public baths, and airplane engines for the takeoff. Certain sequences are also punctuated with modern rhythms that have no illustrative function. Banks of sound are used.[172] The engineers create a very precise frame, spatializing the sound sources, reproducing the sequences, and amplifying certain sounds. As in film, sound effects engineers can render not only any sound frame, but also suggest it in movement and in evolution. Just like the dissolves used in narrative transitions, Lepage uses sound morphing to quietly and coincidentally move from place to place or object to object. This is how, in the same way that the porthole in *The Far Side of the Moon* in turn represents a washing machine, a rocket, a plane, and a scanner, the soundtrack gives direction to guide the audience's perception.

The equipment is adjusted to create the right ambience, and increasingly, the sound source is computer generated rather than analogue or solely analogue, as in *Zulu Time*. Most of the tones of the soundscape have a specific psychological function, such as conveying anxiety, solitude, or drunkenness. So the voices at the airport, the conversations in the bar, and the humming of engines heard from inside the plane cabin are processed by composer Michel F. Côté to suggest a frame as well as a psycho-physiological state. Everything unfolds as if the soundscape were in fact perceived by one of the protagonists, along the lines of the subjective camera. This is why the sounds in the hotel bar are all amplified, as if stripped of perspective: everything is heard through the ears of the drunken hostess who returns to the room in which she had a strange sexual encounter. Côté and composer Diane Labrosse multiplied their voices eight times over, in the scraps of conversation in the bar, to recreate the way someone waking up with a hangover perceives sound. Likewise in the plane, the low vibration of the engines contradicts the apparent tranquility of the flight attendants and foreshadows the final catastrophe. When the divers search for the wreckage of the plane, the soundscape brings the scene to life and makes few props necessary: just the odd seat and aircraft debris. The audience is plunged underwater: the space between the stage and the bridges becomes the underwater space. The simultaneous information (sound, light, slowed gestures, the weight and dress of the protagonists) creates not only the sense of witnessing an underwater scene, but also of being able to touch the water. It's as if the set were an aquarium or as if we were being shown an image of the dive, and yet there is nothing at all onstage: no water, projected images, or screen. The stage image has the dimensions of a movie screen in a panoramic theatre, and the scene is played out at the screen, which is unfurled several times during the performance. The far-off voice of singer-songwriter Carlos Gardel, who died in a plane crash in Colombia in 1935, is one of the production's first sounds. The aircraft in *Zulu Time* was flying over South America, connecting Lima and New York, when it went down in the Gulf of Mexico with 237 passengers, a journalist tells us over the monitors. The voice processed as if heard underwater thus evokes its disappearance. Côté talks about a "requiem, a sort of expressionist sound tableau."[173] The soundtrack communicates a range of information, multiplies it by layering so that it takes on a metaphorical reach, which is common in Lepage's productions, in this case in the form of a song.

The action onstage is always framed, underlined, and commented upon by a sound discourse that isn't language based. The productions mainly use an accompanying soundtrack for sound. This has obvious advantages in terms of easy manipulation. However, sometimes one or more musicians appear onstage accompanying the show live, and are actors at the same time (*The Busker's Opera*). They appear in *The Seven Streams of the River Ota*, in *Zulu Time*, and to some extent, in *Jean-Sans-Nom*. This, of course, is not uncommon. In fact many creators, such as Brook and Mnouchkine, use live musicians integrated into the stage to varying degrees, most often positioned along its edge. Plus, image technology calls for sound technology, and with the idea of the total show, the desire to mix aesthetics, genres, and artistic areas is rendered by mixes and contrasts of prefabricated elements: images, sounds, and sets, evolving or created in real time. Live music is one of the most commonly chosen options. There is a clear coincidence between the manipulation of the different technologies and the manipulation of sound instruments. Is this a holdover from silent film, with the musician on the side of the stage? In *The Seven Streams of the River Ota* music is often used as a substitute for words that are incomprehensible to one or another of the protagonists. *Zulu Time* uses virtually no words. The few lines are at times even recorded. This universe, particularly in *The Busker's Opera*, also borrows from cabaret: often silent pieces succeed one another, around the chatter of the captain. For *Zulu Time*, Lepage surrounded himself with actors who were not terribly familiar with acting with a text.[174]

Live background music is therefore used in shows that make minimal or particular use of language. *Jean-Sans-Nom* and *Zulu Time* are virtually musicals. There is a lot of dialogue in *The Seven Streams of the River Ota*, but communication is always contradicted, ill-used, and in jeopardy. The actors talk a great deal precisely to try to be understood. The sound technologies surround but also replace or reinforce the actors' words.

When musicians are present, there is a constant interplay between tradition and modernity in the instruments. Because each show uses both digital and analogue sound, the contrast is dynamic: a trademark and the idea behind all explorations and productions. In Lepage's musical universe, the use of old instruments not only serves the idea of resurgence, but also multiplies effects of meeting, intersection, or, to use the musical term, "mixing." Music is one of the areas in which Lepage has the least practical knowledge, and it is the area in which he gives the creator the greatest freedom. He spent a total of five minutes discussing music with Michel F. Côté before inviting him to come on board for *The Seven Streams of the River Ota*, impressed by the fact that Côté has few preconceived ideas, aside from some notions about jazz. Lepage quickly identified coincidences or possible convergences between him and Côté, who when composing uses equipment that fits perfectly with the director's world. According to Côté, he offers a "combination of technologies [that brings together] traditional sound, acoustic sound, and digital sound."[175] In addition to traditional percussion instruments, such as gongs, bells, wind chimes, the Japanese *ki*, and the water-phone (a stainless steel resonator bowl filled with water), there are more common instruments such as the snare drum, the high hat, the bass drum, and the extended drum set, equipped with more elements than usual. These two sorts of instruments are set up in an arc around the seated musician. Some are processed acoustically: the musician runs a bow along the side of a cymbal equipped with a pedal-activated microphone, which achieves inflections between "the traditional American violin and the Far Eastern string instrument."[176] The electronic components are MIDI (Musical Instrument Digital Interface) controllers, drum pads whose sound changes depending on how fast or hard they are hit. These controllers are also connected to synthesizers that emit sound sequences programmed using a sampler; for example, the Amsterdam sequence features an aggressive electric guitar sound. Essentially, with MIDI controllers the drummer becomes the bassist. Metal percussion instruments equipped with contact microphones electronically modify an originally acoustic sound. These pads and contact microphones are distributed throughout the ensemble, a veritable floating floor of sound, peppered with all kinds of sensitive and reactive surfaces: wood, copper, plastic, and others. Each of these surfaces reacts differently depending on what it is and how it is connected.

Côté exploits the triad of electronic music: the sequencer, the sampler, and the synthesizer, the synthesizer enabling the use of the first two. This is even more apparent in *Zulu Time*, where Côté relies on the possibility of capturing the sound of the sampler and using it in different ways for unlimited transformation and repetition. He creates a bank of sounds that he reintroduces into his sound environment by hitting the drum pads. The show's soundscape is primarily made up of electronic music and by "the musical tools specific to new trends,"[177] including the sequencer-sampler-synthesizer trio. Côté first proposed two DJs, each in a tower, like in a nightclub, but Lepage was set on the composer being onstage in this show. The idea of two DJs remained, but in the form of a jam band. Since there would be limited space on the towers and percussion wouldn't suit such a technological show, new digital synthesizers – drum machines – had to be used. Inspired by the theremin wave device, he would come up with the D-Beam, which controls sound and effects via hand movements interacting with a beam of infrared light.[178] Patented by Interactive Light, the D-Beam is a light device that uses digital sound information like a motion detector.[179] Also accompanied by a bass and an accordion suspended under the bridges or played upside down, the show opens to the music of a psaltery playing along to an old Gaelic tune. These instruments are more than an opposition between past forms and new technology; they are testimony to an essential relationship in all of Lepage's work:[180] how to integrate one aesthetic into another or how to make the mix of genres work. In *The Seven Streams of the River Ota*, this quest is expressed through a juxtaposition of equipment and sound sources, while in the techno-cabaret *Zulu Time*, it is more isolated interludes confronted and juxtaposed by numbers. The first robot number, created by Louis-Philippe Demers and Bill Vorn, suggests different ages of music. Robots emerge from the set and, in a light display, make noise by rattling their metal parts. They hit the structure: the stage system becomes a sound system, like in Greek theatre, which combined place and sound system into one construction. This passage refers to the three ages of music: the past, with percussion on the structures, a sort of return to the music of origins; the present, with the factory aesthetic of music somewhere between industrial and techno; and the future, with robot musicians.[181]

Within the musical world of productions, historical range is important, as with any technological medium Lepage uses, which always serves at the same time for meta-discursive and trans-historical reflection. Tradition and modernity therefore coexist through the musical instruments onstage, often with one of them dominating: the tradition of percussion in *The Seven Streams of the River Ota*, techno modernity in *Zulu Time*, and rock and jazz in *The Busker's Opera*. For *Jean-Sans-Nom*, the distribution is a little more ambiguous. The way the instruments are processed suggests mechanical organs worthy of Captain Nemo, while either a synthesizer or keyboard controls the percussion instruments set on the metal frame.

When Lepage decided to place musicians in plain view it was also to have the music as close to the action as possible, as we see in other theatrical forms. Sound intervenes on dramatic action, but also sometimes on another sound source already being heard. The evolution of the music for *The Seven Stream of the River Ota* is significant in this sense. The first version didn't have live music, and yet in the later versions it became an essential element. It overcame ongoing communication problems between the characters and had a strong emotional impact on the audience in every country the show toured. The performance aspect of this accompaniment and the emotional aspect of the music combined electrical and electronic bursts with ancient and delicate tones, as heard in the circular sound of the waterphone and the notes of the wind chimes scattered to the wind. Côté was hired just before the creation of the second version of *The Seven Streams of the River Ota*. The soundtrack was once again limited: a Koto chant and Robert Caux's music for the Terezin scene. Côté simply observed and improvised. This is accompaniment in its truest sense: omnipresent, but discreet. At one and the same time the storyteller comments on the story and the editor looks to enhance a film sequence. Côté brings this work closer to that of a musician in the theatrical traditions of the Orient who watches and accompanies, using sound to mark out the place and time of the story and the performance, delicately filling moments of silence, but also introducing or underlining the tensions, the crises, and the punchlines. Live music draws sequences out by slowing things down and holding notes as long as possible. A particular sound base develops, which becomes temporal and dreamlike material.

What occurs throughout *Zulu Time* is the perfect synchronization of the action and the musical commentary. The musician grabs the information from mid-air and punctuates it. The musical score achieves an uncommon precision, one sometimes found in productions where the musician is close by or, more often, in film. The soundtrack is worked to the quarter of a second and emphasizes the dramatic weight of a given scene. During the march of the deportees from Terezin, the sequence is repeated faster and faster, between the mirrored walls. The same people walk and then run after leaving their musical instruments. Côté hits his percussion instruments violently and with greater and greater resonance. The scene's emotional impact is not only the result of the music, but also of the musician's effort, his gestures, and his physical movements in the midst of all the percussion instruments that surround him. In *Zulu Time*, the musicians are at the centre of the set, which allows them to suddenly intervene as a new actor or as a musician or both at the same time. Like DJs, the musicians who are perched high in their towers and share the same beat are practically dancing with their instruments, carried away by what they are playing while watching the action. The protagonists of this action become conductors in a way, setting the rhythm of the accompaniment through their action, even though they may not be aware of it. The musician has more latitude than the sound engineer to slow down or accelerate a phrase, to improvise. This is where the D-Beam becomes particularly useful, with the optical sensor allowing for broad and immediate interaction with the manipulator. In addition, this visual intervention and the manipulation involved, because the hand plays with the beam, reinforces the impact of the live act. While the musician adapts to the tempo of the stage, he controls the sound sources. However, the use of pads that play pre-recorded sound sequences and the soundtracks launched by the sound technicians complicate this control. The recorded track, when launched by the musician hitting a pad, is just another instrument or additional range in the score. He controls this musical intervention. He knows how long it will last and how loud it will be, and can change it while it is being played. If it's launched by the sound technician, then the background the musician has to line up with is just a mechanical rhythm that can't be changed.

Onstage, the musician thus uses a panoply of instruments both traditional and technological, but also recorded sound supports. This returns to the idea of an orchestra, working in layers. Côté's music is in part technological because it is based on technological means of reproducing sound. It is a distinctive combination: a mix of music, using a soundtrack but based on the presence of the musician commenting on what he sees.

SOUND TECHNOLOGY:
A NEW SORT OF PROTAGONIST

Jazz is the most common musical reference in Lepage's productions. It's used as a sort of new universal language that is found in the airports, clubs, and cafés of the world (*Zulu Time, The Busker's Opera*) and in the American and Dutch apartments (*The Seven Streams of the River Ota*). It is even one of the initial subjects of *Needles and Opium*. In the technological and dehumanized universe of *Zulu Time*, jazz is part of the resistance, a relic of intimacy and of sensitivity in the face of machines. Lepage insisted on its presence in *Zulu Time*, whereas Côté recommended techno. Côté wound up creating new arrangements of standards (*Time After Time*). He put a bass onstage and reintroduced a few acoustic percussion sounds. The same applied in the original movie soundtracks, no matter when and where the film is set. Just as Lepage doesn't doubt the ability of his audience worldwide to read the screen and have appropriate audiovisual reactions, he counts on an understanding and the shared emotional impact of jazz, which does not exclude references to other music.[182]

Jazz influences casting, whether the singers – the hostess and other characters in *Zulu Time,* or the junkie crooner in *The Seven Streams of the River Ota* getting into the collective bathtub, enthused by the acoustic effect of the reverberation of his voice on enamel – or whether records played or allusions to the lives of famous singers. During his trip, Philippe writes a postcard. He leaves Florence to explore the village of da Vinci's birth, the last step on his journey of rite of passage. The postcard provides the opportunity for a particular use of sound and technology. The text of the missive is faltered through, almost spelled out, by a Roland digital percussion pad, the Octapad. When one of the pads is struck, the Octapad delivers a preprogrammed message, in the form of vocal, rather than musical, sequences: eight syllables: "A," "MI," "JE," "TE," "PAR," "LE," "VIN," and "CI," from which Lepage creates the text for the postcard. On the side of the stage, Daniel Toussaint, the composer and musician, hits with a mallet to compose messages that are perceived through preprogrammed sound effects (pauses, tremors, repetitions):

> *Ami, je te parle.*
> *Je pars à Vinci le vingt.*
> *À part le site, le vin,*
> *J'assimile le mythe Vinci.*
> *À six mille milles, assis,*
> *Je parle à Vinci.*
> *My friend, I am talking to you.*
> *I am leaving for Vinci on the twentieth.*
> *Aside from the place, the wine,*
> *I am assimilating the da Vinci myth.*
> *Six thousand miles away, seated,*
> *I am talking to da Vinci.*[183]

The sound-effect message is perfectly coherent. Philippe gives the date of his departure for Vinci, talks about the wine and the vineyard that surrounds the village, and recounts the extent to which he has immersed himself in the Italian artist's work: "J'assimile le mythe Vinci" (I am assimilating the da Vinci myth). He is so immersed that from where he is ("À six mille milles, assis" [Six thousand miles away, seated]), he feels as though he is talking to da Vinci. "What could have been just a technological gadget (although it remains a gadget, albeit appealing and impressive) turns out to be at the service of people, intimate communication, and even communion. The frontiers of space and time disappear."[184] In fact, Philippe meets Leonardo in a bathhouse! Sound technology again takes over from the protagonist's words, in a discourse that is purely vocal rather than musical. Thus, as of 1986, Lepage introduces a playful relationship with technology and makes language the poetic basis of a game with words, but above all with sounds. Language takes on an almost virtual presence, emerging and talking as much to the eyes as to the ears and, even further, to an understanding that it achieves through surprise.

On the lateral screen a dotted line moves in waves, constantly bending out of shape. In *Elsinore*, Lepage uses oscillograph technology. This line of light vibrates with the voice it filters, in this case Lepage's voice, transformed to varying degrees by a computer. It is an effective form of stage direction, like having the name of the protagonist before each line. It intensifies the different ways the voice is processed with nuances of oscillation: "a medical description" or a clinical report, like a lie detector that conveys the character's internal state. Sound is made visual: the oscillograph conveys sound impulses through light. The line of light reappears during the duel, following vocal movements, but the curve becomes an electrocardiogram, and it slows as Hamlet dies. Sound technology in this case is a mere graphical witness that any sound console offers, caricatures medical equipment, an ontological witness of the protagonists it analyzes. It is an inner witness, because it thumbs its nose at outward appearances, like electrodes do.

In the second phone conversation in *The Seven Streams of the River Ota* between Sophie, Hanako, and an awkward American interpreter, musical accompaniment becomes the fourth protagonist of a "symmetrical quadrilateral."[185] Sophie calls Hanako from a phone booth, the latter having returned to Hiroshima and visible in the interpreter's booth stage left. The American interpreter is in the translation booth stage right. He interprets the French conversation of the two women, dubbing it in a muted voice. The conversation is punctuated with silence; words are few and far between. The conversation circulates among the three protagonists, each in their own space. The two interpreters are on the same level, flanking the facade. Sophie is in front of the facade, at the corner of the porch. The musician is in a practically symmetrical position stage left. The music is thus a fourth speaker. It repeats certain sequences, utters short phrases, and inserts itself as lines in the vocal exchanges. It responds to a different semantic – the musician speaks "arbitrary words" – but it functions with the semantic of other protagonists.

The music becomes dialogue rather than accompaniment. It is an additional voice weaving the discursive material of the show. More than a translation, a sort of musical equivalent of the interpreter's English words, the music is the poetic emergence of a new voice, understandable in other ways.

When the D-Beam is used in the *Zulu Time* tours, the music, while accompanying the action, becomes a show. It uses its similarity with concerts or nightclubs, but it is still peripheral, positioned at the edge of the stage. At the beginning of the X-ray scene, Côté leaves his tower and walks along one of the bridges, carrying his console to set it on a sheet of Plexiglas attached to the edge of the bridge. Facing him, Diane Labrosse does likewise. Each of them initiates sounds, modifies them, interrupts them, and links them together with a hand or arm gesture. Each seeks to dominate and overwhelm the other through the use of sound technology. But this challenge is both musical and technological in its impact and reach. Côté is using a synthesizer while Labrosse is using a sampler. A symbolic duel – but one that is recognizable through the characteristics of each piece of equipment; for example, the sampler makes it much easier to change intensity, to produce more complex sounds, and to make them last longer – is played out between two instruments that can produce or reproduce almost any sound. It is a duel between analogue and digital sound. Details disappear and all that remains is a confrontation between two universes of sound. Sound becomes metaphorical, through the reference to electronic games,[186] but also through a return to a certain form of musical accompaniment. The end of the duel occurs at the same time as the sadomasochistic relationship ends between the spy and the plane's pilot, below, in their hotel room. The gagged man is strangled against the background of these enraged machines.

Sound production sometimes has a direct physical effect onstage: the oscillograph in *Elsinore* is the first instance of this. It is interesting to note that the strongest example of this sort of effect is not technological in the slightest. Earlier mention was made of the sand drawing by a man contemplating his neighbour in the bar on the central stage of the set of *Zulu Time* – two tables with chairs. When the man leaves the bar, the drawing remains visible on the screen. Côté arrives onstage and pulls out a bow from the bass case that the man left on the side of the stage. He approaches the table, kneels down, and plays with the metal tabletop, as he did with the trash-can cymbal in *The Seven Streams of the River Ota*. He strokes the bow along the edge of the table, producing a particular metallic sound. The video image shows that the vibrations of these sounds make the sand move on the table. The image blurs in a nice soft-focus effect, a sort of cloud suggesting the permanent loss of memories: the face of the woman he came across fades quickly in the drawing creator's memory, and the table becomes a metaphor for his psychic apparatus, or, at least, for his memory. Diane Labrosse does the same thing on the other table. In this case, there is no drawing to disturb, just a surface of sand that, under the effect of the sound, moves to form a star. The two tables thus hold magnificent organic shapes in ochre on a black background, vibrating with each vibration. The effect, which is very simple to create in terms of equipment, is striking, spectacular, and poetic.

The sound source is being exploited for its semantics, but also for the physical effect it has. Sound physically changes the set, like a character moving an object or a machine running onstage, an invisible protagonist with active waves. Music acts and performs, carrying its creator along with it. The more visible it is, the more varied its visible effects are, the more the musician becomes part of the set. The musician becomes the protagonist in a performance he no longer simply accompanies from the side. The musician occupies the bridge high above or the metal proscenium in a playful allusion to the musician's family name: Côté, or "side." Performance to performance, Côté moves toward the centre of the stage as he plays. In addition to being a musician, he becomes a performer in the theatrical sense of the term: he plays different characters in the two productions.

From performance to performance, sound technology takes on a new role. From mere amplification, necessary from the point of view of space and symbolism to break the solitude and allow for a sense of nearness across a set that can be an obstacle, it takes on the qualities of a protagonist: visibility, lines, movement, and such. Previously, it would have become the subjective experience of a protagonist, whose perception is shared with us. The originality of Lepage's soundscape lies in these two relationships to the protagonist. Based on the model of film, reusing sound archives as stage direction, the soundtrack becomes a metaphor and highlights the dramaturgical accents in the productions that use less of the musician and his technology onstage. Instead, the appearance of the musician enriches the definition of space and time, synchronizing sound and action and integrating sound into the heart of the story. With or without the musician, sound technology invades the stage, first as a humble messenger, then gradually taking part in the dialogue, then monopolizing a sequence or taking on a visual role. In these productions, live music makes up for inadequate language and enables or re-establishes communication. It draws on its most ancient roots. Percussion talks – the Octapad in *Vinci* – and sound technology in *The Seven Streams of the River Ota* becomes a speaker on the phone and music begins to draw. Just as Lepage does with images, he stages sound, rather than just using sound technology. He strives to rethink a medium we thought we knew. Sound is an emotion, of course, but also a vibration, that in Lepage's work is conveyed through light and ripples of sand. Sound is a wave, but also space and time, juxtapositions of recorded tracks and sounds captured live using a broad, porous range of time. Nothing is insignificant in the use of sound technology, or any of the other multiple theatre technologies involving light, photography, cinema, video, and virtual environments. Lepage tries everything on this curious stage that exhibits, explores, and diverts technologies, making them visible, visual, incidental, and magnifying them without being taken in by them.

PART THREE

Experimentation in the Visual Laboratory: Echoes of Chaos

LEPAGE'S PRACTICE: FROM RESOURCE TO SYSTEM

Robert Lepage's productions are very much influenced by currents that existed in embryo in Théâtre Repère productions (including *Circulations*, *Vinci*, and *Tectonic Plates*) and they are constructed in the tradition of collective creations. They take a healthy step back and redefine notions of writing and the writer, and the roles of all the contributors. The concept of the work in progress was not entirely new in Quebec when Lepage made it one of the conditions for creating productions. During the main period for collective creations, the end of the 1970s, Quebec audiences were invited to penetrate the mysteries of a creative process they normally only saw in the result. This invitation was part of a larger redefinition of social statuses during this period. Creators also periodically produced serial productions, inspired both by a tradition of the press and a television genre. The audience was invited to return several times to the production's venue to follow the scenes.[1] As the story evolved, new parts would sometimes be added and material redone, a combination of additions and redefinitions of the story or

the scenic design. Both the perception of the show and the equipment were changing. Beginning with *The Dragons' Trilogy*, Lepage
opened his shows to the public as of the first version – referred to
as a "rough cut." The notion seemed obsolete that creation results
in a definite finished product or a definitive show: the "version,"
the only instance that can currently be seen, is substituted for
the "creation." This requires the participation of the audience.
This seems fairly obvious, now that the practice has become more
widespread – although it is far from being the most common one –
but at the beginning of the 1980s, and in Quebec City moreover,
the approach was far from commonplace. It would definitely be
a factor in Lepage's success and would become systematic and
interwoven with an "appropriated approach to work."[2] Starting
with *The Dragons' Trilogy*, each show was created in at least three
phases, except for some of the commissioned shows, where Lepage
had to conform to another process.[3]

The first version of *The Dragons' Trilogy* was created at
Quebec City's Implanthéâtre, on November 12, 1985 – there would
be five performances by November 16 – with four performers: Marie
Brassard, Jean Casault, Marie Gignac, and Robert Lepage. The show
was ninety minutes long plus an intermission. The four actors played
eleven characters among them. In the second phase, beginning
May 20, 1986, the show grew to three hours with two intermissions,
and nineteen roles were distributed among eight actors: the initial
four plus Richard Fréchette and Yves-Érick Marier.[4] Then more
protagonists were added and the story expanded, with various
scenes and intersections, and as a result the show was longer. The
actors further solidified their performances and took on roles that,
until that point, had circulated interchangeably among them. The
story now painted a portrait that covers fifty years of Quebec life, set
around two little girls, Françoise and Jeanne, through their life and
descendants and through three Canadian Chinatowns. The third
version, which ran six hours, continued to explore these characters.
It was *the* event of the Festival de théâtre des Amériques in 1987,
for which it was created.[5] This framework would be the beginnings
of the creative approach that Lepage would use from then on. For
this show, each period of creation lasted three weeks.

The Seven Streams of the River Ota was created in three
phases over three years, each totalling about six weeks of collective

work.[6] The successive versions were just different ways of telling the same story. They changed how characters meet, which can result in the creation, elimination, or modification of a character: Jana Čapek was no longer the common thread, having been replaced in this capacity by Hanako who, depending on the version, is a blind, widowed *hibakusha,* mother to David the publicist, or a woman who remained single: Jeffrey 2, previously her husband, becomes her brother.

In the first version, three boxes or parts were created: first, "Mirrors": Terezin, New York, Paris, and the artist Jana Čapek revisits her memories of the Terezin camp; second, "Thunder": Hiroshima, Jana Čapek receives Pierre Lamontagne,[7] a young Canadian who has come to take calligraphy courses – *butoh* courses in the versions that follow; and third, "Theatre": Mishima's *Madame de Sade* is performed. The second version added two new boxes: first, "Amsterdam": Jeffrey is sick with AIDS and is in contact with Ada, whom he already ran into in New York and whose mother was interned at Terezin where she met Jana Čapek; and second, "Moving Pictures": the meeting at the origin of the entire show. In 1996 "Theatre" became "Words" and Mishima was replaced by Feydeau.[8] Two more boxes were added: first, "Two Jeffreys," in which the New York scene becomes independent; and second, "The Interview," in which Jana is interviewed by Patricia Hébert, the wife of the Quebec diplomat. Pierre Lamontagne's girlfriend, Sophie Maltais, becomes his mother, who gave birth to him in Japan, at Hanako's house. "Every time we did a new version, I had a character change," Marie Brassard explains good-naturedly, during a Festival de théâtre des Amériques press conference.[9] This transformation of the work is typical, and it is the result and condition of a Lepagean idea that has found the place and means necessary for its expression.

THE RESOURCE: THE HEART
AND FOCAL POINT OF THE REHEARSAL

Since the Théâtre Repère years, Michel Bernatchez has been Lepage's administrator and part of the artistic process. Stationed at the heart of a constantly evolving collective work, a work in progress, he is the key element in a production that, even before becoming widely known, is being shared and disseminated, and that, even before being recognized in Quebec, began with the first international tours. Like the rest of the team, Bernatchez was required to respond to the immediate creation, which was risky and innovative compared with what was on offer in the world of theatre in the 1980s. While the evolution was logical, rethinking his role seems more impressive on an administrative than on an artistic level. The changing character of the productions requires many and distinctive rehearsals, adapted to each show, and that requires the administrator's involvement:

> one of the fundamental problems I see in a lot of theatre, at least in Quebec and Canada, is the tendency to prepare all theatrical dishes the same way. [...] [whereas there are] three weeks of rehearsals in English Canada and [there are] six to eight in Quebec. [...] And people in production circles are rarely aware of [the particular requirements of each project]. [...] Michel Bernatchez has always been able to define and shape the technical aspect of whatever project we're working on by focusing on the artistic content and then adapting his own work to the particular challenges of the creation. [...] [He] doesn't deal only with problems and finances [...] Sometimes, he'll look at a project and say it doesn't justify the degree of technical complexity we've developed.[10]

The connections between the creative and administrative systems mean that the final product hits the market faster: producers[11] and their buying assistants are working without a net. Consequently they have found a new means of financing by looking for customers abroad and supporting productions with early public presentations. When Lepage performed in Avignon (1987), as he was just gaining recognition as a creator in Quebec – something European festivals accomplished – he had an ingenious method for finding co-producers or buyers who would get involved earlier and earlier and in greater and greater numbers for each project, resulting in major tours.[12] It isn't easy to convince an institution to become a partner or buyer for a show in progress, when they know full well that the current version is not the show in its finished state. Only Toronto's World Stage Festival twice took the risk of presenting such a show as a world premiere. From then on, the production plan differed from the traditional plan, exemplified in the Shakespeare Cycle of the 1980s: "fewer co-producers that decided together to do a project around an artist."[13] This meant increasing, in two-party contracts with Ex Machina, the number of co-producers likely to host the show, while guaranteeing it a share of the investment – generally thirty thousand euros per collaboration[14] – before the show was created.

This way of working is marketing American-style, reminiscent of start-ups and the Internet economy. Things move quickly after the launch of a product: the technical dimensions give way to financing and marketing. Marketing Lepage's shows, unfinished products, still in their first generation – like a piece of software or a computer concept – involves moving quickly, taking risks, and engaging a strategic process based largely on communication and financing, which are Bernatchez's terrain. Lepage's shows are like software: users know that their interation will soon be obsolete and will be replaced every eighteen months by a new version. Lepage's success is primarily due to the visual, narrative, and dramaturgical quality of his shows, made possible mainly because of a marketing effort that knows how to sell an unlikely offering.

Having more co-producers or buyers for a show extends its run, which means that its lifeblood – the actors and the technicians – are mobilized longer. The director and the designers remain free. This could be one of the reasons behind the turnover of actors from performance to performance, while designers and technicians tend to stay for a number of productions: Ex Machina keeps the technicians in closer contact with the machine than the actors, again reinforcing the semantic weight of the company's name. For example, the duo of Jacques Collin and Carl Fillion for image and stage design has been part of the troupe from *Elsinore* to the present day.[15]

A number of teams worked on Lepage's creations in the early years, but with Théâtre Repère, while he was co-artistic director from 1986 to 1989, there was a certain continuity among the actors. Later on, Lepage became the artistic director for French theatre at the National Arts Centre in Ottawa, from 1989 to 1993 – and received international commissions for directing, during which he would work with actors associated with the venue in question. But beginning with *The Dragons' Trilogy*, he wanted to be able to bring together different people without creating a permanent team. It just happened that all of the actors would continue working with him, although not exclusively. Richard Fréchette, for example, who was part of the second phase of the creation of *The Dragons' Trilogy*, was asked back for *The Seven Streams of the River Ota*. Marie Brassard took part in more than seven Lepage shows, co-writing *Polygraph* and then acting in the Shakespeare Cycle, *The Seven Streams of the River Ota*, and *The Geometry of Miracles*, in which she was the only actor from the early days to play opposite Lepage again. Marie Gignac played in *Tectonic Plates* and *The Seven Streams of the River Ota* and continues to work on projects with Lepage as an actress and playwright. These three actors have also pursued careers as actors and directors with other creators.

Actors moving from company to company and straddling several shows is common in Quebec. There are fewer barriers than in Europe. There are a number of explanations for this, including the fact that actors don't settle in one place, the desire to experiment, as well as migratory intermixing and the status of companies, which are subsidized for a particular show rather than through operating grants. The shows go on tours that last a number of years and visit several continents. *Polygraph* is without a doubt the show that was most seen, because it played multiple performances in more than 15 countries from May 1988 to February 1995, was then restaged in 1998 in Japan and in Italy, and then again in Spain in 2000. It went on a new tour in Italy and Spain.[16] *Needles and Opium* was staged 184 times from March 1992 to January 1996; *The Seven Streams of the River Ota* had a similar run: 168 performances in three and a half years, from August 1994 to March 1998.[17] Before that *The Dragons' Trilogy* ran nearly seven years, from November 1985 to August 1992, in 19 countries and 36 venues. In just 14 months, *The Far Side of the Moon* had racked up 81 performances, from February 2000 to April 2001, and the show was still touring in 2014, with Yves Jacques taking over the acting after June 2001.

For every solo show since *Needles and Opium*, Lepage has handed over his role to another actor. This means that the show can continue a run that he can no longer accommodate without stopping work on other creations. So after having created *Needles and Opium* in Quebec City in 1991, and performing the show in Montreal, Ottawa, New York, Frankfurt, Munich, Maubeuge, London, Florence, and Stockholm, Lepage handed over the role to Marc Labrèche.[18] The list of this show's tours provides a sense of the scope of such an operation: performance dates and locations cannot always be grouped together, which means that actors have to be available for at least two years. Problems arose for *The Seven Streams of the River Ota* and *The Geometry of Miracles*: tour fatigue and the requirements of other shows under way at the same time resulted in casting changes.

Lepage puts together his team and chooses his actors through encounters and a keen sense of curiosity: he doesn't hold auditions for his shows, but he brings together people who have caught his eye or indicated their interest. Lepage had seen Bosnian émigré and avant-garde director Tea Alagić[19] on video before inviting her to play Olgivanna Lloyd Wright in *The Geometry of Miracles*; dance-actor Rodrigue Proteau was spotted in performance with physical theatre company Carbone 14 in Montreal. Lepage looks for people to work with him and draws on their special resources. This non-exclusive relationship with the actors and the demands of touring could explain his fragmented approach to creation: it's harder to find six consecutive weeks when the entire team is available than to find three periods of two or three weeks.

Lepage's creations have involved particular teams, but also a physical framework that has evolved from locations that are available rather than chosen, to a fully designed location for exclusive use: La Caserne. The early productions were rehearsed in all sorts of places: universities, small theatres, and other sites. Resources and facilities were paltry, which had a definite impact on the aesthetic and the means deployed. The rehearsals for *The Dragons' Trilogy* were held in a room on Rue Saint-Paul that Théâtre Repère was going to vacate after the second phase of creation. Inspiration for improvisation was found in the reality of where the show was created, and the show used the lighting found on-site. The warehouse in which the entire show was performed two years later reflected the aesthetic of the site of its creation.

Lepage then began to work in very different locations. He soon wanted a home base to work on projects. After having made

connections between a multitude of countries and people, he would
bring them together in Quebec City, as if simply pulling on their
strings.[20] La Caserne was not just the result of a desire to limit travel
and creation costs, but it also fit with his idea that creative work is
influenced by place. La Caserne is an all-purpose site, the result of
the director's fifteen years of experience. When he said he wanted
to set up shop in Quebec City in 1993, the municipality offered him
an old firehouse, built at the beginning of the twentieth century.[21]
It had been abandoned in the 1980s and was slowly sinking into the
crumbling ground on the shores of the St. Lawrence. The envelope,
the layout, the circulation of people, electricity, and electronic
information … every detail of George-Émile Tanguay's 1902 design
was studied by architects Jacques Plante and Marc Julien, stage
design consultant Michel Gosselin, engineer Louis Larouche,
and contractor Lauréat Pépin during the development of the site.
Lepage wanted a space that met all the requirements of creation.
All sorts of images would be created there. It had to accommodate
theatre as well as opera rehearsals, be used as a film or television
set – most of *Nô* was shot at La Caserne, and it accommodated,
with great difficulty, the metal scaffolding stage set for *Zulu Time*.
In short, it is a multimedia centre. Lepage's La Caserne is a site for
creation, a space for development and rehearsal, which can, on
occasion, open its doors to the public.

> The heritage facade
> and the black cube
> of La Caserne,
> Quebec City.
>
> PHOTO
> Yves Fillion

   In many respects, the architectural structure designed
by Lepage and his collaborators also uses the site as scenery. A
fibreglass moulding of the original facade – the Second Empire
facade – is detached from the building, raised on jacks, and
almost self-supporting. It was created by Martin Beausoleil, a
specialist in television sets. Behind the facade is a glass wall with
aluminum frames. Certain support columns were moved to free
up as much space as possible for the stage and to allow for a true
stage to emerge. The work took seventeen months, and the site
was inaugurated on June 2, 1997.[22]

   La Caserne also houses offices for Ex Machina's and
Robert Lepage Inc.'s administrative staff, and, since 2004, the
adjoining building has been used as an administrative annex. It's
also equipped with two rehearsal studios, a small set and carpentry
workshop, and rooms used by the designers or rented to small companies that work with Ex Machina as partners.[23] The designers set

> Black granite clads
> the back wall
> of La Caserne,
> Quebec City.
>
> PHOTO
> Ludovic Fouquet

up their workshops at La Caserne: Jacques Collin for the creation
of images and Carl Fillion for stage design until 2004 – one of the
doors of his workshop led directly onto the stage.

The major achievement of this project is stage one, a
black box attached to the Second Empire facade, the heart of
the building. It's a large cube measuring 18.25 by 16.45 metres
and has an under-beam height of 9 metres. The sides of the cube
have a variety of openings. An immense metal curtain makes it
possible to open the room to the street to bring equipment in,
but also to extend a show onto the street or gather an audience.
The windows of workshops and offices that run along the three
other sides can be closed off like the main opening. Collaborators therefore have direct access to the stage and can watch
the rehearsals, project images, provide information from their
windows or from the bridges that run the length of the walls.
Information circulates very quickly in this tightly packed area,
which also provides room for many work spaces: it's a veritable
nave and a strange compromise between a national theatre not
restricted to only domestic performances, a Renaissance academy, and a multinational enterprise. All sorts of researchers,
scientists, and artists are invited to work in the space either on
Lepage's projects or to participate in colloquia, meetings about
technology, or other events, for which La Caserne regularly rents
out space. Collaborations with technology industries and Laval
University would develop later on. "Lepage wants to recreate
the spirit of the Renaissance workshops, where playwrights,
architects, painters, and sculptors mix with scientists."[24] This
idea of workshops is clear in Lepage's intentions, although he is
aware that Quebec City is no modern-day Florence.[25] La Caserne
is at one and the same time part of the world of the theatre and
a laboratory workshop, like Svoboda had started in 1957 at the
National Theatre in Prague, with his retinue of engineers and
technicians, uncommon professions in the world of theatre at
the time. La Caserne has taken up the torch for this experiment,
although designed for a single company.

The stage is equipped with forty removable trap doors
that measure 223 by 114 centimetres. From the surface of these trap
doors, there is a usable height of 12.5 metres rather than 30, and a
width of almost 16 metres, dimensions that many theatres would

The cube seen
from the bridges
at La Caserne.
The windows of
the workshops are
on the opposite
wall, overlooking
the work space.

PHOTO

Ludovic Fouquet

envy. There are highly accessible anchoring and power-source points, thanks to perpendicular, movable beams. These points can even be extended right into the street, using a uniquely designed bridge that can transport lighting and sound. The entire back of the building, opening onto the short Rue Bell, is polished black granite with carved diagonal grooves, framing the large metal curtain. These are at one and the same time vanishing points, veiled references to the Renaissance and perspective, but also a metaphor for a theatre that, behind the heavy metal curtain, places man at the centre of the set.

Lepage's universe is found in this opposition of the two facades. Two aesthetics are expressed in two different forms: firehouse and theatre, old and new, traditional facade in worked and warm stone in the front, avant-garde granite facade in the back, stripped of any ornamentation, dug out like certain Japanese rock gardens. However, both function as a curtain: they mask and foreshadow the theatre activity going on in the heart of the black cube. This opposition becomes the *dramatis personae* of any venture into architecture, just as it is in Lepage's practice.

Lepage chose Quebec City, his hometown, as the location for this centre, a city that has regularly served him as inspiration,[26] and in which he came up theatrically. While Quebec City is the official capital of the province, locating the centre there clearly thumbs a nose at Montreal, the cultural capital. His point is not to spurn Montreal – Lepage puts on a show there about once a year – but rather to get away from its bustle. After long periods spent on the road and creating overlapping productions in several countries or theatres at the same time, Lepage feels the need to withdraw. The isolation is necessary for him, not so much to retreat to allow the fruits of his reflections to emerge, but to have the complete attention of his collaborators. Quebec City was chosen for its distance from Montreal. For Montreal actors, it means moving away from their usual surroundings and, for the others, it means being immersed in a quiet city. During the phases of creation, the participants "have nothing better to do" than to enter their creative bubble.

FROM OPENNESS TO VERTIGO: LEPAGE'S APPROACH

The creative principle that underlies Lepage's creations is merely an update of the underlying principle of collective creations: the actor is a creator.[27] For Lepage, the actor is a co-author; other creators are present, but the actor is invited to participate in story development. This applies even for repertory pieces; Lepage allowed himself a great deal of freedom and did a lot of work at the table on the plot of *Elsinore* and *A Dream Play*.[28] The classics are usually marked by stronger, more restrictive scenography that requires that the actor be used in a particular way, which results in more limited research and freedom: acting off balance in the cube of *A Dream Play*, a truncated silhouette and parody of the movie screen for *Coriolanus*, theatre within a theatre for *The Tempest* in the Shakespeare Cycle, for which there was a public rehearsal for the first part. This involves devising a specific sort of involvement of the performer. This quest has translated into an increasing propensity to invite performers who aren't specialized in text-based theatre, even in theatre itself, to work from their own world to create a theatrical tale.

During a round table at the Festival de théâtre des Amériques, the actors from *The Seven Streams of the River Ota* talked about the work process, centred first around the table. Lepage began by sharing his ideas with them: seven boxes, seven streams, seven sliding Japanese doors, a house, and a garden. The idea of including concentration camps came up, which could intersect with Hiroshima and Chinese opera. At the beginning, there were seven cities (New York, Paris, Beijing, Prague, and so on) and seven rivers. He explained what had touched him during his visit to Japan, showing them different documents, having them watch Alain Resnais's film *Hiroshima mon amour*, in which the words of Marguerite Duras resonate so intensely and ended up being the source of the play's title.[29] Then he waited for reactions, as he had done for *The Dragons' Trilogy* and would do again for *The Geometry of Miracles* and *Zulu Time*. Lepage seeks reactions to the stimulus, which vary in number and specificity, from the people he has brought together: "When we start working on a project, I'll have more questions [for the actors] than answers."[30] The actors have the sense of starting from scratch, with "practically nothing to go on,"[31] and of truly building the show, the connections they gradually develop, creating "a sort of matrix that generates characters, places, and situations."[32]

Lepage is driven by instinct and spontaneous reaction, as a result of his beginnings in improvisation. So it's not surprising that the first thing he asked the nine creators of *The Seven Streams of the River Ota* was to react through drawings. Then words were added, and everyone was invited to suggest ideas and test connections and extensions of the narrative: "We could be in Hiroshima and a woman ..." or "There could be a Quebecer on a calligraphy internship ..." Disparate, incongruous suggestions emerged, and they were sorted through and integrated, an effort was made to bring elements closer together through the notes and transcriptions of all these discussions, notes made by one or more of Lepage's assistants on laptop. During *The Geometry of Miracles*, for example, remarks constantly circulated, as did all sorts of documents. A veritable library was cobbled together near the work table: books on architecture, on Wright in particular, on the avant-garde at the turn of the century, and on Gurdjieff. At the beginning of this phase of creation, new books, photocopies,

and snapshots were brought in by each of the designers, who
reported on their inquiries. The long rectangular table became
a site of convergence.

It is around this table, rather than a fire, that a first audience is tested, to ensure that the story comes across effectively.
There is something comfortable, oral, and collective in this initial
gathering – with the content of the message considered more than
its speaker, content that is immediately absorbed in the collective
work taking shape. It's as if the theatrical work in the strict sense
of the term is postponed – even held back – to concentrate on the
creation phase inspired largely from the very thing it questions:
writing. In fact, the work at the table, the progressive drafting of
notes, and the accumulation of archives all reproduces the classic
conditions of writing a story. Lepage has gotten rid of the author,
but then more than a dozen authors are found, chained to the work
table! Scribes are designated, not to replace the author, because the
author is collective, but to write down what is said.

The way space and elements are distributed in La Caserne's
large black cube is meaningful: the long rectangular table recreates
the rectangular wooden set, each on opposite sides of the cube.
Two spheres coexist in the space: the table facing the stage, the
planning space facing the experimentation space, a first step toward
the show. Participants move back and forth between table and stage
during the final period of rehearsals. Quite often, an idea everyone
agrees on is tested out immediately onstage: everyone gets up and
improvises in small groups. Using a few props, the actors sketch out
a realistic or poetic illustration of an anecdote or an image discussed
around the table. This approach produces the result through the
actors' work alone, and at the same time what is produced is merely
the product, the trace, or the residue of what was said around the
table. Every improvisation done in groups of two or four is the fruit
of a story told by twelve. Once again, it's an echo.

Work is done at the table at every stage in the creation.
Work resumes at the end of the journey, the point at which writing
takes place. The actors return to the table to write their text from
the transcript of discussions, from improvisations, from Lepage's
notes, if any, but also from their own memories and emotions.
This writing with many hands and in many phases is effortless
and is a textual echo of the exchanges that have occurred as

Collaborative creation
in rectangular form,
a classic work scene
at La Caserne.

PHOTO

Ludovic Fouquet

much as retranscription. The writing occurs at the end of the creation process. It's rarely the foundation of it, except in solo productions such as *The Far Side of the Moon*, because Lepagean theatre of images is put down in writing only once the images are established: "Theatre isn't literature. Theatre is about writing. And literature and writing are two different things. People tend not to realize that. Writing is an ongoing process. It's full of unfinished sentences, crossed-out words. And when I'm told my writing is awkward, it stimulates me."[33] This practice, which was tried and tested with *The Dragons' Trilogy* and *The Seven Streams of the River Ota*, resulted in the emergence of Marie Brassard, who didn't refer to herself as "the author of the text" and who didn't see herself writing in any way other than through improvisation. She has since written and staged a number of productions, by practising this retranscription, dreamlike in the case of *Jimmy, créature de rêve*. This practice also made it possible for some of the actors to make the move to directing, such as Marie Gignac. But it also exposes the designers to the risk of using a text that may be weak, depending on the contributors' suggestions. The contributors are actors first and foremost, with varying levels of curiosity and experience, and they don't always have a complete command of the language of expression. Communication among an international cast like for *The Geometry of Miracles* required exchanges in English and occasionally in French, when a francophone actor didn't understand something or needed French to express himself.[34] Some feel a language barrier, and while they can take part in the conversation, they can't always express themselves fully. The result is an often impressionist text, that at times resorts to cliché, which reduces the poetic range and the humorous distance that other creations allow.[35]

Generally speaking, the text is not the crux of Lepagean theatre. Wilfully funny, realistic, and laconic, it shines more for its power to make contact than for what it expresses; the last solo productions, however, place new importance on the text. While the approach is not uninterested in words, it's not primarily literary. But Lepage doesn't create theatre without text, even with *Zulu Time*, which is the most radical experiment in this sense; he doesn't ignore text completely. He reserves a special place for words, the word more than the text, and the tale more than the literary narrative. The idea of the storyteller, a tutelary and archetypal image, hovers over all of Lepage's creations. A long way from text-centred French theatre, Lepage's practice deals with the text but doesn't start from the text; it leaves space for the text, but decentres it. In fact this practice leaves nothing in the centre, other than a clear desire for constructing scenography, with every element becoming a satellite in this characteristically loose conglomeration. This is why there are many scenes without words in Lepage's work. The scores aren't exclusively textual or verbal; the typescripts of the first solo shows are good examples of this. They break down the show into sequences that are more descriptions of actions, images in the process of appearing, rather than lines.

But there are also departures from this principle. *The Dragons' Trilogy* and *The Seven Streams of the River Ota* have scenes with text that is strong, poetic, and dense: Hanako's description of her garden, the spare dialogues between Nozomi and Luke O'Connor, Hanako's translation problems with Rimbaud. These two shows demonstrate that collective writing isn't necessarily superficial or weak, which is not to suggest that there isn't the occasional excess of cliché. In his solo shows, Lepage doesn't have as many intermediaries between his ideas for scenography, dramaturgy, and scriptwriting. The writing in *Vinci* is skilful, and the writing in *Needles and Opium*, primarily at the service of the image, uses poetry and metaphor, in a whole that works in snippets. It becomes a mosaic text, as can be said of certain treatments of images since Svoboda, in particular. In Quebec City in 2001, *The Far Side of the Moon* received four Masques awards, including one for the writing, which shows a deft blend of humour, emotion, and demonstration. During the creation of this production, Lepage had surrounded himself with contributors with proven writing skills, which in a sense calls into question the premise of collective writing, which seems fairly uneven from one show to the next, presupposing more than simple intuitions and generous acting.

It is undoubtedly to make up for this unevenness that since *The Dragons' Trilogy* Lepage has at times relied on a shared language that is physical rather than verbal, a more certain means of getting around the local to find a universal language, which he succeeds at in his use of projected images. In *The Dragons' Trilogy* and *The Geometry of Miracles,* in addition to gathering around the table to find the words, a common language was created from common movements: *tai chi* for *The Dragons' Trilogy* and exercises inspired from Gurdjieff's sacred dances for *The Geometry of Miracles*. In the final phase of work, elements are drawn both from the work at the table and this language of gestures. This language is initially developed independent of any dramaturgical reflection or reference to the story, and of course that is precisely where the most effective communication can happen, requiring only the body as a common lexicon.

Every day of rehearsals for *The Geometry of Miracles* began with dance exercises, which Lepage didn't take part in, leaving the actors to their work. Rodrigue Proteau was the rehearsal coach, and he drew inspiration from movements taken from Gurdjieff's dances.[36] As the days passed, the exercises fused the actors in a common dynamic, ensuring visual effectiveness – resulting in the most beautiful tableaus of the show, such as the scene of Svetlana's accident intersecting the "dance of the heron" performed by Gurdjieff's disciples – as well as group unity, trust, and mutual respect. This is the sense in which Lepage explains that *tai chi* was a key element in the creation of *The Dragons' Trilogy*: "We have to discover a language specific to each show. Getting there can be as simple as doing a bit of exercise and warm-ups … anything, even if the language is not precise, the important thing is that the bodies move together."[37]

Every show thus shares common preparatory work (vocal, physical, and textual), but because a form of physical exercise often occurs in the initial phases of choreography, it is seen at once as a warm-up, getting in shape, and shared material likely to be used in the creation. *Zulu Time* connects the actors in a common energy, the reinterpreted Zulu dance, with an opening marked by acrobatics and the talents of contortionists or actors suspended from the scaffolding stage set.[38] These exercises are therefore an essential alternative to work at the table. Used more at the beginning of rehearsals, they are also a way of postponing the moment of confronting the story and the stage: indirectly, the show is being tamed. As these danced sequences become increasingly homogeneous, the story is put together, sometimes integrating choreographed movements. The great discovery at the end of rehearsals for *The Geometry of Miracles* was how the exercises of Gurdjieff's disciples, practised in particular at Château Le Prieuré at Fontainebleau-Avon, France, can be placed anywhere, superimposing themselves on the gatherings of the architect's apprentices, particularly once Gurdjieff finds himself at Wright's Taliesin Fellowship in Spring Green, Wisconsin.

Lepage's creative work very quickly became structured around a few themes that simultaneously exploit the notions of chaos and order, inspiration and system, chance and planning. The frame is meant as stimulating limitation.

> I spent only three weeks at Knapp in Paris, but one of
> the principles I came away with is that the more you
> impose barriers, limits of time and space, the more the
> work and the show benefit […] I've always worked
> that way. But it was the first time I imposed this prin-
> ciple on a group [during *The Dragons' Trilogy*]. At
> times it was traumatic, but by the second phase, we
> started to believe more in the method because it had
> produced results for the first phase.[39]

While the creative work uses the principle of the work in progress, limitations are nonetheless imposed. A time limit is set on each stage of creation even before it begins: Lepage's creation gains meaning and impact in gathering and urgency. Urgency is an integral part of the early shows (*The Dragons' Trilogy*) and is illustrated in the Shakespeare Cycle, with the three plays being created in five weeks during a residency in Maubeuge, France, in 1992. The time limit is in keeping with a very definite framework for scenic design and idea for the set: film in the case of *Coriolanus*, the rehearsal room angle for *The Tempest*, a two-tiered stage for *Macbeth*. Over the years, the desire to create in urgency has transformed into a desire to create within a framework, during clearly defined working hours. Work for Ex Machina is planned more than one year in advance of the dates for each phase of creation. The pace of work for the last phase of creation of *The Geometry of Miracles* is typical in this. Rehearsals began at half past nine every morning, broke at one o'clock, and resumed again from seven to ten in the evening. During the first four weeks of rehearsals, the actors worked at set times, six days a week. Lepage was managing to get in seven hours of daily rehearsal, while freeing up the afternoons. After a few days, everyone settled into the pace. Space and schedules allowed the creation to blossom, without any real urgency, or at least with an urgency concealed by regularity, as often happens in creative residencies.

But the afternoon provided a break only for the actors, freeing up the stage for the technicians and designers. The actors didn't see the technicians and designers, or saw very little of them, which in a way left the actors to pure, quiet research, relieved of the duty of performance. It was as if two teams were in rehearsal every day, using the same space and converging more or less directly on the same stage. Every day the set would come together a little more, whether perceptibly or not. When rehearsals resumed, the lighting would have evolved, elements such as the projectors would be better positioned. The actors didn't necessarily realize that there were twelve more than the day before, but their addition allowed for increasingly refined moods. This fixed schedule, aside from encouraging a fairly calm creative rhythm, also allowed the show to evolve along two trajectories.

Lepage is the great unifier in this process. He starts from nothing, combining questions and instincts, without knowing exactly where he is going or exactly what the show will look like. This is why so much effort goes into making the actors feel comfortable: they aren't used to working so out in the open and following the trail of coincidences, and they generally hate uncertainty. For Lepage, preparing the actors means getting them to see that he too is letting himself be guided. What is troubling for them during rehearsals is that Lepage knows exactly how the set has to be, while many shadowy areas in the story remain.

The third and final phase of work on *The Geometry of Miracles* started with wiping clean the slate of the story and the narrative elements generated in previous phases. Although the same doesn't apply to the scenic design, because the approach remained similar: the set was the same and ideas that closed out the previous phase of creation were reused. During the first weeks, the actors worked by trial and error while the technicians' work was more advanced. They built a kinetic set without knowing exactly what would go on inside it: movements of the revolving stage, fire, rain, moving screens, and so on; the set was ahead of the story. So when improvisations began around Taliesin, the white tent was already set up and suspended, and the lighting planned. Lepage had anticipated certain images or, more precisely he had imagined a *pièce à tiroirs* (a story within a story), and the creative work consisted of exploring its possibilities. The whole team had to get rid of preconceived ideas and approaches and be open to new directions. The resistance of the actors is not unlike the attitude of the audience in these works in progress, who remain attached to the version they originally lit upon. In our own experience, the first version is always the strongest and is the favourite of the audience, as though the newness, the mastery, and the balance of later offerings can't compensate for the impact of discovery.

Lepage navigates his vessel through uncertain waters or more precisely through fog, which for him is the basis of receptiveness.[40] But he imposes areas where navigation isn't permitted, areas he doesn't want to cover again for the time being. The actors willingly adopt this notion of chaotic work, making them feel as though they aren't being directed, while sensing the extent to which, through this trial and error, Lepage finds the answer to certain instincts or acts without prior judgement when he proposes opening a "door." Thus the diplomat couple emerged from an improvisation around a photo booth and connected with the idea of having theatre within theatre in part of *The Seven Streams of the River Ota*. The director works from his material as it emerges. His strength lies in the ability to orient the creation from the work done at the table without appearing to do so, to connect with, through conversations and experiments, the instincts that initially drove the work and to arrive at a collectively created show, while pursuing his own intuitions. "Chaos is necessary. If there is only order and rigour in a project, the outcome will be nothing but order and rigour. But it's out of chaos that the cosmos is born – the order of things, yes, but a living, organic, changing one. This is where true creation lies."[41]

This principle is explicit in *The Far Side of the Moon*, when Philippe explains the nuances between cosmos and chaos to the bartender, who doesn't see the difference between cosmonauts (Russian) and astronauts (American). The cosmonaut is supposed to be searching for the cosmos, therefore order and organization; for the Greeks, the harmonious organization of creation was synonymous with beauty.[42] Lepage untangles the usual dichotomy between the cosmos – "involving conviction, certainty, order" – and chaos – "involving doubt, uncertainty, disorder" – making them "two faces of the same phenomenon, and specifically the phenomenon of the theatrical act."[43] Complementary steps or, rather, steps necessary from chaos toward the cosmos and balance. Eight days before the first public rehearsal of *The Geometry of Miracles*, the team still didn't know exactly how to play the architect, who tended to be the pretext rather than the protagonist of the tale. This is revealing of Lepage's work, which progresses without necessarily answering questions that, in another context, would come before any dramatic research. Lepage put off this decision to the end of the process so that he could experiment. This desire to put off the dramatic composition nourishes the research, at the price of actor anxiety. During this period, Lepage preferred a "cubic version" that would have more actors playing Frank Lloyd Wright. In his eyes, the solution would be found in improvisation, in building the character.[44] The meal scene at Wright's Taliesin

Fellowship was played again, using a silhouette seen from behind, an easily reproducible image from actor to actor.

Lepage's interventions have mainly to do with rhythm. In giving actors a great deal of freedom in their performances, Lepage constructs his tableaus with precision without being rigid, like blocking in film, in which one marks the ground, studies the movements of the camera, and repositions elements according to the framed image. Sometimes, a scene has to be replayed for greater clarity, particularly if he feels that the lines involve codes or innuendos raised around the work table that the audience isn't in on. For the Fellowship scene, Lepage insisted on the coherence of the text and on the importance of distinguishing accents, particularly once the scene started to be worked text in hand, four days before the public rehearsal. He listens to the actors' lines with a musical ear, and he isn't afraid to suggest improvisation that replaces lines with an invented language in Slavic tones. Once again, concern for the general colour wins over precision. The visual aspect and placement is first, followed by the sound aspect, and only then the semantic aspect: structure prevails over words.

To set a deadline for this creative process in motion and ultimately produce a performance, Lepage uses a system of one to four public rehearsals to close the creation phase. These are not to be confused with the first performances that can come close on the heels of the creation phase: the public rehearsal directly follows rehearsals; it is held in the same place and presents, in a cross-disciplinary coming together that benefits the production, the show at its current stage of development, which is incomplete and has gaps in the material. Holding public rehearsals is a practice that is becoming more common, but Lepage used it very early on, and it's an essential part of his creative process.

The idea of urgency, which doesn't conflict with the notion of trust in chance and coincidence, runs through Lepage's practice. He doesn't allow himself the time or the means to polish a production in studio; he wants this to be done in public during the tour, because it's only at that point that the material seems to truly come to life for him.

But the public rehearsal always comes too soon for the players involved. La Caserne thus reveals its capacity for metamorphosis. In a few hours on the morning of March 9, 1998, the rehearsal space was transformed into a performance space with a capacity for about one hundred. The large work table was replaced by benches; what was already at times an area for observation became plainly *a place for viewing*. The control areas were also set up. The black-box space turned out to be perfectly designed for such a performance: the hallways that border the studio – and therefore the set, taking up almost the entire width – serve as the wings, and the black walls of the studio act as legs, providing three accesses to the stage. The public rehearsal allowed the actors and technicians to size up the venture in practical terms: props management, moving people and objects, costume changes, and set changes. There had been run-throughs before, but they didn't bring together all of the elements used for every scene. This feverishness – receiving final costumes in the hours before the show, discovering the important props only the night before the premiere – is common in theatre. What is specific to Lepage is that the narrative choices haven't been made at this critical moment. While not a traditional premiere, a public rehearsal inserted in the work in progress still marks the end of the research process. On the morning of the dress rehearsal, Lepage dictated the places and different ideas to his assistant, but in particular he asked the actors, who continued to work on the scenes among themselves, to meet back in the afternoon to continue to develop the story. There was still only a basic structure of thirty-one scenes, to varying degrees written, or rather, transcribed. From this general framework, nine scenes would not be performed because they were not advanced enough. Clearly the public was being invited to watch a show still under development, but now open to others.[45] The mysterious heart of the black box became a public space. The energy and exchanges were no longer centripetal, but were beginning their first movements outward.

 INTERVALS AND OVERLAPS IN PHASES OF WORK

The fact that these phases of creation are so close together in time doesn't mean that they are simply juxtapositions, the result of approaches or problems that Lepage solves one after the other. They are one of the ways of organizing the chaos around the run-through of a given work. The dates of the many later phases are set during the first phase of rehearsals. Things aren't all settled in a single phase. The time between the phases is part of the process; it may even be more important than the phase when everyone comes together. The intervals are generally quite long between the stages of work: from five to eight months. Thus the creation of *The Dragons' Trilogy* stretched over a year and a half, from October 1985 to June 1987, with intervals of six and twelve months between the three phases of creation. *The Seven Streams of the River Ota* involved three phases spread over three years, from January 1994 to May 1997, with a major reorganization one year after the final phase. The creation of *The Geometry of Miracles* was condensed into one year, with phases separated by five and seven months, from February 1997 to March 1998. The break becomes an essential moment of gestation. It takes into account people's availability, but it also reflects a production strategy that provides time for the technological, dramatic, scenographic, and musical development of a show. Integration work begins during this break that couldn't really be done during rehearsals. This time is also used for reading, research, and even travel, on the theme of the show. Far removed from the creation team, each person can assess the group's work and their own contribution to it. All this of course applies to collectively created shows; for repertory pieces, the approach is different, although similar.

The technological shows, because of the equipment expertise required – managing equipment and exploring new con-figurations – are necessarily built in several stages. The technical fine tuning takes a lot of time. The ideas of a director like Lepage aren't necessarily based on technological realities. They pose the challenge for designers creating images and new and poetic environments, which require research that can't be done during the rehearsals at the risk of holding up all the contributors. Michel Gosselin, technical coordinator for *Zulu Time*, said: "The greatest challenge was to assume we would achieve what we wanted to without knowing whether the equipment existed. There was also a share of improvisation and risk. There are surprises every day, and we keep asking technology to do things it wasn't designed for."[46] Just as with his actors, Lepage also asks the designers, the "technologicians" (a Lepage expression) to propose ways to create the images, sets, and atmosphere he envisions. These images and devices often find an expression onstage: sometimes, an accident is exploited. Here too, chance, a new expression of stage improvisation developed by the actors, can be a driver. Where a "traditional" show – such as the Shakespeare Cycle – can be created in a few weeks and in a single phase of work, the technological shows require breaks in their creation so that each contributor can develop material individually. And one can easily see that this break of several months isn't a luxury when one has to create one hundred 3-D illustrations (*Jean-Sans-Nom*) or virtual-animation loops in relief (*The Tempest*).

The break also allows participants to work on the disciplines involved in certain shows. Lepage had to lose weight and gain strength and flexibility to perform the acrobatics for *Needles and Opium*, a show that required him to be harnessed and suspended from wires. The breaks between phases of rehearsals allowed actor Marco Poulain, an electric bass player – he plays in *The Busker's Opera* – to learn double bass, an instrument that he plays convincingly in *Zulu Time*. At the same time, after the first phase of work, Michel F. Côté experimented with techno, meeting DJs, trying out their equipment, and improving his skills on the sequencer. The break is also used to find new co-producers, get confirmations of involvement, and put together the tour. Each step of creation allows the production – the administrator, the producers, the production manager, who started work before the first rehearsal – to better identify the intention, aesthetics, and particular qualities of the show and its technical requirements.

The phases of creation for a show don't fall along a straight line. In fact, the rehearsal and occupancy schedule for La Caserne shows that phases of creation overlap and that several shows are developed at the same time: like individuals, they cross paths. The designers and technicians don't all need the same amount of time to fine-tune their work; as a result some are freed up before the new phase of creation of the same show. For instance, the final phase of work for *The Seven Streams of the River Ota* in May and June 1997 came between the first two phases of creation of *The Geometry of Miracles* in February and July 1997.

The show isn't designed as an independent block or a closed unit that takes its place in the chain of creations. Lepage needs to provoke intersections, like so many pauses, moments that encourage coincidences and continuums. He works on several projects at once, as one would mark out one's world or the

route with pegs for better climbing. Lulls are not allowed, and
neither is a sense of certainty. Lepage seems to be reassured when
there are still other riddles to solve. Having overlapping phases
of creation fits in with the need for chaos, the same "obligation
of uncertainty."[47] Not only do rehearsals alternate, but multiple
projects often intersect within a single phase of rehearsals. While
Lepage was working on the third version of *The Geometry of Miracles*
in February and March 1998, he was monitoring the development
of images for *The Tempest* and thinking about another project with
one of the actors from *The Geometry of Miracles* during some of
his afternoon breaks. He was editing *Nô* during the first phases of
The Geometry of Miracles. Similarly, during the rehearsals for *Zulu
Time*, he was editing *Possible Worlds* (2000).[48] All of this is now
possible in Quebec City at La Caserne, whereas he used to have
to go from rehearsals in Montreal or Stockholm to editing in Paris
or Montreal.[49] The effect of different phases of work happening in
parallel is seen through the similar treatments. One even gets the
sense at times that a workaround for a stage or narrative sequence
is found in the work on another show, which lends support to the
idea that Lepage pursues the same work from performance to
performance: "Each show is the resource for the next; this is why
you find a lot of *Vinci* and *The Dragons' Trilogy* in *Carmen*. Not
only in its visual aspect, style, or aesthetic, but also in what it talks
about, in the impressions it creates."[50]

    By requiring that the production team work on different
projects at once, Lepage reveals the secret of his stimulation. A
break during a rehearsal means moving to another project. The
virtual images in *The Tempest* plunged Lepage into a different
world than that of *The Geometry of Miracles*, a show that used
few images – or at least ones that raise few challenges – and was
built from a collectively written text. These breaks allowed the
designer to shift his attention from *The Geometry of Miracles*,
which had its moments of crisis, stagnation, doubt, incubation,
and resistance from the actors. It also provided the opportunity to
try out ideas for scenic design when they posed a problem in the
first project. Crossovers are fundamentally restorative for Lepage,
with one show reacting to another. What he merely sketches in
A Dream Play, he develops fully in *The Seven Streams of the River
Ota* – the periods of creation of which overlapped – using what

was advanced in *A Dream Play*. The evolution of the set in the box is testimony to this: *The Seven Streams of the River Ota* realizes the ideal model of the closed box. After this, Lepage would treat the box as an angle and container (*A Dream Play*) or suggest a symbolic box (*The Geometry of Miracles*). The opera *1984* would pick up this line of thought again, literally recycling the cube from *A Dream Play* inside a circular set.

Ideas can cross over to different forms of performance, from the stage to the screen, for example, with the mirror panel used as a table in the film *Possible Worlds* and in the show *The Far Side of the Moon*, both created in 2000. In *Possible Worlds*, a high-angle dolly shot shows objects floating in the water, a reflective aquatic surface that, when the camera stops moving, is transformed into the shimmering surface of a shining table. It's the stylized image of photos being developed in a tray, and the objects are clues photographed at the scene of the crime by the young inspector. The protagonist is at the end of this table, just barely visible from the waist up and extended by the reflection of his image on the table. The same treatment appears in *The Far Side of the Moon*: in a hotel bar, Philippe waits for a cosmonaut visiting Montreal. To suggest the location, a wall clock is projected and the mirror panel is inclined toward the audience, almost horizontally, 1.5 metres high. Lepage is sitting on a bar stool; only his chest is visible, divided in two and inverted on the surface of the mirror.

It was during one of the overlapping intervals that Francis Leclerc shot his film version of *The Seven Streams of the River Ota*, which had a real impact on the final stage version of the show. In fact, the outside perspective he offered helped the designers take a step back and re-evaluate scenarios, logic, and story outlines that they had not been able to or didn't want to get rid of during the final phase of creation. In the film, which is seven times seven minutes long, each part opens on the symbolic and strangely reverent image of a protagonist. This goes back to one of the original ideas for the show of making each box coincide with a symbolic protagonist, an idea that was progressively dismissed for more links between the protagonists.

Over time, the overlaps are tempered somewhat. With each work, the creation and reflection time for each phase is extended. There is no longer the same urgency; there is no longer a compulsion to have many projects going at once. Instincts are developed more and explored in greater isolation. Certain projects were delayed, such as the show *Kà* staged for Cirque du Soleil in 2004, which resulted in gaps in phases of creation and a commensurate extension of the breaks. The projects spend longer in rehearsal; at the same time Lepage has more time to gather information around an idea. For instance, for *La Casa Azul* there was a reading and the beginnings of work on scenic design – a canopy bed, a mirror, a room with an accentuated perspective – over two years before the first phase of work in November 2001. The true development of the text only started in June 2001 for a show in December.[51] The preparatory work was long, but the creation time was cut by a third, because there were only two phases of rehearsals. Similarly, two years earlier, a Spanish-Quebec project in Salamanca around *La Celestina* and the opera *1984* in London were in planning, leaving time not for actual preparatory work, but to awaken interests and stir up curiosity in a wealth of images, sensations, and knowledge. This is what made *The Andersen Project* possible, which Lepage initially had no interest in doing. Lepage was commissioned to do a show about Hans Christian Andersen for the two-hundredth anniversary of the author's birth, but the tales didn't resonate with him, nor did the biography that was then proposed to him. It was in reading the author's journal that a troubled, hidden face appeared that echoed in Lepage's imagination and story.

Ideas circulate from one project to another, either to provide solutions or to provide a counterpoint. The sobriety, manual movement of elements, and thinking about the group from *The Geometry of Miracles* is contrasted with the high-tech aesthetic and gigantism yet solitude of *Zulu Time*. Similarly *The Far Side of the Moon*, performed solo with a small team, contrasts with the final version of *Zulu Time*, a techno cabaret with its increasing number of people – six musicians rather than two, the involvement of Peter Gabriel, and the search for new numbers. *Zulu Time* is the opportunity for a technological spectacle, whereas *The Far Side of the Moon* uses technology parsimoniously, in a sober set reminiscent of the first solo experiments. The crossover between projects creates a vital force of opposition. The work advances by diversifying; it finds itself, and gains unity and strength, not through concentration but by opening up. Lepage finds unity in quantity and intersections.

By studying rehearsals, I was able to get a sense of how Lepage makes changes, which can dominate the creation process and make Lepage lose control, for the sake of receptiveness. *The Geometry of Miracles*, which had disappointments and aborted efforts, is an example of an outcome that Lepage had always been able to avoid, with so much room accorded to the evolution of material that it took precedence over the story and set management. Suddenly Lepage, the maker of images and teller of tales, let himself be mesmerized by the malleability of the material, and lost his final perspective, the power of unification that is his strength. *The Geometry of Miracles* was the result of a great deal of assembled material, but also endless change. Lepage, who had proven his method and his control, lost control, and the transformation of material became the most important thing for the theatre company. He relegated aesthetic and dramatic concerns to second and third place.

In *The Geometry of Miracles*, explorations led to anecdotes and concepts being oversimplified, when one considers the body of knowledge the actors accumulated. Of course, collective creation leads to all sorts of interventions and suggestions that have to be sorted, selected, and organized. In this show, the form outshone the substance. By more than one account, the show's set demonstrated the designer's maturity in visible notions of theatricality, visual sequences inherited from film, and simultaneous action. The images – as long as the sand was in place – were both strong and sober, playing magnificently with scale and references. However, the material doesn't seem to have been controlled effectively, revealing a poor choice of dramaturge: actress and improvised playwright Rebecca Blankenship.[52] In *The Busker's Opera*, the text, a simple pretext for a cabaret, is hard to understand, and it would have benefited from dramaturgical awareness. Faced with material that has been collected but not digested, juxtaposed, and is difficult to organize, Lepage advocates change and malleability as a means of redemption and organization. Even before gaining control of the story, he suggests that nothing be set in stone. The method had worked before, but with less conceptual and biographical material, more seasoned actors, and, most importantly, final control by a director.

The sand was removed from the box during the performance of *The Geometry of Miracles* in Salzburg: Lepage, assisting in the

montage, rediscovered the beauty and interest of the empty wooden
box and no longer wanted the medium, and the team agreed. And yet
the entire show was built on the sand, on the contrast and convention
that presumes the presence of the sand as the frame of a number of
interior scenes. This square of the desert, a basis for an imaginary
world he explored, provides the formal and symbolic beauty of the
entire show. Of course, removing the sand made it possible to reveal
the machinery and ropes used in the show, but this falls into the realm
of demonstration. Lepage lets himself be seduced by the formal
aspect of his work, which explains the difficulties during rehearsals,
as well as the reception by the public, during the first two thirds of
the show's run. All we saw was an effective application, polished,
but simplistic, of some of Wright's architectural principles. Lepage
contemplates the object he creates; suddenly he switches from the
role of director to that of audience. And it was only once he agreed
to rework the foundation of the story by actually introducing the
character of the architect to the stage and making greater use of the
architect's conceptual material, his principles, and his speeches, that
the show found balance and strength.[53] Was this journey necessary?
Was it for him alone to see the interest and relevance of the project?

The transformation of material is the basis of this practice. There are many examples of formal evolution of a show, the
most successful being *The Seven Streams of the River Ota*. When
talking about one of Lepage's shows, it's hard to know which
stage is being referred to, because the show described can differ
from what another person saw at another stage on the tour. These
phases of creation are not counted by the designers, who refer to
a "Vienna version," or a "Chicago version," and so on. Scenes are
developed throughout the process, resulting in new and ephemeral
images, even when a sequence appears to have found its form.

The set doesn't change, as suggested when discussing
the rehearsals for *The Geometry of Miracles*. And while the set
evolves slightly throughout the course of *The Seven Streams of the
River Ota*, this is more to do with internal organization and prop
changes. The set doesn't change when Lepage reworks *Elsinore*,
lopping off over an hour of the performance, or *The Seven Streams
of the River Ota*. The initial theatrical instinct remains, from the
first sketch and the first trials of the set, made up of mobile screens
and the Monolith, of the Japanese facade, or the wooden box. The

setting hardly changes, but the rest changes or disappears. The receptacle remains, but the echoes are infinitely varied.

LEPAGE'S STAGE:
A MULTICULTURAL SPACE

Lepage's stage is a space for encounters, confrontation, and visual creation. This space exposes actors, shadows, and sound, visual, and kinetic technologies to many cultural references. On the whole, that mixing echoes with landmarks in a history of the image, calls cultures into question, and may propose a new meaning of "métissage," or the blending of cultures. From his first productions in the café-theatres of Quebec City, Lepage builds his productions on the generally visual foundation of a culture explored; initially the popular culture of tabloids (*L'attaque quotidienne*), then literary culture (*La ferme des animaux*, 1979, and *Dix petits nègres*, 1981), then, very soon thereafter, film culture, and then more specifically theatrical culture. Lepage questions the foundations of Québécois, American, and European culture and, more broadly, the way other cultures are seen.

 ### EXPERIMENTING WITH THE UNKNOWN

The main theme of productions such as *Vinci* and *Needles and Opium* – travel – is a recurrent idea and commonly used basis for stories. It is central to *Zulu Time*, a show that enters the airport, the point of departure and arrival for travellers, "emblem of our strange modern solitude. [...] The airport offers a curious paradox: outside of space and borders, almost outside of time, it is a crossroads of many cultures."[54] Journeys connect in the form of vehicles of all sorts: the train (*The Dragons' Trilogy*, *The Seven Streams of the River Ota*, and *The Geometry of Miracles*), the car (*The Geometry of Miracles*), and the plane, from takeoff in a seat (*Vinci*) to the aircraft cabin, solid in *Zulu Time* and lighter in *The Far Side of the Moon*, and in *The Dragons' Trilogy* by way of Gambier the pilot miming while stretched out on his suitcase set down in the sand. The characters are travelling or in transit, always uprooted, quite often strangers to themselves. In *Circulations* they help weave a web through their

connections to different points on the globe, underlining how easy
it is to circulate. The travelling protagonists become increasingly
mobile from show to show, as does Ex Machina, with its members
and productions criss-crossing the planet.[55] In leaving for Venice
to commit suicide, Madeleine makes encounters that change her
plans: *Tectonic Plates* explores the notion of collision to get at
the encounters and solitude of individuals adrift. Geology is just
another way, in this case symbolic and scientific, of suggesting the
intercultural. A much-needed retreat from a day-to-day world,
distance that allows for analysis and discovery of oneself, of others,
or of others through oneself, and vice versa, travel, in the tradition
of *Bildungsroman*, is above all a rite of passage. This is not to say that
there aren't caricatured protagonists disinclined toward encounters.
For Lepage, "strangers are not an enemy, a rival, a threat, or a god;
they are an opportunity for encounters and evolution."[56]

These encounters first emphasize differences that, in
addition to being morphological or physical, are cultural and
manifest themselves through language: two languages attempt a
conversation. This is part of Lepagean theatre which, while visual,
is primarily an effort in communication, set against a backdrop
of solitude and lack of understanding, particularly in the solo
productions. There are multiple languages, often because people of
different nationalities share the same space. The characters speak
French, English, Chinese, and Japanese in Canada in *The Dragons'*
Trilogy, and they speak Japanese, French, German, Czech, and
English, and sing in French, Japanese, and Italian in *The Seven*
Streams of the River Ota. The productions, through the simultaneous use of different languages, make the idea of "original version"
obsolete: the languages cohabit, and a show like *The Seven Streams*
of the River Ota is performed practically in the same languages
no matter what country it visits; meanwhile an English version
and a French version were created for *The Far Side of the Moon*.
While the text isn't necessarily essential, language is primordial,
another example of the oral versus the literary.

Lepagean theatre stages attempts at conversation between
cultures. This is what happens at the beginning of *The Seven Streams*
of the River Ota, when Luke O'Connor tries to speak Japanese with
Nozomi's mother-in-law, or when the Englishman Crawford arrives
in Quebec City and tries to talk to the merchants, including the

Chinese shopkeeper (*The Dragons' Trilogy*). The protagonists are often confronted with one or more foreign languages, which they command to varying degrees, along with the commonly admitted prejudices of members of the culture of departure, generally Québécois. In *The Dragons' Trilogy*, the character of the Chinese man, a launderer, is the victim of sarcasm and mockery by two little girls, repeating what they have learned from adults. Laying bare prejudices provides access to other cultures by showing the exotic and even incomprehensible side of them. In *The Seven Streams of the River Ota*, this involves the colourful scene of Pierre's arrival at Hanako's house when he discovers the reality of *tatami* mats, or the scene in the Osaka restaurant in which Patricia describes sushi – reminiscent of *Empire of Signs* – or explains different Japanese traditions, from tea to *sumi-e* (ink painting).

Lepage has often expressed the need to explore a larger territory, because "disorientation is necessary to theatre."[37] This propensity for the foreign undoubtedly has its origins in Lepage's early passion for geography and his later attraction to Asian cultures. But above all it shows a consistent desire to use the power of an uninitiated gaze onto another reality rather than the pompous assurance of encyclopedic knowledge. In the uninitiated gaze, Lepage finds theatrical material that exploits the cliché in all its forms. Despite the presence of a few professors – the medical examiner teaching his courses in *Polygraph* and, in *Tectonic Plates*, Jacques Macman, an art history professor, or Madeleine who we first meet as a student and then as a professor – in Lepagean theatre, culture is primarily experienced empirically. It is perceived through the naïveté of the traveller making discoveries. Lepage has a weakness for students, who are both prisoners of their knowledge and grappling with their initial research, their initial experiments, and their initial confrontations; for example, Philippe in *The Far Side of the Moon*, and Frédéric confronted with an unfamiliar workplace in *The Andersen Project*. We watch Pierre discover Japan and *butoh*, like his mother, Sophie, earlier in the play, personifying the "door" through which the audience can become part of the story and project themselves onto. This stranger who discovers a culture could be any Westerner travelling abroad and is an image of the audience, which sees itself onstage. This theatre elicits our reactions to the unfamiliar and what is inside us that is unfamiliar. Lepage explores exchange as a form of relationship with the other.

Certain characters are plunged further into another culture. Françoise, in *The Dragons' Trilogy*, marries the son of the Chinese man and goes to Toronto, which is yet another source of disorientation for the young girl from Quebec City. She learns a few words of Chinese, and Lee picks up a few words of French. They communicate in broken English. It is not an innocent choice that Françoise speaks the language of the colonizer with Lee. Once her daughter Stella, with whom she spoke French, is placed in an institution, she can no longer lean on her culture, only on her memories. Françoise is then acculturated and plunged into a sort of no man's land. Other characters willingly abandon their culture and adopt another: Jana Čapek escapes her surroundings and her role as avant-garde artist to go live in Hiroshima, Japan, and practise Zen. A symbol of acculturation in her dress, shaved head, philosophy, and learning of the language, she seems more integrated into her new culture when she is faced with Western caricatures. The plays suggest that openness to a different culture, through the distancing required from one's own, offers an understanding of the characteristics of one's own culture, while opening the person up to a few universal ideas. Any movement toward distant shores has repercussions in the proximate: openness to a macrocosm is just one way of understanding the microcosm.

Lepage's cultural references contain this dual movement between the near and the far. "The obsession we have with discovering other cultures is usually intimately linked to the discovery of our own culture,"[58] Lepage explains, justifying his thirst for travel, encounters, and this way of considering the globe as a space that is easy to understand, often emotionally, through focus on short anecdotes that speak to larger themes. "If you want to be universal, first look at what is going on in your kitchen. I was interested in starting with little stories like the one I had heard about a disfigured woman who was hiding a lipstick and every once in a while she would put lipstick on."[59] Lepage's intelligence consists in not making this approach a simple game of opposition between the kitchen, the key site of dramatic composition and Quebec life, at least until 1980, and Japanese trivia, but superimposing two potential readings on a single element. The kitchen becomes an allegory for the Universe. This is one of the strengths of *The Far Side of the Moon*, superimposing international themes over Quebec stories, images of the universal history of humanity, such as the space race, with images of home movies. In this production, Lepage crosses many Québécois themes and preoccupations, and deals with Quebec's notorious frictions with the rest of Canada; this is the show that is the most completely international or at least Western: the Ph.D. student character could just as easily have been French, Swedish, or American.

Between near and far, between microcosm and macrocosm, there is someone who intervenes and allows for exchange rather than mere contact: the translator. Lepage doesn't obliterate identity and, in an attempt at realism, he has actors talk in the mother tongue or language of expression of their character. When the protagonists don't use French, he projects the translation, but more often, he integrates the translation into the story. In *The Seven Streams of the River Ota*, Hanako has made it her profession to study conncections between cultures. In a monotone voice, she translates Feydeau in Osaka, while the actors talk faster and faster. Later on, she explains her work in literary translation, in which she is constantly moving between cultures trying to find linguistic equivalents. This involves more than just words: the entire culture of the target language has to be considered when translating poetic images and concepts, and the culture of the source language has to be familiar. Talking about words implies talking about cultures, as suggested by the title of the box in *The Seven Streams of the River Ota*, Part Five, "Words":

> HANAKO: I'm working on a translation of an anthology of French poetry. It's very complicated because the language is much richer than in the government documents I usually translate. So it's hard to find equivalent expressions in another language. For example, Baudelaire often uses the word "spleen" and in Japanese there is no equivalent.[60]

This character embodies Lepage's approach, which is a matter of conveying meaning in spite of and through cultural difference. "Conveying," in other words, in motion, connecting two cultural realities, being both the bridge and the boatman, two figures that, not surprisingly, are found in Lepagean theatre. *Zulu Time* is built around the idea of international code and features a mobile bridge.

These metal bridges connect the towers of the set – at times control
towers – and therefore connect airports, different countries, and
continents. They are also what allow the protagonists to cross over,
even turn upside down! A symbol of passage, the bridge is mobile,
like meaning, language, and convention. It adapts to the levels of
the action in *Zulu Time*, like the translator has to adapt to levels
of language. This makes transmission and understanding possible.
Generally speaking, the cultural arena and, more particularly, the
world of fine arts, serves as a common medium for exchanges,
performing the function of boatman. In *The Dragons' Trilogy*, Yukali
has come to see Pierre's installation in a gallery. She doesn't speak
French, and Pierre stammers a few words in English. This divide
leads to misunderstanding and anxiety, to the point that Yukali
makes as if to leave. He holds her back and tries to explain what he
was trying to achieve, through broken word games in English: this
"installation" (in English) could be called "constellation" he tells her:
"*C'est un sky trip*." In Pierre's work, an illuminated garland encircles
a central light bulb. With this light, he discovers Yukali's painted
dragons. Clumsily, she tries to explain her creative process: "To
make the light come out of my painting." And he, just as clumsily,
tries to show her that her work is more interior, more urgent:
"You, you plug in you, me I plug in the wall!" he says sardonically
about the inspiration and power connection for his constellation.
Each speaking in their own fashion, the two artists find common
ground over Pierre's installation, the prelude to a love affair already
suggested by the pair's entry into the space of the installation.

When journalists questioned them about the differences in
the treatment of the Asian theme, having noted a return to the Orient
with *The Seven Streams of the River Ota* ten years after *The Dragons'
Trilogy*, the actors answered: "We travelled there!"[61] From interest
in or fascination with something foreign, they had moved to a more
interior approach. Although they knew they had merely touched
on the reality of the Orient, their journey there had nevertheless
taken place. This shows the importance of the claim of a neophyte,
but curious, gaze. Generally speaking, foreigners aren't mocked
in Lepagean theatre, but the way foreigners are seen is mocked, at
the same time as it explores how to move beyond local character,
through bridges that Lepage puts up here, there, and everywhere,
aerial constructions over differences.

Cultural references
intersect in *The
Dragons' Trilogy*
when Pierre creates
a light installation in
the centre of which
Yukali will place
her ink drawings.

PHOTO

Claudel Huot

THE STAGE:
A SPACE FOR UNLIKELY ENCOUNTERS

Lepage places himself firmly in the intercultural, in this "space between." He uses links, he observes, he connects, and he strives to provoke collisions, in a movement that is similar to the "mélange of individuals and mind-sets"[62] evoked by Serge Gruzinski to define "crossbreeding": a raging flood, a movement, that troubles the elements like water is troubled when agitated, as our perceptions and normal ideas would be troubled. The term "mixing" suggests the idea of energy greater than the individuals and mind-sets that it shakes, stirs, and overturns. But while the elements are purposely mixed and troubled, they are no less contained. The stage not only creates a site to exhibit these crossings, it also contains and channels them. We have looked at the sets as successive versions of stage boxes. Generally speaking, the entire stage is home to and a frame for the stream of elements that are blended together upon it. What I described in the phases of creation of the productions is found

in this idea of "an amorphous cluster in perpetual movement,"[63] such that we can define the culture and such that Lepage seems to conceive it through opposition to a stable and well-defined system. Whether clouds or waves, the stage is crossed by flows that carry with them the seed of improbable encounters.

Lepage knows that theatre is a "collecting art," and it is this premise and claim of the federative power of theatre that drive him more toward a blended, open, and deliberate practice. In 1993 he recalled how, when *The Dragons' Trilogy* was created, the creation team was influenced by dance, music, and film, essentially everything but theatre:

> I'm a follower of people, not necessarily connected with the theater [...] For me, theater will always be very, very much alive but not necessarily in the theatrical tradition. My taste comes from when I was 12 years old and saw Genesis or Laurie Anderson or some performance artist who had put paint on himself. I've seen a lot of theater, but that's not what woke up my taste to become a director; nontheatrical things were much more theatrical than the theater I was seeing.[64]

A recent graduate of the Conservatoire, he wanted to test the theatre and its capacity for resistance and to define its territorial limits, and he threw himself into the exploration as a topographer or cartographer:[65] first of all through the language and framing of film, the world of the tabloids, and a great diversity of meanings of objects and props, and then through multilingualism, outgrowth, and planetary movements, an outburst of action and duration. We can imagine Lepage's practice as a territory divided into the land of theatre and the land of film. Lepage always remains on the theatre side of the border, with both feet firmly planted, but he is increasingly on the border, at times even hugging it.[66] The border is the line that he twists and moves, but he never crosses it. When he makes movies, he uses the same map, but the land of theatre is always in sight. The influence of theatre is more limited in his movies, but the reverse is not true, on the contrary.[67]

He moves away from the border to explore cinematic terrain, penetrating a little further with each film. *Possible Worlds* is a more radical exploration of film narrative, tortuous and complex, but above all an obvious formal exploration of parallel lives. It's the age-old relationship between psychoanalysis and cinema: it talks about a mental universe broken down into multiple avenues. There, the colours fade; all that remains is white, pulling Lepage toward cinematic composition. He also dives into the archives of cinema: detective movies with *Le confessionnal* and vampire movies with *Une histoire de vampire*, an abandoned project combining the theme of transplants with superstitions about vampires. *Possible Worlds* provides malleable material that could assimilate any subject. This is the case, literally, in the fog, pale reflections that take up the entire frame of the image. The temptation no longer resides in masterful composition as in a monochromatic approach to the image, a reflected image in which everything tends to merge or ends up disappearing.

Lepage then seems to have addressed the question of the evolution of his theatre with other practices through an awareness that "theatre always comes last, in the sense where it is the meeting point of all other artistic forms."[68] Crossbreeding primarily occurs through centripetal movement in a lopsided acculturation; he makes theatre predominant at the service of a polymorphic and polysemic gaze that can adapt to any sort of spectacle, including cinema. His approach is based on having a richer discourse and vision, while gradually mastering the rules of each area he borrows from.

Within his territory and the space of his theatre practice, Lepage is remarkably ubiquitous. This is undoubtedly because while he keeps expanding his areas of exploration – into dance, puppetry, virtual environments, architecture, opera, robotics, biology, and the conquest of space – he shrinks the territory. The frontiers move closer to where he is standing, until they are almost in contact with other frontiers that used to be diametrically or largely opposed. The practices come close enough together to create the feeling of fusion. But Lepage's territory, while it increases boundaries, also juxtaposes the frontiers without erasing them. It is true that in their being so close, they can be considered reflections, and we can see across another line, a sort of palimpsest gaze. While theatre remains in the fore and always visible, it is invaded: it is condensed into a magnetic centre, the vital core, the heart of the kingdom. It is not a neutral place between two lines, but rather the place where encounters happen, where everything is possible: "a zone of uncertainty in the sphere of the unknown,"[69] but rich in new potential.

The analogy of the centripetal movement of frontiers toward the centre of Lepage's territory – a slow shrinking – is played out at La Caserne in Quebec City, where all the contributors assemble. Creators, actors, and technicians all strain toward the centre: Studio 1. Individuals and frontiers, beings and mind-sets reconnect at the centre of the blended practice. The name of the place is evocative: La Caserne – in this case meaning the firehouse, or alternatively the garrison house – is like a fortress at the centre of a symbolic and physical territory.[70] Its nerve centre is a black cube, Studio 1. This sober, geometrical receptacle virtually contains all the circulations and offerings. It is destined to showcase them and shows only them. Monumental and durable in Quebec City, the receptacle is ephemeral and partial onstage. There is therefore a parallelism between this parabola of Lepage's territory and the box/screen dialectic, a movement that tends to flatten volume and make the space a surface. More than a parallelism, it is the same dialectic at work – and to be continued.

The stage walls, whether physical or symbolic, full or truncated, embody these frontiers. Their mobility, as in *Needles and Opium, Elsinore, The Seven Streams of the River Ota, A Dream Play, The Geometry of Miracles, The Far Side of the Moon, The Busker's Opera*, and so on, is like the movement of frontiers in Lepage's territory. These fluctuating lines redraw all sorts of figures. For the space of an instant or longer, the walls contain the crossbreeding that they help create by simply moving closer together. They are a bit like a contracting surface that drives everything within it toward the precipice, like a wall of flames pushing animals toward the far reaches of the forest. The idea of actors pushed around by moving frontiers (that is, in their theatrical habits) is found in their having to coexist with the neighbouring frontiers of other practices. The actors find themselves having to move the frontiers themselves, guardians, defenders, and individuals penned in within their limits. They sometimes handle the technology themselves: placing microphones, filming sequences, turning devices on and off, in the same way that they move panels and set up some of the props. Marie Brassard remarked that the effect of this is to create "the spirit of the troupe:

you have to muck in. We don't have time [to think or to have stage fright]; everyone is responsible for everyone else."[71] Sometimes, as in *Jean-Sans-Nom*, the actors have a harder time while being pushed around by their normal topography and being squeezed by moving walls, impalpable frontiers of canvas, virtual projections, and light. This is the only instance in which the universe is reduced to a piece of working scenery 4 metres wide by 3 metres deep and that, with the projections, only a small portion – the far reaches of the forest – can be used by the actors. The flipped-over cube for *A Dream Play* also put the actor in an uncomfortable position.

In parallel to this centripetal dialectic, Lepage tries to have new figures onstage. Beginning with *The Seven Streams of the River Ota*, he tries more broadly and more systematically to open up to other artistic forms: "Rather than just using actors, I would also like to get video artists, dancers, contortionists, and others involved."[72] This desire would lead to opera, musical sequences, *butoh*-like choreography, magic acts, and drawing-workshop scenes to be integrated into the show, periodically bringing new sorts of performers to the stage. The principle was established. It's interesting to note that the desire expressed for *The Seven Streams of the River Ota* describes a show staged five years later, the building of a universe in the form of the spiral. In fact, opening the stage up to dancers, video artists, and contortionists, which Lepage describes in 1993, doesn't reflect what would become *The Seven Streams of the River Ota*, but rather *Zulu Time*, and in part foreshadows the approach for *The Damnation of Faust* and *Kà*. Also, *Zulu Time* plays with frontiers, bringing together different disciplines and performers who at the same time were looking to perform in places beyond the frontiers, outside of institutions, large hangars, or big tops.[73]

This stage receptacle contains a peaceful coexistence between things that can be dated technologically: the moving image coexists with shadows formed by a candle, the psaltery comes a bit before the sampler (*Zulu Time*), the computer-generated image shares the stage with a viola and a flute (*Elsinore*). There is no rivalry, no hierarchy of impact, and no modernity: merely simultaneous operation. The historical meta-discourse of each technology is a component of any work, any use of technology, but this history of the medium, often told by the story, is confronted with many other visual and sound elements. In this receptacle, elements are close to one another, often in contact or at least visually superimposed. Poetic shortcuts are then created and offer a layered vision that functions by bringing together crossbeam elements in a transversal reading. This results in "spontaneous generation": the creation of new elements through contact – superimposition and juxtaposition – rather than through penetration. Lepage's gaze is a superficial one. If there is a history of the gaze, then it is a history of the surface of images that is offered. Even though he talks about a circle of origins and the theatre of the future as a circular set,[74] what he creates show after show is fundamentally obverse, meant for the eyes of the audience accustomed to seeing all sorts of different screens.

Lepage composes an increasingly shallow image: a shift from the large performance area is clear from *The Dragons' Trilogy* to *The Damnation of Faust*. The actors move in front of a background that draws closer and closer. This is clear on the tiny stage for *Jean-Sans-Nom* and comes up again in *The Far Side of the Moon*, with its long, narrow set. Lepage makes little use of open panels and depth, keeping the actor virtually tacked on the grey backdrop of

panels, during Philippe's thesis defence or during André's weather scene in front of the satellite image. The set is deep and wide in *The Geometry of Miracles*, but the full area is never used.[75] And the screen that closes out the sandbox space reinforces the impression of two-dimensionality of this stage image. The Lepagean actor, who creates images within the receptacle, cannot make large movements or run around, except in *Zulu Time*. It's quite obvious that during the upside-down tango or the trash copulation on a bungee cord, the energy and the movements of the actors are limited to the width of the bridge, a simple line in the width of the set. The feeling of two-dimensionality is never compromised. When Pierre Maltais does dance exercises, he crosses the entire set in *The Seven Streams of the River Ota*, but again it's a lateral movement along the garden of raked stones.

Dual obverse stages (*Tectonic Plates*, the Stockholm version of *La Celestina*, *Zulu Time*) double the audience's viewing possibilities, while maintaining a degree of proximity. The show provides two views, but whether it is seen from one side or the other doesn't change much: it is a simple inverted image, but still an image. Lepage composes flat universes that make ingenious use of the possibilities of perspectivist modulations and openings, but the aim is not so much to suggest depth as to reproduce in large format screen representations of our videosphere world. These encounters create poetic forms, often through the play of shadows, visual distortions, or simple shared conventions. The particularity of this association and unique propagation is that a trace of the parent remains visible in the element created: one plus one equals three! We see the projected image, we see the actor before the image, and we can meld them into a single vision, in the same way that, in *Needles and Opium*, we can make out a cup or a part of a trumpet. We see the light and, at the same time, we read the message formed by all the scenery elements that spell out the word "cool" in shadow on the screen. Used with other elements, the elements don't fade away; they remain perceptible, while creating a poetic vision. Lepage knows that in crossing, and therefore in his practice, the whole is larger than the sum of its parts.

The white screens in *Elsinore*, the screen in *Needles and Opium*, and the low wall in *Vinci* mark out a neutral space, at the same time as they contain it. However, the Lepagean receptacle forms a space that is more free than neutral, to the extent that a

The two-dimensionality of the stage is apparent in *Zulu Time*.

PHOTO

Emmanuel Valette

few connotations survive: the Japanese roof of the wooden facade (*The Seven Streams of the River Ota*), the window of the washing machine in *The Far Side of the Moon*, or at least the material of the panels reminiscent of school blackboards, the clocks that indicate the time zones, attached to metal beams, and the monitors (*Zulu Time*). This free space offers leeway in interpretation that allows for rapid changes. It's a bit like rooms in a museum, places that juxtapose all sorts of cultural products, through intersection or chronology, visited by very different people.[76] The receptacle is like a museum space that can constantly change what's hanging on the walls. The receptacle always opens a crack: the stage is never sealed. One side tips and everything can escape and change. Lepage understands the multiple meanings and visual richness of this grouping of elements at the centre of a receptacle, but, at the same time, he is seeking accidents, encounters, and crossings. He makes a point of reversing and inclining his building, of opening it a crack for a few moments to let light pass through and the unknown to enter. The audience witnesses these openings in real time. One of the responses to this centripetal dialectic is the explosion, the breach, and the opening that contradicts, for a time, the unavoidable contraction of the form becoming surface.

ORIENTALISM AND MULTIMEDIA: A NEW BAROQUE?

Lepage uses the term "baroque" to describe not only the proliferation of aesthetics and technologies he has used in his many borrowings, but also an energy that he attributes to his encounter with Japan,[77] a contemporary Japan he discovered along with its traditional culture. However, his notion of baroque also refers to canons of the European baroque, which Lepage seems to be less aware of. This baroque comes from two sources, both European. Lepage's reading of Japan is strongly marked by Orientalism (that is, a European gaze on Japan), and the baroque canons found in it are principally those of the Western sphere. What Lepage says about Japan and what he calls baroque apply in part to what is said here about this genre: an aesthetic of the heterogeneous and of saturation.

The upside-down tango and the bridge in *Zulu Time*.

PHOTO

Ludovic Fouquet

A BAROQUE-DOMINATED READING
OF THE ORIENT

Very early on, Lepage was fascinated by the Orient, mainly Japan, China, and, in an academic way, Indonesia, a fascination laden with many teachings and fantasies. These two ideas are similar in Lepage's practice and his pedigree, and they are synonyms for encounters or dreams: for him the Orient is a seminal medium. Lepage uses instinct and fantasy when it comes to China, of which he has only theoretical knowledge, allowing him to create *The Dragons' Trilogy*; Marie Brassard was able to appreciate the accuracy of his interpretation during the Chinese tour of *Polygraph*.[78] The opening line of *The Dragons' Trilogy* is in this sense an artistic credo: "I have never been to China."

    The Orient has been part of Lepage's work from the first productions: a reproduction of a Japanese *sumi-e* style painting on the canvas backdrop in *En attendant*; a tie bearing the Japanese inscription *kamikaze* that Philippe wears in *Vinci*. In these two productions, the reference to the Orient, while anecdotal, contrasts with the rest of the story, almost incongruously but as a metaphorical backdrop. Lepage integrates dissimilar elements drawn from another culture. The work on *The Dragons' Trilogy* was the opportunity to better define the clichés and fantasies of the Orient that define Orientalism, seen as a resource and an opportunity for renewal or formal borrowing: *tai chi* was used as a gestural register, even before it was used in the group's work to bring people together and inspire their creativity. *Bunraku* puppeteers and *kabuki* costumes are used in the same way. References are Chinese, but also increasingly Japanese. In the 1980s, Lepagean theatre stood clearly apart from local productions for its use of foreign cultural elements. In this sense, he could merit the title "baroque," meaning "an irregular pearl" among round pearls, according to Portuguese etymology. A heterogeneous mix of the baroque, therefore one that doesn't fuse, is contained in Lepage's reading of the Orient, precisely in his discovery of Japanese artistic practice and, more broadly, of its system of thought.

    Lepage first travelled to Japan only in 1993 – to stage *Macbeth* and *The Tempest* at the Globe Theatre in Tokyo. He found the place to be very exotic. During a phone interview, he said

The Dragons' Trilogy redefines clichés and fantasies of the Orient, including those of the geisha.

PHOTO

Érick Labbé

that it was like living in a Nintendo game, alluding both to the
frenetic lifestyle and the incomprehensible signs that, as a good
reader of Barthes's *Empire of Signs*, Lepage felt bombarded with.
In his own way, he underlines the extreme difference between
Japan and the Western world, in the tradition of Orientalists.
Travel writers have been providing a baroque reading of the
Far East since the nineteenth century, Loti first among them,
spreading a perception that is expressed through literature, fine
arts, and travel writing. People used to travel with journals or
sketchbooks, observing and taking notes. Later on, they would
bring cameras, video cameras, and microphones. The traveller
observes, is astonished, compares, analyzes, and dreams, because
Orientalism is as much an academic activity as an imaginative
one. But above all, travellers express themselves. Orientalism is
first and foremost a discourse for the representation of the other,
the evocation of the outside world, the faraway, indeed the other
outside, attitudes, and activities evoked earlier in the gaze on
the foreign developed in this practice. Many avant-gardists had

a decisive encounter with Orientalism; one simply has to think
of the following:

> Artaud's interest in Balinese theatre, Indian thought,
> Ezra Pound's interest in Chinese calligraphy and
> Confucianism, the interest of the surrealists and the
> Grand Jeu group in Eastern spirituality where they
> sought the exact opposite of the "Western culture"
> that they rejected – to the more recent interest of the
> Tel Quel group in Chinese thought, and of Barthes
> in this semi-imaginary Japan that he defined as an
> "empire of signs."[79]

Each has helped create the myth, each has forged a reading, often
utopian, that became their founding myth. Guy Scarpetta discovered Japan in 1984. This trip seems to have been an important
moment in the thinking that led to his essay *L'impureté*, an essential
step in that it provides new elements of heterogeneity. His trip to
Japan occurred almost at the same time as his discovery of certain
European baroque works;[80] everything intersects, but above all, and
this is obvious in the form of the text, everything is intertwined.
Here the divine inspiration of European baroque is replaced by the
proliferation of vertically stacked signs: neon lights, ideograms,
and such. With the Japanese baroque, there is a movement of the
lines of demarcation, *habitus* (lifestyle), and perspective. What
Scarpetta discovers, virtually at the same time as Lepage, is the
decompartmentalization and cohabitation of everything, and the
seamless integration of extreme modernity within a framework of
extreme tradition. A kitsch through proximity is also evident, either
through the contrast of elements from different styles – and the
inversion or levelling, indeed the renewal of value systems, rules,
and criteria of composition inspired by the baroque – or through
the simple chromatic contrast, or, rather, through its intensity.

Lepage explains his conception of the Japanese baroque
through the "transparency, which allows them to put a lot of things
in a huge pile and still see it all clearly. The density of Japanese culture
is so great they have no difficulty inserting other cultures into their
own, like a sheet of paper slipped into a pile."[81] For Lepage, the
association with Japan is a powerful trigger, an experience based on

Calligraphy lesson in
The Blue Dragon.

PHOTO

Ludovic Fouquet

completely different conventions. "When I directed *The Tempest* in Tokyo, I was told that this character would be played by a *kabuki* actor, that character by a Noh actor, and the other by a Western-style actor."[82] Like many creators, in Japanese theatre he found enough to feed his "multi-" instincts: multidisciplinary, multilingual, and so on. Using actors of different origins that don't belong to "the same artistic community,"[83] who will "perform together but not in the same way," multiplying aesthetics, not being afraid of disharmony and difference, are all examples of the multidisciplinarity that is part of Lepage's approach. He is very much aware that he wouldn't do this had he not gone to Japan, "at least not to this extent."[84] He refers to the example of Brook, while admitting that he doesn't go as far as the director who virtually made "theatrical anthropology."[85] Referring to the very different aesthetic worlds of the new performers that he assembled for *The Geometry of Miracles*, Lepage explains that he briefly thought that these differences would result in an "incompatibility," but that it was actually good to integrate them, that this was precisely the "baroque of the theatre," that this "diverts, destabilizes the actors, the audience, and the critics […] because the world strives to find stability in the theatre, to find formulas."[86] We can see the extent to which the chaos sought in the development of material is in line with what Lepage calls baroque.

In Japan he sees things that legitimize his practice and give him the permission to follow the path he anticipated during his first journeys and prepared in advance. From a great distance, he rediscovers what was simmering in his kitchen. The shock is not so much the shock of something new popping up in his artistic field, but rather the affinities that, beyond time and space, the designer was able to discover elsewhere. The fundamental thing is therefore in this recognition, even though the notions of superimpositions and all of these "borrowings [that] multiply" are also indebted to "the CNN global village in which we live, where we know every-thing about everyone almost instantly."[87]

In Japan, Lepage also discovered an empire of transparency created by the country's incredible density. He uses a geographical approach in talking about Japan to Rémy Charest:

> On my first visit to Japan, I was fascinated by the minuteness, by the maximized use of living space, and therefore by the forced transparency of every-thing in the country. Japan is a country made of rice paper – the walls of houses are literally made of it – so boundaries are always a little ethereal, hazy; they're made of air. There are countless demarcations, hier-archies, territories within territories, but they're all transparent.[88]

Loti helped forge an oversimplified representation of Japan: spare interiors, plays of light through *shoji* screens, the kindness of the *mousmés*,[89] in the same way that, later on, a reading of Tokyo was forged as "urban chaos," that Scarpetta and Lepage echo, a reading that today is called into question. The ethereal, hazy frontiers made of air that Lepage references relate directly to the design of the *shoji* screens. They also relate to the metaphor of territory regarding the practice and the description of images in *Possible Worlds*, bathed in a pale light and filled with white.[90] In one of the first versions of *The Seven Streams of the River Ota*, the *shoji* screens are manipulated and assembled like a small house behind the protagonists, and then everything is torn down leaving nothing onstage. From the *shoji* screens on the set of *The Seven Streams of the River Ota*, Lepage discovered and adopted a kinetic use of several screens, a Japanese influence. Since this show, rails and runners have always been part of the stage, guiding the panels, partitions, and screens that act as doors (*The Far Side of the Moon*, *The Damnation of Faust*, *La Casa Azul*, and *The Andersen Project*). The evolution of the panel-based set prompted a Japanese reviewer to refer to the Japanese facade of *The Seven Streams of the River Ota* as baroque: "One has to appreciate the baroque-like structure on stage which contained a large world in a small rectangular frame."[91] Transparency is at the origin of what Lepage and Scarpetta call "Japanese baroque" as a juxtaposition, a coexistence in a small space. The space is full because it is clearly delimited. The empty space that Lepage discovers is dense. Recalling Michel Tournier's lectures comparing Canada with Japan,[92] he becomes aware that "The Japanese live in apartments the size of handkerchiefs, which means that they have to create a considerable interior space." But he quickly discovered a highly codified organization of space that nonetheless arranges empty spaces: "These are planned empty spaces [Zen gardens, the stage in the Noh theatre] that don't exist in daily life. In a world where everything is built up and occupied, an empty space, precisely because it's not built up, is in fact a full space."[93] This quality is a key to Lepage's stage design: empty space, of modest dimensions in which an often solitary character projects, in the figurative sense or not, his or her interior world. The solo shows are in fact those that best reflect this. This also explains the relatively small size of many of the sets. Philippe is alone in the small hotel room in *Needles and Opium*. The receptacle – the coming together of the set and the box revealing its value – becomes a meditation space, a space full of a shared imaginary realm, of an exhibited object, and of a few projected visual traces, painted or traced in chalk. If Lepage's walls are the mirror of our dreams, then the set in its entirety is the reflection of our imagination, the trace of our thoughts.[94]

The Far Side of the Moon is one of the most obvious examples of the symbolic density of space. Like the rock emerging from its bed of foam or a gravel sea, condensing energy, meaning, and poetry, the porthole becomes the element around which empty space becomes denser and is organized and personalized. This has connections with Zen thought, but also with European baroque. The set is almost empty to showcase the ornament, and it is through this ornament that it connects with the baroque. The ornament is showcased, made meaningful through its very economy. Lepage never does "everything ornament." He stops before ornamentation grows, just when the ornament swells. More and more, he creates a sober, monochromatic space, punctuated with a few props as few and far between as in a traditional Japanese interior. This is very clear in *The Far Side of the Moon, La Casa Azul,* and even in *The Damnation of Faust.* Despite its rainbow colours, its acrobats, its use of series of European baroque elements, and references – five Christs on the Cross, five acrobats appearing at the crossing of the beams of the set, during the evocation of the Resurrection – the show opens on a sober, empty set, in shades of grey blue.

The vacuum hose highlights the value of ornament as a device. *The Far Side of the Moon.*

PHOTO
_____
Ludovic Fouquet

There are therefore two possible approaches to Japan: one based on emptiness and the other on the proliferation of signs that through saturation make use of fullness. This opposition can create an impression of the baroque. Loti refers to "the land of pretty little trifles,"[95] grasping the asceticism and the sensory overload, sobriety, and the colourful. His vision of an "unimaginable splendour, a spectacular sparkle,"[96] while based on what he saw, was prepared by an opposite vision of rigour and sobriety. Loti doesn't set them in opposition, but understands that these are two aspects of the Japanese identity. He grasped them in the same gaze and in the same place. His vision is built on a dream of the emptiness and the shadow and on the just-as-exotic appearance of colours and contrasts. Lepage inserts himself in this deliberately multiple path, seeking not only shadow and tranquility, but also artificial light, frenzy, a technological shadow, the *shoji* screens, and neon. And this is where we find the opening image of *The Seven Streams of the River Ota.* In this show, Lepage multiplies spaces and juxtaposes characters and eras. The scene that has a *kabuki* lion run into a Quebec actor coming out of a phone booth is typical. The trajectory of the show as a whole is close to the baroque that Lepage noted in certain Japanese productions. He moves from a Japanese reconstitution strongly marked by Noh sets, to Feydeau's kitsch stage design, by way of a concentration camp, Dutch interiors, American apartments, and so on. There are many purposely surprising costumes, characters, and styles of dwellings.

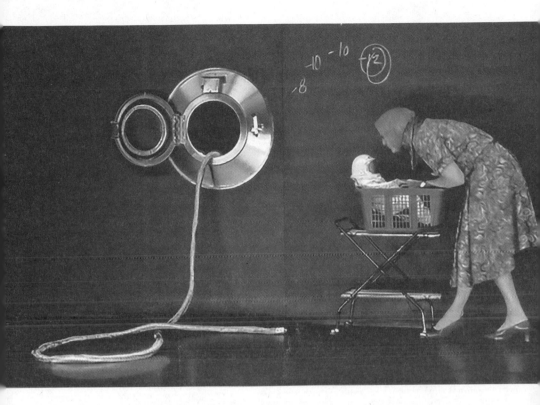

Similarly, it makes sense that *The Damnation of Faust* was created in Tokyo: Lepage felt even freer to delve into the baroque while working in Japan. The mix of acrobats, dancers, and singers, using weightlessness, exploiting new vertical movement, is reminiscent of the circus: the acrobatics were managed by Alain Gauthier from Cirque du Soleil. The stage is heterogeneous, vertical, and spectacular, and it confronts the acrobats and the actors with violent sounds and images. Lepage creates a contrasted, fragmented, and multifaceted malleable space.

On each trip to Japan, Lepage assimilated new information about Japanese people and culture. He went to see two *kabuki* plays each day for two weeks during his first visit, and he explored all sorts of artistic forms of expression. He also discovered Hiroshima – with a guide who was an enlightened lover of Shakespeare and of the theatre in general and a *hibakusha* himself – and the city's stark contrasts, the power of life and death, reconstruction and laughter over the ruins. This was all a stimulus and changed the way Lepage saw Japan, while keeping his fantasies alive. Lepage doesn't try to reproduce Japanese theatre or pretend to be a specialist, but he integrates different notions of its theatre into his own practice, without fear of the "traps of projection and utopia" like Scarpetta, during his first trip to Japan.[97] Lepage knows he needs a door into a story: his gaze as a Westerner and a neophyte will serve as a prism, and the discovery will become part of the story. The trip to Japan acts as an intermediary that allows him to advance more firmly along the path of heterogeneity, although a Japanese heterogeneity. This heterogeneity would see the number of different constructions in a sober space increase, and would reconcile meditation before a space, full by virtue of being empty, with the dive into a colourful space, whether traditional or technological. In Japan Lepage experiences what he qualifies as baroque and he uses these elements in his practice. As of the first trip, we can detect clear heterogeneity in his theatre, much stronger than before 1993.

TENSION AND SPATIAL ORGANIZATION: THE ULTIMATE EMBODIMENT OF THE BAROQUE

The organization of the stage, the set design, and certain drama-turgical aspects of Lepagean theatre suggest pictorial, sculptural, and architectural baroque – verticality, flight, weightlessness, machines – as it developed in Europe. One of the avenues for work on *Elegant Universe*[98] was the life and rival work of baroque artists Bernini and Borromini, crossed with string theory; a complex game of echoes between baroque circumvolutions and advanced cosmological theory. The baroque goes beyond a simple anchor in the Orient and infiltrates how he thinks about theatre, which tends to assemble the arts, like the baroque. Both a recurring component of art and historical phenomena occurring between the seventeenth and eighteenth centuries, the baroque has incredible and malleable energy, irregular shapes, and copious ornaments. It uses allegory and surprise; it works with new ranges of colour, and reserves a special place for light, bringing the space created to life often against a backdrop of darkness, making it more like the stage of a theatre. Penetrating architecture, it offers a new syntax to built elements that are part of a representation in which the audience-visitor takes part.

Another meaning of the term "baroque" was offered by Scarpetta in 1985 as part of his thinking about the notion of impurity as a mark of his era. The baroque is a timeless space of dialogue, which encourages intersections, influences, and resurfacing. The great church altarpieces, mainly in Italy and Germany but also in Spain, superimpose clouds and swarming wings and bodies, on two levels. They exaggerate the baselines and are surrounded by dynamic lines like cabled columns, golden rays, and balusters. The stone becomes weightless and the sky parts. Painted ceilings offer the illusion of being pierced and opening onto a mystic sky.

The baroque often uses figures in flight: angels, the Assumption, and other figures, part of a tradition of being carried away or taking flight that is common to baroque painting, statuary, and theatre. In contrast to the figures on the "lower level," caught in a "system of weight," there are swirling figures in a "system in weightlessness."[99] They are captured in mid-movement, arms extended, bodies arched, feet no longer on the ground weighted in stability, but on the contrary, in the disequilibrium of the intermediary position, "midway between two positions."[100] Christian art responds to this mythological taking flight with the mystical rapture, two subjects that justify the vertical orientation in baroque art. Baroque always involves movement, either with the characters flying or wearing a tightly pleated dress, or the gaze is "enraptured," to use the baroque term, to the point that we sometimes call something baroque when a work creates a sense of the "preponderance of the kinetic over the static."[101] The flame could be a metaphor for the baroque. A trembling glow, a vertical mark gleaming red against a backdrop of darkness, a twisted column made of light is "the continual metaphor of boundless baroque forms, infinitely multiplying forms, deformed and anamorphic as if infinitely consumed by the infinite."[102] The flame, with its endless, ephemeral tendrils gives form and light to the folds, which are one of the strongest marks of the baroque for Deleuze.[103] The idea of the baroque might be represented by infinite, multiple, and omnipresent folds. Everything becomes an eruption in a world that fosters only dynamic opposition. The line confronts the curve, the ground confronts the sky, sinking confronts elevation, even submerging confronts vanishing into the heavens. The baroque repeatedly uses the "concurrent display of opposites […]: emptiness and plenitude, light and shadow, disappearance and appearance, major and minor, form and formlessness, *Eros* and *Thanatos*."[104]

Through the idea of transcendence that creates weightlessness, rotation, and an opening toward the sky, baroque vision devices make the eye a focal point.[105] This tradition of immersive seeing is what landscape painting accomplished in a grand and convincing fashion in the nineteenth century. The tradition involves experimentation, exploring the very process of seeing, a proven vision that could extend into "transvision," that is "seeing beyond vision."[106] With regard to virtual environments, there exists an idea of "super-vision." The immersion in the baroque vision creates a feeling of penetrating the image or, more precisely, of the image spreading to reach, envelop, and submerge us. This same idea emerges in most memories of visits to or visions of baroque buildings and paintings, which because of the vitality of their architectural lines have a real power over the audience, drawing them in. The baroque requires that the eye move, whether by tipping the head back to see the thick clouds painted and sculpted on the ceiling, or by requiring that the gaze try to find a direction in which to read the layered, frenetic waves, the vertical perspective, this partially open sky.

Lepage's set is more like the stage of a movie theatre with its rectangular screen. But while it is built on a rectangular base set on the ground, within the frame there are many vertical lines and vertical movements, creating an opposing tension. Besides, Lepage increasingly builds vertical sets, with scenes superimposed, high structures, and so on. The box is stretched to become a tower. For Lepage, the proscenium is the reflection of the "inner conflict of man, [of] his frictions;"[107] it is therefore vertical when he believes in divinity and battles with heaven, and horizontal when he battles with his neighbour. The man who abandons religion no longer has a vertical connection to heaven: "Scanning has become horizontal because for Sartre, Brecht, and company, as for Wenders in film, man is in conflict with his neighbour."[108] Whether film is a new place of worship or, on the contrary, deconsecrated, it reverts to theatre. Lepage notes this horizontal orientation along with the fact that "people want to be witnesses to transcendence." Therein lies the secret of Lepage's baroque: reconnecting with transcendence independent of religious discourse, keeping the movement without the metaphysical backdrop, returning to vertical patterns, while his leanings toward cinema drive him into an entirely different relationship. The idea of transcendence crops up again here: something is stronger than we are, and we can let ourselves go. Lepage thus introduces transcendence in his theatre, but a new sort of transcendence.[109] Moving closer to the baroque creates a number of intersections: a fairly similar approach to light that makes light and darkness the zero and one of this theatre, like "the two levels of the world separated by a thin line of waters"[110] and an approach that frequently moves from shadow to light, into so many chiaroscuro. We can also draw connections between the baroque cabinet or canvas, Lepage's stages – and theatre in general – and the *tokonoma* (display alcove), recesses on a dark background on which light battles dark, plunges into it, and flows forth from it. The purest or most powerful light and the thickest darkness links Japanese references to their European counterparts with a single baroque system. The baroque vision and Lepage's vision are dazzled visions, the light erupting on a dark background through flames, reflections, sinuous trails of light coming from an invisible source, and so on.

This theatre contains what Deleuze calls "derivative forces," a system of compositions that is in tension with the ground and being engulfed, as opposed to a "primitive force," which tends toward flight and ecstasy. *Zulu Time* can be interpreted through this tension: murder, alcohol, solitude versus flight, the upside-down tango, and ecstasy. This derivative force is precisely that of Madeleine, arriving in Venice with the intention of committing suicide by drowning; in other words, by being engulfed and drifting (*Tectonic Plates*). It is also what paralyzes François, prostrate in the sauna and shot from overhead (*Le confessionnal*). This derivative force is even a regressive force: the image of François shot from overhead is followed by a shot of his mother's swollen belly when she is pregnant with him. She ends up engulfing him because he commits suicide by slashing his wrists in a large bathtub and sinking into the water. Many of Lepage's protagonists float this way, carried along by a derivative force, a metaphor of their idleness and loss of bearings, until a meeting changes this force into a primitive life force.

The term "transcendence" primarily means anything that rises above a certain level, in addition to the broader idea of pushing oneself to new heights. It can be a centralizing idea: the cosmos in *The Far Side of the Moon*, painting and dance in *The Seven Streams of the River Ota*, an opportunity for characters moved by a passion that is greater than them and that opens up onto something larger. The choice of the cosmos is highly symbolic; it

offers an opportunity to talk about one's place in it and to position oneself as a microscopic subject. When Philippe films himself for a video intended to be viewed by possible extraterrestrials, he is aspiring to transcendence. The camera is symbolically placed above him, and he is seen in miniature with his head raised. The scene has fun with the idea of the existence of aliens, but more importantly uses religious symbolism. Showing the protagonist in miniature introduces the idea of the smallness of man faced with the divine, like a child faced with his father. One could say that the cosmos plays the role of a father for Philippe, through the figure of the cosmonaut.[111] The actor, raised up and transported outside his workaday reality, is the object of a real or symbolic upward aspiration that is a pronounced vertical movement that becomes flight. One expression is the final ascension of Marguerite in *The Damnation of Faust*: an immense ladder crosses the entire width of the set and Marguerite confidently starts to climb it, while the lights go out[112] and the shadows of purgatory remain on the ground.

Lepage's set has the same capacity for weightlessness as baroque architecture. Movement isn't merely suggested: the set rotates and rises. It also unfolds (*The Busker's Opera*), and the screen becomes a kinetic panel, swirling like a character elevated in the midst of the clouds. We have seen how often these panels appear in kinetic sets, opening up, growing longer, and turning upside down. Walls turn into a curtain (*The Seven Streams of the River Ota*, *The Far Side of the Moon*, *The Damnation of Faust*), the mirror panel in *The Far Side of the Moon* often rotates, like the screen in *Needles and Opium* and *The Geometry of Miracles*, while the cube in *A Dream Play* moves in every direction, inclining and changing the actors' points of equilibrium. It seems logical that in such spaces confusion between interior and exterior would be at work, another characteristic of the baroque. The cable column suggests reversibility in a fixed spiral, and the rotating panels and elements compound the commotion. We move from place to place with each revolution of the panel of *Needles and Opium* and *The Far Side of the Moon*, and the panel with mirrors on one side carries the audience off in its flight. The audience sees themselves appearing weightless as reflected in the slightly inclined mirror behind the actor. Likewise, when the audience sees halos of projectors or

Frida Kahlo's canopy bed rotates, transforming in full view of the audience. *La Casa Azul.*

PHOTO

Yanick MacDonald

pilot lamps in the room slide away, take flight, and disappear from the polished surface, they too have the sensation of flying. The audience in *La Casa Azul* is unsettled when the canopy bed rotates: suddenly they are no longer sure of their angle of view. Death has descended near Kahlo through an opening in the bed's canopy. While the two women recall one of Kahlo's recurring dream's – she follows a little girl into a dairy, going in through a window – the bed tips and the upper panel becomes perpendicular to the ground. The canopy remains wide open, and we see the two women through this improvised frame, suggesting the window or the door that Kahlo created in her dream. The bed slowly returns to horizontal, and little by little we discover the bottom of the bed, with Death on the ground, arms and legs moving slowly in the void, as if weightless, almost swooning like Bernini's *Ecstasy of Saint Teresa*. Slow motion and the transformation of the image onstage provide the audience a direct experience of the movement of the bed from one position to another. While they still perceive the roof as a wall, before the bed returns to the ground, there is an intermediary step that plays on discord. This gap is where the poetry and the power of the image reside.

   With the flying character, Lepage creates rapture or mystical transcendence in a vision that is more prosaic than in baroque art. Elevation and flight, while the same, are merely a stage rendering of the disruption of perception that results from the consumption of hallucinogenic substances: marijuana, opium, or heroin. The rapture is hallucinogenic, in the symbolic flight in *Circulations, Needles and Opium*, and *Zulu Time*. In *Zulu Time*, the actor, who we see hanging from a wire, bolts upright after being administered a mix of medication and alcohol by the hostess. This form of transcendence is merely a pagan, contemporary, and disenchanted version of the mystical rapture and of ecstasy, with opium replacing religion.

   The vertical orientation of the set becomes more important the more flying emissaries there are. Taking flight is sometimes metaphorical; in particular, with the use of mirrors that from *Coriolanus* to *The Far Side of the Moon* disrupt the perception of a scene by creating the impression of weightlessness. In *The Damnation of Faust*, taking flight is replaced with suspension: characters appear hanging from ropes, hurtling down the set to fall into the lap of their mistresses, sitting at the bottom of each jamb. Summoned by Mephisto, these hellish beings suddenly appear and drop head first as if they were crawling along the wall, while others climb the wall from bottom to top. They ignore notions of top and bottom to create a ballet of forms moving in every direction. And *Kà*, the first Cirque du Soleil show directed by Lepage, uses this effect with even more spectacular results: the hanging actors perform on a giant touch screen. In *La Casa Azul*, taking flight becomes a form of resistance, with movement opposing immobility. So it is an interesting choice that the bed is a massive, heavy construction of straight-grained wood: we don't expect it to move and float in space, even less than we expect Kahlo to move and float. The movement of the elements and protagonists in this show stages a battle between weight and grace, illness and health, and, in the end, life and death.

While the fight for life and the relationship of the Mexican artist to this strange visitor are inspired by the life story of Frida Kahlo, they connect more deeply to one of Lepage's themes: the dark attraction and the omnipresence of death, another feature of the baroque. Skeletons figure in the director's world. They occupy space, they imitate the living, they create allegories reminiscent of *vanitas*, and they encourage reflections on life. In *Polygraph* a skeleton is visible onstage, manipulated like a string puppet from the flies, and appears to have a life of its own. It takes off when approached by a police officer, in burlesque flight and baroque weightlessness. The skeleton appears throughout the show as part of the theme of forensic pathology. In the final scene, entitled "Death," the top of the wall crumbles, just as a naked corpse falls on the lab cart: the corpse of François who has just killed himself. A doctor is pushing the cart along the wall stage right, just under the inclined mirror, while we hear the final monologue of *Hamlet* recited offstage by Lucie: "To die, to sleep, perchance to dream ..." François's body is reflected, and, through a trick of a change in lighting, the reflection of the mirror is transformed to show the skeleton from earlier in the place of the body.

This is classic *vanitas*, which foreshadows Frida Kahlo's world with a strange acuity. Not only did she have a mirror installed on the ceiling of the canopy bed above her to observe herself while painting self-portraits, but she also had a brightly

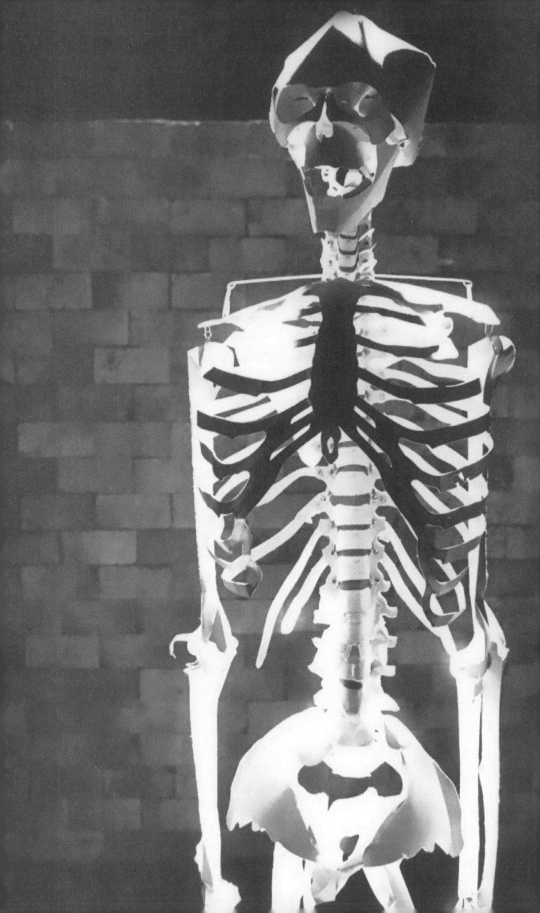

painted wooden skeleton put up![113] This cohabitation of life and death is a feature of Mexican culture, death being a mere extension of life and expressed in an artistic language that combines Western religious baroque with local figures and ancestral beliefs. Kahlo lives in companionship with death. She refers to it in her notebooks, at once as a friend and a repugnant companion, the "bald old whore." The reading that Lepage offers, through actor Lise Roy, who plays multiple secondary roles, is based on this ambiguity. Death, *La Pelona*, even becomes the double, the reflection, and the other self of the artist, who appears to be talking to herself. The final scene brings them face to face, on either side of the frame of the standing mirror with no glass, Death simulating Kahlo's reflection. Kahlo lures Death with a jewel and, grabbing his hand, pulls him over to her side of the mirror. She puts Death in the wheelchair in her stead, and it is Death that she sends off to the opening of her exhibition, wheeling him offstage.

A recurring derivative force, death runs through all of Lepage's productions. Protagonists commit or attempt to commit suicide and are witness to suicide, such as a man jumping in front of the metro while Lucie looks on in *Polygraph* and the medically assisted suicide of Luke in *The Seven Streams of the River Ota* or of the mother in *The Far Side of the Moon*. Homicide sometimes appears instead of suicide (*Circulations, Tectonic Plates, Polygraph, Possible Worlds*). An obsessive fear in the baroque, death did not represent a repudiation of life; in Lepage's work it appears in the form of props as a contrast and a visible dynamic opposition: the 3-D scythe in *The Tempest* and the mini-coffin in *The Far Side of the Moon* – a pencil box filled with pebbles. Hiroshima is an intersection of opposites that provided Lepage the initial shock that triggered his creative process. He expects to find desolation, but he discovers life and flowers, and he learns that the first things rebuilt after the bomb were two bridges: "a Yin bridge and a Yang bridge, one with phallic shapes and the other with vaginal shapes. For life to return to Hiroshima."[114] The theme of sexuality runs alongside the theme of death, through constant nudity related to the notion of surpassing oneself – the gymnasium and Mount Olympus that Lepage refers to[115] – which is not inconsistent with the baroque emphasis on the body, this extravagance of the body, carnal despite the context of Catholicism:

The skeleton
in *Polygraph* is
manipulated like
a string puppet.

PHOTO

Claudel Huot

> If you want to reveal life and the instincts to survive
> and reproduce, you often have to approach them
> through death. *The Seven Streams of the River Ota*
> entirely centred on this contrast. Nothing in the cen-
> tury represents death, nothingness and desolation as
> much as the atomic bomb. And yet, for us, it inspired
> a very living, extremely sensual show. Over time, I've
> learned that recurring appearance of death and suicide
> in my plays has produced the opposite effect, that it
> has led us towards life.[116]

Childhood as a source of symbols, regrets, and dreams marks many of Lepage's creations, and the return to childhood, through different resurgences, always begins through contact with death. An absent being leaves an empty space on the set (*The Dragons' Trilogy, Vinci, Needles and Opium, Elsinore, The Seven Streams of the River Ota, Zulu Time, The Far Side of the Moon, The Andersen Project*). The omnipresence of the shadow is one way of conjuring the spectre. The dramatic action contained in two-dimensionality is another way of addressing the place of the deceased. The theme of death is a strong visual source, for a dynamic look that explores the potential of the image onstage.

Lepagean transcendence also appears as an expression of the ubiquity of the gaze exploring a set that stages it. The set, like the baroque object or monument, is built like a vision machine, examining the gaze and making it a central element. And this *miembro divino*[117] common to the baroque and Lepage makes it possible to work on sharing the visible, by multiplying the possibilities and the impasses. Lepage's sets are built for a moving eye, but an eye that can sometimes be fooled and caught in a labyrinth of illusions. The tiny cameras in *Elsinore* and *The Far Side of the Moon* are like many individual, ubiquitous gazes. The porthole in *The Far Side of the Moon* is reminiscent of the eye of baroque painting and of the mirror, which is merely a reflecting version of the eye, it too rounded like an eye. This baroque omnivoyance influences the creation of vision sets. And, besides, the idea crops up on Lepage's stage and film sets and justifies the mirrors and use of technology. The impression of a low-angle shot, an opening to the sky, is created onstage, an opening that isn't always placed above the audience but rather in front of them. The vertical panel passes for horizontal, by convention. This shift in convention is created by inclining the real or simulated performance area. Inclining the stage, which first appeared as an influence of film on Lepage's practice, can be seen in light of his baroque heritage, which often uses visual tilts: characters are angled 45 degrees on certain tombs or even more in *trompe l'oeil* architecture. When the image is inverted, the tacit convention required by the audience makes them enter the scene. This is not an immersion in a totalizing image, but rather immersion that the audience participates in, their gaze creating the metamorphosis and overall movement. Their gaze is captured to penetrate a new image with highly dynamic lines. The line of vision changes, the earth rears up, shots straighten up, twist, stretch as far as they can. This is how the table and the Monolith in *Elsinore* move, and how we go from the main character in *Jean-Sans-Nom* seen running in profile to an overhead view of him. These foreshortened and overhead images let us in on the secret, of course, but also have us participate in the framing. They assume the movement of the eye, either the eye of the camera or the eye of the audience.

Flames emerge from the heart of *The Damnation of Faust*, when Marguerite sings about how her passion has burned her, foreshadowing purgatory for her and the infernal flames awaiting Faust. These flames occupy the entire length of the set and are the largest ever in Lepage's shows: they grow as Marguerite sings. Faithfully rendering what she is saying, the flames are also the trademark of a culminating show, one of Lepage's most baroque. The flame is again a shape that is always similar and yet never identical. The approach is baroque: repeating the same shape until the head swims – the repeated shape creating the impression of depth – and a predilection for fragments, themes that are oddly echoed in serialization and fragmentation. Repetition with variations is one of the features of pop art, but it is also what directors like Lepage do with their idea of a non-transparent montage. In live performance as in fine art, the figure is repeated through the use of reflection, not simply setting figures side by side, but complex montages that combine doubling the image, reflection, inverted reflections, and possibly superimposition. Today breaking down the subject through fragmentation is reinforced through the practice of sampling that, using a sampler for sounds or editing software for images, generalizes the montages in loops of short sequences. However, this infinite spiral deliberately marks a return to the point of departure, the movement to the new loop, which at the same time helps make an archaic technology visible: the scratch characteristic of the needle on a vinyl record, the distortion of the voice in old microphones, the echo of radio, and so on.

The stage design for *The Damnation of Faust* is based on this sort of repetition, accentuating what the baroque began by mechanizing it. Lepage uses the same silhouettes on the four levels of his set: hussars, women in hoop dresses, scholars in their studies, ballerinas, demons, and so on, in fairly simple typologies of easily identifiable costumes and colours. These similar silhouettes move in different directions, in twenty-four identical boxes – the same tables for scholars, the same guardrails, the same image twenty-four times over – to more effectively disrupt and create a feeling of vertigo and number. The figures, apart from the figures of the three protagonists, dissolve into their own repetition. The process is highly visible; for example, when Faust is in his library drinking the contents of his flask, eighteen other boxes on three levels reproduce the same tableau: a table, a scholar, and lateral projections of library shelves. Faust is lit only by a projector and is identifiable by his beard. The figure becomes, as in the human whirlwinds in baroque paintings – clusters of bodies entangled or winged punctuation – a malleable element. It contributes to an overall figure in which it remains perceptible, but is no longer the means of recognition. It is also the use of repetition that could constitute this new baroque. If, as a result of the crossbreeding from which it emerges, baroque increases the number of encounters, intersections, and protagonists, then it behaves as a simple broken mirror making a kaleidoscopic, multiplied. and possibly fragmentary representation from an initial group, with no regard for weight. The image can be upside down, like the hanging creatures in *The Damnation of Faust*. Technology takes over for the figures created by the baroque; it increases the repetition. The expansion of the material thus expands the gaze: the eye is invited to spin and rotate in all directions. The *shoji* screens and the screen panels move and slide where movement could only be suggested in baroque churches. They open onto an empty centre, an empty core that the actors and the images will fill, in which everything is played.

A series of silhouettes during the horse race in *The Damnation of Faust*.

PHOTO

Eric Mahoudeau /
Opéra National de Paris

VERTICAL AMBIGUITY

The latest creations show signs of thinking about the screen and
the interval, which is original in Lepage's work. Baroque transcendence gives impetus to a greater vertical orientation on the set and
mobility of the gaze. However, what's important is no longer the
origin of this transcendence or its possibilities, but the surface on
which everything is laid out, a surface that expands so that it is no
longer the main element of the set, but, like the door mentioned
earlier, the thing through which everything is seen. Screen, image,
set, and cube, everything is a threshold. The screen set is a logical
response to a Japanese question, but is also reminiscent of the
composition of baroque productions. The screen in *Jean-Sans-Nom*
is always present, and the entire show is seen through this tableau,
just as *The Damnation of Faust* takes place in this row of symbolic
monitors. Half the scenes in *The Andersen Project* play out on a
strange screen with rounded edges (nicknamed "the conch").[118]

The screen is both the backdrop to the stage and a medium for the projected image. The screen grew for *La Casa Azul*, and the stage is even sparser, with nothing more than the screen, a few props, and legs. This screen refers to cinema or television with a 16:9 aspect ratio, through blue snow similar to that of a waiting monitor. There is no more depth in the strict sense with this screen, or, rather, there are no more points of reference. Where theatrical tradition used a perspectivist illusion, the set of *La Casa Azul* keeps this impression, but without any pretence at figures or icons: everything assumes its place on the flat blue screen, a place without depth but that nonetheless hosts 3-D figures.

To achieve this paradoxical space, the creation team tried to create "gobe images,"[119] using leg panels that make an image appear and disappear in a space where the permanent screen surface (other than the scrim screen) and the light beam of the projector are no longer distinguishable. The screen panel moves sideways or rotates, and it literally disappears into the blue, taking the image with it. This system of gaping holes that are invisible to the audience and supposed to emit or swallow a light beam, is similar to the baroque architectural ideal of "a room in black marble, in which light enters only through orifices so angled that nothing on the outside can be seen through them, yet they but illuminate or color the decor of a pure inside."[120] This description applies equally well to this set and to La Caserne, and it describes the baroque *studiolo*, traditional Japanese constructions,[121] or a work by Le Corbusier, seemingly far removed from the preoccupations of the baroque: the Convent of La Tourette in France. In fact, inside La Caserne, there are no openings and no light other than electric and the indirect light from the workshops if the blinds are open. On the set for *La Casa Azul*, like in the baroque chapels and *studiolo* of Florence, Urbino, and Gubbio, the low-angled light comes from invisible openings. These spaces create the effect of an autonomous interior, an interior that doesn't need an exterior – an empty core – because no rays of light are captured and there are no openings on this flat background. The baroque trademark lies in this autonomy of the interior and independence of the exterior, often contrasted. And the fact that the facade of La Caserne is designed as scenery detached from the structure only extends the analogy: "Far from being adjusted

The screen is both the stage backdrop and a medium for the projected image. *The Andersen Project.*

PHOTO

Érick Labbé

to the structure, the Baroque facade only tends to thrust itself forward,"[122] while the interior remains closed.

Does this light that "slides as if through a slit into the middle of shadows," according to Deleuze quoting Leibniz, come from a small basement window, a thin angled opening, through intermediary mirrors? In fact Deleuze refers to a large number of small mirrors that seal a white light in this space without openings that he calls "monad."[123] Lepage uses this sealed light and white mirrors for his sets in his image-based shows, in the form of screens or actual mirrors, most often two-way mirrors, like the screen panels in *La Casa Azul*. Like a sort of two-dimensional column, they turn on their own axis and disappear.

The set showcases the very evolution of its design. The stage coincided with the outline of a box, a horizontal outline of a performance area. Then this outline was raised and righted like a screen. The consecrated area is reduced; it becomes a surface rather than an area, like what happened in Hiroshima. In this process, area becomes a space for images to be projected onto, and the evolution of this work shows the extent to which any part of the stage, no matter where it is, is a potential screen. If the stage acts as a showcase, a surface for presenting objects, then the effect of showcasing the sign in this way makes every element a potential surface for real or symbolic projection. So, it's not the box and the receptacle that are so essential, but rather their outline. The frame dominates: staging means setting a limit; it involves organization within a frame. This frame sometimes coincides with one of the sides of the set box, closing off the space onstage, but gradually, while the reference space rights itself, the box is no longer the main criteria for defining the stage. All this is similar to the *tokonoma* (display alcove) that Lepage refers to in *The Seven Streams of the River Ota*. The recess denies its own depth, for a surface of shadows shining with a few reflections or striped with a bit of paint, or a strangely two-dimensional flower arrangement. The box becomes a surface around a recess of shadows from which the image emerges.

This is what we have already observed in the evolution of Lepage's sets, which are basically obverse despite a few attempts at theatre in the round. The proscenium opening gradually loses its depth, until it reaches a minimal depth, fostering the idea of the screen image[124] – because this flat, infinite space, like Turrell's recessed light, almost palpable but penetrable, becomes screen-like. The two-dimensional surface has no more depth than the screen. It's a unique depth in the case of *The Andersen Project* with the conch that is both like the *tokonoma* and a work by Turrell or Kapoor. There is depth, more than 1 metre in fact, but because the surface is white and rounded, the impression of depth isn't apparent when seen head-on. The projected images often repudiate it, but when the actor moves and walks in the screen – which for a time becomes a subway platform or a room in a pavilion at the 1867 World's Fair – the depth is obvious, and surface changes to depth. During Frédéric's nightmare, while he is facing the lit ramp and in the image of the opera house, we see the announcement of the cancellation of the performance of his libretto. Suddenly, he no longer knows why the performance has been cancelled and, feeling faint, he falls and rolls in the rounded edge of the screen. The image disappears when he falls, revealing the materiality of the set. The actor doesn't merely face the screen; he performs in it, rolls and sits in it, during a scene waiting for a metro in Paris. The image of the bench is lined up with the rounded part of the screen, so the actor can lean on it as if he were sitting. This is what happened in the movements of the frames and the rails in *The Seven Streams of the River Ota*, and what the sets of *Jean-Sans-Nom* and *The Damnation of Faust* responded to. With *La Casa Azul*, everything unfolds surrounded in blue, an infinite space that displays figures in an endless luminous depth at the same time as on the flat surface of the screen. The actors are performing in a space without reference points, most often two-dimensional. It is a vertical set with two axes: everything seems to be set for an overhead view, but everything is also seen from the front, with the actor standing in the outline of the screen.

The size of Lepage's symbolic screen gradually grows. There is a regular progression from *Coriolanus* to *The Damnation of Faust*. The screen occupied almost the entire proscenium opening at the Opéra de Bastille, and the largest touch screen ever was used for *Kà*.[125] But more importantly the usable surface for the image grows as well. Like a computer monitor, the entire surface of the screen is used. While the set shows the influence of the screen, in some incarnations (*The Damnation of Faust, La Casa Azul, Kà*) it draws on the visual organization of the computer monitor. Where icons on a monitor – files, images, text, tables – can be moved in any direction and to any location, on the monitor the elements that make up the stage image occupy the entire surface. Like the icons, indications of potential files, they can be superimposed, but, unlike icons, the transparency of one element over another is real, hence the idea of the palimpsest. We get used to organizing the computer screen's desktop using the entire surface, and opening many files, which are superimposed as icons and control windows. This mosaic surface is full, top to bottom and left to right, whether on game consoles, televisions, or computer screens.

Our screen-based perception is the outcome of channel surfing and generalized compartmentalizing, and we have become accustomed to tracking different pieces of information at the same time.[126] Lepage has accustomed us to protagonists being elevated in the proscenium opening. Thus, in the image of *Jean-Sans-Nom*, the actors use an unusual surface, in its rectangular form, filling it top to bottom. Similarly, the rectangular screen delimited by the structure in *Zulu Time* – a symbolic screen when a screen is mimicked under the moving bridges and a real one when the large screen is unfurled – is used in different ways. The mobile bridges make the icons move, and so the actors and elements onstage move, reminiscent of the electronic sweeping of the televised image. The bridges are the lines, and the actors the points of lights scurrying to create the image with their rapid sweeping. During underwater search for the plane wreckage, everything that is high under the bridge is a screen image, and the lighting creates the impression of water; the void becomes full, and light becomes matter.

The influence of the computer is particularly noticeable in the composition of images for the correspondence read in voice-over in *La Casa Azul*. The handwritten text of the letter appears on the screen, along with the envelope, sometimes shown on both sides. A stamp is placed on the upper right hand of the screen, as if the screen were the envelope. Documents are added as the scenes dictate: a portrait, the reproduction of a painting as a background, like sheets of paper emerging from the envelope. Everything is laid out on the screen as if it were desk, with the photo of the things found on it, such as the envelope, the handwritten pages, and so on, the computer screen – another desk with files of various sizes – but also like the brain, a personal and organic desk that brings together a range of visual information when it discovers the letter: a sort of cubist vision. Lepage is no longer projecting a unified image or a simple large-format reproduction, but rather a composite image, developed using a new aesthetics and approach. The screen, via the projected image, is seen as a flat surface every inch of which will be used. However, this surface remains ambiguous, like the surface that appears in du Bouchet's poem "Fire Where It Shines":

> Depth here
> whole sea-surge on a field's wing
> takes to the air.[127]

The image is first projected onto the scrim, but lined up with what appears onstage; different projected layers can be detected: the bed, a panel, and a character. At one point, there are four

A handwritten letter by Frida Kahlo and other elements are arranged over the entire surface of the image like on a computer desktop. *La Casa Azul.*

PHOTO

Jacques Collin and Lionel Arnould

surfaces receiving the projector's veil of light. The actor's body is inserted in the centre of these projections, not transparently or superimposed on the projected images, but through a desire to give the actor his own area of visibility. The projection hugs the singers in *Jean-Sans-Nom* and covers them in *La Casa Azul*, creating the impression that they are surrounded, a two-dimensional projection that inserts 3-D elements in its "depth." Lepage tries to integrate the actor into the projected image and, more specifically, to the screen, but to accomplish this, he realized he didn't need 3-D imagery. The important thing is to make the very notion of the screen evolve, to create discord. In his later creations, everything takes place in the depth of the proscenium frame[128] and one of the main points of interest in *The Damnation of Faust* is precisely this constant but changing wall of monitors. With *The Busker's Opera*, Lepage fully exploits the mobility of the plasma screen, which can move anywhere in the proscenium opening, but also in the depth of the stage: it can move both perpendicular and parallel to the audience, and it can be raised

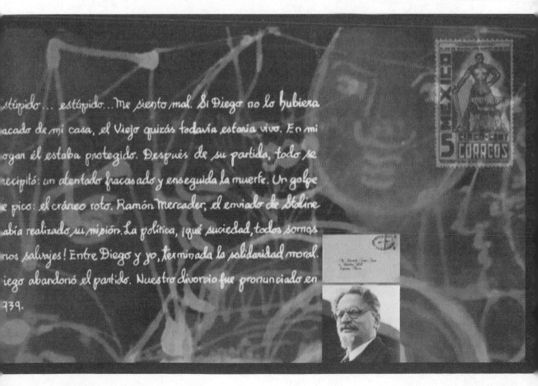

and lowered using a hydraulic hook. The plasma screen transports the image, superimposing itself on the actors along a symbolic veil, a fragment of which it makes visible through its very materiality. Like any monitor, the plasma screen doesn't require any distance between the source of projection and the screen, but here the box is flat and the interval is surface.

In the same way that he developed the object, Lepage has developed a multiform conception of the screen that assumes that we have a polysemic vision of it. The screen is not physically transformed, but it becomes conceptually more flexible; it is a hybrid surface, or, more precisely, a surface with changing density. Because air is often what penetrates the screen – in talking about Japan, Lepage indeed refers to boundaries "made of air"[129] – or water, in any case an element that changes the symbolic density. A new form of this variation in density is accomplished with the mobility of the conch screen in *The Andersen Project*. The concave screen can move back or advance toward the house. Made of spandex canvas, it can even swell for magnificent zooms. The image literally moves toward or away from the audience. The actor sometimes stands in the screen or faces it, and the impression that the image changes size is even more striking. We experience zoom ins and zoom outs. The conch reaches the edge of the stage with a statue set on its edge where Lepage moves about sitting on trunks. Once animated images are added, the audience's gaze is drawn into a twofold movement.

The change in density is also created by piercing or even symbolically breaking open the screen's surface. This opening up of the surface is used consistently as another form of the detachment raised earlier as one of the more common fantasies in the relationship between the actor and the screen. In *The Seven Streams of the River Ota*, the opening takes the form of an alternation between acted and projected scenes that coincides with the sliding of the *shoji* screens. This same alternation is used in *The Andersen Project*, between the scenes with the conch and those with the sex-shop booths and phone booths, clearly obverse. In *La Casa Azul*, Rivera pretends to hit the fresco he has painted, which was turned down for the Rockefeller Center. The projected image falls apart, and the fresco explodes into fragments that fall to the ground. Earlier, the red image of a sun was gradually

The digitized fresco cracks. *La Casa Azul*.

PHOTO

Jacques Collin and Lionel Arnould

The explosion of the fresco is visually spectacular, while a realistic soundtrack amplifies the experience. *La Casa Azul*.

PHOTO

Jacques Collin and Lionel Arnould

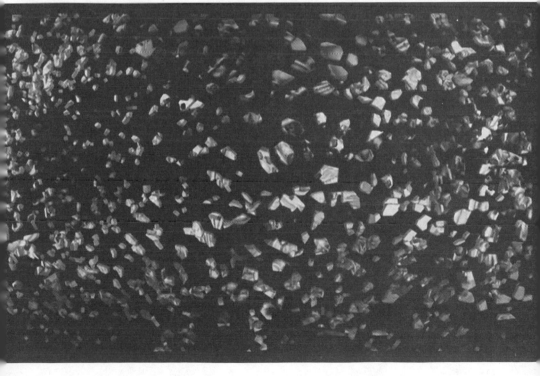

covered by a round shadow that eventually hides it. All that is left is a colourful vibration, a dusty haze of white around a circle of shadow. This can create the impression of an opening on the surface of the screen, all the more so since the actors are standing within the outlines of the shadow: Rivera and Kahlo comb each other's hair, under the ritual invocations of a Mexican divinity.

Lepage's set is a surface of shadow of varying density and depth, an upright surface for actors and images that rotate and are elevated and superimposed. But it is significant that the shows open and close on a clearly two-dimensional blank surface. An affinity for monochrome arises naturally in the evolution of this practice:[130] monochrome, including in the *shoji* screens, is the ultimate meeting of surface and depth. When the colour is black or grey, as in the backgrounds for later productions, its material is the shadow. Lepage distills hybrid presences between surface and depth, drawn from the history of painting and cinema or a computer semantic, even the traditional Japanese dwelling. There are many references from the history of painting; for example, the works of Mark Rothko, Clyfford Still, and Barnett Newman. The physical confrontation with the canvas happens through the emotion generated by the colour and, sometimes, as with Newman and Still, through the emergence of colours on the canvas. Newman calls his emerging bands "zips." The contrast is often violent, creating the feeling that the canvas is ripping, a rupture or piercing of what was a monochrome surface: "The rip and the accident sustain the presence of the event, and make the pattern erupt in the field of the colour."[131] The same applies to the images emerging from the blue background in *La Casa Azul*, while the red figures run across the monochrome length in *The Damnation of Faust*, red stripes on a blue background, or the splash of fire of Clary's red hair in the grey tinted environment of the projected illustrations in *Jean-Sans-Nom*. We penetrate Lepage's images through these rips, breaches that rupture chromatically with their environment. Like a monochrome canvas, the screen's surface and, more broadly, the set, offers a face-to-face encounter that becomes immersion. Monochromatic white runs through several scenes of *The Andersen Project*. In one of the scenes, the conch moves closer to a statue, Jean-Baptiste Clésinger's *Woman Bitten by a Serpent*, at the Musée d'Orsay. This marble statue on

The monochromatic stage set creates tension in *Jean-Sans-Nom*.

PHOTO

Vincent Jacques

the white background of the conch creates a monochromatic effect from which Frédéric emerges, dressed head to toe in black. Earlier he had taken part in a psychology session for the dog of his ex-girlfriend Marie. Sitting on a stool in the conch, he floats in the screen's total whiteness, and he's an albino no less![132] Audience and actor come together in a single impetus. Piercing the screen's surface, they are both encouraged to take flight and discover that the shadow contains all the images, that the surface is mobile and changing, that the gaze is free, and that movement is a rotation after takeoff. This is often the perception that Turrell's work creates when, standing at the edge of what appears to be an unlimited, pure, and luminous surface, we are tempted to plunge in, but contact with the surface never comes.

The screen in *The Andersen Project* is well designed as an ambiguous surface. Frédéric, an albino, appears to float against the white backdrop during a dog psychology session.

PHOTO

Érick Labbé

Originally, the breach is an opening in a fortified enclosure. We have compared the box, the cube, and La Caserne to a fortress. In this case, the breach is the intersection of the box and the screen. It moves the screen closer to the box, giving it depth, and the box to the screen, emphasizing a surface while piercing it. The opening is the optimal point of this centripetal dialectic, its expression at the same time as its point of dislocation. The spandex surface in *The Andersen Project* swells at one point. The screen changes form, through creases. And we see the folds on the surface at the end of the scene, before the material is retracted. The retractability of spandex – the idea was to be able to aspirate the screen and the image – goes back to a whole psychoanalytic backdrop of the image pierced like the comforting recess, like an abyss, which the works of Anish Kapoor refer to, increasing the emptiness in the monochromatic surfaces. The latex surface grows deeper, a flat surface that suddenly has depth. The veil of projection acquires a broader and more ambiguous range of movement, something that started with the tilted spandex screen in *Needles and Opium*, which the suspended actor walked on. Like the screen in *Noise, Sounds, and Sweet Airs* (1994), it loses its shape under the pressure of a man holding an axe and pressing himself against the screen. The breach, like the centripetal dialectic, is rendered by the aspiration making the monochrome surface an aspirating space or an abyss. The breach is the encounter that Didi-Huberman refers to, a dimension "where the objective distances collapse and where the *there* becomes unlimited, rips itself from the *here*, from detail, from

The screen distorts as it rotates. *Needles and Opium*.

PHOTO

Jacques Collin

visible proximity."[133] *La Casa Azul* and *The Andersen Project* offer
the experience of this place where the "*there* becomes unlimited."
At some moment in each show the image is torn; for example, in
Elsinore when the tapestry behind which Polonius stands becomes
the foreground – the Monolith screen – when it is pierced by the
swipe of a sword. The breach that results is another name for the
translator, an essential boatman, or for the "doorway protagonist,"
recurrent in Lepage's work. Lepage's stages, which fit with many
characteristics of art history and are part of a history of images, try
to physically open that which contains the image, with the same
symbolism as the ritual opening and closing of the painted image
in the altarpiece, of the relic, or of the exhibition of the Latin *imago*.
At the same time they help construct this archetypal idea, from
before the *eidolon* and the *imago*, of the image that opens up and
contemplates us, and then engulfs us, an image that is a threshold,
not only of a door but of a border. There is no anxiety before the
gaping openness of the image: Lepage combats the anxiety by taking
flight; he doesn't let us fall, he takes us higher. The breach is what

draws the audience onto the stage: it's the path or the entryway. It is what makes the use of technology not artificial; the breach fills Lepage's world with humanity or, rather, it is a pathway to humanity.

This breach often takes the form of frame openings: doors, windows, the symbolic lens of a black box, a viewfinder, and so on, in sets that, fundamentally, are inspired by the cranium. We witness the process of creating and rendering images, which operate between gaze and memory. And then the breach disrupts the tight weave of the image and memory. The vertical surface summons a memory of the gaze, through a memory of the image, and the influence of the baroque makes possible every form of coming closer, angle of view, and colour. It allows or reinforces the clashes that activate memory. The influence of the baroque, which finds a surprising extension in the computerized set and a serene completeness in the traditional Japanese environment, allows Lepage to become more radical in his ideas of how to use the screen to go beyond the mythical arrangement of the quarry, by refining the stage image, while making it more unstable – the "ridiculousness" that Loti refers to. All the echoes surge into the breach and are jostled about: the box breaks open, releasing the echoes while the screen reflects them make for an instant. The breach creates a draught that prevents stability, and for Lepage, this is essential.[134] The baroque is another term for uncertainty and questioning, but there is no anxiety inherent in it. Memory swirls around above chaos, and the gaze hangs on to what emerges and then disappears. Elevation and bedazzlement remain.

As an obvious and easily penetrated breach, a hole develops in the screen to represent a lunar eclipse. *La Casa Azul.*

PHOTO

Yanick MacDonald

PART FOUR

The Visual Laboratory in Conclusion

In many ways, Lepage's practice is a symbol of the evolution of the theatre of images, trying its hand at different aspects without adopting all of them. There is intermingling, borrowed from crossbreeding, or echoes, because there is a receptacle: Lepage's visual laboratory is closed and defined. But like Turrell's recesses of light, he can create the impression of "vastness," which is the basis of nineteenth-century landscapes. Traditional theatre has always used spatial constraints, in particular the proscenium stage box. By intensifying it with the use of technology, Lepage turns his stage box into a set under surveillance that values the old delimitations while thumbing its nose at them. He places a box onstage, knowing how many partitions, limits, and constraints are needed for the mix to work. Trajectories are defined, and the echo is created within the box.

The ambiguity of space is fundamental. It's part of the tradition of a theatre of images, with Wilson at its head, the stage for which was set by the evolution of theatre at the turn of the nineteenth century. Beginning at the end of the 1880s, advances in lighting lifted the image from the painted canvas and allowed it to occupy space. The image was freed from its medium and its duty of representation, at the same time discharging theatre of the obligation of three-dimensionality. Just as the canvas can be pure surface, the stage can be a two-dimensional space. And this started at the beginning of the twentieth century, before the screen appeared onstage – simply consider the obverse productions of the

Royal Swedish Ballet. A recurring issue in the theatre of images, the ambiguity of space created by the screen remains, regardless of the medium used: broadcast or projected images, screen or monitor, and in rooms where the audience faces the stage, a variation of the proscenium stage model. Sellars uses many obverse and satellite windows in his use of the monitor; Wilson uses immense paintings cut into ambiguous strips; show to show, Dumb Type enlarges the surface of the screen and reduces the depth of the set, the actors' movements replaced by real or symbolic inlaying. The screen diverges from the painted canvas because its icons can change, but the essence remains its obverse nature, with attempts made to divert it through screens of different types: angled screens, lamellar screens, translucent screens, and so on. Lepage uses layering in the form of vertical sedimentation, creating a palimpsest. The screen surfaces and the set as a whole invite successive deposits that aren't always palpable: images are projected onto it, patterns are found on them, elements such as actors, objects, and other panels frame them. The audience also adds their own layers in the form of connections and memories. What is happening with the conch in *The Andersen Project* is not so much a vertical sedimentation as a penetration to the very heart of this sedimentation and the heart of the emerging image.

The audience is invited to penetrate this space which, from the cave to the virtual environment by way of the baroque, asks the question of how it should be penetrated. Mirrors, cameras, screen surfaces of all sorts, and microphones: everything needed to amplify, reflect, and observe the space, and to track the echo is there. The stage in the form of box under surveillance becomes, through the design of the theatre material and the audience's involvement, the cranium. Through technology, Lepage reconnects with something that is at the origin of theatre: the place where talking and acting happen becomes the place from which we see and from which we understand. When we enter Lepage's visual laboratory, we are moving into ourselves, contemplating our own range of colours and our own space: technology as a new catharsis? Of course, mirrors make space appear larger and multiply surfaces. By penetrating our flesh barriers like clinical investigators, they also expand our interior space. In Lepage's work, the mirror is both an instrument for introspection and an echo that uses the double (the twin, a recurring figure) and ends up breaking down certainties into reflections ad infinitum. The mirror, which was to cover the sides of the square box that was supposed to contain the actor in *Elegant Universe*,[1] is also the breach or an opening in the frame. Through the mirror the echo finds its impulse, and space can be delimited (the partition) while being expanded (the reflection), in the end transforming the echo (the reflected message). The breach is featured in every technological echo raised; the idea has long existed in Lepagean theatre: the screen-like opening in *Coriolanus* with the actor emerging from the symbolic screen, the spandex surface the actor walks on in *Needles and Opium*, the surface of the Monolith pierced with a door lined up with a cut-out in the projected image – a gap that allows Lepage as an actor to work in it – the first translucent surfaces of stage design in *The Seven Streams of the River Ota*. All of this sets the stage for the breach, even before the screen surface downstage becomes commonplace.

The breach is the metaphor for the encounter, the obligatory opening onto another, at the same time as it is the eye's focal point on the mélange that occurs in Lepage's receptacle. Whether on the set or in rehearsals, there is a closed area in which different elements are jumbled together, mixed together by Lepage's initial impulse, "a creator of contact." The breach connects with archetypes of the Japanese and European baroque, taking on new roles, while happily coming back to that of the screen: the scrim, the plasma screen, or the giant touch screen. There is an endless rivalry between chaos and harmony in this stirred-up visual laboratory on Lepage's stage.

The visual and poetic concern for the stage image, stretched between puppet theatre and quarry, allows Lepage to strip his stage. The revival of *The Dragons' Trilogy* in 2003 marked a return to these minimal sets, as did *The Far Side of the Moon* and *The Andersen Project*. A return toward a physically stripped set, but in a frame that is upright and aesthetically sublime. Lepage is not seeking the perfect image,[2] in slow motion that would suspend time to better set out the image, something that can be found in the evolution of Robert Wilson's work.[3] In Lepage's work there is an undeniable sense of the image that was in part behind his quick rise to fame. His first images are recognizable through the power of their pragmatics, like the reversal of the point of view in *Circulations*. Images make the image in a way; they are striking and remain with the audience long after the show, without becoming too precious. This is what emerges in certain scenes in *The Geometry of Miracles*, with characters in slow motion on monochromatic, intense backgrounds – a blue screen during the scenes in the desert at Taliesin – and particularly in *The Damnation of Faust*, with intense contrasts between the red sculptural figures of demons and the white figures of the women on a colourful background. Striking images occur most particularly in *The Andersen Project*, when we hear the Danish tale while contemplating superb images (the tree from the story and then the dryad within it, a cart, and so on, against backgrounds of intensely dramatic skies). Certain sequences in *Kà* could also give in to this temptation, but this approach seems to better suit the genre and aesthetic of Cirque du Soleil which functions by tableau, combining physical skill, visual surprise, and the artistic beauty of the whole. Unlike Wilson, Lepage has few pictorial influences; his references are primarily cinema, photography, and even music. However, his stage creations increasingly refer to the visual arts and, in the film *Possible Worlds*, he keeps coming back to a particular painting by Pedro Pires, representing the cottage that appears in the film: looking head on, we see a normal image, but in profile or at a slight angle, the image is distorted, because the surface of the canvas is made up of several truncated and juxtaposed pyramids. The slightest movement around the painting disrupts its reading. This effect is typical of Lepage's practice, in which the scenes drawn from the painting are in movement and offer visual inversions, creating visual impact more than "formal organization."[4] Herein lies the difference between Wilson's approach and Lepage's approach. In Lepage's work, the image is above all thought of as impact, final form, visual intuition, constantly transforming, and having multiple meanings. Whereas in Wilson's work, the image can lose its "figurative function," its power of representation, to "reference itself." In Lepage's work, the image doesn't operate in a closed manner, on itself, but in relationships.[5]

Lepage demands that theatre speaks a contemporary language, and above all that language must be visual. He seems to be saying that we can't practise theatre today as if there had been no photography, cinema, computers, the Internet, virtual environments, and the evolution of the visual arts. Like Sellars, who claims to address the "post-rock generation" when he stages an opera, what's specific about Lepage is that he takes into account all of these technological languages and brings them together in a space that draws from visual media, but that is and remains a space for theatre, indeed a space for theatres, because it has a permanent *mise en abyme* or Droste effect of small theatres and puppet theatres. His theatre vies with these technological universes; it absorbs them, conquers them, but is transformed in turn. This is accomplished without any real conflict, because Lepage doesn't set theatre and technology against each other: he stages technology, he dramatizes it as he does with everything he treats.

For him, theatre comes last; the gaze comes first. It is the visual aspect that is most important, beyond the technological, sculptural effort and before the exploitation of a repertoire. The eye is the grammarian of this language, creating a syntax that combines elements by creating coincidences. The eye circulates between the two "openings" that are also thresholds. From the eye to these openings, the path is in turn winding or dazzling. But the eye explores; it circulates and it too is drawn by this visual laboratory of images, by this practice that proposes a new way of seeing.

EPILOGUE

Eight years have passed since this book was published in French, eight years during which, while pursuing creative work and teaching, I have continued to appreciate and view Lepage's creations.[1] During this time, there has been a definite shift toward a genre not investigated before: opera. Since 2005, Lepage has staged eight operas and lyrical plays: *1984* (2005), *The Rake's Progress* (2007), *The Nightingale and Other Short Fables* (2009), *The Tempest* (2012), and the four parts of Wagner's *Der Ring des Nibelungen*, performed between 2010 and 2012 at the Metropolitan Opera in New York. In addition, he has continued his theatrical work, creating six plays: *Lipsynch* (2007), *The Blue Dragon* (2008), *Eonnagata* (2009), and *La tempête* (a 2011 production of Shakespeare's *The Tempest*, performed outdoors at Wendake, a Huron First Nations reserve situated on the St. Charles River, fifteen minutes from downtown Quebec City), as well as *Spades* (2012) and *Hearts* (2013), the first two in a series of four plays entitled Playing Cards. All this creative work is in addition to *The Image Mill*, an astonishing sound-and-light undertaking in the port of Quebec City, created in 2008 to celebrate the four-hundredth anniversary of the city, and staged every summer since then, in addition to an architectural lighting version called *Aurora Borealis* presented year-round.

Since 2005, the way Lepage talks about his work has changed. He lays claim more explicitly to certain recurrent themes, some of which I pointed to in this book.[2] In April 2007 Lepage was awarded the Prix Europa in Thessaloniki, Greece, an opportunity for a two-day encounter with him during which he looked back on his career and talked to researchers and long-time allies. So, well after 2005, this was a moment to look back on the journey, and for Lepage to take stock. At about the same time Stéphan Bureau conducted a series of interviews televised on Radio-Canada and published later in print.³ No doubt the reflection these experiences allowed Lepage is connected to the simplification, return to the source, and exploration of new territories we are seeing now. In November 2012, when I found myself back at La Caserne to attend a rehearsal of *Hearts*, the second play in the Playing Cards series, and then returned a few days later only to discover part of the set for the Russian version of *Elsinore*, a padded cube, set at an angle on a wooden structure, I recognized familiar elements, and I sized up the differences.

This book had pointed to the importance of puppets in Lepage's career (and their impact on stage design) and of the baroque (a European baroque, at a time when people were talking only of Japan). The use of puppets has continued in *The Nightingale and Other Short Fables*, based on a group of short operas by Stravinsky, which borrows yet again from an Asian form of puppetry, in fact from several Asian forms, because the centrepiece, *The Nightingale*, includes references to Japanese *bunraku*, Chinese shadow theatre, and Vietnamese water puppets or *mua rôi nuac*, and a secondary

piece, *Fox*, uses techniques inspired by the Indonesian *wayang kulit* for the shadow puppets.

For this Ex Machina collaboration with the Canadian Opera Company (Toronto), Lepage explains that the idea for the puppets was inspired by the medieval bestiary (a compendium of moral tales featuring animals such as the nightingale, fox, cat, hen), but also, for *The Nightingale*, in which a tiny bird expresses the ancient Chinese emperor's fear of death, inspired by the idea that small figures can express feelings that are larger than life – which for Lepage is one of the characteristics of opera. In the libretto for *The Nightingale*, the emperor's palace is situated at the water's edge, giving Lepage the idea of working with Vietnamese water puppets, which are manipulated by performers immersed in pools of water – a traditional theatrical form he and puppet designer Michael Curry saw performed while travelling in Vietnam. The power of the show lies in a rare union between singer, puppet, and Chinese shadow play. In *The Nightingale*, as in Japanese *bunraku* (but without having the puppeteers fade into the background by dressing in black), the character-puppet is at times indistinguishable from the puppeteer-actor, all of them dressed in magnificent jewel colours of ruby, turquoise, and gold. A strange relationship develops between the singer and the puppet, with the singer manipulating the puppet who is supposed to be singing, a perfect duo, which is even more impressive given that the opera performers had to learn puppeteering and how to move while standing waist-deep in water and wearing wetsuits under their colourful costumes. Lepage placed the 67,000 litre pool of water in the orchestra pit, leaving the musicians in full view onstage. Carl Fillion created a set that with its wooden terraces and risers makes the link with sets for *bunraku*, Noh, and Vietnamese puppets, adding a tree that grows and takes shape and a screen backdrop, positioned slightly above the musicians. The result was quite masterful: the singers looked at ease with their puppets and conveyed a sense of playfulness, a visual finesse, and a tremendous sense of lightness, despite the technical constraints of installing the pool of water in the various types of orchestra pits at different theatres.

In the second part of the show, *Fox*, a moral tale about a boastful rooster and the sly fox intent on eating his harem of hens, Lepage creates a playful, striking shadow theatre: inspired by both

White shadow puppets. *Fox*.

PHOTO

Michael Cooper

Chinese shadow play and *wayang kulit* puppetry in reverse (white forms behind a translucent screen with the audience side of the forms lit to make them appear even whiter). He plays with a visual blurring between acrobats miming and using their limbs to form the outlines of the Chinese shadows and the fact that their legs and feet are visible beneath the screen. Once again, Lepage shares the imaginative process; he shows us both the shadow and what created it; the audience is like a child looking on in wonder as an animal appears on the wall, at the same time seeing the two hands lit by the candle. The principle is simple, but the execution is sublime, and at times the team of conjurors can be seen on the audience side creating the shadows that will be shown on the backdrop screen; at other times just their feet can be seen behind the screen. The stroke of genius is in this reversal, in which Lepage creates white shadows and plays with transparency more than with shadow.

In 2013 Lepage restaged *Needles and Opium* with Marc Labrèche, with its much-talked-about hypnosis and airplane scenes, in which the actor is suspended and manipulated. And similarly, the *Hamlet / Collage* (2013), a new creation of *Hamlet* in a version specially created with the famous actor Yevgeny Mironov, again featured the inclined, padded cube from *A Dream Play* and *1984*, pursuing the exploration begun with *Elsinore*: a module in which the actor is unstable, destabilized, basically, manhandled.

One has the impression that the need has waned in Lepage to reference technology, to borrow from other worlds (photo, film, film sets), and to use this material to create the underlying world, implicit in the story. It is as if he has less of a need to *justify* his borrowing or to make it as explicit. The later plays are not built as obviously on the symbolism of the image. They continue to explore the relationship with the image, but make a resolute return to the storyteller's quarry and the box as theatre. There is more limited use of technology and more space for play, handicraft, and dramaturgy.

That said, more than ever his stage is a space for a multi-disciplinary practice and multicultural encounters. And this applies in particular to his approach to opera. By bringing all of his worlds with him, Lepage creates from this total art an even more all-encompassing art. At the very least, he puts things onstage that we are not used to seeing there, such as video, circus arts, and puppets.

Both images:
Modelling in
Hamlet / Collage.

COMPUTER
SIMULATION

Carl Fillion

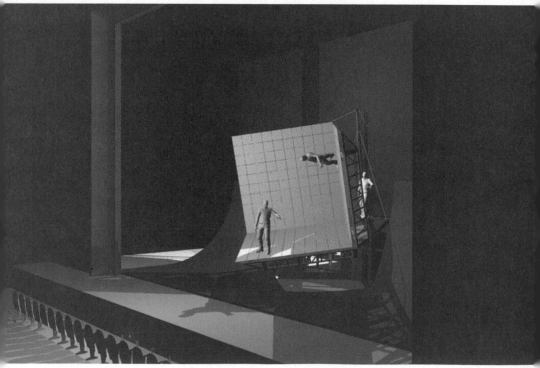

THE LURE OF GEOMETRY
(CUBES, MILLS, AND CIRCLES)

Much has happened since this book was first published in French. In 2005 as I was completing the French edition, Lepage had just finished creating *Kà* for Cirque du Soleil to be performed on an immense touch-screen stage at the MGM Grand in Las Vegas, Nevada. Expanding on ideas first presented in *The Andersen Project,* with *Kà* Lepage drew us into the image, deep into a malleable screen: the shell. He pursued this vertical image, rising up from the stage, becoming pure image.[4]

   The Blue Dragon, a spinoff of *The Dragons' Trilogy* co-written with Marie Michaud, for which I attended the world premiere in Châlons-en-Champagne in 2008,[5] confirms my thinking articulated in this book: the ambiguity of the surface; the proscenium opening as an image – like a computer desktop, a wholly usable surface; the shift of the image; and the increasing number of boxes as in the set for *The Damnation of Faust*. In *The Blue Dragon*, Lepage continues with the interplay of the opening and closing of boxes he began in *The Seven Streams of the River Ota*, but whereas for that show the stage set was on only one level, by *The Damnation of Faust* the action occurred on five different levels, each used in turn as a curtain, then as a border, and then as a screen. Now in *The Blue Dragon*, the acting structure or apparatus is again like a small theatre, with the potential for simultaneous boxes, because there are two playing levels. In Michel Gauthier's set design, which often divides the stage into panels, there is a new reference to the world of comic books – which appears quite rarely in Lepage's work: once in the naming of Théâtre Hummm…, one of his first theatre companies, and then in the allusion to Clark Kent, a.k.a. Superman, in *Circulations*. To create *The Blue Dragon*, Lepage actually started working from his memories of *The Blue Lotus*, the classic 1936 comic in *The Adventures of Tintin* series in which the hero Tintin pursues a drug-smuggling gang to Shanghai, but Lepage ran into problems with Hergé's estate and as a result could not fully exploit these references.[6] Regardless Lepage was able to forge in the story and on the set a rewarding exploration of Chinese calligraphy (Pierre Lamontagne, a visual artist in *The Dragons' Trilogy*, in *The Blue Dragon* is now running

Both images:
Modelling in
Hamlet / Collage.

COMPUTER
SIMULATION

Carl Fillion

a gallery in Shanghai and working on his calligraphy – a medium close to that of the graphic novel): Lepage has moved from working with the image on the screen to the panel of a comic-book grid.

> And this is precisely what the set looks like: eight boxes stacked two storeys high, suggesting the interior of a loft, an art gallery, or a restaurant, with amazing simultaneous scenes or sequences "in boxes," like the three-part account of Pierre and Xiao Ling's [meeting and] relationship: we see the young girl giving Pierre a dragon tattoo in a tattoo parlour, and then the next box shows them sharing a bike, and, finally, in the last box, Pierre meets his son with Xiao Ling. These eight boxes can join to form a single one or break down to become more intricate through unfurling screens and curtains.[7]

The Blue Dragon is filled with wonderful theatrical moments that create fluid scenes and surprising shifts (movements from place to place, bike tours with Shanghai's cityscape in the background). The set is a magical box with components that rise up to become a floor, a table, or the conveyor belt in a sushi bar, changing and developing, with a new, more specific hook in the projected graphics, among them references to contemporary art, as Xiao Ling shows a series of self-portraits.

But at the show's premiere, I noted that the box (the set) was more advanced in development than the story, and that the story was weak, with its rather shaky foundation of "China as explained by Wikipedia." I figured this would get sorted out later on. Yet when I saw the show again a few months later, it had not. This confirmed the dramaturgical shortcomings that can at times limit the impact of Lepage's shows, but that are also one of the marked changes since 2005: a dramaturgical evolution. The cube transformed into the comic-book panel, the starting unit in and on which Lepage creates brilliant compositions; playing with simple geometric shapes is still one of the keys to his universe.

Cube and circle were also behind the success of the opera 1984:[8] the scenography, the sense of the stage saved Maazel's confused score, which borrowed liberally from twentieth-century music. The music was universally panned, but Lepage received widespread praise for his direction, confirming his skill as a stage manager, particularly of choruses (working with his very first set designer, Carl Fillion, who would step away from Lepage's theatrical productions to follow him into opera with Toronto's Canadian Opera Company). The set consisted of a circular form, a sort of optical silo that opened endlessly onto vertigo-inducing interlocking cubes (apartments, shops, the boardroom, and so on), and contained an impressive number of walk-ons, surprising given that the stage house at the Royal Opera House is not large.

The circle is, of course, the circle of the eye of Big Brother, omnipresent on screens, or symbolically present in the form of sliding circular partitions, like an eye blinking. The circle and the cube form complex combinations, created by manipulating fairly simple cubic modules. Lepage again uses the inclined cube, first explored in A Dream Play, to suggest the madness of the protagonist, who is tortured, the cube being padded and small compared with

The cube in 1984.

COMPUTER
SIMULATION

Carl Fillion

the large silo, evoking Room 101, where the character is placed in isolation. I found this same inclined cube (even a double cube) at La Caserne in November 2012, suggesting that the restaging of *Hamlet* as a Russian solo show would explore the theme of madness. The inclined cube creates disorientation. The geometric module, the boxes that open and unfold, create this initial disorientation that makes it possible to accept everything, to construct everything, and to tell everything that is to be told.

The geometric module is undoubtedly one of the points of departure for Lepage's staging of Wagner's complete Ring Cycle, a major undertaking at New York's Metropolitan Opera that ran from 2010 to 2012. In the Ring Cycle, an initial disorientation allows the telling of the whole story. A single set piece can become anything, the gigantic and the epic, a set that is almost light and minimalist, even though a great deal of work was required to ensure that the Met's stage could support the weight of this unusual acting apparatus and that no other opera performed in this opera house involved such lengthy technical work. (Of course, the team would say they didn't have enough time!) Bob Eisenhardt and Susan Froemke's documentary film *Wagner's Dream* (The Metropolitan Opera, 2012) depicts the genesis of *The Ring* and is a tremendous resource for following the team's research, the initial refinements, the incredible challenges, the first technical tests, and the performers' exploration of the set and their learning how the stage apparatus worked. This documentary film shows the advantage of following a project from initial discussions to the premiere.

When designing the acting structure for the Ring Cycle, Lepage proposed a sketch with clean lines – even though the set weighs several tons – based on the idea that Wagner is depicting the creation of the world, but as described by Germanic, indeed Icelandic, legends. The result? A cyclorama partially obscured by a floating mobile partition made of twenty-four large planks and, on the ground, a floor made of planks the same width as those of the wall. This is clearly Lepage's customary set, with its tension between box and screen. But the surface is ambiguous in a new and different way.

Lepage takes what he started in *Elsinore, A Dream Play, La Celestina,* and *1984* to extremes: the mobility of actors via the mobility of the set, the screen, and the easily dismantled set

The scale model for *1984*.

SKETCHES

Carl Fillion

becoming one. Continuing with the suspended mobile screens used since *Vinci*, Lepage creates a set that is pure screen. It is a screen that, because it can be broken up plank by plank and set at different angles, can create geometric forms that correspond to the images, whether projected or not, in a very effective blurring. As with Svoboda, there is no screen as such; instead, almost-organic modules that receive and freely distort the images are used.

In *Das Rheingold*, which opens the Ring Cycle, Lepage demonstrates the versatility of the modular set by having the audience witness it being created out of nothing, as he did with *Kà*, but this time using a simpler yet more dexterous approach – which effectively sums up Lepage's evolution in later years – and at the same time introducing the protagonists and the set transformations to come.[9] A blue line appears to float in the darkness. During the musical prologue, the audience can make out vertical rectangles in the shadows: a cliff that rises up from a muted blue, and then this mass of shadow leans over and starts to undulate, like breathing, a wave song that swells with the music. This is a magnificent rendering of the opening note, held for more than two hundred measures, gradually generating other notes and symbolically an entire world. Returning to the source of *The Edda*, a group of poems and mythological Icelandic tales, Lepage tries to make his set a tectonic plate, as it must have emerged and split in Iceland, where the plates that separate Europe and North America meet – and this is clearly one of Lepage's themes. It is what will fuel his imagery of the union of fire and ice, rock and water, projected onto the set.

One of the features of Lepage's opera stagings is how in step they are with the music, their rhythmic sense, and their profound understanding of composition rendered in space. The end result is stunning in these shows, because there are no distractions, no set changes or major movements, because the set remains unchanged for the four parts of the cycle. Everything is accomplished by rotating the mobile plank screen, which creates all of the spaces required and makes the set a frame where movement renders the music, but which the audience can forget when it remains motionless for long stretches during oratorios. Lepage does not distract; he is at the service of the music. His actors seem to have understood this, and they are completely absorbed in the strange positions their performance requires (suspended, walking on a vertical axis, sliding along the planks until they disappear over the edge, and so on).

It is a curved surface that swells and that holds all the locations within it. When the planks are vertical, it is a fortress; by forming terraces and showing two sides, it is an ocean floor – actually an underwater cliff with three mermaids perched on it (the three singers are suspended from bungee cords); inclined, it is a menacing cliff above Brünhilde; rounded, it is the wall of a cave; and more pronounced, it is the steps of a staircase, and so on. The position of the planks and different projections provide for infinite possibilities, a virtual extravaganza, playing on a dark background. The three faces of the planks are different dimensions, forming an irregular triangle, with one short side and two of about equal size. This is a three-sided screen, building on Lepage's repertoire of screens that had either one side or two (symbolically, the mirror-Sputnik from *The Far Side of the Moon*, which is not really used as a screen). Here, images can be projected onto three sides, and the planks' rotation changes how the projected images are read.

The Ring's universe, as shown by its opening and closing images, is a perfect example of Lepagean theatre of images. Lepage describes his set as a sort of breathing sculpture or a living being, one that paints itself – because the images are generated by the movement of planks or actors – but above all as something "hypnotic [...] that slowly builds up and gathers you and grabs you and pulls you into the story."[10] One could replace the word "story" with the word "image." But in this case, there is not only a breach: it is the image and the screen that break apart, that create a breach and carry us into it.

There is a magnificent scene in *Das Rheingold* when Wotan and Loge descend a staircase toward a small white door. They exit. The planks right themselves, come together to spin and form a coil, suggesting a staircase seen from above. It is a hypnotic transition that builds before our eyes, disturbing because of the way in which it disrupts our orientation, making what was vertical horizontal; Wotan and Loge appear at the door and start descending the staircase. They are suspended from bungee cords, and the dual interpretation is disturbing: we can see them suspended in front of the inclined planks, giving us a bird's-eye view of them going

downstairs, at the same time as we see them suspended in front of a set. It is a nice twist, and Lepage made the right choice in having them do an about-face to appear to have passed through the door into a new space, lit in orange. They have arrived among the dwarves.

The set is the most unsettling in *Siegfried*, the third opera in the cycle, when the planks move while images of flames are projected; they are disturbing because they appear to have no substance. Some planks are straight, others are starting to turn, and suddenly the audience no longer knows whether the flames are immaterial or tangible scenery. The flames whirl, and then the set freezes and is solid once again. It is a gripping oscillation, a kind of to-and-fro movement.

Twenty-four rotating planks create a highly versatile stage set in *The Ring*.

PHOTO

Yves Renaud, courtesy Metropolitan Opera

The technical dexterity of the set – as well as the independent operation of each of the twenty-four planks and their ability to move in full rotation, thanks to counterweights – lies in the fact that the images can be piloted through the movements of the set and the actors. The position of each plank is controlled electronically, allowing it to move independently or in unison with the others, just as Craig had a score for his screens and Svoboda had one for the placement of his columns and modules for *Hamlet*. But what is new here is the fact that the mobility of what is on the stage (planks and actors) makes it possible to manage and change the projected images and to make it feel as though the set is alive, as though it is a reactive surface, or a tactile surface, like a touch screen: this is how the mermaids from the opening scene, suspended from bungee cords and seemingly perched on an underwater cliff, make the pebbles around them move as their tails move or as they change position. This is what Lepage means when he says that the set breathes or paints itself. Lepage is continuing in his quest, which he began in *The Andersen Project*, to have the actor guide the image and erase his shadow; but this time he has created a set far more malleable than the "conch," the screen that is both the backdrop to the stage and a medium for the projected image.

Moving planks bring fire to life. *Siegfried*.

PHOTO

Yves Renaud, courtesy Metropolitan Opera

In the final scene of *Das Rheingold*, the characters walk along a rainbow to Valhalla. The centre of the set returns to a vertical position and, as in *The Damnation of Faust*, the protagonists (the acrobats standing in for them) appear to be seen from above and are then seen as upright when their shadows are projected

onto the ground. The disorientation, breach, and verticality of the image are made possible by a set that no longer has a specific form, or that takes the form of a side view of the symbolic box that Lepage uses in many variations, but in this case fringed. It cannot only lean, rise, and fall, as in *Elsinore* and *The Far Side of the Moon*, but each of its elements can also rotate, creating a spiral. The planks become like blades turning around a central axis, a product of both the square and the circle, a blurring Lepage commonly uses and that is quite vivid in a tectonic reading of this set: it can be read as a rounded surface of grey rocks, while the planks above, lit in red, suggest lava. The screen becomes solid, the image tears, becomes fringed, and takes on depth; the image becomes a set. It is no longer a box that contains an ambiguous screen-surface or a screen that breaks into layers, but instead a floor that is at once screen and house, surface and mass, wave and rock. The image becomes an object and not simply an ambiguous depth. It is intentional depth, the depth of the proscenium opening (a smaller proscenium arch surrounds the apparatus), because the set is designed as a recess in a large wall. The apparatus does not fill the proscenium opening at the Met, but instead is surprising for its seemingly small size: a human-sized opening, characteristic of Lepage's sets.

No discussion of the use of geometry in Lepage's set design would be complete without mention of *The Image Mill*, commissioned for the four-hundredth anniversary of Quebec City in 2008. This was the largest projection ever in the world, across the huge expanse of eighty-one grain silos that serve as one immense screen.[11] Lepage chose the site in the Old Port of Quebec City so that the light and images projected onto the grain silos set at the water's edge would create a play of magnificent reflections on the water. *The Image Mill*, with its ability to draw and hypnotize crowds, is an example of the quarry as imagined by Lepage: a city-scale quarry – one with a wall 600 metres long. On summer evenings in 2008 the Louise Basin came to life with the history of Quebec City, and the show could be seen for free from several vantage points in the city. People gathered, attracted by the light and the colourful shadows. The show was so successful that new and different versions of the show have followed on the same site, and their popularity has endured.

The Image Mill projections reflect beautifully in the calm waters of the Louise Basin in the port at Quebec City.

PHOTO

Ludovic Fouquet

Detail of *The Image Mill*, Quebec City.

PHOTO

Ludovic Fouquet

Gigantic projections are used along with a more conventional form (sound and light), in impressive technical conditions: the dimensions, the ability to adapt to the venue and to the shape of the silos in this massive mill, and the quality of the soundscape that continues to dazzle even after several years. Lepage and his team demonstrated their visual inventiveness, particularly in the transitions between images, in how they push the limits of the split-screen, isolating part of the set, using the shape of the silos to evoke, for example, cigarettes or gun cartridges or piano keys, turning all surfaces of the massive mills into a projection screen, in the same way that Svoboda used different shapes for his Poly-ekran sets. Those who are familiar with the site are impressed by the variety of projections created from this architectonic base, combining tubes, squares, and rectangles, and integrating trees and reflections into the water. A great deal of research was done at La Caserne using a mock-up several metres long to test a range of possibilities for projection. In 2011 a move was made to 3-D, which by all accounts was not very successful, but which offered a chance to rethink entire sections and to create a more appealing definition of space within the images. When I saw them again in 2012, the creation had a feeling of volume and space despite the fact that it is only a 2-D projection. One can sense how the experience of *Jean-Sans-Nom* fuelled this effort. *The Image Mill* uses an oversized screen in an outdoor show before a large audience and serves as a showcase for ambitious technical feats and content (it is a page of history, touching, brazen and accurate, the content of which has changed over the years).[12]

With *The Ring* and *The Image Mill*, one could assume that Lepage is continuing on a course of technical dexterity, magnitude, and omnipresent technology. But this is not the case; in fact, the opposite is true if his most recent projects – those from the past three years – are anything to go by.

A 360-DEGREE THEATRE

Lepage's most recent project, the Playing Cards series is a group of four plays being developed around the symbolism and numerology of playing cards and the tarot deck.[13] All four are to be performed on the same set – the realization of Lepage's dream of a 360-degree theatre, a goal he has been striving toward since starting out and a form he tested in *Growing Up* (2002–2004), one of two concerts he staged for Peter Gabriel. The 360-degree theatre is also a way of returning to the much-discussed storyteller circle, because the audience is seated around the set, just as Lepage describes the audience around the fire in his personal mythology of the theatre. It should come as no surprise, then, that in shows in the Playing Cards series we find the shaman character running around the circle of the set. Lepage has been talking about circles for a long time, but up until 2005, this form remained primarily a founding myth. Lepage tackled many more frontal sets, sometimes bi-frontal sets, influenced by film, even though his staging involves deconstructing and manipulating the set in every direction and showing it to us from every perspective through video, effectively thumbing his nose at the front-facing approach.

The circle is the face of this project and indeed the driving force behind it, since Playing Cards is the result of a commission from a group of circular arts venues around the world. They are former circus venues built as permanent structures or nineteenth-century gas reservoirs converted to permanent or one-time performance spaces, operating under the name Réseau 360° (360° Network). They are an initiative of Philippe Bachman, director of La Comète, Scène Nationale (Châlons-en-Champagne, France), who asked Lepage to create a first show that could tour these spaces, beginning in 2005.

So in a sense this commission launched the Playing Cards project, giving it its richness and limitations; Lepage's team discovered once the first instalment had premiered that not all the venues could accommodate the stage design. As a result, as for *The Nightingale*, there was a long process of adapting to the technical specifications of each venue. As I write this epilogue, it remains unclear whether the series will tour widely, because while the set fits the dimensions of the various theatres, not all have the right grid for the apparatus and lighting that needs to be suspended above it.

Spades, the first show in the Playing Cards series, somewhat confirms Lepage's use of the stage as the source of a theatrical language that develops a visual, sound-based, musical, and only incidentally text-based language. The point of departure is a stage-object, a bit like the adjustable puppet theatre of his early career, always an extension of the box used in different forms throughout the shows. But with a new twist, because with *Spades*, Lepage is no longer playing quite so much with the lure of the screen. At least it is more subtle, because the performance space is not designed precisely as a reference to the screen, a box-like surface to free oneself from, but instead the actors emerge from it and create sequences steeped in television culture: TV images are seen directly on flat screens lowered from the grid, or they come to life on the set. But more than just a two-dimensional temptation, it is a televisual memory, a screen memory (to use Lepage's words) that is at play, basically, re-immersing us in TV images from the war in Iraq and its legitimation by the U.S. government.

As a general rule with this show, as with all the latest Lepagean creations, there is a slight departure from the screen and a return to the quarry, or more specifically to the box; so it is no surprise that the set contains thirty-six trap doors. *Spades* marks a return to a more homespun theatre, playing with trap doors

rather than image technologies. This provides for a compelling visual blurring, a box that is unfolded, although more like a game board. A surface with trap doors, from which people, beds, and pool ladders emerge, all elements that define a space, in part by delimiting it.

A double circular stage surrounds the central performance space, which is also circular, and acts as a sort of double sidewalk, with rings that can turn in either direction, so that they move toward one another.[14] These sidewalks, like those in *The Dragons' Trilogy* or the steps in *The Seven Streams of the River Ota* and *The Blue Dragon*, create a foreground behind which tableaus are formed with action in parallel. Actors emerge from trap doors as if they were hand puppets. These trap coors in the circular stage create all kinds of spaces and allow the movement of players and props. Travellers walk along airport corridors with rolling suitcases, an image Lepage is fond of (the travellers can walk in the same direction or toward one another), but it is the shaman scene that demonstrates the true genius of the set: during an encounter near Las Vegas between the compulsive gambler and the shaman, a man undresses as he walks against traffic, transforming first into a shaman and then into a bird flying over the desert. The shaman stretches out his arms and picks up speed, as the sidewalks turn faster. It is such a simple scene in its construction, but beautiful nonetheless.

Proximity is guaranteed to some extent by the venues for this show, with the audience gathering close to the fire. The proximity is a welcome change from the distance of some of later shows performed in huge rooms.

With *Hearts*, the second show in the series, circle and the quarry come together in a set that at times is surrounded by a scrim, which closes off the space as in a nineteenth-century panorama. As a result, *Hearts* features not only projection, but also immersion in the image, on a screen that has been transformed into a circular box. The scrim projections (excerpts from Méliès's films, photos taken by Nadar in Algeria) pass through the screen and light up the house, plunging the audience into the image. The images rotating in the front of house create a pleasant effect, the result of the video projector on the turntable – the sidewalks referred to in *Spades* – and the image rotates along with the set. The images and the actors'

Gambling in Las Vegas in *Spades*.

PHOTO

Érick Labbé

and storytellers' shadows are therefore visible on the scrim, in the front of house, and on its walls, forming the interlocking walls of the symbolic quarry. But unlike panoramas, the audience is not in the centre of the circle, but instead the audience watch the action within the circle, projected onto translucent walls. In the February 2014 production in Montreal, the elements identified during rehearsals in November 2012 are evident in the show, the success of which lies – aside from the quality of the acting – on how narrative, image, and set are moulded from visual intuitions and research into early mechanical processes for recording images. There is an obvious connection between Méliès's early effects, Nadar's portable laboratory of collodion-on-glass negatives, and the set for the show. But more than that, the *Hearts* derives its power from how Lepage pulls a narrative thread from these technical elements, weaving it through to connect magic, the image, and politics around the figures of Nadar and Houdini in Algeria.

A GEOMETRIC APPROACH IN *THE TEMPEST*

In July 2013 at the Grand Théâtre de Québec, Lepage staged a new opera, *The Tempest*, by British composer Thomas Adès, based on the work by Shakespeare. It demonstrates Lepage's ongoing theatrical musings on the cube and the circle, and about how to play with the theatrical box, in this case, the theatrical cage.

In the stage design, Lepage does not give in to the effortlessness of the image or of seduction (he makes sparing use of video) and lets the theatre's special magic take over, specifically the magic of the proscenium theatre, in the form of the La Scala opera house, where the entire story unfolds in Lepage's version. It is a long way from Lepage's 3-D version in 1998, but also a long way from the low-tech version of 1992, which takes place in a rehearsal room. In other words, more than just a staging of Shakespeare's *The Tempest*, we are watching a performance of *The Tempest* at La Scala, and therefore Prospero's magic, the apparitions, and the visions are expressed through theatrical effects. The stage design is a brilliant homage to the stage machinery of proscenium theatres and at the same time a lesson in theatre.

In this stage design, Lepage goes back to manoeuvring around a box, or rather, in this case, presenting an initial box as an apparatus and showing it to us from every angle. But Lepage offers more than just a box: as with the puppet theatres or the house in *The Seven Streams of the River Ota*, this box is a little theatre. And in this case, the theatre is a real building: La Scala, in all its eighteenth-century splendour. We move around the stage and break through the "sacred" boundary of the fourth wall (though this idea was not yet established in the eighteenth century).

Lepage is at his best when he uses visible objects to create images, when he engages the audience by revealing the trick, which in this case means seeing the performance from the wings (in the first act, the opera house, bridge, and so on are viewed upside down) and then from the house (in the second act, the opera house becomes translucent and can reveal what is going on behind it, like the canvas flat, so the audience sees what is being prepared, how things are being moved, and so on). Then in the third act, we are in the middle ground: the house and the wings are seen in cross-section and in profile after the audience has witnessed the reality backstage at the Grand Théâtre

The Tempest stage set recreates the theatre La Scala (Milan, Italy), as if it were seen in sectional view.

PHOTO

Louise Leblanc

de Québec. A set is built before our eyes and, in a few seconds, large painted canvases are unrolled, two inclined platforms are moved (one for the stage and below stage, the other for the parterre around the orchestra pit), and the La Scala opera house re-emerges, in all of its glory, with all of its little boxes for the audience. But the opera house is seen in cross-section. So the audience sees half of a prompter's box and the characters preparing to leave it.

The third part, which takes place in this middle ground that is no longer fully front facing, but instead on an angle, even fractal, offers an interesting blurring of perspectives. When the curtain opens, not only is there a tremendous aesthetic shock – the action is taking place onstage at the Grand Théâtre de Québec today, whereas the first two acts took place at the eighteenth-century La Scala by convention – but also the audience cannot distinguish between the architecture of the actual place and the waiting scenery. We no longer know where we are: no doubt at the back of the stage, near the scenery stores, or on the side, like at the Opéra Bastille in Paris, where scenery can be left waiting for the upcoming acts. So there is a blurring because the audience is put off by the rough metal structure before them, unsure whether it is the raw structure or a piece of scenery. There is collusion between the costumed actors and the stark appearance of the backroom, as if suddenly the actors are no longer acting on the set, but in the wings, underlining the fact that we are indeed in a theatre. And we don't at all expect to come back to this place in La Scala afterward. The audience is even disappointed to see the magical banquet or wedding masque treated conventionally, a theatrical banquet with food props set on a large table, and even a somewhat tawdry handling of Ariel bursting in, who spreads the arms of the chandelier that lifts her as if she had wings, her feet in metal talon-like shoes, a sort of kitsch Lady Gaga in concert. It is a bit disappointing, particularly for anyone familiar with the play and how the banquet masque, like the spirits in the play, disappears into the air – as Lepage staged it in this theatre in 1998, using video and 3-D effects.

So we can no longer refer to the front and back of the performance space, or at least not exclusively: Lepage does not simply have us move from one side of the curtain to the other; he also takes us into profile, along the dividing line of the curtain – the curtain the liberated Ariel uses to escape, symbolically scaling it and disappearing (in actual fact, the singer is raised by a sling and pretends to wrap her legs around the curtain as if she were climbing a rope). This is in addition to the emotion, the surprise of seeing the final set built before our very eyes, much like the magic of the proscenium theatre in which an entire palace can be built with a few painted canvases and flats, much like Lepagean palimpsest and virtual environments.

Cubes, mills, circles: more than ever Lepage is using a geometric approach, guided by a visual intuition that assumes a particular, architectonic organization of the stage.

CONTINUING COLLECTIVE CREATION

Since 1986, Lepage has regularly confronted the theatrical intuitions and desires developed during his solo creation period. Solo creation doesn't mean solitary creation for Lepage, but rather a more pared-down team and the chance to act again, bringing his intuitions up against the reality of the stage. And Lepage has done this like clockwork: in 1986 with *Vinci*, in 1991 with *Needles and Opium*, in 2000 with *The Far Side of the Moon*, and in 2005 with *The Andersen Project*. Every five years, he has gone back to work and returned to the stage. And yet, since *The Andersen Project* in 2005, there have been no further solo efforts. There are a number of reasons for this: for a long time solos toured first with him and then with Yves Jacques. Lepage even took over his role again for *The Andersen Project* for a few dates in December 2012, playing it in French and in English (even though he hadn't played the role in English for five years). During this period, Lepage acted in a few films, including Martin Villeneuve's *Mars et Avril*, but he has largely dedicated himself to opera (*The Ring*, four operas staged in less than two years, required an enormous time commitment spread over five years) and, finally, he developed projects collectively. Actually, for the past four years Lepage has had plans for a solo show about memory, and he has begun to work on this show about his youth in Quebec City – titled *887*, after the house number on the street where he lived. Lepage plans a small set, mainly video, and a very small team will rehearse in Le Periscope theatre, set in the neighbourhood where he grew up. This show is expected to be created in France in 2015 and has been announced as part of the programming for the Pan American Games in Toronto in 2015.[15]

Whereas up until 2005 there had been a balance between the sweeping sagas of collective creations and solo work, Lepage has since focused more on collective creation, with varying degrees of success. I believe there was a problem with this approach to creation for projects like *Lipsynch*, *Eonnagata*, and *The Blue Dragon* (which is really a joint effort with Marie Michaud rather than a collective creation). Meanwhile with the Playing Cards series (*Spades* and the subsequent *Hearts*), one has the impression that Lepage is back to steering through the chaos of collective creation with joy, intuition, and insight.

Lipsynch, a sweeping saga about the human voice as the vehicle of identity and as the key instrument of film (with respect to dubbing), confirmed my comments about multilingualism and collective creation in my discussion of *The Geometry of Miracles*: the shortcoming of not having a common language (being limited to only basic English, which means remaining within the confines of cliché). *Lipsynch* also confirmed my comments about the limits of crossbreeding, raised in relation to Lepage's *Métissages* exhibition (suddenly the languages of Babel are no longer communicating) and the weaknesses in each person's contribution. For example, on the team for *The Seven Streams of the River Ota*, everyone was fluent in French and was used to collective creation or ready to dive into improvisation and research (and no doubt had an artistic background more suited to this type of creation than the teams for *The Geometry of Miracles* and *Lipsynch*). For *The Seven Streams of the River Ota*, the subject itself – the impact of Hiroshima on Japanese and European protagonists and on history – may have been a better source of inspiration. Something didn't take in the play's alchemy, and many elements were reused: tricks, characters (Ada Weber in *The Seven Streams of the River Ota*), sequences (on the plane, in particular), in a show that was both long and unsuccessful; the full version lasted over nine hours. Of course, there were some gems in the play, successful moments, some fine acting (in particular from Rick Miller, an actor with astonishing range who appeared in Lepage's *Zulu Time*). In addition, sequences explored the connection between voice and memory, and voice and cinema. But when I saw *Lipsynch* at the Festival de théâtre des Amériques in Montreal in 2007, the recipe didn't work, the cake didn't rise (to use Lepage's metaphor for the gestation time required for shows, referenced in the book of interviews with Rémy Charest).[16] Of course, this is not to say that the project didn't evolve, because it toured until 2012, and I think the intention developed; in any event, that's what people who had seen it reported.

Marie Michaud was part of the first team for *The Dragons' Trilogy*, but she did not find the same creative inspiration with Lepage in *The Blue Dragon*, despite all the paths they cleared and connections they found during the research stage (conveyed in *EX MACHINA: Creating for the Stage*). What resulted was an uneven show, formally beautiful, touching at times, interesting in its use of calligraphy and the construction of simultaneous scenes, bringing back characters from *The Dragons' Trilogy*; but again it didn't work, although there are some strong passages featuring Pierre Lamontagne. The connection between the kitchen and the world, between the small story and the larger story, was not as compelling as in *The Dragons' Trilogy* and *The Seven Streams of the River Ota*.

I found *Eonnagata* even less successful. It was an uneven show that ultimately fell flat, but contained many striking scenes that capture Lepage's magic, with a simple stage on which are scattered a few objects to represent the world of the main character, Chevalier d'Éon: tables, a partition screen, a kimono, and silent sliding leg panels to frame the different perspectives. This show did not spring spontaneously from Lepage's mind; it was a response to an offer from the dancer Sylvie Guillem and Canadian choreographer Russell Maliphant, a triumvirate approach to exploring the genre through the figure of the Chevalier d'Éon, a colourful character who was an eighteenth-century author, diplomat, French spy, cross-dresser, traveller, and patron of the royal courts of France, England, and Russia. Although Lepage's physical ability is clear as he works alongside two world-renowned dancers, the final impression was again of something that did not take.

These juxtaposed worlds, in which everything melts together into a Lepagean aesthetic of familiar images, nevertheless are still more successful in the intention than in *The Blue Dragon*. For example, the Japanese element is introduced with classic

Lepage simplicity: a small riser and an actor dressed in a kimono seen from behind, seemingly very tall. A long stick extends from his sleeves, holding them in position: Maliphant emerges from the kimono, smaller than the character, like a child or a dream, and launches into a duo, a pas de deux that finishes in a perfectly orchestrated execution. In a brisk movement, the dancer just has to remove the stick (which has become a sabre), so that the Japanese woman's mask collapses, as if she were swooning. Later on, there is a kimono dance in the shadows, each person taking turns inhabiting it as in *The Seven Streams of the River Ota*: a beautiful interplay of Chinese shadows, intensified by Sylvie Guillem's grace in drawing very graphical shadows. An epistolary scene using a voice offstage (people corresponded regularly at the time) shows the knight in London sending and receiving a great deal of correspondence; Guillem traces invisible letters with a swift sword, a moment in dance that verges on interesting, but that is too illustrative or schematic. All three will speak for the knight downstage, depicting facets and periods of the Chevalier d'Éon, at times speaking perfect English (Maliphant) and at times over-the-top Gallicized English (Lepage, reusing an approach from *The Andersen Project*). They use a table, which becomes a tomb, dance barre, and mirror, multiplying the facets of this enigmatic character.

What is missing from these three shows is a dramaturgical approach, a way of rummaging through the literary and historical material. And that is what makes the difference in Playing Cards and the operas, where in fact, Lepage deals with specialists from the outset and where there is a literature, a framework, even a guide; Lepage refers to this when he says he let himself be guided by Wagner's score and libretto for *The Ring*. He composed neither the music nor the libretto, so he simply had to react, to follow the guide, a guide that offers tremendous freedom to anyone who knows how to heed it, and Lepage is a natural reader of music.

In the three shows under discussion (*Lipsynch*, *Eonnagata*, and *The Blue Dragon*), there are obviously strong visual successes and even a respectable creative impulse based on the clash of disciplines and their mutual enrichment. The centralizing perspective, the organizer of chaos, which Lepage is so good at, is swept away in the movement and is unable to take a step back. He does this more

easily in the latest collective adventure, Playing Cards, but guided
by playwrights and advisors. In fact, Peder Bjurman, who with
Adam Nashman and Lepage co-authored *The Far Side of the Moon*,
is dramaturge for both *Spades* and *Hearts*, and this collaboration is
essential to the show's success, undoubtedly as important as the
visual approach and the way Lepage has of intertwining threads to
tell a story. Likewise, for *Hearts*, the French magician Philippe Beau
was a consultant for the show's magic effects. His involvement went
beyond merely consulting on magic; he is knowledgeable on the
origins of film, spiritualist movements, and the history of magic,
which was invaluable while work was being done in November 2012.
The link between origins of photography, cinema, and the political
life of the Second Empire (with Nadar or the magician Houdini
going to Algeria to document the country of show European magi)
is truly powerful in the 2014 production.

Does Lepage need an open, stimulating structure, and
a resource that is rich in connections to launch into collective
creation? That is precisely what he had with Playing Cards, a series
for which the symbolic world of the card game came to him when
Réseau 360° (360° Network) made its proposal. But clearly a theme
and a visual avenue came together to form the pathway for creation:
what was being proposed was a show built around a circular stage:
"it came to me: a game of cards, that's it. Everyone is seated around a
table. It seemed like a good pretext. And it's a resource that contains
the idea of math, chance, fortune, and superstition. It's a very rich
and playful point of departure, an idea that I still champion in
theatre, the idea of the play."[17]

From this already tenuous theme, Lepage develops a new
thread: the Arab world, the origin of card games, along with mathe-
matics, astronomy, great poets, all of which are longstanding themes
in Lepage's world. Yet Lepage has rarely looked at Arab culture in
his work, aside from the terrorist theme in *Zulu Time*: "Research
into the origin of cards invariably leads back to the Arab world. The
tetralogy's four parts, each independent and yet interrelated with
the others, will make up a cosmos dealing with our past, present
and future relationships, our exchanges, and sometimes too, our
culture shocks when encountering the Arab way of life."[18] This is
how he explains what prompted him to address Muslim culture
(and one can already guess the story for *Spades*):

> Arab-Muslim culture had a major influence over
> European culture and, in turn, American culture. At
> a time when the Islamic world is stigmatized and seen
> as something dark, I thought it would be interesting
> to create a series of shows that deals with our relation-
> ships to Muslim culture. It's a way of drawing closer to
> our own origins, through these influences, to imagine
> things that came from other places and that helped
> create our culture.[19]

A creative avenue developed from the symbolism of the four playing-card suits (like the resources in the earlier discussion of the
Repère system). Spades suggest soldiers or war; hearts, also called
the cups, Lepage says, evoke the world of belief – religious, but
also magical; diamonds represent the world of business; and clubs
represent the world of labourers and farmers. *Spades*, then, deals
with war, specifically the war in Iraq, with Las Vegas as the anchor
location. Las Vegas is obviously a symbol of the world of gambling,
but during exploratory work around the table, Lepage's team soon
discovered that a model village had been built not far from Las
Vegas, in the desert, to train G.I.s to attack Iraqi villages. "The action
juxtaposes two desert cities, at the moment in history when the
United States invades Iraq. On one side is Las Vegas, a caricature
of the Western world's values, and on the other, Baghdad, bombed
by President Bush in the name of promoting democracy."[20] And in
this reconstituted Vegas, as in the reconstituted villages, personal
stories cross paths with history, the lonely come to lose themselves,
and people who are searching come seeking answers. Hotel rooms
become a camp, a moving walkway in an airport becomes a games
table, and everything is created and torn down with the opening and
closing of the trap doors, as one would deal cards. The connection
between theme and visuals combined with greater collaboration
in playwriting are what make this new collective creation work.

The same thing occurs with the second instalment, *Hearts*.
Quite clearly, the team is solid and diverse: circus performer,
actor and actress trained at the École internationale de théâtre
Jacques Lecoq in Paris, which explains the physical approach,
author-creator, but also magician (Philippe Beau evokes anecdotes
of nineteenth-century magicians, the beginnings of spiritualism,

spirit photographs, photograms, and even films by Méliès; in short, anything to do with illusion, whether directly or indirectly). When I watched the second work session around the table in November 2012, it was obvious that the team of authors and actors was strong, drawing on a range of practices and recent research, but also that most people were fluent in the language they were working in. The fact that everyone during rehearsal had a better command of a common language (French and sometimes English) contributed to the quality of discussions and improvisations and helped in the choice of scenes to keep or discard, guided at this stage by simple connections and echoes. And when I saw the show in Montreal in January 2014, all these intuitions were confirmed.

Since this part of Playing Cards addresses belief, wide-ranging research was done into different religions – and of course into Islam, as well as into a possible Christian-Muslim confrontation – and into the belief in spirits (Victor Hugo is raised, mediums, the beginnings of photography), the early films of Méliès, magic tricks, and so forth.

One session dealt with the theme of the family unit with an in-law from another culture (in Quebec, a young Muslim man is introduced to the family of his non-Muslim girlfriend, and vice versa). Improvisations occurred, drawing on clichés, accents, attitudes, perceptions of the other culture, but also trying to find more universal or specific motives (with the choice of an alcoholic, homosexual, and jealous character, and so on). English is spoken with an accent as a foreign family tries to talk to the young male or female francophone. After having tried both versions, Lepage suddenly proposed playing both situations at once, with the choice of language defining whether we are in the first or second situation (the actor who plays the father does so for both families, and so on). Everything becomes clear, everything falls into place, the cliché is no longer a cliché, and we understand when the situation flip-flops. Lepage creates space, and suddenly it takes off, everything is clear and understandable. Lepage has the power, as I have noted, to play with chaos, to seemingly control it while only directing parts, channelling ideas, but brilliantly, thanks to his sound intuition and listening skills. This phase of rehearsals marked a return to collective creations at their best. No doubt because, in more than one sense, Lepage seemed to be coming back to earlier practices.

A RETURN TO HIS ROOTS?

There is both a desire to simplify and a move to revive or recreate Lepage's old shows. Undeniably, *The Nightingale* and *The Tempest*, but above all Playing Cards (because with opera, a lot more depends on the budget and teams available), mark a return to a more handcrafted, less technological, theatre, and the next solo show, titled *887* confirms this direction. So it is no surprise that Lepage used the thread of chinoiserie for *Nightingale*, as Stravinsky did. Lepage returns to this dream of the East (Orientalism) that fed many of his early shows.

> I guess a bit like what a lot of rock bands did 10, 15 years ago, the "unplugged" thing, saying: "Well, this is a good song, but would it be as good if we did this on an acoustic guitar instead of a synthesizer [...]?" [...] So it's going back to basics, and I feel I'm entering this new phase of my work where I'd like to present things in a more simple way, hopefully, and discover the real strength of it and not count on technological crutches [...] I'm interested in the whole writing process more and more, and less by the staging process.[21]

Lepage made these remarks at the premiere of *The Blue Dragon*, which still relied a great deal on technology, but which marked the beginning of the return to the story and the storyteller. Above all, it marked a return to the sources of creation, in this case, Asia. *The Blue Dragon* was a way of returning to *The Dragons' Trilogy*, a flagship Lepage show, built entirely on dreams of Asia and clashes of cultures. At the end of *The Dragons' Trilogy*, Pierre tells his mother he is leaving for China. His mother responds by repeating the opening sentence: "I have never been to China."

The Blue Dragon catches up with Pierre Lamontagne in 2007, still in China, in Shanghai. But the play doesn't pick up where Lepage left off. We encounter the same character twenty years later. And while there are echoes of the trilogy, above all there are echoes of Lepage:

Pierre Lamontagne returns in *The Blue Dragon*.

PHOTO

Ludovic Fouquet

Because the show is a response to his journey as a
director after *The Dragons' Trilogy*: the collective tale,
the cultural encounters, narration through the image,
technology, scenography between box and screen.
Lepage's entire world is represented, combining questions of identity, filiation, quest, and artistic initiation.
It's all there, to the point that one might think it's
all a rehash, but instead it blazes the trails that fuel
Lepage's creation.[22]

Lepage is returning to themes by taking pleasure once again in
telling stories and manipulating objects. And as luck would have
it, Playing Cards and *Hamlet* – the working title for the restaging
of *Elsinore* – are two projects with a scenography based on the
manipulation of elements, as I described in this book.

In fact, in 2013 Lepage returned to two of his flagship
creations, after having staged a brilliant recreation of *The Dragons'
Trilogy*. His restaging of *Needles and Opium* with Marc Labrèche,

with Canadian Stage in Toronto and at the Grand Théâtre de Québec in Fall 2013, meant coming back to a show created twenty-two
years earlier, and in that restaging we could see the point to which
his early works were seminal in that they contained the seed of this
world of images, the storyteller tinkering in a visual laboratory
and sharing it. Lepage also announced a recreation of *Hamlet*
in Moscow, with Yevgeny Mironov, one of Russia's best-known
actors. He started from the stage design and ideas developed
in 1995 with *Elsinore*, but enriched them with all the research
done since. This includes all the stage work in particular around
the cube, the manipulated object, but also all the knowledge of
Shakespeare, the history of theatre, and Russian culture that
Lepage discovered during his performances in Russia, which
may explain the working title of *Hamlet / Collage*. For this play,
Lepage also added the perspective of Roman Dolzhanskiy as
dramaturge, I think as much for his knowledge of Shakespeare
as for his ability to weave ties between cultures.

> Model of the set
> for the restaging of
> *Needles and Opium.*

The plan to create a performance space for Ex Machina
in Quebec City makes even more sense given this return to the
source. This is a project that Lepage has been talking about for
years. Plans were even put forth to develop one of the highway
access ramps dug into the cliff under the Old City and abandoned
some years ago. Instead the performance space, Le Diamant, was
confirmed in 2014, to be constructed in three heritage buildings
next to Théâtre Le Capitole. With this venue (which will seat 750),
Lepage expects to present first-run plays and work on revivals
of his own repertoire. A cultural venue equipped with all of the
top-of-the-line equipment required by today's artistic productions,
Le Diamant will present the highest quality international shows
and will contribute to making Quebec City a world-class cultural
destination. Le Diamant will host productions by Ex Machina and
Robert Lepage, but will also serve as a performance venue for the
Carrefour international de théâtre de Québec and the Quebec
Opera Festival as well as international touring productions, circus
shows, small-scale operas, and other artistic programming. So
in its final development, Le Diamant will be used by many other
cultural organizations, in addition to Ex Machina.[23]

> COMPUTER
> SIMULATION
> _____
> Carl Fillion

> Digital modelling for
> the recreated set in
> *Needles and Opium.*

> PHOTO
> _____
> Ludovic Fouquet

"It's going to be a wonderful, crazy, transformable space," said Lepage, noting he'd also like to build an international acting company within the theatre. "We're going to start not only presenting our own work in our own city, in La Caserne-Quebec, like we should have been doing all these years, but we'll also kind of have our repertoire. So we'll be providing all of this old stuff and try to rediscover it maybe in a new light, in a more simple way – try to shed skins and try to find the essence of what these pieces were about."[24]

Lepage will be finding the essence of the plays, throwing open the trunks, looking back on creations, and asking himself how to reinvent them. Lepage's visual laboratory will be enriched through the act of rediscovery and rereading, something that can be pointless when it is mere citation or navel gazing, but this sort of pitfall is rarely seen in Lepage's world, if only for his complete openness to new encounters and challenges. We must not forget that cross-pollination fuels his work. And clearly Lepage's visual laboratory has found real momentum in the uncharted world of opera.

OPERA AND *THE RING*: VIRGIN TERRITORY

Opera is truly Lepage's greatest departure and evolution since 2005, and confirmation of his ease and the power of his vision.

He has worked on stage designs for wildly different musical projects with different budgets and sets, but clearly, he has made his mark, because he has been invited to work with the most prominent opera and festival houses: the Saito Kinen Festival in Matsumoto, Japan, the Opéra Bastille in Paris, La Monnaie in Brussels, the Metropolitan Opera in New York, to name just the main ones. Opera is definitely what works best for him, perhaps because he can infuse it with his entire visual universe, his desire to involve the audience, and to get the performer involved in a more playful approach, but also because he can work from an existing libretto (that has its own story and that is solid, but not necessarily written in stone, because Lepage prefers open drama and enigmatic plays). The main thing is that Lepage has to become part of a score, for it is evident, from opera to opera, that he has a clear, even impressive, feel for music.

When this book was first published, Lepage had staged only Schoenberg's *Erwartung* (meaning "expectancy") and Bartók's *Bluebeard's Castle*, two short works. *Erwartung*, with a cast of three characters, uses madness as a pretext for an unstable world and dazzling visual inversions, fitting perfectly within Lepage's stage universe. It was created in collaboration with Rebecca Blankenship, who worked on *The Seven Streams of the River Ota* and who has often been an artistic consultant on his operatic journey.

With each subsequent creation, he has used an approach based on the world of the libretto and the composer's era, and then a choice is made, often visual, that will give the adventure direction. It may be an open book, or in *The Damnation of Faust*, it may be a whole library (its twenty-four boxes like library shelves, twenty-four boxes like film's twenty-four frames per second, no doubt at the root of the connection Lepage makes with Muybridge's time-lapse photography, evoked through skeletons of horses galloping for the "horse in motion"). For Stravinsky's *The Rake's Progress* with Toronto's Canadian Opera Company, the approach is film landscapes, a large cyclorama, and an inclined stage. I have indicated the scenographic choices for the operas that follow. *The Rake's Progress* was an interim step, a means to master and better understand the world of opera, based on film imagery and a few elements of Lepage's world (in particular, the cube from the mental asylum and the inversions).

The staging of *1984* marked Lepage's true beginnings in opera, confirming the first attempt in *The Damnation of Faust*. And then came the seemingly small-scale form of *The Nightingale*, which suddenly established Lepage over a larger territory, because the show toured more extensively and confirmed that his direction and intuitions were sound and that he has a remarkable way of getting the performers to step far outside their comfort zone. The first operatic works were smaller scale forms, not always considered full operas. Lepage received many proposals to stage a work or his choice of works. The recent public recognition for *The Ring* has brought Lepage into the circle of bona fide opera directors.

In interviews, Lepage refers to the fact that "in opera everything is larger than life, that it is a world of tragedy, archetypes, and excess."[25] He points to and understands, even profoundly respects, the central place of the voice, how opera singers work differently with their bodies ("because it is a body that produces the voice"). He has found all sorts of ways to respect the body's positions and the need for projection, but at the same time was not afraid to take the performers onto unstable ground and moving planks (the Valkyries straddle them like horses, or slide along them as if on toboggans). The voice is one of the things, along with gestures, that controls the technology on the sets, like in *The Ring*: the performer's voice can control and his or her silhouette triggers projection effects, so the performer has a new role – and in this sense, Lepage becomes part of a larger movement of theatre and visual artists who are exploring the potential of interaction and notions of reactive space, ideas raised earlier in this book.

Above all, the detour through singing provides Lepage a distance that interests him. Not realism, rather a stylization, an openness to infinite possibilities, a vocal quest, as he experimented with in *Lipsynch*:

> And because the text is sung, it establishes a necessary distance. In fact, realism in opera is, to all intents and purposes, impossible. Whether one looks at Brecht, Mnouchkine, or others, the quality of their work relies in part on the fact that they modify the voice. In what I consider to be the most successful theatre plays, not one phrase is pronounced by an ordinary, realistic or normal voice.[26]

There must be a connection between the sound and musical world of his shows – the fact that he has staged concert performances – and his attraction to the lyrical world. At the outset, the first project was the result of a commission: *Erwartung* and *Bluebeard's Castle* were proposed by the Canadian Opera Company to an at-the-time dubious Lepage.

But what is most obvious in Lepage's past creations, and particularly those since 2005, is how he sees opera as a total work of art (*Gesamtkunstwerk*), like Wagner, who asserted it as such.

Opera is a form that brings together all art. This is undoubtedly where Lepage is at his best, even managing to upset the orthodox contingent pickled in their shared beliefs (and following the opera with the score open on their knees, wanting to see *their* Ring Cycle, *their* Mozart). While respecting the world of music and his musical performers as singers, Lepage is not afraid to use the world of film, circus, puppets, shadows, traditions from different countries onstage, in short, a blending that he used in his theatre and that profoundly regenerates the lyrical world, a world that has the potential for openness, but that has often stifled it. Lepage relies on the many trades found within opera houses, but he tends to add others that are less common (acrobats, engineers calculating the weight and range of apparatuses, programmers and computer graphic designers to create reactive images). This is why the Wagner expert Georges Nicholson was able to say in *Wagner's Dream* that this is the staging of *The Ring* that Wagner would have wanted. Or that never before had there been a "vrai *Ring*, pour le ring" ("A true [Wagner's] *Ring*, [designed] for the [boxing] ring"). "We are actually having the vision that Wagner had when he was composing," when he witnessed the first tests of the planks and the evolution of acrobats, in January 2009, near Quebec City. And that Wagner was not satisfied with the 1876 stage design, not happy with how the creation of the world by the Gods was represented: "We have the vision Wagner had when he was composing."

Although I saw *The Ring* only on film in a movie theatre, I was nevertheless able to feel the vibration of its music and immerse myself in this tale that falls somewhere on the continuum between legend and dream. There were no real effects, no showing off, but instead there is an economy, a reserve, a way of giving music and song its place, without stepping aside, but providing the visual space for the singing and the music to develop, a superb screen, a polymorphous and dreamlike stage, through the images he creates, suited to this excessive, lyrical, and passionate music. It was a very effective balance.

For me it was pure Lepage, but a mature Lepage, one who is not afraid to simplify and reduce, or rather who is not so much trying to make opera, in the large-scale sense, but rather bringing his vision to opera, his visual and theatrical savoir faire and his sets like human-sized theatrical boxes. There is something at once respectful and irreverent (the sexy mermaids), but above all visionary, in the sense of wonder. Lepage remains completely at the service of Wagner's opera, while taking us into his own world of dazzling images. Like the characters in *The Ring* who want to melt gold, he takes us into his visual laboratory and creates images that are all the more compelling for their apparent simplicity, but unsettling, new, and musical.

While Lepage's visual laboratory is still fuelling his experiments, he is increasingly self-assured in putting together "multi" presentations, but ones that are spare, confident in their intuitions and in those who execute them. While the laboratory is more than ever visual, his lab assistants are better able to share their protocols; they even embellish and carry us into stories, making the scientist a storyteller, the researcher an artist, the actor an author, and the singer an acrobat. It is a laboratory that, while ensuring its foundations – La Caserne has developed and continues to be a place for experimenting with projects, which could be developed in a few years at Le Diamant – Lepage increasingly pursues activities that are at the crossroads (film, theatre, opera, sound and light, urban installations), constantly making the boundaries a little more porous, and striving to keep upending work benches and shelves filled with books of spells and potions. Everything is upended, but nothing breaks. Or more, everything is upended and everything is transformed, leaving us in wonder, ready to become chemists ourselves.

NOTES

INTRODUCTION

1.   Ève Dumas, "Atterrissage en douceur," *La Presse*, June 9, 2001.
2.   Marc Cassivi, "La face cachée de la lune," *La Presse*, March 4, 2000.
3.   Don Shirley, "*Far Side of the Moon* shines in brief run," *Los Angeles Times*, October 30, 2000.
4.   In 1980, after the failure of the referendum that saw Quebec nationalism disintegrate as the receptacle of all hopes and constituent of collective practice, many directors turned to new approaches: image based theatre, which emerged from experimental theatre, is a response to a prevailing feeling of helplessness.
5.   Rémy Charest, *Robert Lepage: Connecting Flights*, Wanda Romer Taylor, trans. (Toronto: Alfred A. Knopf Canada, 1998), 23.
6.   Ibid.
7.   Ibid. Referencing the Latin term *deus ex machina*, literally meaning "God from the machine," used in Greek tragedy to resolve a plot problem by suddenly introducing a deity or divine being, who would descend to the theatrical stage suspended from a crane or other machine. See "Deus Ex Machina," in *The Classical Tradition*, Anthony Grafton, Glenn W. Most, and Salvatore Settis, eds. (Cambridge, MA: Harvard University Press, 2010), 263–64.
8.   The Latin term *machina* evokes both the machine and invention, and the Greek terms *machine* or *méchané* combine contrivance and trick, which have the common root *médonai*: "to invent, to assemble, and to devise."

PART ONE

Puppet Theatre and Quarry:
Two Models in the Visual Laboratory

1. Transformations are "a key theatrical element," writes Aleksander Saša
    Dundjerović in *The Theatricality of Robert Lepage* (Montreal: McGill-Queen's
    University Press, 2007), 56, referencing "Lepagean trademarks, particularly
    the interaction of performer, objects, and visual imagery." – Ed.
2. They were the only graduates that year not to have job offers upon graduation.
3. According to Robert Lepage, named "from an onomatopoeic line that
    constantly recurs in a well-known comic strip by a cartoonist called Fred,"
    referring to the *Philémon* comic books and the pseudonym for author Frédéric
    Othon Théodore Aristidès. Quoted in Rémy Charest, *Robert Lepage*, 134.
4. Ibid., 144.
5. In combination with physical resources, as discussed in Aleksandar Saša
    Dundjerović, *The Theatricality of Robert Lepage*, 52: "During rehearsals,
    Lepage surrounds himself, as Jo Litson observes, with lots of props and
    gadgets 'to hide behind and work out what it is you are trying to say
    and convey'," citing Jo Litson, "Playfull Theatre of Coincidences,"
    Weekend Australian Magazine, December 29, 2000, 10. – Ed.
6. "The remarkable artist Robert Lepage (Did you see him on TV Sunday night
    during the LNI match improvising on New York? Incredible!) won the award
    for *mise en scène*," Robert Lévesque, *Le Devoir*, November 10, 1986, 5.
7. In highly broken English, the Quebec librettist tries to describe the puppets
    he wants to use to an international audience at a meeting in Stockholm, half
    miming the animal or naming it in French.
8. *Sumi-e* (ink painting) is a Japanese pictorial practice that combines colour and
    gesture in a highly physical calligraphy.
9. Lepage played a country singer, a kitsch figure that foreshadows the very
    cheeky Parisian Mona Lisa in *Vinci*.
10. Robert Lepage, *Vinci* (1986), unpublished.
11. "In the beginning God created the heavens and the earth. Now the earth was
    without shape and empty, and darkness was over the surface of the watery
    deep" (Genesis 1: 1–2).
12. The financial constraints of the early productions developed into an aesthetic;
    an empty stage allowed the object to be showcased.
13. The creator, in justifying the choice of object, fills it with poetic, historical,
    and other content, an easy task because the object acts as a container or
    receptacle. The object's potential therefore resides largely in the physical
    potential of the content, or around the effect of that content on a character.
14. The language-study program *English without Tears* (!) dictates the words that
    Louise can use in this foreign land. When she has lunch with the man who
    saved her life, none other than Clark Kent, alias Superman, the conversation,
    as trite as can be, is an awkward rehash of the lessons on a meal in a restaurant
    with all the declensions of the culinary lexical field.
15. Irène Roy, *Le Théâtre Repère, du ludique au poétique* (Quebec City:
    Nuit blanche éditeur, 1994), 53.

16. Robert Lepage, quoted in Pierre Lavoie, "Points de repères: entretien avec les créateurs," *Cahiers de théâtre JEU* 45 (1987): 178.

17. Diane Pavlovic, "Du décollage à l'envol," *Cahiers de théâtre JEU* 42 (1987): 90.

18. Ibid., 102.

19. Marie Brassard, Jean Casault, Lorraine Côté, Marie Gignac, Robert Lepage, and Marie Michaud, *La trilogie des dragons*, preface by Michel Tremblay (Quebec City: L'instant même, 2005), 22–23.

20. Marie-Louise Paquette, "Circulations," *Cahiers de théâtre JEU* 35 (1985): 153.

21. Ibid.

22. For example, the story of the little horse that doesn't know how to whinny, or the one about the zebra that has to go to the tanning salon to get his stripes.

23. Josée Campanale received the Prix Jacques-Pelletier for the best set design in 1996 for this production.

24. Marie Brassard et al., *La trilogie des dragons*, 142–43.

25. By the time *Elsinore* was performed in London, the lengthy and overly involved set changes had been simplified to the point that the length of the performance was reduced by one hour.

26. In describing the wall in *Polygraph*, Jerry Wasserman, "Robert Lepage," in *Modern Canadian Plays*, vol. 2, 5th ed. (Vancouver: Talonbooks, 2013), writes: "Physically and metaphorically, the wall dominates the stage. It stands variously for the wall in François's garden, the wall between his and Lucie's apartments, the ramparts of Quebec City, and the 'fourth wall' in naturalistic theatre itself, smashed to pieces by the raw presence of the actor in Lepage's metatheatrical dramaturgy – literally when François's naked body crashes through it in the play's spectacular climax. Characters clamber over the wall and slide down it. At one point, the wall bleeds. The opening scene equates it to both the Berlin Wall and the septum bisecting the human heart." (33). – Ed.

27. Georges Didi-Huberman, "La plus simple image," *Nouvelle revue de psychanalyse: Destins de l'image* 44 (Autumn 1991): 82. In the analysis of the cube's potential emptiness, Didi-Huberman talks about this shape as a box, which is what it is first and foremost for Lepage.

28. Ibid. Because it is absolute manipulability, Didi-Huberman compared the cube to a toy in the hands of a child (a sewing spool to develop a Freudian metaphor) which, just like a toy, can be used in unending games of deconstruction and reconstruction.

29. Robert Lepage in Rémy Charest, *Robert Lepage*, 91.

30. *Egozentrische Raumlineatur* (*Egocentric Space-Delineation*, 1924).

31. The point of transition from a static stage to a kinetic stage, for Craig, with this fifth stage that emerges after the Greek amphitheatre, the boards of the *commedia dell'arte*, and the proscenium stage. Quoted by Jean-Jacques Roubine, *Théâtre et mise en scène, 1880–1980* (Paris: PUF, 1980), 94.

32. Josef Svoboda, *Josef Svoboda* (Prague: Theatre Institute, [1966] 1971), 2.

33. Discussed in Antoine Vitez, "Antoine Vitez about his staging of *Hamlet*," *Acts of Congress of the French Society Shakespeare* 4 (1983): 260–71.

34. Prompt script of the full version from November to December 1996 (Paris, New York).

35. This cohabitation is the point of departure for Tanizaki's approach in his essay *In Praise of Shadows* (1933), the Japanese aesthetics of which are referenced a number of times in this production.

36. Nickname for the character Jeffrey O'Connor, self-attributed in order to distinguish himself from the other character, Jeffrey Yamashita, nicknamed Jeffrey 2.

37. These bunks are also boxes, beds on non-existent outside walls, that contain the actors.

38. Rémy Charest, *Robert Lepage*, 92.

39. Ibid., 91.

40. This actually made objects and actors slide around. On October 26, 1994, . ten days before the premiere of *A Dream Play*, the actor playing the lawyer Johan Rabaeus fell during a rehearsal and broke two ribs.

41. Georges Didi-Huberman, "La plus simple image," *Nouvelle revue de psychanalyse: Destins de l'image* (1991): 81.

42. Agnès, Indra's daughter, doesn't age; instead she does adopt the clothing styles of each era. In fact she says that, for gods, a century is but a minute.

43. Lepage, suspended from a rope, flies above the rooftops of Paris, as if attached to a helicopter. Later he "flies off" in a dream in an image of clouds.

44. Sophie Faucher, *La Casa Azul: Inspired by the Writings of Frida Kahlo*, Neil Bartlett, trans. (London: Oberon, 2002), 37.

45. Since childhood, Lepage has suffered from alopecia.

46. Various actors in discussion with the author.

47. David Clermont-Béïque, *Digging for Miracles*, documentary film (Montreal: In Extremis Images, 2000).

48. But in the early days creating *The Andersen Project*, this fluidity was just as much at work in a one-man show: from one evening to the next, characters disappeared (the neighbour), came back (Rashid, the young Moroccan), and so on and so forth.

49. Denis Bablet, *Edward Gordon Craig* (New York: Theatre Art Books, 1966), 92–103.

50. Didier Plassard, *L'acteur en effigie. Figures de l'homme artificiel dans le théâtre des avants-gardes historiques (Allemagne, France, Italie)* (Lausanne: L'Âge d'Homme / Institut International de la Marionnette, 1992), 47.

51. Pliny, *Natural History*, Book 35.

52. Ludovic Fouquet, interview with Robert Lepage, "Du théâtre d'ombres aux technologies contemporaines," in *Les écrans sur la scène*, Béatrice Picon-Vallin, ed. (Lausanne: L'Âge d'Homme, 1998), 327.

53. Rémy Charest, *Robert Lepage*, 120.

54. Quoted in Rémy Charest, *Robert Lepage*, 120, referring to Laurie Anderson, *Stories from the Nerve Bible: A Retrospective 1972–1992* (New York: HarperCollins, 1993).

55. Maurice Maeterlinck, "Menus propos—le théâtre," *La Jeune Belgique* 9 (September 1890): 334.

56. Paul Claudel, *Le soulier de satin* (Paris: Gallimard, 1957), 13.

57. Georges Didi-Huberman, *Devant le temps* (Paris: Minuit, 2009), 249.

58. An allusion to the imaginary world of the image used since Lepage's beginnings.

59. Georges Didi-Huberman, *Devant le temps*, 250.

60. Walter Benjamin, "Paris: Capital of the Nineteenth Century," *New Left Review* I/48 (March–April 1968): 77–88.

PART TWO

The Visual Laboratory of the Imagination: Technological Echoes

1. Yves Jubinville, "Les plaques tectoniques," *Spirale* 98 (1990): 7.

2. Chantal Hébert and Irène Perelli-Contos, "Les écrans de la pensée ou les écrans dans la théâtre de Robert Lepage," in *Les écrans sur la scène*, Béatrice Picon-Vallin, ed. (Lausanne: L'Âge d'Homme, 1998), 173.

3. Lepage's strongest use of images is in *Le moulin à images* (*The Image Mill*), which according to Bruno Lessard, "Site-Specific Screening and the Projection of Archives: Robert Lepage's *Le Moulin à images*," *Public: Art / Culture / Ideas* 40 (2010): 71, created "a montage of images ... archival materials, paintings, photographs, films, etching, and engravings" to celebrate the four hundredth anniversary of Quebec City.

4. Alain Lercher, *Les mots de la philosophie* (Paris: Belin, 1985), 234.

5. These wax portrait-masks were first mentioned in Pliny's *Natural History*, Book 35, Chapter 6.

6. Régis Debray, *Vie et mort de l'image* (Paris: Gallimard, 1992), 28.

7. Homer, *Iliad*, XXIII, 59–107.

8. Jean-Pierre Vernant, *Myth and Thought Among the Greeks*, Janet Lloyd and Jeff Fort, trans. (New York: Zone Books, 2006), 326.

9. Ludovic Fouquet, interview with Robert Lepage, "Du théâtre d'ombres aux technologies contemporaines," in *Les écrans sur la scène*, Picon-Vallin, ed., 328.

10. Pliny, *Natural History*, Book 35.

11. Later, in the eighteenth century, drawing in profile was very much in fashion, pioneered by one of Louis XV's ministers, Étienne de Silhouette.

12. Philippe Dubois, *L'acte photographique et autres essaies* (Paris: Nathan, 1990), 115.

13. Frédéric Maurin, "Au péril de la beauté: la chair du visuel et le cristal de la forme chez Robert Wilson," *La scène et les images*, Béatrice Picon-Vallin, ed. (Paris: CNRS Éditions, 2001), 58.

14. Originally published in French as *L'Œil et l'esprit* (Paris: Gallimard, 1961). In *The Merleau-Ponty Aesthetics Reader: Philosophy and Painting*, Galen A. Johnson, ed., Michael Smith, trans. (Evanston, IL: Northwestern University Press, 1993), 121–49.

15. Chantal Hébert and Irène Perelli-Contos, *La face cachée du théâtre de l'image* (Quebec City: Les Presses de l'Université Laval, 2001), 47.

16. Robert Lepage, *Vinci* (1986), unpublished.

17. Chantal Hébert and Irène Perelli-Contos, *La face cachée du théâtre de l'image*, 92.

18. Paul Valéry, *Introduction à la méthode de Léonard de Vinci* (Paris: Gallimard, [1895] 1968), quoted by Chantal Hébert and Irène Perelli-Contos, "La tempête Robert Lepage," *Nuit blanche* 55 (April–May 1994): 8.

19. Denis Bablet, *The Revolutions of Stage Design in the 20th Century* (Paris and New York: Leon Amiel, 1977).

20. Aleksandar Saša Dundjerović, *Theatricality of Robert Lepage*, 193. – Ed.

21. An effect also used in the New York episode of *The Seven Streams of the River Ota*, with the exposed light bulb hung in the communal bathroom that the protagonists turn out at the end of scenes, and in *The Far Side of the Moon* with the cord from the lamp in the wardrobe.

22. Marie Brassard, Jean Casault, Lorraine Côté, Marie Gignac, Robert Lepage, and Marie Michaud, *La trilogie des dragons* (Quebec City: L'instant même, 2005).

23. Ibid.

24. Robert Lepage in discussion with Pierre Lavoie, "Points de repère, entretiens avec les créateurs," *Cahiers de théâtre JEU* 45 (1987): 178.

25. In the first plans for *Polygraph*, a film adaptation of the play by the same name, the lower half of the space is covered with metal plates, a blurry mirrored wall around François as he takes a lie detector test. A bird's-eye view of the play even creates a modern, geometric version of the quarry: a small metal room, a box that hems in the protagonists and projects reflections on its walls.

26. The Pepper's ghost is a visual effect making a ghostlike image appear in an inclined glass that reflects a hidden subject, created by John Henry Pepper in 1863 and used by the magician Robin in Paris on the Grands Boulevards.

27. Hero of Alexandria discusses the ability of progression of light, reflection, and the use of mirrors in *Catoptrica*. *Mechanica et Catoptrica*, Volume 2, Part 1, of *Works*, L. Nix and Wilhelm Schmidt, eds. (Leipzig: B.G. Teubner, 1900).

28. Frédéric Maurin, "Au péril de la beauté: la chair du visuel et le cristal de la forme chez Robert Wilson," *La scene et les images*, Picon-Vallin, ed., 58.

29. This is truly stage lighting and not lighting effects, achieved by projectors equipped with gobos (patterned screens), creating the impression of sculpting the light.

30. In *Zulu Time*, a technological cabaret number created by Bill Vorn and Louis-Philippe Demers is a luminous, flickering ballet, completely liberated from the tubular metal structure. White stripes cover the set, breaking it up, thumbing its nose at it, and drawing against the darkness.

31. Guillaume Apollinaire, "Zone," *Alcools*, Anne Hyde, trans. (Berkeley: University of California Press, 1965), 5.

32. The Super Scan's only limitation is with regard to vertical movements, because it cannot point upward.

33. This image is particularly obvious in the production, with two batteries of projectors superimposed in columns on the metal frame that surrounds the stage. This arsenal was installed in the wings and wasn't visible to the audience.

34. In *Elsinore*, Lepage created an interactive video performance with multimedia effects by Jacques Collin and video animation by Michel Petrin. – Ed.

35. An event that brought together Quebec government departments, the French ministry of culture, the *Association Française d'Action Artistique*, and hosting organizations.

36. This is what marked Lepage in the production *[OR]* by the Japanese group Dumb Type. "They began from the principle that they would use whiteouts rather than blackouts. All of a sudden, there are no more shadows and their absence haunts us." Ludovic Fouquet, interview with Robert Lepage, "Du théâtre d'ombres aux technologies contemporaines," *Les écrans sur la scène*, Picon-Vallin, ed., 317.

37. Paul Virilio, *War and Cinema: The Logistics of Perception*, Patrick Camiller, trans. (New York: Verso, 1989), 81 [emphasis in original].

38. *Elegant Universe* is based on Brian Greene's classic book on string theory and modern cosmology: *The Elegant Universe: Superstrings, Hidden Dimensions, and the Quest for the Ultimate Theory* (New York: W.W. Norton, 1999).

39. The central character in *The Andersen Project* purposely refers to the look that kills in discussing Eurydice and Orpheus.

40. The red light photographers use in their darkrooms.

41. "I wanted to make this show starting not from a theme, but rather from a painting by da Vinci that I had seen in London and that had struck me: *The Virgin and Child with Saint Anne*, which is projected throughout the show." Carole Fréchette, "L'arte è un veicolo, interview with Robert Lepage," *Cahiers de théâtre JEU* 42 (1987): 114.

42. Cocteau's *A Letter to the Americans* is another source of inspiration for this production.

43. Likewise, the signs of the zodiac appear in the centre of the set, while struggles for power start to unfold in the castle's corridors and antechambers.

44. Jacques Collin (projection designer), in discussion with the author, Quebec City, June 1997.

45. Philippe Dubois, *L'acte photographique*, 126.

46. The point here is not to debate the relevance of the idea of photography as mortification, but obviously this is at work in Lepage's reflections on the medium.

47. The statue Frédéric contemplates in *The Andersen Project* is of Eurydice. He refers to the look that kills, a forbidden look that he can no longer turn on his ex-girlfriend Marie, whom he compares to this statue, embracing one in the place of the other.

48. "From a real body, which was there, proceed radiations which ultimately touch me […] like the delayed rays of a star." Roland Barthes, *Camera Lucida: Reflections on Photography*, Robert Howard, trans. (New York: Hill and Wang, 1981), 80–81.

49. John Berger and John Mohr, *Another Way of Telling* (New York: Pantheon, 1982), 87.

50. "There is an explosion, an enormous flash that pulverizes men and leaves the trace of their shadow on the walls. This is really the idea of the photo booth and the flash." Ludovic Fouquet, interview with Robert Lepage, "Du théâtre d'ombres aux technologies contemporaines," *Les écrans sur la scène*, Picon-Vallin, ed., 327–28.

51. Philippe Dubois, *L'acte photographique*, 77.

52. Jean Guerreschi, "Territoire psychique, territoire photographique," *Les cahiers de la photographie* 14, "Le Territoire" (Paris: Laplume, 1984), 67.

53. Guerreschi, 66.

54. Ibid., 67.

55. Ibid.

56. Roland Barthes, *Camera Lucida: Reflections on Photography*, Robert Howard, trans.

57. Ludovic Fouquet, interview with Robert Lepage, "Du théâtre d'ombres aux technologies contemporaines," in Picon-Vallin, ed., *Les écrans sur la scène*, 327.

58. In the same way that in 1977 Roy Rogers tried to explain the shroud of Turin by a flash photolysis that would fix a shadow, a flash, and an impression. Quoted by Marie-José Mondzain, *Image, Icône, Économie* (Paris: Seuil, 1996).

59. Serge Tisseron, *Le mystère de la chambre claire, photographie et inconscient* (Paris: Champs / Flammarion, 1996), 176.

60. "An experiment, showing how objects transmit their images or pictures, intersecting within the eye in the crystalline humour, is seen when by some small round hole penetrate the images of illuminated objects into a very dark chamber. Then, receive these images on a white paper placed within this dark room and rather near to the hole and you will see all the objects on the paper in their proper forms and colours." *The Notebooks of Leonardo da Vinci peinture*, vol. 1, Jean Paul Richter, ed. (Mineola: Dover Publications, 1970), 44. – Ed.

61. Philippe Dubois, *L'acte photographique*, 127.

62. Sigmund Freud, *An Outline of Psycho-Analysis* (New York: W.W. Norton, 1969), 13.

63. Sarah Kofman, *Camera Obscura of Ideology*, Will Straw, trans. (Ithaca, NY: Cornell University Press, 1999), 22.

64. Philippe Dubois, *L'acte photographique*, 276.

65. Ibid.

66. Serge Tisseron, *La mystère de la chambre claire*, 167.

67. Philippe Dubois, *L'acte photographique*, 273, referring to the story of Gradiva, she who walks, first told by German novelist Wilhelm Jensen in *Gradiva* (1903) and then retold and analyzed by Sigmund Freud, "Der Wahn und Die Traume in W. Jensens *Gradiva*" (1907) = *Delusion and Dream: An Interpretation in the Light of Psychoanalysis of "Gradiva," a Novel, by Wilhelm Jensen, which Is Here Translated*, Helen M. Downey, trans. (London: George Allen and Unwin, 1921). The text can be read as a psychoanalysis of the nineteenth-century imagination.

68. Dubois, *L'acte photographique*, 17.

69. Freud, *Delusion and Dream*, ibid.

70. Philippe Dubois, *L'acte photographique*, 172.

71. Ibid., 274.

72. Ibid., 278.

73. Lis Moller, *The Freudian Reading* (Philadelphia: University of Pennsylvania Press, 1991), 42. – Ed.

74. Sigmund Freud, "A Note Upon the Mystic Writing Pad," *General Psychological Theory*, Philip Rieff, ed. (New York: Simon & Schuster, 1963), 207–212.

75. Philippe Dubois, *L'acte photographique*, 280.

76. Ibid.

77. Ibid.

78. Rémy Charest, *Robert Lepage*, 121.

79. Jacques Aumont, Alain Bergala, Michel Marie, and Marc Vernet, *Aesthetics of Film*, Richard Neupert, ed. and trans. (Austin: University of Texas Press, 1992), 37.

80. Ibid., 47.

81. Dominique Villain, *Le montage au cinéma* (Paris: Cahiers du cinéma, 1991), 14.

82. The metal containers for rolls of film are commonly called "boîtes" in French meaning "boxes." Each can today contains around 300 metres of film, or ten minutes' worth.

83. Marie Brassard also attended the Conservatoire at the time Lepage studied there, and she joined Théâtre Repère in 1985. "She has been an important collaborator in Lepage's work ever since, as well as an independent film and theatre actor. She formed her own company, Infrarouge, in Montreal in 2001, and has toured internationally with it, writing, directing, and performing," according to Jerry Wasserman, "Robert Lepage," *Modern Canadian Plays*, vol. 2, 5th ed. (Vancouver: Talonbooks, 2013), 30. – Ed.

84. Solange Lévesque, "Polygraphe," *Cahiers de théâtre JEU* 48 (1988): 154. Published in English as Robert Lepage, Marie Brassard, and Gyllian Raby, *Polygraph* (London: Methuen Drama, 1997).

85. Solange Lévesque, "Polygraphe," *Cahiers de théâtre JEU* 48 (1988).

86. Marie Brassard, Jean Casault, Lorraine Côté, Marie Gignac, Robert Lepage, and Marie Michaud, *La trilogie des dragons*, preface by Michel Tremblay (Quebec City: L'instant même, 2005).

87. Marcel Martin, *Le langage cinématographique* (Paris: Les Éditions du Cerf, 1985), 96.

88. Ibid., 97.

89. Lepage in conversation with the author.

90. "Substitution of one shot for another through the momentary superimposition of an image over the previous one that fades." Marcel Martin, ibid., 97.

91. The architect solves a riddle by drawing a climbing spiral, foreshadowing New York's Guggenheim Museum.

92. Marcel Martin, *Le langage cinématographique*, 97.

93. Rémy Charest, *Robert Lepage*, 121.

94. Paul Virilio, *The Vision Machine* (Bloomington: Indiana University Press, 1994), 21.

95. Beginning in 2008, Lepage's *The Image Mill* has projected light and images onto Quebec City's grain silos set at the water's edge in the port at Quebec City, creating a projection screen 600 metres wide, one of the largest in the world.

96. Flies are the space above a theatre stage which is behind the proscenium, into which scenery is raised.

97. Because the size of a photogram on film is larger than that of its photographic cousin, filmed sequences can be read without projection.

98. Placing two rushes side by side during editing, using the splicer today, but previously done with spots of glue of varying degrees of transparency.

99. When Coriolanus is banished, he leaves the stage by stepping over the edge of the rectangular frame and exiting downstage. Similarly, during the movie scene that was edited out of *The Geometry of Miracles*, journalists and other spectators recognize Wright with his mistress and follow them. The line of people heads toward the screen, raises the square of fabric, and steps through the wooden frame, therefore the screen, to exit.

100. A same framing of bodies occurs in *Elsinore*; in particular, in the scene where Hamlet and Polonius are in the library. The rectangular opening of the Monolith lets the audience see Hamlet from the waist up and only the legs of Polonius, who has climbed a ladder. The cuts are precise and explicitly refer to what is outside the field of the image or outside the shot.

101. Like the doors in Velázquez's painting *Las Meninas*, in which the doors frame
      and showcase the protagonists, like the frames of paintings hanging on the
      wall.

102. Jacques Prévert, "La famille tuyau de poêle," in *La pluie et le beau temps*, folio
      collection, no. 90 (Paris: Gallimard, [1955] 1997), 197.

103. *GEO*, a travelling magazine, or *Mac OS*, a computer magazine, depending on
      the evening, in performances in Paris. The audience could actually read the
      article!

104. This is how the audience enters the photo booth through the camera in
      The Seven Streams of the River Ota.

105. *Mise en scène* by O. Krejča, Théâtre National de Belgique in Brussels.
      I mention Svoboda's stage set because it received most media attention.
      The photos of the production appear in every book on theatre and were
      therefore likely seen by Lepage. This stage set is perhaps also the most
      fundamental for him because of all stage designers, Svoboda is the one he
      refers to most often.

106. In fact, we go from a single source of projection to three sources.

107. Jacques Collin in discussion with the author, Quebec City, April 2001.

108. Ibid.

109. Edmond Couchot, "La mosaïque ordonnée," Raymond Bellour and Anne-
      Marie Duguet, eds., *Communications* 48 (Paris: Seuil, 1988): 80.

110. Jacques Collin, in discussion with the author, Quebec City, April 2001.

111. However, in *The Busker's Opera*, what the video monitors is visible on a flat
      screen, the only piece of equipment in plain view. The cameras and cabling are
      in the shadows.

112. Frédéric Maurin, quoting *L'image mouvement* by Gilles Deleuze in "Usages et
      usures de l'image. Spéculation on *La Marchand de Venise* vu par Peter Sellars,"
      Les écrans sur la scène (Lausanne: L'Âge d'Homme, 1998), 78, free translation.

113. In one of the last scenes, Philippe is talking in the dark, lit by the monitor that
      then turns toward the audience like a curtain of light, blinding it while a quick
      scene change takes place. This is an obvious reminder of the light table in
      The Seven Streams of the River Ota. Philippe disappears, and when the monitor
      turns toward the back of the stage again, we see his mother (Lepage dressed as
      a woman) in a wheelchair.

114. This is how the monitor is suggested in the peepshow booths in *The Andersen
      Project*: when the character inserts a token to see the video, a light is triggered,
      mimicking the illumination of the monitor with the same variations in light.

115. Jacques Collin, in discussion with the author, Quebec City, April 2001.

116. Jacques Collin, in discussion with the author, Quebec City, June 1997.

117. Anne-Marie Duguet, "Dispositifs," *Communications* 48 (1988): 227.

118. Ibid.

119. Ibid., 229.

120. Frédéric Maurin, "Usages et usures de l'image." In *Les écrans sur la scène*,
      Picon-Vallin, ed., 77.

121. William Shakespeare, *Hamlet*, act 2, scene 2.

122. Throughout the duel and the play, the double keeps up this confusion,
      wearing the same hairpieces when needed. During the recording, the
      audience isn't always sure who is being filmed.

123. Jean-Luc Marion, *La croisée du visible* (Paris: PUF, 1996), 15.

124. Ibid.

125. Ph. Dubois, M.-E. Mélon, and C. Dubois, "Cinéma et video: interpenetrations," *Communications* 48 (1988): 273.

126. Ibid., 283.

127. Robert Lepage as quoted in *The 7 Faces of Robert Lepage*, documentary film directed by Michel Duchesne, Télé-Québec, 1997.

128. Jacques Collin, in discussion with the author, Quebec City, February 1998.

129. Which would be in keeping with Cyrano de Bergerac, whose tale *Voyage dans la lune* confirmed Lepage's musings around this production. Robert Lepage, in discussion with the author, Le Havre, November 2000.

130. In a first version of *Elsinore*, Lepage uses a smokescreen, in the opening of the Monolith, a screen partition made of plastic the colour and consistency of smoke.

131. As at the Théâtre de Quat'Sous in Montreal, where it was created.

132. The stage set for *The Tempest* by Denise Guilbault, Victor Pilon, and Michel Lemieux at the TNM (February–March 2005) accomplishes this to perfection, by updating Pepper's ghost on a large scale and with video. The virtual characters are Ariel and those who are shipwrecked. The intention here is to use spectres rather than bodies, to summon presences that could only emerge from the mind of an embittered Prospero.

133. Shakespeare, *The Tempest*, act 4, scene 1.

134. This screen has a particular capacity for polarization. It reflects the light of the projection because of metallic particles mixed with the paint on the wood panels.

135. Robert Lepage, in discussion with the author.

136. Shakespeare, *The Tempest*, act 4, scene 1.

137. Quebec equivalent of the French "Molières," but with the impact and diversity of the American Oscars. There is an award for every genre of theatre.

138. Philippe Quéau, *Le virtuel, vertus et vertiges*, Milieux collection, INA (Seyssel: Éditions Champ Vallon, 1983), 56.

139. This is the case for all attempts at simulation, whether vehicle simulators, computer-aided design software, or computer-aided design and manufacturing software.

140. Although in the first versions, created by the company Mirage, the boulders look more like rum babas.

141. Philippe Quéau, *Le virtuel, vertus, et vertiges*, 18.

142. Ibid., 22.

143. On Mark Reaney's creations, see Frank Bauchard, "Théâtre et réalité virtuelle, une introduction à la démarche de Mark Reaney," *Les écrans sur la scène,* coll. Th XX (Lausanne: L'Âge d'Homme, 1998), 225–45, or see Reaney's portfolio at http://www2.ku.edu/~ievr/reaney/. The site also includes his conference papers and histories of and excerpts from each production.

144. "The first time I saw the *butoh* dancers, Sankai Juku, for example, something struck me. A guy was dressed as a Japanese soldier, covered in rice powder. He was moving on the stage. All of a sudden, he took off incredibly quickly, so fast that the rice powder remained where it was and disappeared. It's a bit like the extension of the idea of the shadow. [He refers to the quarry.] Then theatre evolved, technology evolved and in the twentieth century, we started to erase shadows [...]. Another show talks about shadows: *[OR]* by Dumb Type. They started from the principle that rather than having blackouts, they would have whiteouts. All of a sudden, the shadows are gone, and we start to obsess about their absence." Ludovic Fouquet, interview with Robert Lepage, "Du théâtre d'ombres aux technologies contemporaines," in *Les écrans sur la scène*, Picon-Vallin, ed., 327.

145. The Polyekran, invented by Josef Svoboda, included a wall of 112 cubes (that is, a 112-part screen) onto which two projectors show 15,000 slides over 11 minutes. First presented at Brussels World's Fair in 1958 and again in Montreal at Expo 67.

146. It's precisely because of the Parisian protagonist's shadowy side (voyeurism that drives him to watch porno films in narrow, dirty booths) in *The Andersen Project*, in one of its first versions, that he ends up setting fire to himself in the booth of a sex shop. The fire eradicates his shadowy side at the same time as it engulfs him entirely. The actor is burned in the shadow of the stage (projection on the scrim of video flames).

147. Carl Fillion (set designer), in discussion with the author during the creation of *Jean-Sans-Nom*, Quebec City, 1999.

148. From time to time the pages of books throw a translucent veil over action played with illustrations.

149. Their white faces are nonetheless brighter than the matte white of the illustrations.

150. Expression borrowed from Jean-Louis Weinsberg, *Les chemins du virtuel*, 98.

151. Jean-Pierre Miquel offers a nice description of two large magazines, containing an entire canvas palace, that he was involved in mounting during the Festival de théâtre de Parme in 1957. Preface to the work by Alain Roy, *Dictionnaire raisonné et illustré du théâtre à l'italienne* (Paris: Actes Sud, 1992), 7–8.

152. This doesn't mean that proscenium arch set-up is light: the wooden structure surrounding the stage, as well as the machinery in the flies and below stage obviously contradict this.

153. "Computers have an announced lifespan of three years; video equipment, five." Christine Van Assche, Editorial, "New Technologies," *Parachute* 84 (October–December 1996): 5.

154. Ibid.

155. Rémy Charest, *Robert Lepage*, 16.

156. Ibid.

157. The screen expands in a kind of vertical ambiguity, as discussed below.

158. Rémy Charest, *Robert Lepage*, 17.

159. Marie-Madeleine Mervant-Roux, "Faire théâtre du matériau multimédia. La nouvelle *Laterna Magika*," *L'oeuvre d'art totale*, Élie Konigson, ed. (Paris: CNRS Éditions, 1995), 301–24.

160. Robert Lepage as quoted in Duchesne, *The 7 Faces of Robert Lepage* (third word, "Solo").

161. Created in 1986 and hailed by the critics, this production received the Prix Coup de Pouce at the Festival d'Avignon in 1987, among others.

162. *Vinci* uses ingenuity to bring the Italian artist and scholar to light. The sound design is one of these ingenious means.

163. Sipping her Coca-Cola in a Burger King, the *Mona Lisa* talks about "Gainsbourg, fat Régine, Darry Cowl: the ugliest children in the history of genetics!" Then she explains that she is a translator at the Louvre for the guides, and ends by introducing herself: "Careful: fragile work of art!"

164. During the show opener "Come Talk to Me," Peter Gabriel rises from beneath the stage in an English phone booth. He sings into the phone and then emerges from the telephone box, holding the handset. While walking forward on the stage (actually on a treadmill), he stretches out the cord, almost to its full extent of 20 metres. At the end of the song, he goes back into the booth, which is lowered through the stage floor.

165. The "white telephone" is an essential part of a dramatic construction based on sudden twists and ignorance of an outside situation. It is used more frequently in film than onstage.

166. This is how Frédéric can tell this modern fable, inspired by Andersen, and recount his experience in Paris in recent weeks. He weaves a speech drawn from the fable and confession and touches on the personal when he addresses the public at the Palais Garnier.

167. Lepage still has to change his voice, but the effects are done by the mixer, just as the visual effects were the result of what was stored on the console. With sound, we talk about an "effects rack," which generally allows for reverberation.

168. Marie Brassard understood this perfectly in her solo production *Jimmy creature de rêve* (2001). Constantly split in two, her voice is transformed by the same mixer, but diffused as if it comes from somewhere other than where she is.

169. Rémy Charest, *Robert Lepage*, 123.

170. Ibid.

171. The set confirms that we are in Feydeau's *The Girl from Maxim's*.

172. The list and the description of these sequences are impressive. Studios can be equipped with a digital inventory of any number of different wind sounds or bell sounds.

173. Michel F. Côté (composer), in discussion with the author, Quebec City, April 2001.

174. Specifically Marco Poulain and Rodrigue Proteau. Proteau spent a long time working with visual theatre companies, such as Carbone 14, where words are fairly rare onstage.

175. Michel F. Côté, in discussion with the author, New York, December 1997.

176. Ibid.

177. Michel F. Côté, in discussion with the author, October 1999.

178. The D-Beam or Dimension Beam owes its name to the famous expression from *Star Trek*: "Beam me up, Scotty," used when a character wants to be tele-transported. "To beam" is a term used for disseminating waves or programs. The "D" is for "Digital," of course.

179. Once an object enters the beam, the beam records the information and transposes it digitally. If the hand is very close to the beam, then the sound is intense. Sounds can be programmed and developed or changed through a sequence of gestures. The change caused by the movement is therefore anticipated like, for example, slowing down, raising in pitch, and so on. This beam is available on certain Roland SP-808, Groovebox MC-505, and other synthesizers, as is the case in *Zulu Time*.

180. While the psaltery suggests a bygone era, it's also a symbol of transition. A plucked string instrument, it is the forerunner to the spinet and the harpsichord.

181. Didier Léglise (composer), in discussion with the author, Paris, September 2001.

182. Like rap throughout *The Andersen Project*. From the credits, the rhythms and the rap of the group IAM seem out of place (we have come to see a production about Andersen), but are justified by the young Moroccan character who listens to the group on his Walkman.

183. Robert Lepage, *Vinci* (1986), unpublished.

184. Diane Pavlovic, "Du décollage à l'envol," *Cahiers de théâtre JEU* 42 (1987): 93.

185. Michel F. Côté, in discussion with the author, New York, December 1997.

186. The aesthetic of sounds produced, like that of the equipment, is reminiscent of video-game consoles. The light ray symbolizes the joystick on today's consoles.

PART THREE

Experiments in the Visual Laboratory:
Echoes of Chaos

1. This is what the audience had to do for *The Seven Streams of the River Ota*, for example, a seven- to nine-hour show performed over two or more evenings.

2. Jean Saint-Hilaire, "The créateur se penche sur l'avenir du théâtre," interview with Robert Lepage, *Le Soleil* (Quebec City), January 22, 2000.

3. *La Casa Azul*, created December 6, 2001, only had two phases of creation.

4. Implanthéâtre in Quebec City, from May 20 to 27, 1986, or nine performances.

5. *Green Dragon* premiered on June 3, 1987, in a warehouse in the Old Port of Quebec, commissioned for the occasion; *Red Dragon* premiered on June 4 and *White Dragon*, on June 5. The entire six-hour production was staged for the first time on June 6.

6. In 1997, there were new changes before the performances in Chicago. These were adjustments, rather than the product of a period of creation: Patricia interviews Walter, her ex-husband, now the Canadian ambassador to Japan.

7. This is the same character as in the film *Le confessionnal*, then named Pierre Maltais.

8. Feydeau's play takes place in a lighter atmosphere than that of Mishima. An anachronism also motivated the change: Mishima had not yet been translated into French in 1970.

9. Marie Brassard, press conference with the team of *The Seven Streams of the River Ota*, round table discussion at the Festival de théâtre des Amériques, June 1997, Montreal.

10. Quoted in Rémy Charest, *Robert Lepage*, 103–105.

11. Menno Plucker for Australia, North America, and Japan; Richard Castelli for Europe and sometimes Japan; Michael Morris for the UK. They act as producer agents.

12. "Eighty per cent of Ex Machina's revenue is generated from the sale of shows internationally," the *Journal du Québec* noted, October 24, 1996.

13. Richard Castelli (producer), in discussion with the author, Sevran (Paris), March 2001.

14. Jean-Pierre Vézina (executive director of Ex Machina), in discussion with the author, Quebec City, April 2001.

15. The same applies for the assistants, the lighting and costume designers, but particularly for the technical team that manages each project.

16. These revivals had new and foreign producers. Marie Brassard, the co-playwright, directed the actors and provided artistic direction.

17. Twenty-eight venues and 68,726 spectators.

18. Marc Labrèche played in a new Ex Machina production of *Needles and Opium* presented in Toronto by Canadian Stage, in co-production with Théâtre du Trident, Quebec City, and Théâtre du Nouveau Monde, Montreal, in November 2013.

19. Kristina Mendicino, "A Televisual Inferno: Tea Alagić's preparadise, sorry now," *TDR: The Drama Review* 50: 4 (2006): 171. – Ed.

20. This is the impression created by the fact that the Dramaten actors came from Stockholm in the summer of 1997, as did the soloists for *The Damnation of Faust* later on.

21. A narrow tower adjoins the Second Empire facade, topped with a copper dome. Firemen used to dry the firehoses inside the tower. It was reinforced with a metal framework and has a winding staircase that serves every floor.

22. "The restoration of the historical elements apparently cost $830,000 (in Canadian dollars), or 11% of the total cost assessed at $7,430,000. The built portion accounts for 54% of the budget, or slightly more than $4,000,000, and professional fees were $1,263,000." "La Caserne Dalhousie sera inaugurée en mai," *Le Journal de Québec*, October 24, 1996.

23. Such as Mirage Multimedia, which created the images for *The Tempest*, and Casting Cauffopé, which worked on publicity.

24. Christine Borello, "Mettre en scène, c'est écrire," interview with Robert Lepage, *Théâtre / Public* 117 (1994): 83.

25. Robert Lepage as quoted in *The 7 Faces of Robert Lepage*, documentary film directed by Michel Duchesne, Télé-Québec, 1997.

26. To the point that a route was created in Quebec City of the shooting locations and references that appear in Lepagean theatre.

27. This explanation of the creative process and its impact on technology is based mainly on *The Geometry of Miracles*, the final phase of creation of which was studied at length in February and March 1998.

28. Lepage reversed how the story unfolds.

29. The film's narrator talks constantly about "the seven delta streams of the Ota River," a river that crosses the city, and of its rhizomes, which would be seen in the aerial views of the city after the bombing.

30. Robert Lepage, quoted in Duchesne, *The 7 Faces of Robert Lepage*.

31. Marie Brassard, quoted in Duchesne, *The 7 Faces of Robert Lepage*.

32. Chantal Hébert and Irène Perelli-Contos, *La face cachée du théâtre de l'image* (Quebec City: Les Presses de l'Université Laval, 2001), 21.

33. Robert Lepage, quoted in Duchesne, *The 7 Faces of Robert Lepage*.

34. Using English also fosters sensitivity to and passion for the story, as the actors get caught up in expressing themselves in a language that isn't their own. The use of English and the presence of American actors seem to encourage a certain emotional, biographical exaggeration: "He *really* loved that woman, *but* ... *She* has *never* ignored ...," the actors tending to rely heavily on adverbs in their sentences in English.

35. French was a more universally shared language during the creation of *The Seven Streams of the River Ota*, the effect of which can be felt.

36. One of the foundations for the work was the Peter Brook film *Meetings with Remarkable Men* (1979), which features a number of dancers.

37. Robert Lepage, quoted in Pierre Lavoie, "Points de repères: entretien avec les créateurs," *Cahiers de théâtre JEU* 45 (1987): 203.

38. This production also uses the Zulu code as a point of departure, which, through twenty-six words, establishes an international language – a reflection of the desire to create a universal language.

39. Robert Lepage, quoted in Pierre Lavoie, "Points de repères: entretien avec les créateurs," *Cahiers de théâtre JEU* 45 (1987): 179–80.

40. On a number of occasions during rehearsals, Lepage would have to deal with the actors' crises of doubt, the first occurring at the end of three weeks of work.

41. Rémy Charest, *Robert Lepage*, 84.

42. A play on words follows: the cosmonaut is inspired; the astronaut is well financed!

43. Robert Lepage in discussion with Edgar Morin, quoted in Chantal Hébert and Irène Perelli-Contos, *La fache cachée du théâtre de l'image*, 25.

44. And as he often does, he would then find the justification for this idea or instinct. He would see strong symbolism in the fact that Marie Brassard, who plays Olgivanna, puts on her husband's coat and wig, to then play Wright. In effect, she is the two protagonists and becomes Wright's soul, something his life story bears out.

45. Lepage opens the first public rehearsal by explaining that the audience is invited to see, "displayed in great detail, the moments that they hope to present in the final version."

46. Florence Laly, *Les nouveaux modes de creation théâtrale en lien avec les nouvelles technologies*, DEA thesis, Paris III (2000), 19.

47. Françoise Coblence, *Le dandyisme, obligation d'incertitude* (Paris: PUF, 1988).

48. "*Possible Worlds* (2000) is his first feature film in English, adapted from the play by Toronto's John Mighton." Jerry Wasserman, "Robert Lepage," in *Modern Canadian Plays*, vol. 2, 5th ed., 32. – Ed.

49. During the fall of 1994, while he was rehearsing *A Dream Play* in Stockholm during the week and editing *Le confessionnal* in Paris on the weekend, he started the first phase of creation of *The Seven Streams of the River Ota*.

50. Carole Fréchette, "L'arte è un veicolo. Entretien avec Robert Lepage," *Cahiers de théâtre JEU* 42 (1987): 123.

51. Théâtre de Quat'Sous, Montreal, December 5, 2001.

52. It wasn't her first time acting as dramaturge, but her contribution didn't prevent this oversimplification of the material.

53. This evolution can be seen in David Clermont-Béïque's documentary *Digging for Miracles* (2000), which follows the production for almost three years. Based on excerpts of performances and rehearsals, one can guess how the show finally integrated elements that were rejected during the first phases of work.

54. Marie Laliberté, "*Zulu Time* at the Carrefour international de théâtre," *Voir* (Quebec City), May 11, 2000.

55. Except for Africa, a continent that Lepage hasn't yet toured and that doesn't seem to fuel his imagination.

56. Solange Lévesque, "L'œil de la culture, un regard sur le travail de Robert Lepage," *Possibles* 17: 2 (Spring 1993): 73.

57. Jean Saint-Hilaire, "Le créateur se penche sur l'avenir du théâtre," interview with Robert Lepage, *Le Soleil* (Quebec City), January 22, 2000.

58. Rémy Charest, *Robert Lepage*, 45.

59. Laura Winters, "The World Is His Canvas, and His Inspiration," *New York Times*, December 1, 1996.

60. Robert Lepage, *The Seven Streams of the River Ota* (London: Methuen Drama, 1996), 98.

61. Press conference with the team of *The Seven Streams of the River Ota*, round table discussion at the Festival de théâtre des Amériques, June 1997.

62. Serge Gruzinski, *The Mestizo Mind: The Intellectual Dynamics of Colonization and Globalization* (London: Routledge, 2002), 19.

63. Ibid., 25.

64. Matt Wolf, "Robert Lepage: Multicultural and Multifaceted," *New York Times*, December 6, 1992.

65. Lepage loves geography and he has collected atlases and travel stories from a very young age.

66. "At Ex Machina, we want to see how far we can push theatre into the territory of film." Jean Saint-Hilaire, "La face cachée d'Andersen," *Le Soleil* (Quebec City), February 2, 2005.

67. The fact that he shot a film version of *The Far Side of the Moon* doesn't make this any less so: the treatment is really more cinematic for *Nô*, the movie adaptation of *The Seven Streams of the River Ota*.

68. Brigitte Fürle, "Le théâtre comme point de rencontre des arts, une interview avec Robert Lepage," *Theaterschrift* 5–6 (1994): 210–29.

69. "No man's land," definition, *Le Petit Robert* (Paris: Dictionnaires Le Robert, 1993).

70. This black austere building resembles a fortress in its impenetrability and sobriety. And during the Québécois cabal of April 2001, which set Lepage and critics against one another, La Caserne, flying a terse banner that read: "Artists are free and have no accounts to render to medi@cracy [in the French original, Lepage's clever compound, 'médi@crité,' speaks more of the media's general ineptitude than to the concept of 'mediocracy'…"] was very much like a fortress under siege with a creator fighting for his independence.

71. Press conference with the team of *The Seven Streams of the River Ota*, round table discussion at the Festival de théâtre des Amériques, June 1997.

72. Robert Lepage, quoted in Brigitte Fürle, "Le théâtre comme point de rencontre des arts," *Theaterschrift* 5–6 (1994): 221.

73. This is what blocked its distribution after the last version in June 2002 in Montreal.

74. "I think we're moving toward a spherical theatre, or a theatre of man in his position in the universe. There will be directors to sculpt the frame of this stage. It's nothing new, really. Shakespeare's theatre was called the Globe," Jean Saint-Hilaire, "Robert Lepage, le créateur se penche sur l'avenir du théâtre," *Le Soleil* (Quebec City), January 22, 2000.

75. Except for very slow, very dreamlike dances, but they only occupy a single line along the entire width of the set, like the heron dance sequence. The line of dancers crosses Svetlana's table vehicle, climbs over it, and then continues, without deviating from its course.

76. Lepage often refers to museums in his work: an art gallery in *The Dragons' Trilogy*; a photo exhibition, the Dome of Florence, and London's National Gallery in *Vinci*; the Hiroshima Peace Memorial Museum in *The Seven Streams of the River Ota*; and *The Far Side of the Moon*, where a puppet cosmonaut gives an inaugural speech in the entrance of one of the rooms of the Montreal Biodome.

77. The term "baroque" is the title of one of the seven parts of the documentary that the director Michel Duchesne devoted to Lepage during the creation of *The Seven Branches of the River Ota*, as quoted in Duchesne, *The 7 Faces of Robert Lepage*.

78. On the relationship with China, see Rémy Charest, *Robert Lepage*, 31. Also, Lepage says: "Marie Brassard [...] told me when she got back [from the *Polygraph* tour to Hong Kong] how much of what we had imagined of China was true to life."

79. Guy Scarpetta, *L'impureté* (Paris: Grasset, 1985), 36.

80. Guy Scarpetta saw the Turners at the Tate Gallery a few weeks before leaving for Japan.

81. Rémy Charest, *Robert Lepage*, 41. Also: "These games of superimposition create a kind of 'pizza' style of working. In contemporary theatre especially, the companies always have a very baroque side to them, which creates a strange effect. They have no problem performing the role of a samurai to the music of Brahms or mixing very disparate techniques in the same show. [...] the confusion caused by the baroque nature of their work is very difficult for international festivals and distributors who want to produce it" (41–42).

82. Ibid., 42.

83. Robert Lepage as quoted in Duchesne, *The 7 Faces of Robert Lepage*.

84. Rémy Charest, *Robert Lepage*, 43.

85. Robert Lepage as quoted in Duchesne, *The 7 Faces of Robert Lepage*.

86. Robert Lepage, free translation from *Digging for Miracles*, documentary film by David Clermont-Beïque (Montreal: In Extremis Images, 2000).

87. Rémy Charest, *Robert Lepage*, 43.

88. Ibid., 38.

89. From the Japanese word *musume* ("girl"). The three texts by Pierre Loti on Japan, *Madame Chrysanthème* (1887), *Japoneries d'automne* (1889), and *La troisième jeunesse de Madame Prune* (1905), are all marked by the same casualness, combining intuition, the acuity of a universally curious gaze, a poetic sensibility, but also hasty remarks that ambiguously repeat many clichés.

90. This film has many shots of windows and walls that are a clear echo of the Japanese interior, although the action takes place in Canada.

91. Minoru Tanokura, "Hiroshima: *The Seven Streams of the River Ota*," *Asahi Shimbun* (the Asahi daily), October 11, 1995, translation by the Délégation du Québec à Tokyo.

92. Michel Tournier, *Des clés et des serrures* (Paris: Chêne / Hachette, 1979), an essay often quoted by Lepage.

93. Rémy Charest, *Robert Lepage*, 41.

94. Like in Japanese interiors, the colours of Lepage's sets are matte, solid, often light, even sometimes pale grey (*The Far Side of the Moon*). The walls of *The Seven Streams of the River Ota* conjure dreams of the colour of fresh butter, evoked by Loti and Claudel.

95. Pierre Loti, *Madame Chrysanthème* (Middlesex: The Echo Library, 2007), 66.

96. Pierre Loti, letter of November 6, 1885, to his sister Marie, *Julie Viaud ou Pierre Loti, coureur des mers et coureur de rêves* (Paris, Galerie Régine Lussan, 1994), n.p.

97. "And then after a moment, doubt surfaces: am I not entirely fabricating a 'postmodern' Japan, but an Orient as projective and mythological as the avant-garde imagined? [...] pure projection of my preoccupations as a European author of the end of twentieth century? Is it impossible, when it comes to the Orient, to escape the traps of projection and utopia?" Guy Scarpetta, *L'impureté*, 38.

98. This project was developed between 2005 and 2007, but finally abandoned, inspired by the eponymous physicist Brian Greene. "String Theory" seeks to connect the infinitely large image of the theatre to the infinitesimally small image of quantum physics. At stage one of development, Lepage gathered Greene and string musicians. The project is believed to have been in co-production with the Lincoln Center for the Performing Arts in New York.

99. Gilles Deleuze, *The Fold: Leibniz and the Baroque* (London: Continuum Books, 2006), 32.

100. Jean Rousset, *La littérature de l'âge baroque en France. Circé et le paon* (Paris: José Corti, 1954), 163.

101. Marcel Brion, "Baroque et esthétique du movement," *Études cinématographiques*, 14–15.

102. Christine Buci-Glucksmann, *The Madness of Vision: On Baroque Aesthetics* (Athens, OH: Ohio University Press, 2013), 121.

103. Gilles Deleuze, *The Fold: Leibniz and the Baroque*. Fire is what accounts for the extraordinary folds in the tunic of Bernini's *Saint Teresa*, the pleats being a metaphor for the fire that consumes her.

104. Christine Buci-Glucksman, *The Madness of Vision*, 13.

105. What was new about the baroque was that it accorded to the gaze "a new category of seeing that ascribes an epistemological and aesthetic capacity, an ontological *optikon*, to the gaze," Christine Buci-Glucksmann, *The Madness of Vision*, 2. The eye here is qualified as "miembro divino" (Graciàn). Hence the constant use of the *mise en abyme* of the gaze, through the figure of the painter, the mirror.

106. Christine Buci-Glucksmann, *The Madness of Vision*, 121.

107. Jean Saint-Hilaire, "Robert Lepage, le créateur se penche sur l'avenir du théâtre," *Le Soleil* (Quebec City), January 22, 2000.

108. Ibid.

109. Not like Olivier Py, who, after Claudel, exploited the religious and passionate vein of theatre, or Valère Novarina who instituted the word "transcendence" and the very inspiration of these words as a new transcendence. It is no coincidence that the circus, which also uses a vertical plan that combines religious transcendence and physical excellence, is also present in Lepage's creations. The suspended actor in *Needles and Opium* is also an acrobat using bungee cords, just like the aerial acrobats in *The Damnation of Faust* and *Zulu Time*.

110. Gilles Deleuze, *The Fold: Leibniz and the Baroque*, 44.

111. A symbolic meeting with the father takes place during the rendezvous with the Russian cosmonaut in a hotel bar in Montreal. The true father is never evoked.

112. The ladder is often used in Lepage's world (*Elsinore, National, Capital Nationale, La Celestina*, and so on). It is the central element in *The Tempest*, which Lepage staged at the Tokyo Globe Theatre in 1993.

113. Marie Brassard introduces a similar morbid superimposition at the beginning of *Polygraph*: she appears naked, and then her body is lit by anatomical slide projections: muscles, veins, organs, and bones are superimposed on her flesh, so that she seems transparent, the seemingly phosphorescent image of a skeleton.

114. Rémy Charest, *Robert Lepage*, 86.

115. Ibid., 75–81.

116. Ibid., 87.

117. Christine Buci-Glucksmann, *The Madness of Vision: On Baroque Aesthetics*, Dorothy Z. Baker, trans. (Athens, OH: Ohio University Press, 2013), 2.

118. Robert Lepage, in discussion with the author.

119. Carl Fillion (set designer), in phone discussion with the author, December 2001.

120. Gilles Deleuze, *The Fold: Leibniz and the Baroque*, 6.

121. Tanizaki describes the light filtering through *shojis* to the most out-of-the-way rooms as unreal reflections, almost dreamlike or like the horizon at dusk: "The mobile partitions and the golden screens, in a darkness that no outside light ever penetrates, capture the very tip of light from a far-off garden, separated by I don't know how many rooms." Éloge de l'ombre (Paris: Publications Orientalistes de France, 1977), 60.

122. Jean Rousset, *La littérature de l'âge baroque en France*, 168, quoted in Deleuze, *The Fold: Leibniz and the Baroque*, 32.

123. Gilles Deleuze, *The Fold: Leibniz and the Baroque*, 45. Tanizaki similarly describes the indirect light that passes through certain *shojis* to light up the *tokonoma*.

124. Borrowing from photography and film.

125. Designed by Holger Förterer, the touch screen reacts to the performers' movements via an infrared-sensitive camera above the stage and computer software that tracks their movements.

126. The relative briefness of scenes in Lepage's plays and films also shows the influence of television. Zapping and watching several channels at the same time are very common in North America.

127. André du Bouchet, *Where Heat Looms*, David Mus, trans. (Los Angeles: Sun & Moon Books, 1996).

128. A few weeks before the premiere of *The Andersen Project*, the technical creation team noticed that Lepage was acting in the wooden proscenium set on the stage like it was the great frame of a painting. But there were no plans for Lepage to move about on this frame, which was made of light plywood. The frame had to be reinforced to accommodate his movements. This anecdote shows the extent to which Lepage always explores how to act within a frame, which can be distorted and left behind. Rémy Charest, *Robert Lepage*, 38.

129. Rémy Charest, *Robert Lepage*, 38.

130. A phenomenon seen in Lepage's films.

131. Denis Riout, *La peinture monochrome, histoire et archéologie du genre* (Nîmes: Éditions Jacqueline Chambon, 1996), 69.

132. Frédéric is in fact an albino. His pale skin, transparent irises, and white hair form a sort of version in negative of Andersen, as if the values of a daguerreotype of the writer had been inversed, visible during the credits.

133. Georges Didi-Huberman, *Ce que nous voyons, ce qui nous regarde* (Paris: Les Éditions de Minuit, 1992), 194.

134. "The world strives to find stability in theatre, to find a formula, and that is what creates boring institutions." Robert Lepage, free translation, *Digging for Miracles*, documentary film by David Clermont-Beïque (Montreal, In Extremis Images, 2000).

PART FOUR

The Visual Laboratory in Conclusion

1. This project was developed between 2005 and 2007, but finally abandoned.
2. "Theatre is too polished today. We spend a lot of time and energy to make things polished." Robert Lepage, free translation, *Digging For Miracles*.
3. Comparison and reflection borrowed from Frédéric Maurin, "Au péril de la beauté: la chair du visuel et le cristal de la forme chez Robert Wilson," in *La scène et les images*, Béatrice Picon-Vallin, ed. (Paris: CNRS Éditions, 2001), 58.
4. Ibid.
5. Ibid.

EPILOGUE

1. With the exception of *La tempête* (2011), I have seen all of Lepage's productions since 2005. I watched the Cirque du Soleil productions (*Kà* and *Totem*) on video and attended one of the Metropolitan Opera's worldwide movie-theatre screenings of his production of Wagner's *Der Ring des Nibelungen*.

2. Following the publication of *Robert Lepage, l'horizon en images*, I convinced Ex Machina to publish some of the play scripts with the same publisher. Some of the play scripts published in French include *La trilogie des dragons* (2005), *La face cachée de la lune* (2007), and *Le projet Andersen* (2007); all are published in Quebec City by L'instant meme. I also assembled a collection of Lepage's sketches, archives, and hundreds of photos of his shows that in part inspired the team to put together the heavily illustrated book *EX MACHINA: chantiers d'écriture scénique* by Patrick Caux and Bernard Gilbert (Sillery, QC: Les éditions du Septentrion, 2007), published in an English translation by Neil Kroetsch as *EX MACHINA: Creating for the Stage* (Vancouver: Talonbooks, 2009).

3. Stéphan Bureau, *CONTACT, the encyclopaedia of creation*. Interviews with Robert Lepage originally broadcast on Radio-Canada (television) in 2007, published in print as Stéphan Bureau, *Bureau rencontre Robert Lepage* (Montreal: Amérik Média, 2008).

4. The vertical image is a technique explored again later in Wagner's *The Ring*.

5. Ludovic Fouquet, "L'envol du dragon. *Le Dragon bleu*," in *Cahiers de théâtre JEU* 128 (September 2008): 25–28.

6. Robert Lepage, in discussion with the author.

7. Ibid.

8. Opera by Lorin Maazel, based on a libretto by J.D. McClatchy and Thomas Meehan, in turn based on the novel by George Orwell. Staged at London's Royal Opera House, 2005.

9. This is an aesthetic of polyvision sets that has been used since Craig and Svoboda.

10. Lepage's remarks in the documentary *Wagner's Dream*, by Bob Eisenhardt and Susan Froemke, 2012, Bob Eisenhardt, ed., Susan Froemke and Douglas Graves, prod., released by Metropolitan Opera, New York.

11. Bruno Lessard, "Site-Specific Screening and the Projection of Archives: Robert Lepage's *Le Moulin à images*," *Public: Art / Culture / Ideas* 40 (2010): 71.

12. The creative adventure of *The Image Mill* has been faithfully recorded in the documentary *The Image Mill Revealed* (Marie Belzil and Mariano Franco, Les Productions du 8e art, and the National Film Board of Canada, 2009). The directors followed Lepage's team during the three last months before the opening of the festivities for Quebec City's four-hundredth anniversary.

13. Jerry Wasserman, "Robert Lepage," in *Modern Canadian Plays*, vol. 2, 5th ed. (Vancouver: Talonbooks, 2013), 31. – Ed.

14. As has been done since the nineteenth century with stages equipped with moving sidewalks or as Piscator experimented with in *The Good Soldier Švejk* (1928), based on the novel by Jaroslav Hašek; a production in which two moving sidewalks create a soldier's journey as he wanders through a war-torn world.

15. "Robert Lepage, Veronica Tennant to Show New Pan Am Games Works: Canadian Artists among Dozens Commissioned for Arts and Culture Festival in 2015," Canadian Press, April 1, 2014.

16. Rémy Charest, *Robert Lepage*, 125.

17. Lepage in interview for "Jeu de cartes 1: Lepage joue son a tout," Éric Moreault, *Le Soleil* (Quebec City), June 9, 2012.

18. Description of the project from La Caserne's website.

19. Lepage in interview with Manuel Piolat Soleymat, in "Les beautés de la culture islamique," for *La terrasse* 201, France, September 7, 2012.

20. Description of the production on La Caserne's website.

21. Lepage in discussion with Victoria Ahearn, "Robert Lepage Going 'Back to the Basics'," Canadian Press, January 9, 2012.

22. Ludovic Fouquet, "L'envol du dragon. *Le Dragon bleu*," *Cahiers de théâtre JEU* 128 (September 2008): 25–28.

23. Sylvie Isabelle (communications director, Ex Machina), in discussion with the author.

24. Lepage in discussion with Victoria Ahearn, "Robert Lepage Going 'Back to the Basics'," Canadian Press, January 9, 2012.

25. Robert Lepage, quoted in Caux and Gibert, *EX MACHINA: Creating for the Stage*, 68.

26. Ibid., 77.

CHRONOLOGY OF ROBERT LEPAGE PRODUCTIONS

All shows and other works excepting films were created, designed, directed, and performed by Robert Lepage in collaboration with the creators listed.

Abbreviations used:

AD: Assistant Director; C: Costume Designer; CC: Collective Creator; CH: Choreographer; D: Dramaturg; DIR: Director; I: Image Designer; L: Lighting Designer; M: Music Director; P: Producer; S: Sound Designer; SD: Set Designer

Not all creation teams are listed. The shows depicted in images in this book are listed as a priority.

1979

Arlequin, serviteur de deux maîtres
– by Carlo Goldoni

P: Cégep de Lévis-Lauzon (Lévis).

L'attaque quotidienne

CC: Richard Fréchette; P: Théâtre Hummm... (Quebec City); opened at bar Le Zinc (Quebec City).

La ferme des animaux
– based on George Orwell's Animal Farm

CC: Paule Filion, Michèl Laperrière, Suzanne Poliquin; P: Théâtre Hummm... (Quebec City); opened at Centre François-Charron (Quebec City) and was invited to the Association québécoise du jeune théâtre festival.

1980

L'école, c'est secondaire

CC: Camil Bergeron, Denis Bernard, Michel Nadeau; P: Théâtre Repère (Quebec City); toured high schools in the greater Quebec City area.

Oomeraghi ooh!
– by Jean Truss, translation and adaptation by Josée Campanale
> P: Les Marionnettes du Grand Théâtre de Québec (Quebec City).

Saturday Night Taxi
> CC: Richard Fréchette, Francine Lafontaine; P: Théâtre Hummm...
> (Quebec City); opened at Centre François-Charron (Quebec City);
> restaged at Le Hobbit café-theatre (Quebec City) in 1981.

 ## 1981

Le coq
– adaptation of *La zizanie*, cartoon by Albert Uderzo and René Goscinny
> P: La Troupe Méchatigan (Sainte-Marie-de-Beauce).

Dix petits nègres
– based on Agatha Christie's *Ten Little Indians*
> P: Cégep de Lévis-Lauzon (Lévis).

Jour de pluie, rêves de nuit
– by Gérard Bibeau
> P: Les Marionnettes du Grand Théâtre de Québec (Quebec City).

1982

À demi-lune
> CC: Johanne Bolduc, Estelle Dutil; P: Théâtre Repère (Quebec City);
> opened at L'Anglicane (Lévis).

Clodiko, bric-à-brac
– by Luc Simard
> P: Les Marionnettes du Grand Théâtre de Québec (Quebec City).

En attendant
> CC: Richard Fréchette, Jacques Lessard; P: Théâtre Repère (Quebec
> City); opened at Le Hobbit café-theatre (Quebec City).

Pas d'chicane dans ma cabane
> CC: Michel Bernatchez, Odile Pelletier, Marco Poulin; P: Théâtre
> d'Bon Humeur (Quebec City); opened at Centre François-Charron
> (Quebec City).

Les rois mangent
> CC: Théâtre d'Bon Humeur (Quebec City); opened at Centre
> François-Charron (Quebec City); performed at Théâtre de la Bordée
> (Quebec City).

1983

Carmen
– adaptation of the opera by Georges Bizet

> **P:** Théâtre d'Bon Humeur (Quebec City); performed at Théâtre de la Bordée (Quebec City).

Coriolan et le monstre aux mille têtes
– based on William Shakespeare's *Coriolanus*

> **P:** Théâtre Repère (Quebec City); opened at Théâtre de la Bordée (Quebec City).

Dieu et l'amour complexe
– collage of writing by Woody Allen

> **P:** Conservatoire d'art dramatique de Québec.

1984

Le bal des bals
> **P:** Parks Canada; opened at Artillery Park (Quebec City).

Circulations
> **CC:** François Beausoleil, Bernard Bonnier, Lise Castonguay; **M:** Bernard Bonnier; **P:** Théâtre Repère (Quebec City); opened at Théâtre de la Bordée (Quebec City).

Ligue nationale d'improvisation
– improvisational comedy

> **P:** Radio Canada.

Partir en peur
> **P:** Théâtre des Confettis (Quebec City).

Solange passé
– by Jocelyne Corbeil and Lucie Godbout

> **P:** Théâtre de la Bordée (Quebec City).

Stand-by 5 minutes
> **CC:** Jean-Jacqui Boutet, Ginette Gay, Louis-Georges Girard, Martine Ouellet, Marie St-Cyr; **P:** Théâtre de la Bordée (Quebec City) in cooperation with Théâtre de l'Équinoxe, restaged at Théâtre Paul-Hébert the following season.

1985

À propos de la demoiselle qui pleurait
– by André Jean

> C, SD: Monique Dion; I: François Lachapelle; L: Denis Guérette;
> S: Robert Caux; P: Théâtre Repère (Quebec City); opened at Centre
> International de Séjour de Québec; new version performed at Théâtre
> du Trident (Quebec City), January 1986.

Comment regarder le point de fuite
– solo show

> P: Théâtre Repère (Quebec City); opened at Implanthéâtre (Quebec
> City); performed again at the opening of the multidisciplinary show
> Point de fuite in which Robert Lepage also had a role.

Coup de poudre

> CC: Josée Deschênes, Marin Dion, Simon Fortin, Benoit Gouin,
> Hélène Leclerc; P: Théâtre Artéfact and Parks Canada; opened at
> Artillery Park (Quebec City).

Histoires sorties du tiroir
– by Gérard Bibeau

> P: Les Marionnettes du Grand Théâtre de Québec (Quebec City).

Suite californienne
– by Neil Simon (*California Suite*)

> P: Théâtre du Bois de Coulonge (Sillery); performed at Théâtre du
> Vieux-Port du Québec.

La trilogie des dragons (*The Dragons' Trilogy*)

> CC: Marie Brassard, Jean Casault, Lorraine Côté, Marie Gignac,
> Marie Michaud; L: Lucie Bazzo, Louis-Marie Lavoie; S: Robert Caux;
> SD: Jean-François Couture, Gilles Dubé; P: Théâtre Repère (Quebec
> City, for the two first phases) and Festival de théâtre des Amériques
> (Montreal, for the third phase); opened first phase, November 1985;
> second phase, May 1986, Implanthéâtre (Quebec City); third phase,
> June 1987 (Montreal).

1986

Le bord extrême
– based on Ingmar Bergman's *The Seventh Seal*

> DIR: Michel Nadeau; S: Robert Caux; SD: Monique Dion;
> P: Théâtre Repère (Quebec City); opened at Implanthéâtre
> (Quebec City).

Comment devenir parfait en trois jours

– by Gilles Gauthier, based on the novel *Be a Perfect Person in Three Days* by Stephen Manes

> **P:** Théâtre des Confettis; opened at Implanthéâtre (Quebec City) and performed more than five hundred times on tour in the province of Quebec.

Le groupe sanguin: prise 1

– comedy show

> **P:** Groupe Sanguin and Michel Sabourin (Montreal); toured the province of Quebec.

Vinci

– solo show

> **I:** François Lachapelle, Dave Lepage; **S:** Daniel Toussaint; **P:** Théâtre de Quat'Sous (Montreal) and Théâtre Repère (Quebec City); opened at Théâtre de Quat'Sous (Montreal).

 1987

En pleine nuit, une sirène

> **CC:** Jacques Girard; **P:** Théâtre de la Bordée (Quebec City); opened at Théâtre de la Bordée.

Le groupe sanguin: prise II

– comedy show

> **P:** Groupe Sanguin (Montreal) and Michel Sabourin; toured the province of Quebec.

Le polygraphe

> **CC:** Marie Brassard; **I:** Dave Lepage; **L:** Eric Fauque, Robert Lepage; **SD:** Jean Hazel; **P:** Théâtre Repère (Quebec City); opened at Implanthéâtre (Quebec City).

Pour en finir une fois pour toutes avec Carmen

– free adaptation of the opera *Carmen* by Georges Bizet

> **P:** Théâtre de Quat'Sous (Montreal); restaged at Institut Canadien (Quebec City) in 1998.

 1988

Les plaques tectoniques (Tectonic Plates)

> **CC:** Normand Bissonnette, Lorraine Côté, Richard Fréchette, Sylvie Gagnon, Marie Gignac, Michael Levine, François Pick; **C:** Louise Fillion; **I:** Claudel Huot; **S:** Michel Gosselin; **SD:** Michael Levine; **P:** Théâtre Repère (Quebec City) and Cultural Industry (London); opened at the World Stage Festival (Toronto), second version 1989, third and fourth versions 1990, fifth version 1991.

Le songe d'une nuit d'été
– William Shakespeare's *A Midsummer Night's Dream*.
>   **P:** Théâtre du Nouveau Monde (Montreal).

1989

C'est ce soir qu'on saoûle Sophie Saucier
– by Sylvie Provost
>   **P:** Les Productions Ma chère Pauline (Montreal).

Écho
– based on *A Nun's Diary* by Ann Diamond
>   **P:** Théâtre 1774 (Montreal) and Théâtre Passe-Muraille (Toronto);
>   opened at the Saidye Bronfman Centre (Montreal); restaged in
>   Toronto in 1990.

Jésus de Montréal
– feature film, released in English as *Jesus of Montreal*; Robert Lepage acted
the role of René
>   **DIR:** Denys Arcand; **P:** Max Films (Montreal).

Mère Courage et ses enfants
– by Bertolt Brecht (*Mother Courage and Her Children*)
>   **P:** Conservatoire d'art dramatique de Québec.

Romeo and Juliette
– Shakespeare (bilingual version)
>   **P:** Théâtre Repère (Quebec City) and Night Cap Productions
>   (Saskatoon); opened in Saskatoon at the Shakespeare on the
>   Saskatchewan Theatre Festival; toured Stratford, Ottawa, Toronto, and
>   Sudbury in 1989–90.

La vie de Galilée
– by Bertolt Brecht (*Life of Galileo*)
>   **P:** Théâtre du Nouveau Monde (Montreal).

1990

Ding et Dong le film
– feature film, Robert Lepage acted the role of Pharus
>   **DIR:** Alain Chartrand; **P:** Max Films Productions (Montreal).

Les plaques tectoniques (*Tectonic Plates*)
– fourth version, Glasgow and London
>   **P:** Théâtre Repère (Quebec City), Festival de théâtre des Amériques
>   (Montreal), and Cultural Industry (London).

La visite de la vieille dame
– by Friedrich Dürenmatt (French version of *Der Besuch der alten Dame*; known in English as *The Visit*)

> **P:** National Arts Centre (Ottawa) and Productions AJP (Montreal).

1991

Les aiguilles et l'opium (*Needles and Opium*)

> **I:** Jacques Collin, Zilon, Téléféric; **S:** Robert Caux, Yves Laferrière; **P:** National Arts Centre (Ottawa), Les Productions d'Albert (Ste-Foy), and Les Productions AJP (Montreal); opened at Palais Montcalm (Quebec City).

Les Cincos Soles
– performance exercise by the graduating students of the National Theatre School of Canada

> **P:** National Theatre School of Canada (Montreal); performed at the National Arts Centre (Ottawa); restaged at the Carrefour international de théâtre (Quebec City).

1992

Alanienouidet
– by Marianne Ackerman

> **C:** Judy de Boer; **I:** Dave Lepage; **L:** Mike Brunet; **S:** Jean-Frédéric Messier; **P:** National Arts Centre (Ottawa); restaged at Carrefour international de théâtre (Quebec City).

Bluebeard's Castle
– opera by Béla Bartók, and *Erwartung*, oratorio by Arnold Schoenberg

> **C, SD:** Michael Levine; **L:** Robert Thomson; **P:** Canadian Opera Company (Toronto) and Brooklyn Academy of Music (New York).

Cycle Shakespeare: Macbeth, Coriolan, et La tempête (*Shakespeare Cycle: Macbeth, Coriolanus, and The Tempest*)

> **C:** Nina Reichmann; **L:** Maryse Gauthier; **S:** Guy Laramée; **P:** Théâtre Repère (Quebec City), Le Manège (Maubeuge), Am Turm Theater (Frankfurt), and Festival d'automne à Paris; opened in Maubeuge.

Macbeth
– by William Shakespeare

> **P:** Theatre Department, University of Toronto.

A Midsummer Night's Dream
– by William Shakespeare; Royal Shakespeare Company

> Robert Lepage became the first North American to stage a work by Shakespeare at the Royal National Theatre; **P:** Royal National Theatre (London).

Montréal vu par ...

– feature film, Robert Lepage acted the role of the chatterbox

> **DIR:** Denys Arcand, Michel Brault; **P:** Atlantis Films (Toronto), Cinémaginaire Inc. (Montreal), National Film Board of Canada (Ottawa).

Tectonic Plates

– feature film, Robert Lepage acted a minor role

> **DIR:** Peter Mettler; **P:** Rhombus Media (Toronto).

La tempête (The Tempest)

– by William Shakespeare

> **P:** Atelier de recherche théâtrale de l'Outaouais (ART); performed at the Atelier of the National Arts Centre (Ottawa).

 1993

Macbeth and The Tempest

– by William Shakespeare (Japanese versions)

> **P:** Globe Theatre (Tokyo).

National, capitale nationale

– by Jean-Marc Dalpé and Vivian Laxdal (English and French versions)

> **P:** National Arts Centre (Ottawa) and Théâtre de la Veille 17 (Ottawa).

Secret World Live tour

– by Peter Gabriel

> **P:** Real World Tours (London).

Shakespeare's Rapid Eye Movement

– original English version or *Map of Dreams*, collage of dreamlike texts by William Shakespeare

> **P:** Bayerisches Staatsschauspiel (Munich).

 1994

Bad Blood or Viper

– action film, Robert Lepage acted the role of the bartender

> **DIR:** Tibor Takács; **P:** MDP Productions (Los Angeles).

Ett Drömspel

– original Swedish version of *A Dream Play*, by August Strindberg

> **P:** Kungliga Dramatiska Teatern (Stockholm).

Les Sept branches de la rivière Ota
(*The Seven Streams of the River Ota*)

– first phase

> **CC:** Eric Bernier, Normand Bissonnette, Rebecca Blankenship, Anne-Marie Cadieux, Normand Daneau, Richard Fréchette, Marie Gignac, Ghislaine Vincent; **I:** Jacques Collin; **L:** Sonoyo Nishikawa; **S:** Michel F. Côté; **SD:** Carl Fillion; **P:** Ex Machina (Quebec City) with co-producers; opened at the Edinburgh International Festival, August 1994.

Noises, Sounds, and Sweet Airs

– opera by Michael Nyman (original English version), inspired by *The Tempest*, by William Shakespeare

> **P:** Globe Theatre (Tokyo) and Shin-Kobe Oriental Theatre (Kobe).

 1995

Elseneur (*Elsinore*)

– based on William Shakespeare's *Hamlet* (solo show also performed in English)

> **C:** Yvan Gaudin; **I:** Jacques Collin; **VIDEO:** Michael Petrin; **L:** Alain Lortie, Nancy Mongrain; **S:** Robert Caux; **SD:** Carl Fillion; **P:** Ex Machina (Quebec City) in co-production with the Musée d'art contemporain de Montréal and sixteen international co-producers.

Le confessionnal

– feature film released in English as *The Confessional*; script by Robert Lepage

> **P:** Channel Four Films (London), Cinémaginaire (Montreal), Enigma Films (London), Cinéa SA (Paris), Téléfilm Canada (Montreal).

Les sept branches de la rivière Ota
(*The Seven Streams of the River Ota*)

– second phase

> **CC:** Eric Bernier, Normand Bissonnette, Rebecca Blankenship, Marie Brassard, Anne-Marie Cadieux, Normand Daneau, Richard Fréchette, Patrick Goyette, Marie Gignac, Ghislaine Vincent; **P:** Ex Machina (Quebec City) and seventeen international co-producers.

Le songe d'une nuit d'été

– William Shakespeare's *A Midsummer Night's Dream*

> **P:** Ex Machina (Quebec City) and Théâtre Le Trident (Quebec City); opened at the Grand Théâtre de Québec (Quebec City).

1996

Le polygraphe
– feature film released in English as *Polygraph*; script by Robert Lepage
   P: In Extremis Images (Montreal), Road Movies Dritte Produktionen (Berlin), Cinéa SA (Paris).

Le polygraphe
– Japanese version
   P: Shinjuku-Nishitoyama Development Company (Tokyo and Osaka).

Les sept branches de la rivière Ota
(The Seven Streams of the River Ota)
– third phase
   P: Carrefour international de théâtre, Theater der Welt '96 – Staatsschauspiel (Dresden), Kobenhaven '96 (Copenhagen), Schlossfestspiele (Ludwigsburg), Stadsteater (Stockholm), the Brooklyn Academy of Music (New York).

 1997

Les aiguilles et l'opium
– Italian and Spanish versions
   P: Ex Machina (Quebec City), in co-production with Segnali Culture (Rome).

Elsinore
– based on William Shakespeare's *Hamlet*, staging of a new adaptation by Peter Darling
   P: Ex Machina (Quebec City).

Nô
– feature film released in English as *Nô*; script by Robert Lepage
   P: Alliance Communications Corporation (Toronto), In Extremis Images (Montreal).

1998

La Celestina
– by Fernando de Rojas (Swedish version)
   C: Karin Erskine; **L:** Ulf England; **SD:** Carl Fillion; **P:** Ex Machina (Quebec City), Kungliga Dramatiska Teatern (Stockholm).

La géométrie des miracles (*The Geometry of Miracles*)

CC: Tea Alagić, Daniel Bélanger, Jean-François Blanchard, Marie Brassard, Denis Gaudreault, Anthony Howell, Kevin McCoy, Thaddeus Phillips, Rodrigue Proteau, Catherine Tardif; **C**: Marie-Chantale Vaillancourt; **I**: Jacques Collin, Carl Fillion; **L**: Eric Fauque; **S**: Michel F. Côté, Diane Labrosse; **SD**: Carl Fillion; **P**: Ex Machina (Quebec City), Salzburger Festspiele (Salzburg), and twenty-two co-producers.

Kindertotenlieder (*The Song Cycle*)

– by Gustav Mahler

P: Ex Machina (Quebec City), Cultural Industry (London).

La tempête

– by William Shakespeare (French version of *The Tempest*)

P: Ex Machina (Quebec City), Grand Théâtre de Québec (Quebec City), Théâtre du Trident (Quebec City), National Arts Centre (Ottawa).

▉ 1999

La damnation de Faust (*The Damnation of Faust*)

– opera by Hector Berlioz, first adaptation

CH: Alain Gauthier (acrobats), Johanne Madore; **I**: Atsuhi Moriyasu; **L**: Guy Simard, followed by Maryse Gauthier; **SD**: Carl Fillion; **P**: Ex Machina (Quebec City), Saito Kinen Festival (Matsumoto, Japan) in September 1999; Opéra national de Paris, Bastille, in June 2001.

Jean-Sans-Nom

– musical tragedy, based on the novel *Famille-Sans-Nom* (*Family without a Name*) by Jules Verne

I: Jacques Collin; **M**: Robert Charlebois; **SD**: Carl Fillion; **P**: Ex Machina (Quebec City), Gestion Son Image (Montreal), CDC (Nantes, France); performances only on May 3 and 4, 1999.

Zulu Time

CC: Michel F. Côté, Claire Gignac, Jinny Jessica Jacinto, Diane Labrosse, Marco Poulain, Rodrigue Proteau; **C**: Marie-Chantale Vaillancourt; **I**: Bernard Duplessis, Véronique Couturier; **L**: M. Gagnon; **S**: Michel F. Côté, Diane Labrosse; **SD**: Yvon Fortin, Alain Sébastien Gauthier, Lydie Jean-Dit-Pannel, Gordon Monahan, Pierrick Sorrin, Granular Synthesis (software); **P**: Ex Machina (Quebec City), Real World Studios (Box Mill, Wiltshire), Maison des Arts de Créteil (France), Zürcher Theater Spektakel (Zurich), Festival d'automne à Paris.

2000

La face cachée de la lune (*The Far Side of the Moon*)
– solo show

> **CC:** Peter Bjurman, Adam Nashman; **L:** Bernard White; **M:** Laurie
> Anderson; **SD:** Marie Claude Pelletier; **P:** Ex Machina (Quebec City)
> and twenty-four international co-producers.

Métissages
– temporary exhibition

> **P:** Musée de la civilisation (Quebec City); May 2, 2000, to
> September 3, 2001.

Le polygraphe
– Italian and Spanish versions

> **P:** Segnali Culture (Rome) and Théâtre Municipal d'Udine (Italy),
> Mercat de les Flors (Barcelona).

Possible Worlds
– feature film released in French as *Mondes Possibles*

> **P:** In Extremis Images (Montreal), The East Side Company (Toronto).

Stardom
– feature film released in English as *15 Moments*; Robert Lepage acted the
role of Bruce Taylor

> **DIR:** Denys Arcand; **P:** Cinémaginaire (Montreal).

 2001

La Casa Azul
– formerly titled *Apasionada* [*Que viva Frida*], by Sophie Faucher

> **C:** Véronique Borboën; **I:** Lionel Arnould, Jacques Collin;
> **L:** Sonoyo Nishikawa; **SD:** Carl Fillion; **P:** Ex Machina (Quebec
> City), Théâtre de Quat'Sous (Montreal), Ysarca (Madrid); Wiener
> Festwochen (Vienna).

2002

La Celestina
– by Fernando de Rojas, as part of Salamanca events

> Cancelled spring 2002.

Die Dreigroschenoper Songspiel (*The Threepenny Opera*)
– by Kurt Weill and Bertolt Brecht

> **P:** Ex Machina (Quebec City); opened at La Caserne as part of the
> Carrefour international de Québec, May 19 to 26, 2002.

Growing Up
– Peter Gabriel concert tour
  P: Real World Tours (London).

Zulu Time
– new version with Peter Gabriel
  Montreal, June 14 to July 7, 2002.

2003

La face cachée de la lune (The Far Side of the Moon)
– script by Robert Lepage, who acted the roles of Philippe and André
  P: La face cachée de la lune inc. (Quebec City).

La trilogie des dragons (The Dragons' Trilogy)
  CC: Marie Brassard, Jean Casault, Lorraine Côté, Marie Gignac,
  Marie Michaud; P: Ex Machina (Quebec City); restaged at Festival
  TransAmériques (Montreal).

2004

The Busker's Opera
– inspired by The Beggar's Opera by John Gay
  C: Yasmina Giguère; L: Robert Lepage, Laurent Routhier; M: Martin
  Belanger; SD: Paul Bourque, Véronique Dumont, Marie Poulain.

La Célestine (La Celestina)
  by Fernando de Rojas
  L: Étienne Boucher; M: Silvy Grenier; S: Jean-Sébastien Côté;
  SD: Carl Fillion.

Kà
– show created and directed for Cirque du Soleil, MGM Grand (Las Vegas)
  C: Marie-Chantale Vaillancourt; S: René Dupéré.

2005

L'audition
– feature film; Robert Lepage acted the role of a casting agent
  DIR: Luc Picard; P: Cité-Amérique inc. (Montreal).

Le projet Andersen (The Andersen Project)
– solo show
  C: Catherine Higgins; I: Jacques Collin; L: Nicolas Marois; S: Jean-
  Sébastien Côté; SD: Jean Lebourdais; P: Ex Machina (Quebec City)
  in co-production with the Grand Théâtre de Québec (Quebec City),
  Hans Christian Andersen 2005, Théâtre du Trident (Quebec City);
  opened at Théâtre du Trident (Quebec City), February 2005.

1984

– opera by Loren Maazel, based on the novel by George Orwell

> CH: Sylvain Émard; I: Lionel Arnould, Jacques Collin; L: Michel Beaulieu; SD: Carl Fillion; P: Big Brother Productions (New York), co-produced with Royal Opera House (London); opened May 2005.

2006

Dans les villes

– feature film; Robert Lepage acted the role of Jean-Luc

> DIR: Catherine Martin; P: Coop Vidéo (Montreal).

No-Vacancy

– short film; Robert Lepage acted the role of Éric Millette

> DIR: Gaël d'Ynglemare; P: Productions Thalie (Quebec City).

2007

La belle empoisonneuse

– feature film; Robert Lepage acted a minor role

> DIR: Richard Jutras; P: Productions Thalie (Quebec City).

Lipsynch

> CC: Frédérike Bédard, Carlos Belda, Rebecca Blankenship, Lise Castonguay, John Cobb, Nuria Garcia, Marie Gignac, Sarah Kemp, Rick Miller; C: Yasmina Giguère; I: Jacques Collin; L: Étienne Boucher; S: Jean-Sébastien Côté; SD: Jean Hazel; P: Ex Machina (Quebec City) and Théâtre Sans Frontières (Tynedale, Northumberland) in cooperation with Cultural Industry (London) and Northern Stage (Newcastle Upon Tyne); opened in Newcastle Upon Tyne, February 2007.

The Rake's Progress

– opera by Igor Stravinsky, libretto by W.H. Auden and Chester Kallman

> AD: Neilson Vignola, Sybille Wilson; C: François Barbeau; CH: Michael Keegan-Dolan; I: Boris Firquet; L: Étienne Boucher; S: Jean-Sébastien Côté; SD: Carl Fillion; P: Ex Machina (Quebec City) in co-production with Théâtre Royal de la Monnaie (Brussels, Belgium), Opéra national de Lyon (France), the San Francisco Opera (United States), the Royal Opera House (London, England), the Teatro Real (Madrid, Spain); opened at Théâtre Royal de la Monnaie (Brussels), April 17, 2007.

2008

La damnation de Faust (The Damnation of Faust)

– opera by Hector Berlioz, second adaptation

> **P:** Ex Machina (Quebec City) in co-production with Metropolitan Opera (New York), Saito Kinen Festival (Matsumoto, Japan), Opera nationale de Paris (France).

Le Dragon bleu (The Blue Dragon)

– performed with Marie Michaud and Tai Wei Woo

> **CC:** Marie Michaud; **C:** François St-Aubin; **CH:** Tai Wei Foo; **I:** David Leclerc; **L:** Louis-Xavier Gagnon-Lebrun; **S:** Jean-Sébastien Côté; **SD:** Michel Gauthier; **P:** Ex Machina (Quebec City); opened at La Comète at Scène Nationale (Châlons-en-Champagne), April 2008.

The Image Mill

– forty-minute architectural projection and sound-and-light show developed as part of the four-hundredth anniversary celebrations of Quebec City

> **CC:** Steve Blanchet; **I:** Steve Blanchet, Sébastien Grenier-Cartier, Jean-Philippe Turmel; **S** 2008: Jacques Boucher, René Lussier; **S** 2013 and additional music: Bruno Bouchard, Simon Elmaleh. Projected onto the Bunge grain silos in the Old Port of Quebec City; opened June 2008.

2009

Aurora Borealis

– lighting installation inspired by the colours of the northern lights; projected onto the Bunge grain silos in the Old Port of Quebec City; lit every night for five years, ending 2013

> **L:** Martin Gagnon; **P:** Ex Machina (Quebec City) presented by the City of Quebec in collaboration with Bunge of Canada and the Port of Quebec.

Eonnagata

> **CC:** Sylvie Guillem, Russell Maliphant; **C:** Alexander McQueen; **CH:** Tai Wei Foo; **I:** David Leclerc; **L:** Michael Hulls; **S:** Jean-Sébastien Côté; **SD:** Michel Gauthier; **P:** Ex Machina (Quebec City) in co-production with Sadler's Wells Theatre (London) and Sylvie Guillem; opened at Sadler's Wells Theatre (London), April 2008.

The Image Mill Revealed

– documentary film

> Presents the final three months of production before the 2008 premiere of *The Image Mill.*

> **DIR:** Marie Belzil, Mariano Franco; **P:** Les Productions du 8e art (Quebec City) and National Film Board of Canada (Ottawa), in collaboration with Radio-Canada and ICI ARTV (Montreal).

The Nightingale and Other Short Fables

– opera by Igor Stravinsky, libretto after Andersen (*Nightingale*) and Stravinsky (*Fox*)

AD: Sybille Wilson; C: Mara Gottler; puppet designer: Michael Curry; CH: Moses Pendleton, Cynthia Quinn (MOMIX, New York); puppet choreographer: Martin Genest; shadow theatre: Philippe Beau; I: David Leclerc; L: Étienne Boucher; S: Jean-Sébastien Côté; SD: Carl Fillion; P: Ex Machina (Quebec City) in co-production with the Canadian Opera Company (Toronto), Festival d'art lyrique d'Aix-en-Provence, Opéra national de Lyon (France), De Nederlandse Opera (Amsterdam); opened at the Canadian Opera Company (Toronto), October 10, 2009.

 2010

Der Ring des Nibelungen

– opera by Richard Wagner

AD: Neilson Vignola; C: François St-Aubin; automation designer: Tobie Horswill; I: Boris Firquet (*Das Rheingold* and *Die Walküre*), Pedro Pires (*Siegfried*), Lionel Arnould (*Götterdämmerung*); interactive video designer: Holger Förterer; L: Étienne Boucher; S: Jean-Sébastien Côté; SD: Carl Fillion; P: Ex Machina (Quebec City) in co-production with the Metropolitan Opera (New York); opened at the Met, September 27, 2010, for *Das Rheingold*; April 22, 2011, for *Die Walküre*; May 27, 2011, for *Siegfried*; January 27, 2012, for *Götterdämmerung*; and May 7, 2012, for the complete Ring Cycle.

Les grands débordements

– mural on Ex Machina's creation centre, La Caserne, animated at night by an ongoing projection of the Chaudière River

P: MU (Montreal), in collaboration with One Drop Foundation (Montreal).

Totem

– show created and directed for Cirque du Soleil, MGM Grand (Las Vegas)

 2011

La tempête

– by William Shakespeare (French adaptation by Michel Garneau)

Boat designer: Christian Fontaine; C: Mara Gottler; I: David Leclerc; L: Louis-Xavier Gagnon-Lebrun; S: Jean-Sébastien Côté; P: Ex Machina (Quebec City) in collaboration with the Huron-Wendat Nation (Quebec City); opened at the outdoor amphitheatre in Wendake, a Huron reserve near Quebec City, July 2011.

2012

Mars et Avril

– sci-fi feature film, Robert Lepage acted the role of Eugène Spaak's head

Text and DIR: Martin Villeneuve; P: EMA Films (Montreal), Les Productions du 8e Art Inc. (Quebec City).

Playing Cards: Spades

CC: Sylvio Arriola, Carole Faisant, Nuria Garcia, Tony Guilfoyle, Martin Haberstroh, Sophie Martin, Roberto Mori; AD: Félix Dagenais; C: Sébastien Dionne; D: Peder Bjurman; I: David Leclerc; L: Louis-Xavier Gagnon-Lebrun; S: Jean-Sébastien Côté; SD: Jean Hazel; P: Ex Machina (Quebec City), commissioned by Réseau 360° (360° Network) and sponsored by the Luminato Festival (Montreal) in co-production with Teatro Circo Price (Madrid), Ruhrtriennale (Gelsenkirchen), La Comète at Scène nationale (Châlons-en Champagne), Les Célestins-Théâtre (Lyon), Cirque Jules Verne (Amiens), and the Maison de la culture d'Amiens, the Roundhouse (London), the Odéon-Théâtre de l'Europe (Paris), Wiener Festwochen (Vienna), Chekhov International Theatre Festival (Moscow) Østre Gasværk Teater (Copenhagen), La TOHU (Montreal), International Stage at Gasverket (Stockholm), Les Théâtres de la Ville de Luxembourg; opened May 9 to 14, 2012, at Teatro Circo Price (Madrid), as part of Festival de Otoño en Primavera 2012.

The Tempest

– opera by Thomas Adès, libretto by Meredith Oakes, based on the play by William Shakespeare

AD: Félix Dagenais; C: Kym Barrett; CH: Crystal Pite; I: David Leclerc; L: M. Beaulieu; S: Jean-Sébastien Côté; SD: Jasmine Catudal; P: Ex Machina (Quebec City) in co-production with Le festival d'opéra de Québec, the Metropolitan Opera (New York), and the Wiener Staatsoper (Vienna); opened at the Grand Théâtre de Québec (Quebec City), June 26, 2012.

2013

The Image Mill Tribute to Norman McLaren, Animation Pioneer

– projected onto the Bunge grain silos in the Old Port of Quebec City

P: Ex Machina (Quebec City) in collaboration with the National Film Board of Canada (Ottawa) in collaboration with Bunge of Canada, the Port of Quebec, and the City of Quebec; opened June 23, 2013.

Needles and Opium

– second adaptation, performed by Marc Labrèche and Wellesley
Robertson III

> **AD:** Normand Bissonnette; **C:** François St-Aubin; **I:** Lionel Arnould;
> automation consultant: Tobie Horswill; **L:** Bruno Matte; **S:** Jean-
> Sébastien Côté; **SD:** Carl Fillion; **P:** Ex Machina (Quebec City) in
> co-production with Théâtre du Trident (Quebec City), Canadian
> Stage (Toronto), and Théâtre du Nouveau Monde (Montreal); opened
> September 17, 2013, at the Trident (Quebec City).

Playing Cards: Hearts

– festival performance

> **CC:** Louis Fortier, Nuria Garcia, Reda Guerinik, Ben Grant,
> Catherine Hughes, Marcello Magni, Olivier Normand; **AD:** Félix
> Dagenais; **C:** Sébastien Dionne; **D:** Peder Bjurman; **I:** David
> Leclerc; **L:** Louis-Xavier Gagnon-Lebrun; **S:** Jean-Sébastien Côté;
> **SD:** Michel Gauthier, Jean Hazel; performed September 29, 2013, at
> the Salzlager (Essen), as part of the Ruhrtriennale (Gelsenkirchen).

Triptych

– film adaptation of the play *Lipsynch*, Robert Lepage acted the role of
Fox's voice

> **DIR:** Robert Lepage, Pedro Pires; **P:** Les Productions du 8e Art Inc.
> (Quebec City).

2014

Playing Cards: Hearts

– touring production

> **CC:** Louis Fortier, Reda Guerinik, Ben Grant, Catherine Hughes,
> Kathryn Hunter, Marcello Magni, Olivier Normand; **AD:** Sybille
> Wilson; **C:** Sébastien Dionne; **D:** Peder Bjurman; **I:** David
> Leclerc; **L:** Louis-Xavier Gagnon-Lebrun; **S:** Jean-Sébastien Côté;
> **SD:** Michel Gauthier, Jean Hazel; **P:** Ex Machina (Quebec City),
> commissioned by Réseau 360° (360° Network) and co-produced
> with Ruhrtriennale (Gelsenkirchen), La Comète at Scène nationale
> (Châlons-en-Champagne), Les Célestins-Théâtre (Lyon), Cirque
> Jules Verne (Amiens), and the Maison de la culture d'Amiens, the
> Roundhouse (London), the Odéon-Théâtre de l'Europe (Paris),
> Wiener Festwochen (Vienna), Chekhov International Theatre
> Festival (Moscow), Østre Gasværk Teater (Copenhagen), La TOHU
> (Montreal), International Stage at Gasverket (Stockholm), Les
> Théâtres de la Ville de Luxembourg; North American premiere opened
> January 30, 2014, at La TOHU, la Cité des arts du cirque (Montreal).

BIBLIOGRAPHY

Other sources of information about Robert Lepage are available in addition to those listed here. Ex Machina maintains an excellent web archive on Robert Lepage at lacasernc.net; and CBC Radio and Television interviews and videos are available in the CBC Digital Archives at cbc.ca/archives.

I. ROBERT LEPAGE

INTERVIEWS

Ahearn, Victoria. "Robert Lepage Going 'Back to the Basics.'" *Canadian Press*. canadianpress.com. January 9, 2012.

Bernard, Sophie. "L'espace-temps de Robert Lepage." *Convergence, le magazine de la culture numérique* 9 (2001): 9–11.

Borello, Christine. "Robert Lepage, mettre en scène, c'est écrire." *Théâtre / Public* 117 (1994): 82–85.

Brown, Laurie. "Celebrity Speakers: Robert Lepage." April 8, 2009. National Arts Centre podcast. http://nac-cna.ca/en/podcasts/hinterviews/celebrity-speakers-robert-lepage.

Bureau, Stéphan. *CONTACT, the encyclopaedia of creation*. Interviews with Robert Lepage originally broadcast on Radio-Canada (television). Published online and available on DVD. Montreal: Contact TV Inc. 2008.

———. *Stéphan Bureau rencontre Robert Lepage*. Verdun, QC: Amérik Média, 2008.

Carson, Christie. "Collaboration, Translation, Interpretation." *New Theatre Quarterly* 9.33 (February 1993): 31–36.

Charest, Rémy. *Robert Lepage: Connecting Flights. Robert Lepage in Conversation with Rémy Charest*. Wanda Romer Taylor, trans. Toronto: A.A. Knopf Canada, 1997, reprinted 1998. Originally published as *Quelques zones de liberté*. Quebec City: L'instant même / Ex Machina, 1995.

Clarkson, Adrienne. "Robert Lepage's Theatrical Coup: Quebec Native Invited by London's Royal National Theatre to Direct *A Midsummer Night's Dream*." Interview with Robert Lepage, Michael Coveney, and Richard Eyre. *Adrienne Clarkson Presents*. CBC Television. February 2, 1993.

Colman, Geoffrey. "*Playing Cards: Spades*. Post-show discussion recorded on set at the Roundhouse Theatre, London, February 9, 2013." Unpublished. For further information, contact geoff.colman@cssd.ac.uk.

Coulombe, Michel. "Entretien avec Robert Lepage." *Nô, scenario de film de Robert Lepage*. Marcel Jean, ed. Montreal: Les 400 coups, 1998. 95–100.

Crew, Robert. "Quebec Maestro in Top Form." *Toronto Star*. February 21, 1990. F4.

Eyre, Richard. "Robert Lepage in Discussion." In *The Twentieth-Century Performance Reader*. Michael Huxley and Noel Witts, eds. London: Routledge, 2002.

Feldman, Susan. "New Collaboration takes Lepage to Scotland: International Cast Rehearses for *Tectonic Plates*." With scenes from *Tectonic Plates*, directed by Robert Lepage. *Ideas*. CBC Radio. July 7, 1991.

Fouquet, Ludovic. "Du théâtre d'ombres aux technologies contemporaines." *Les écrans sur la scène*. Béatrice Picon-Vallin, ed. Lausanne: L'Âge d'Homme, 1998. 325–32.

Fréchette, Carole, and Lorraine Camerlain. "L'arte è un veicolo, entretien avec Robert Lepage." *Cahiers de théâtre JEU* 42 (1987): 109–26.

Freed, Josh. "Robert Lepage: A Young, Confident Artist." With scenes from *Circulation*, written and directed by Robert Lepage. *The Journal*. CBC Television. December 17, 1984.

Fürle, Brigitte. "Le théâtre comme point de rencontre des arts," *Theaterschrift* 5–6 (1994): 210–28.

Ghomeshi, Jian. "Robert Lepage on Ditching the Plan and Embracing Imperfection: Robert Lepage Talks to CBC's Jian Ghomeshi about the Glenn Gould Prize." *Q with Jian Ghomeshi*. CBC Radio. April 2, 2014.

Gzowski, Peter. "A Bilingual *Romeo and Juliette*." Interview with Robert Lepage and Gordon McCall. *Morningside*. CBC Radio. July 6, 1989.

———. "Method behind Lepage's Award-Winning Play *Circulation*." *Morningside*. CBC Radio. March 7, 1984.

Hébert, Chantal, and Irène Perelli-Contos. "La tempête Robert Lepage," *Nuit blanche* 55 (April–May 1994): 63–66.

McAlpine, Alison. "Robert Lepage." In *Contact with the Gods? Directors Talk Theatre*. Maria M. Delgado and Paul Heritage, eds. New York: Manchester University Press, 1996. 129–57.

Moreault, Éric. "Jeu de cartes 1: Lepage joue son atout," *Le Soleil* (Quebec City), June 9, 2012.

O'Mahony, John. "Aerial Views: The Guardian Profile: Robert Lepage." *Guardian* (London), June 23, 2001. 6.

Ouzounian, Richard. "Lepage's Struggle to Stay Free." *Globe and Mail*. August 12, 1997. A13–14.

Rogers, Shelagh. "Lepage on His New Play *Needles and Opium*." *The Arts Tonight*. CBC Radio. April 11, 1994.

Ruprecht, Alvina. CBC Radio 1. September 10, 1997. Transcript in Ex Machina archive.

Saint-Hilaire, Jean. "Robert Lepage, le créateur se penche sur l'avenir du théâtre," *Le Soleil* (Quebec City), January 22, 2000.

Salter, Denis. "A State of Becoming." *Books in Canada* 20.2 (March 1991): 26–29.

———. "Borderlines: An Interview with Robert Lepage and Le Théâtre Repère." *Theater* 24.3 (1993): 71–79.

Shevtsova, Maria, and Christopher Innes, eds. Chapter 5. In *Directors / Directing: Conversations on Theatre*. New York: Cambridge University Press, 2009.

Shewey, Don. "Robert Lepage: A Bold Québécois Who Blends Art with Technology." *New York Times*, September 16, 2001.

Soleymat, Manuel Piolat. "Les beautés de la culture islamique." *La terrasse* (France) 201, September 7, 2012.

Wachtel, Eleanor. "Canadian Theatre Visionary Robert Lepage." *Wachtel on the Arts*. CBC Radio. July 6, 2011.

PLAYS AND SCENARIOS

Brassard, Marie, Jean Casault, Lorraine Côté, Marie Gignac, Robert Lepage, and Marie Michaud. *La trilogie des dragons*. Quebec City: L'instant même, 2005.

Faucher, Sophie. *La Casa Azul: Inspired by the Writings of Frida Kahlo*. Neil Bartlett, trans. London: Oberon, 2002.

Jean, Marcel, ed. *Nô, scenario du film de Robert Lepage*. Montreal: Les 400 coups, 1998.

Lepage, Robert. *Geometry of Miracles*. [Brooklyn, NY]: Brooklyn Academy of Music, 1999. DVD.

———. *La face cachée de la lune*. Quebec City: L'instant même, 2007.

———. *La trilogie des dragons*. Quebec City: L'instant même, 2005.

———. *Le dragon bleu*. Graphic novel by Fred Jourdain. Quebec City: Les éditions Alto, 2011; published in English as *The Blue Dragon*. Toronto: House of Anansi, 2011.

———. *Le projet Andersen*. Quebec City: L'instant même, 2007.

———. *Nightingale, Fox, and Other Fables: A Chinoiserie for the Twenty-First Century*. Quebec City: Ex Machina, 2011.

———. *Nô*. [U.K.]: Alliance Atlantis, 2000. VHS video.

———. *The Image Mill*. Quebec City: Ex Machina, 2008.

Lepage, Robert, and Ex Machina. *The Seven Streams of the River Ota*. Introduction by Karen Fricker. London: Methuen Drama, 1996.

Lepage, Robert, Anne-Marie Cadieux, and Marco Poulin. *La face cachée de la lune = Far Side of the Moon*. Montreal: Alliance Atlantis, 2004. DVD.

Lepage, Robert, John Mighton, Sandra Cunningham, Bruno Jobin, Tilda Swinton, Tom McCamus, Sean McCann, Gabriel Gascon, Rick Miller, and Ron Proulx. *Possible Worlds*. Montreal: Alliance Atlantis, 2004. DVD.

Lepage, Robert, Marie Brassard, and Gyllian Raby. *Polygraph*. London: Methuen Drama, 1997.

Lepage, Robert, Marie Michaud, and Fred Jourdain. *The Blue Dragon*. Toronto: House of Anansi Press, 2011.

Lévesque, Solange. "Polygraphe." *Cahiers de théâtre JEU* 48 (1988): 154.

Robert, Denise, David Puttnam, Philippe Carcassonne, Robert Lepage, Lothaire Bluteau, Patrick Goyette, and Kristin Scott-Thomas. *Le confessionnal*. Montreal: Alliance Vidéo, 1996. VHS video.

GENERAL STUDIES OF LEPAGE'S PRACTICE

Ackerman, Marianne. "The Hectic Career of Robert Lepage." *Imperial Oil Review* 74 (Winter 1990): 14–17.

Beauchamp, Hélène. "The Repère Cycles: From Basic to Continuous Education." *Canadian Theatre Review* 78 (Spring 1994): 26–31.

Bouchard, Jacqueline. "Le Projet Andersen, de Robert Lepage." *Spirale* 203 (July–August 2005): 55–56.

Bunzli, James. "Autobiography in the House of Mirrors: The Paradox of Identity Reflected in the Solo Shows of Robert Lepage." In *Theater sans frontières: Essays on the Dramatic Universe of Robert Lepage.* Joseph Donohoe Jr. and Jane M. Koustas, eds. East Lansing: Michigan State University Press, 2000. 21–41.

————. "The Geography of Creation: Décalage as Impulse, Process, and Outcome in the Theatre of Robert Lepage." *TDR: The Drama Review* 43.1 (Spring 1999): 79–103.

Burrows, Malcolm. "Levine Meets Lepage: *Tectonic Plates* – Bridging the Continental Drift." *Canadian Theatre Review* 55 (Summer 1988): 43–47.

Campbell, James. "The Lie of the Body." *Times Literary Supplement* (London). March 3, 1989. 222.

Caux, Patrick, and Bernard Gilbert. *EX MACHINA: Creating for the Stage.* Neil Kroetsch, trans. Vancouver: Talonbooks, 2009.

Costaz, Gilles. "Robert Lepage à Paris," *Cahiers de théâtre JEU* 63 (1992): 160–64.

Donohoe, Joseph, Jr., and Jane M. Koustas. *Theater sans frontières: Essays on the Dramatic Universe of Robert Lepage.* East Lansing: Michigan State University Press, 2000.

Dunderović, Aleksandar Saša. *The Cinema of Robert Lepage: The Poetics of Memory.* London: Wallflower Press, 2003.

————. "Creative Spectator: Participation of Global Audiences in Robert Lepage Performance Practices." Ric Knowles, ed. Special issue on Spectatorship. *Theatre Journal* 66.4 (December 2014).

————. *Robert Lepage.* Performance Practioners series. New York: Routledge, 2009.

————. "Robert Lepage and Ex Machina – *Lipsynch* (2007) – Performance transformations and cycles." In *Making Contemporary Theatre: International Rehearsal Processes.* Jen Harvie and Andy Lavender, eds. Manchester: Manchester University Press, 2010. 160–79.

————. *The Theatricality of Robert Lepage.* Montreal: McGill-Queen's University Press, 2007.

Dvorak, Marta. "Représentations récentes des *Sept branches de la rivière Ota* et *Elseneur* de Robert Lepage." In *Nouveaux regards sur le théâtre québécois.* Betty Bednarski and Irène Oore, eds. Montreal: XYZ éditeur, 1997. 139–50.

Fouquet, Ludovic. "Clins d'œil cinématographiques dans le théâtre de Robert Lepage," *Cahiers de théâtre JEU* 88 (September 1998): 131–39.

————. "Du castelet à l'écran: Robert Lepage," *PUCK* 11 (1998): 34–41.

————. "L'envol du dragon. *Le Dragon bleu*," *Cahiers de théâtre JEU* 128 (September 2008): 25–28.

Fricker, Karen. "Cultural Relativism and Grounded Politics in Robert Lepage's *The Andersen Project*." *Contemporary Theatre Review* 17.2 (2007): 119–41.

————. *Making Theatre Global: Robert Lepage's Original Stage Productions.* Theatre: Theory-Practice-Performance series. Manchester University Press, forthcoming 2015.

————. "Robert Lepage." *The Routledge Companion to Director's Shakespeare.* John Russell Brown, ed. London: Routledge, 2008. 233–50.

————. "Tourism, The Festival Marketplace, and Robert Lepage's *The Seven Streams of the River Ota*." *Contemporary Theatre Review* 13.4 (2004): 79–93.

Fricker, Karen. "Risky Business: Robert Lepage and the Cirque du Soleil's *Kà*." = "Le goût du risque: *Kà* de Robert Lepage et du Cirque du Soleil." Isabelle Savoie, trans. *L'Annuaire théâtral* 45 (2010): 45–68.

Fricker, Karen. "The Zero Hour of Cultural (Dis)-Unity: The Problem of Robert Lepage and Ex Machina's *Zulu Time*" = "À l'Heure zéro de la culture (dés)unie. Problèmes de représentation dans *Zulu Time* de Robert Lepage et Ex Machina." Rémy Charest, trans. *Globe: Revue internationale d'études québécoises.* 11.2 (2008): 81–116.

Fricker, Karen, with Brian Singleton and Elena Moreo. "Performing the Queer Network: Divas, Fans, and Families at the Eurovision Song Contest." *SQS* (Journal of Queer Studies in Finland) 2.7 (2008).

Garner, Stanton B., Jr. *Bodied Spaces: Phenomenology and Performance in Contemporary Drama.* Ithaca, NY: Cornell University Press, 1994. 225–30.

Gibson, K. Jane. "Seeing Double: The Map-Making Process of Robert Lepage." *Canadian Theatre Review* 97 (Winter 1998): 18–23.

Gibson, Margaret. "The Truth Machine: Polygraphs, Popular Culture, and the Confessing Body." *Social Semiotics* 11.1 (April 2001): 61–73.

Gilbert, Bernard. *Le Ring de Robert Lepage: Une aventure scénique au Metropolitan Opera.* Quebec City: L'instant même, 2013.

Harvie, Jennifer. "Robert Lepage." In *Postmodernism: The Key Figures.* Joseph Natoli and Hans Bertens, eds. Oxford: Wiley-Blackwell, 2002. 224–30.

————. "Transnationalism, Orientalism, and Cultural Tourism: *La trilogie des dragons* and *The Seven Streams of the River Ota*." In *Theater sans frontières: Essays on the Dramatic Universe of Robert Lepage.* Joseph Donohoe Jr. and Jane M. Koustas, eds. East Lansing: Michigan State University Press, 2000. 109–25.

Harvie, Jennifer, and Erin Hurley. "States of Play: Locating Québec in the Performances of Robert Lepage, Ex Machina, and the Cirque du Soleil." *Theatre Journal* 51.3 (October 1999): 299–315.

Hébert, Chantal, and André Ouellette. "Villes et images de villes dans le théâtre de Robert Lepage," *Ville imaginaire, ville identitaire, échos de Québec.* Lucie K. Morisset, Luc Noppen, and Denis Saint-Jacques, eds. Quebec City: Nota bene, 1999. 67–81.

Hébert, Chantal, and Irène Perelli-Contos. "Les écrans de la pensée ou les écrans dans le théâtre de Robert Lepage." In *Les écrans sur la scène.* Béatrice Picon-Vallin, ed. Lausanne: L'Âge d'homme, 1998. 171–205.

————. *La face cachée du théâtre de l'image.* Quebec City: Les Presses de l'Université Laval, 2001.

Hodgdon, Barbara. "Robert Lepage's Intercultural Dream Machine." In *Shakespeare in Performance.* Robert Shaughnessy, ed. New York: St. Martin's Press, 2000. 194–217.

Holden, Stephen. "Metaphysics and Crime." *New York Times.* October 27, 1990. I12.

Hunt, Nigel. "The Global Voyage of Robert Lepage." *TDR: The Drama Review* 33.2 (Summer 1989): 104–18.

Innes, Christopher. "Puppets and Machines of the Mind: Robert Lepage and the Modernist Heritage." *Theatre Research International* 30.2 (July 2005): 124–38.

Jacobson, Lynn. "Tectonic States." *American Theatre* 8.8 (November 1991): 16–22.

Knowles, Ric. "From Dream to Machine: Peter Brook, Robert Lepage, and the Contemporary Shakespearean Director as (Post)Modernist." *Theatre Journal* 50.2 (May 1998): 189–206.

Koustas, Jane M. "Robert Lepage Interfaces with the World – On the Toronto Stage." In *Theater sans frontières: Essays on the Dramatic Universe of Robert Lepage.* Joseph Donohoe Jr. and Jane M. Koustas, eds. East Lansing: Michigan State University Press, 2000. 171–89.

Lavender, Andy. "*Elsinore*: Robert Lepage." In *Hamlet in Pieces: Shakespeare Reworked. Peter Brook, Robert Lepage, Robert Wilson.* New York: Continuum, 2001. 93–150.

Lefebvre, Paul. "Robert Lepage: New Filters for Creation." *Canadian Theatre Review* 52 (Fall 1987): 30–35.

Lepage, Robert. "Éloge de la technologie bancale." Brunella Eruli, ed. *PUCK* 9 (1996): 39–42.

Lessard, Bruno. "Site-Specific Screening and the Projection of Archives: Robert Lepage's *Le Moulin à images*." *Public: Art / Culture / Ideas* 40 (2010): 70–82.

Lévesque, Solange. "L'œil de la culture, un regard sur le travail de Robert Lepage." *Possibles* 17.2 (1993): 70–76.

Levin, Laura. "Epilogue: Situating the Self." In *Performing Ground: Space, Camouflage, and the Art of Blending In.* Basingstoke: Palgrave Macmillan, 2014.

MacDougall, Jill. *Performing Identities on the Stages of Quebec.* New York: Peter Lang, 1997.

MacKenzie, Scott. *Screening Québec: Québécois Moving Images, National Identity, and the Public Sphere.* Manchester: Manchester University Press, 2004.

Manguel, Alberto. "Theatre of the Miraculous. Where Robert Lepage Walks, Magic Attends. Shoes Speak, Grand Pianos Pour Rain, and Audience Moves from Enchantment to Communion." *Saturday Night* 104 (January 1989): 32–39, 42.

McIlroy, Brian. "Playing Butterfly with David Henry Hwang and Robert Lepage." In *A Vision of the Orient.* Jonathon Wisenthal, ed. Toronto: University of Toronto Press, 2006.

Mendicino, Kristina. "A Televisual Inferno: Tea Alagić's Pre-Paradise, Sorry Now." *TDR: The Drama Review* 50.4 (2006): 171–77.

Poll, Melissa. "Adapting 'Le Grand Will' in Wendake: Ex Machina and the Huron-Wendat Nation's Scenographic Collaboration." Erin Hurley and Hervé Guay, eds. Special issue of *Theatre Research in Canada* 35.3 (Winter 2014, forthcoming).

———. "Making Music Visible: Robert Lepage's *Der Ring des Nibelungen* at the Metropolitan Opera." In *Contemporary Approaches to Adaptation.* Vicky Angelaki and Kara Reilly, eds. Basingstoke: Palgrave Macmillan, forthcoming 2015.

———. "Robert Lepage's Scenographic Dramaturgy: The Aesthetic Signature at Work." *Body, Space, and Technology Journal* 2.11 (May 2013).

Puttnam, Sacha. *Le confessionnal: music from Robert Lepage's film = la musique du film de Robert Lepage.* Toronto: Attic Records, 1995.

Rewa, Natalie. "Clichés of Ethnicity Subverted: Robert Lepage's *La Trilogie des dragons.*" *Theatre History in Canada* 11.2 (Fall 1990): 148–61.

Reynolds, James H. "Acting with Puppets and Objects: Representation and Perception in Robert Lepage's *The Far Side of the Moon.*" *Performance Research* 12.4 (2007): 132–42.

———. "Lepage, Chaos, Needles, and Opium." In *Addiction and Performance.* James Reynolds and Zoe Zontou, eds. Newcastle upon Tyne: Cambridge Scholars Publishing, 2014.

———. "Robert Lepage and Authorial Process." In *Direction.* Simon Shepherd, ed. Basingstoke: Palgrave Macmillan, 2012. 177–85.

———. "Scenographic Acting and the Scenographic Body in the Work of Robert Lepage and Ex Machina." *Blue Pages: The Journal for the Society of British Theatre Designers* (December 2011): 14–15.

Roy, Irène. "Robert Lepage et l'esthétique en contrepoint." *L'annuaire théâtral* 8 (1990): 73–80.

———. *Le Théâtre Repère, du ludique au poétique.* Quebec City: Nuit blanche éditeur, 1994.

Salter, Denis. "Between Wor(l)ds: Lepage's *Shakespeare Cycle.*" *Theater* 24.3 (1993): 61–70.

Shewey, Don. "Set Your Watch to Now: Robert Lepage's *Zulu Time.*" *American Theatre* (September 2002): 26–27.

Soldevila, Philippe. "De l'architecture au théâtre." *Cahiers de théâtre JEU* 52 (1989): 31.

———. "Du hasard et de la nécessité." *Cahiers de théâtre JEU* 45 (1987): 173.

Tommasini, Anthony. "Stravinsky's Tales, Dunked in the Spin Cycle." *New York Times.* March 2, 2011. n.p.

Vigeant, Louise. "Lepage sous deux angles." *Cahiers de théâtre JEU* 96 (2000): 36–39.

Wasserman, Jerry. "Robert Lepage." In *Modern Canadian Plays*, vol. 2, 5th ed. Vancouver: Talonbooks, 2013. 29–34.

Ziraldo, Cristiana. "Lepage's Polygraphe in Italy." *Canadian Theatre Review* (Winter 2001): 16–19.

DOCUMENTARIES ON ROBERT LEPAGE

Belzil, Marie, and Mariano Franco. *The Image Mill Revealed*. Les Productions
    du 8e art and the National Film Board of Canada, 2009. DVD.
Clermont-Béïque, David. *Digging for Miracles*. Montreal: In Extremis Images,
    2000. DVD.
Duchesne, Michel, *The 7 Faces of Robert Lepage*. Télé-Québec, 1997. DVD.
Eisenhardt, Bob, Susan Froemke, Douglas Graves, Robert Lepage, Deborah
    Voigt, Jay Hunter Morris, Peter Gelb, James Levine, Fabio Luisi, Don
    Lenzer, and Richard Wagner. *Wagner's Dream: [The Making of the
    Metropolitan Opera's New Der Ring des Nibelungen]*. Berlin: Deutsche
    Grammophon, 2012. DVD.
Gabriel, Peter. *Secret World Live*. Los Angeles: Geffen Home Videos, 1994.
    DVD.
Lussier, René. *The Image Mill: A Landmark Event Celebrating Québec City's
    400th Anniversary*. Plus *The Image Mill Revealed: An Inside View of How
    The Image Mill Was Created by Robert Lepage and Ex Machina*. Montreal:
    Imavision.com, 2011. DVD.
Robert Lepage. Montreal: National Film Board of Canada, 2009. Online
    resource.
Winkler, Donald, Bill Brind, Marion McCormick, and Anne McLean. *Breaking
    a Leg: Robert Lepage and the Echo Project*. Montreal: National Film Board
    of Canada, 1992. VHS video.

II. THEATRE

THEATRE AND TECHNOLOGY

Assche, Christine Van. Editorial. *Parachute* 84 (October–December 1996):
    4–5.
Bablet, Denis, ed. *Collage et montage au théâtre et dans les autres arts durant les
    années vingt*. Lausanne: La Cité / L'Âge d'Homme, 1978.
Bablet, Denis. *Edward Gordon Craig*. New York: Theatre Art Books, 1966.
———. *Josef Svoboda*. Lausanne: L'Âge d'Homme, [1970] 2004.
———. *The Revolutions in Stage Design of the 20th Century*. Paris: Leon Amiel,
    1977.
Bauchard, Franck. "Théâtre et réalité virtuelle, une introduction à la demarche
    de Mark Reaney." *Les écrans sur la scène*. Béatrice Picon-Vallin, ed.
    Lausanne: L'Âge d'Homme, 1998. 225–45.
Bouchor, Maurice. "The Little Puppet Theatre, Conference." *La Revue Bleue*
    (June 28, 1890): 802–08.
Cahiers de théâtre JEU – Théâtre et cinéma 88 (1987).
Cahiers de théâtre JEU – Théâtre et technologies, la scène peuplée d'écrans 44
    (1987).
Fouquet, Ludovic. "Manipulations différées, un écart marionnettique." *PUCK*
    13 (2000): 92–95.

Grafton, Anthony, Glenn W. Most, and Salvatore Settis, eds. "Ex Machina." In
The Classical Tradition. Harvard University Press, 2010. 263–64.

Kramer, Richard E. " 'The Sculptural Drama': Tennessee Williams's Plastic
Theatre," *The Tennessee Williams Annual Review*, 5 (2002): 1–10, citing Hans
Hofmann, "Search for the Real." In *Search for the Real and Other Essays*.
Sara T. Weeks and Bartlett H. Hayes Jr., eds. Andover, MA: Addison
Gallery of American Arts, 1948. 49.

Maurin, Frédéric. "Au péril de la beauté: la chair du visuel et le cristal de la
forme chez Robert Wilson." Béatrice Picon-Vallin, ed. *La scène et les images*
21 (2001): 49–69.

———. "Spectral spectacle." *PUCK* 9 (1996): 27–31.

———. "Usages et usures de l'image. Spéculation sur *Le Marchand de Venise*
vu par Peter Sellars." In *Les écrans sur la scène*. Béatrice Picon-Vallin, ed.
Lausanne: L'Âge d'Homme, 1998. 71–105.

Norman, Sally Jane. "Acteurs de synthèse et théâtres électroniques." In *Le film
de théâtre*. Béatrice Picon-Vallin, ed. Paris: CNRS Éditions, 1997. 225–60.

Parachute – Nouvelles Technologies 84 (1996).

Picon-Vallin, Béatrice. "Hybridation spatiale, registres de présence." In *Les
écrans sur la scène*. Béatrice Picon-Vallin, ed. Lausanne: L'Âge d'Homme,
1998. 9–35.

———. "La mise en scène: vision et images." In *La scène et les images*. Béatrice
Picon-Vallin, ed. Paris: CNRS Éditions, 2001. 11–31.

Svoboda, Josef. *Josef Svoboda*. Prague: Theatre Institute, [1966] 1971.

Théâtre / Public – Théâtre et technologie 127. Frédéric Maurin, ed. (1996).

Vitez, Antoine. "Antoine Vitez about his staging of *Hamlet*," *Acts of Congress of
the French Society Shakespeare* 4 (1983): 260–71.

THEATRE AND THE INTERCULTURAL

Camilleri, Carmel, ed. *Chocs de cultures: concepts et enjeux pratiques de
l'interculturel*. Paris: L'Harmattan, 1989.

De Marinis, Marco. "L'expérience de l'altérité. Le théâtre entre
interculturalisme et transculturalisme," *L'Annuaire théâtral* 26 (Fall 1999):
84–102.

Hébert, Chantal, and Irène Perelli-Contos. *Théâtre, multidisciplinarité et
multiculturalisme*. Quebec City: Nuit blanche éditeur, 1997.

Lesage, Marie-Christine. "Regards croisés: théâtre et interdisciplinarité.
Présentation." *L'Annuaire théâtral* 26 (Fall 1999): 11–15.

Ouaknine, Serge. "Si près de quelque chose de nouveau …, le théâtre: du
théâtral au virtuel." *L'Annuaire théâtral* 26 (Fall 1999): 16–29.

Vigeant, Louise. "L'espace troué de la mémoire. *Rivage à l'abandon*: œuvre
multidisciplinaire." *Théâtre, multidiscplinarité, et multiculturalisme*. Chantal
Hébert and Irène Perelli-Contos, eds. Quebec City: Nuit Blanche éditeur,
1997. 53.

III. OTHER PRACTICES

AESTHETICS AND THE IMAGE

Art Press – Nouvelles technologies, un art sans modèle? hors-série, no. 12. Norbert Hillaire, ed. Paris: Art Press, 1991.

Asselin, Olivier. "Les corps subtilisés; l'œuvre d'art à l'ère de la photographie et du cinéma." *Cahiers de théâtre JEU* 88 (September 1998): 118–22.

Barboza, Olivier. *Les nouvelles images.* Paris: Éditions d'Art Somogy / Cité des Sciences et de l'Industrie, 1997.

Barthes, Roland. *Empire of Signs.* New York: Hill and Wang, 1982.

Benjamin, Walter. "Paris – Capital of the Nineteenth Century." *New Left Review* I/48 (1968): 77–88.

Claudel, Paul. *Le soulier de satin.* Paris: Gallimard, 1957.

Couchot, Edmond. *Images, de l'optique au numérique.* Paris: Hermès, 1988.

Debray, Régis. *Vie et mort de l'image.* Paris: Gallimard, 1992.

Didi-Huberman, Georges. *Ce que nous voyons, ce qui nous regarde.* Paris: Minuit, 1992.

———. *Devant le temps.* Paris: Minuit, 2000.

———. "La plus simple image." *Nouvelle revue de psychanalyse: Destins de l'image* 44 (Autumn 1991): 75–100.

Freud, Sigmund. "A Note upon the Mystic Writing Pad." In *General Psychological Theory.* Philip Rieff, ed. New York: Simon & Schuster, 1963.

Homer. *The Iliad.* Robert Fagles, trans. New York: Viking / Penguin, 1990.

Maeterlinck, Maurice. "Menus propos: le théâtre." *La Jeune Belgique* 9 (September 1890): 331–36.

Marion, Jean-Luc. *La croisée du visible.* Paris: PUF, 1996.

Merleau-Ponty, Maurice. "Eye and Mind." In *The Merleau-Ponty Aesthetics Reader: Philosophy and Painting.* Galen A. Johnson, ed. Michael Smith, trans. Evanston: Northwestern University Press, 1993. 121–49. First published in French as *L'Œil et l'esprit.* Paris: Gallimard, 1961.

Mondzain, Marie-José. *Image, icône, économie.* Paris: Seuil, 1996.

Plato. *The Republic.* New York: Cambridge University Press, 2000.

———. *Symposium.* Indianapolis: Hackett, 1989.

Pliny the Elder, *Natural History,* book 35. In *Natural History,* vol. IX: books 33–35. Harris Rackham, trans. Loeb Classical Library 394. Cambridge, MA: Harvard University Press, 1952.

Riout, Denis. *La peinture monochrome, histoire et archéologie du genre.* Nîmes: Éditions Jacqueline Chambon, 1996.

Scarpetta, Guy. *L'impureté.* Paris: Grasset, 1965.

Schaeffer, Jean-Marie. *L'image précaire.* Paris: Seuil, 1987.

Tanizaki, Jun'ichirō. *In Praise of Shadows.* New Haven: Leete's Island Books, 1977.

Virilio, Paul. *The Vision Machine.* Bloomington: Indiana University Press, 1994.

———. *War and Cinema: The Logistics of Perception.* New York: Verso, 1989.

THE BAROQUE

Audiberti, Jacques. "Coup d'œil sur le baroque." *Études cinématographiques.*
Paris: Lettres Modernes, 1960.

Bottineau, Yves. *Baroque.* Paris: Mazenod, 1986.

Brion, Marcel. "Baroque et esthétique du movement." *Études
cinématographiques.* Paris: Lettres Modernes, 1960.

Buci-Glucksmann, Christine. *La folie du voir. De l'esthétique du baroque au
virtuel.* Paris: Galilée, 1986. *The Madness of Vision: On Baroque Aesthetics.*
Dorothy Z. Baker, trans. Athens, OH: Ohio University Press, 2013.

Deleuze, Gilles. *The Fold: Leibniz and the Baroque.* London: Continuum
Books, 2006.

Deshoulières, Christophe. *L'Opéra baroque et la scène moderne.* Paris: Fayard,
2000.

Dubois, Claude-Gilbert. *Le baroque en Europe et en France.* Paris: PUF, 1995.

Pacciani, Riccardo. "Baroque et Rococo." In *Histoire Universelle de l'art.* Vittorio
Sgarbi, ed. Paris: Solar, 1988.

 PHOTOGRAPHY

Barthes, Roland. *Camera Lucida: Reflections on Photography.* Richard Howard,
trans. New York: Hill and Wang, 1981.

Dubois, Philippe. *L'acte photographique et autres essaies.* Paris. Nathan, 1990.

Guerreschi, Jean. "Territoire psychique, territoire photographique." *Les cahiers
de la photographie* 14 (1984).

Kofman, Sarah. *Camera Obscura of Ideology.* Will Straw, trans. Ithaca, NY:
Cornell University Press, 1999.

Schaeffer, Jean-Marie. *L'image précaire.* Paris: Seuil, 1987.

Sontag, Susan. *On Photography.* New York: Farrar, Straus, and Giroux, 1977.

Tisseron, Serge. *Le mystère de la chambre claire, photographie, et inconscient.*
Paris: Champs / Flammarion, 1996.

 CINEMA

Aumont, Jacques, Alain Bergala, Michel Marie, and Marc Vernet. *Esthétique du
film.* Paris: Nathan, 1999.

Dickinson, Peter. Chapter 5. In *Screening Gender, Framing Genre: Canadian
Literature into Film.* Toronto: University of Toronto Press, 2007.

Fortier, Denis, and Franck Ernould. *Initiation au son, cinéma, et audiovisuel.*
Paris: Femis, 1996.

Gaudreault, André, and François Jost. *Le récit cinématographique.* Paris:
Nathan, 1990.

Loiselle, André. *Stage-Bound: Feature Film Adaptations of Canadian and
Québécois Drama.* Montreal: McGill-Queen's University Press, 2003.

Martin, Marcel. *Le langage cinématographique.* Paris: Les Éditions du Cerf, 1985.

Nacache, Jacqueline. *Le film hollywoodien classique.* Paris: Nathan, 1995.

Vanoye, Francis. *Récit écrit, récit filmique.* Paris: Nathan, 1989.

Villain, Dominique. *Le montage au cinéma.* Paris: Cahiers du cinéma, 1991.

VIDEO

Bellaïche, Philippe. *Les secrets de l'image video*. Paris: Eyrolles, 1995.

Couchot, Edmond. "La mosaïque ordonnée." *Communications* 48 (1988).

Dubois, Colette, Philippe Dubois, and Marc-Emmanuel Mélon. "Cinéma et vidéo: interpénétrations. *Communications* 48 (1988).

Duguet, Anne-Marie. "Dispositifs." *Communications* 48 (1988).

Wyn, Pascal, and Michel Wyn. *Les boîtes à images*. Quincy: Éditions techniques européennes, 1983.

VIRTUAL ENVIRONMENTS

Art Press – Nouvelles technologies, un art sans modèle? hors-série, no. 12. Norbert Hillaire, ed. Paris: Art Press, 1991.

Couchot, Edmond. "L'Odyssée, mille fois ou les machines à langage." Paris: *Traverses* 44–45 (August 1988).

Maheu, Jean, ed. "Machines virtuelles." Paris: *Traverses* 44–45 (August 1988).

Quéau, Philippe. *Le Virtuel, Vertus, et Vertiges*. Champ Seyssel: Vallon, 1983.

Weinsberg, Jean-Louis. "Un nouveau régime de visibilité." *Les chemins du virtuel, simulation informatique et création industrielle*. Paris: Centre Georges Pompidou, 1989.

IV. MISCELLANEOUS

TECHNOLOGY AND COMPUTERS

Lévy, Pierre. *La machine univers: Création, cognition, et culture informatique*. Paris: La Découverte, 1987.

———. *Les technologies de l'intelligence, l'avenir de la pensée à l'ère informatique*. Paris: La Découverte, 1990.

Scheps, Ruth. *L'Empire des techniques*. Paris: Seuil, 1984.

MÉTISSAGE / CROSS-POLLINATION

Amselle, Jean-Loup. *Logiques métisses. Anthropologie de l'identité en Afrique et ailleurs*. Paris: Payot, 1990.

Diniz, Thaïs Flores Nogueira. "Intermediality in the Theater of Robert Lepage." In *Media inter media: Essays in Honor of Claus Clüver*. Stephanie Glaser and Claus Clüver, eds. Amsterdam: Rodopi, 2009.

Gruzinski, Serge. *The Mestizo Mind: The Intellectual Dynamics of Colonization and Globalization*. New York: Routledge, [2002] 2013.

Lévi-Strauss, Claude. *The Savage Mind*. Chicago: University of Chicago Press, 1966.

———. *Structural Anthropology 2*. Claire Jacobson and Brooke Schoepf, trans. New York: Basic Books, 1974.

Todd, Emmanuel. *Le Destin des immigrés: Assimilation et ségrégation dans les démocraties occidentales*. Paris: Seuil, 1994.

Tousson, Roger. *Mythologie du métissage*. Paris: PUF, 1998.

IMAGE CREDITS

Every effort has been made to trace copyright holders and to obtain their permission for the use of copyright material. The publisher apologizes for any errors or omissions and would be grateful if notified of any corrections that should be incorporated in future reprints or editions of this book.

Photographs are copyright the photographer credited.

COVER

Emmanuel Valette: top (from *The Far Side of the Moon*);
Ex Machina archives: bottom (from *The Far Side of the Moon*)

DOUBLE-PAGE SPREADS

Érick Labbé: pages 6–7 (from *The Andersen Project*)
Emmanuel Valette: pages 62–63 (from *The Geometry of Miracles*)
Eric Mahoudeau / Opéra National de Paris:
    pages 202–3 (from *The Damnation of Faust*);
Ex Machina archives: pages 286–87 (from *The Far Side of the Moon*)
Érick Labbé: pages 294–95 (from *Playing Cards: Spades*)

INTERIOR PHOTOS

Lionel Arnould: pages 277, 279
Jacques Collin: pages 94, 143, 152, 171, 277, 279, 282
Michael Cooper: page 298
Ex Machina archives: page 48
Carl Fillion (sketches and computer simulations):
    pages 37, 157, 169, 301, 302, 304, 306, 330
Yves Fillion: page 213
Ludovic Fouquet (photos and sketches): pages 17, 28, 37, 57,
    79, 129, 136, 184, 213, 215, 219, 248, 253, 257, 312, 329, 330
Sophie Grenier: page 12
Claudel Huot: pages 14, 48, 72, 74, 88, 90, 125, 129, 241, 266
Vincent Jacques: page 280
Érick Labbé: pages 54, 173, 251, 273, 282, 316

Louise Leblanc: page 318
Yanick MacDonald: pages 262, 284
Eric Mahoudeau: page 271
Metropolitan Opera: page 310
Opéra National de Paris: page 271
Yves Renaud: page 310
Richard-Max Tremblay: page 123
Emmanuel Valette: pages 30, 34, 59, 76, 94, 99, 117, 126, 143, 146, 246

INDEX

Consult the Chronology of Robert Lepage Productions for shows not listed in the index.

About the Author

Ludovic Fouquet is a visual artist, teacher, director, and founder of the multimedia theatre company songes mécaniques (Mechanical Dreams) in Blois, France. After training as an actor and dancer, Fouquet earned his PhD studying Robert Lepage's artistic practice and its relationship to technology.

He contributed to the publication of *La trilogie des dragons* (*The Dragons' Trilogy*, L'instant même, 2005). With Robert Faguy of Laval University, he wrote a practical book about the use of stage video, *Face à l'image. Exercices, explorations, et expériences vidéoscéniques* (L'instant même, forthcoming 2015). He prepared a photographic monograph of Lepage's work (to be published).

Since 2000, he has given numerous workshops about the use of image on stage (theatre, visual arts, circus performance) at universities and schools or conservatories, including Laval University's visual arts school and theatre department (Quebec), Université Censier-Sorbonne Nouvelle (Paris), École Supérieure d'Art Dramatique (Paris), and École du Cirque de Québec.

In addition to frequent speaking engagements at French and Quebec universities, Fouquet contributes regularly to numerous theatre and contemporary art magazines, including *JEU revue de théâtre* and *ETC Montréal*.

Fouquet divides his time between France and Quebec and his work between theatre and the making of screenprint and photographic images. Find out more at ludovicfouquet.com and songesmecaniques.com.

About the Translator

Rhonda Mullins is a translator, writer, and editor. She translated Jocelyne Saucier's *Jeanne's Road* and *And the Birds Rained Down*, for which she was shortlisted for the 2013 Governor General's Literary Award for Translation, her second such nomination. In 2007 she was nominated for this award for her translation of *The Decline of the Hollywood Empire* by Hervé Fischer. Mullins lives in Montreal.